Optical
Impersonality

HSM Hopkins Studies in Modernism
Douglas Mao, *Series Editor*

Optical

Impersonality

Science, Images,

and Literary Modernism

Christina Walter

Johns Hopkins University Press
Baltimore

Johns Hopkins University Press
2715 North Charles Street
Baltimore, Maryland 21218-4363
www.press.jhu.edu

Library of Congress Cataloging-in-Publication Data

Walter, Christina, 1975–
    Optical Impersonality : Science, Images, and Literary Modernism
/ Christina Walter.
        pages cm. — (Hopkins Studies in Modernism)
    Includes bibliographical references and index.
    ISBN-13: 978-1-4214-1363-1 (hardback : acid-free paper)
    ISBN-13: 978-1-4214-1364-8 (electronic)
    ISBN-10: 1-4214-1363-9 (hardcover)
    ISBN-10: 1-4214-1364-7
    1. Modernism (Literature). 2. Optics in literature. I. Title.
    PN56.M54W35 2014
    809'.9112—dc23   2013035781

A catalog record for this book is available from the British Library.

*Special discounts are available for bulk purchases of this book. For more
information, please contact Special Sales at 410-516-6936 or
specialsales@press.jhu.edu.*

Johns Hopkins University Press uses environmentally friendly book
materials, including recycled text paper that is composed of at least
30 percent post-consumer waste, whenever possible.

For Rhonda
il miglior fabbro

and

For S.E.W.
who gave his eyes

Contents

Acknowledgments

When I was a graduate student I developed the habit of always turning first to the acknowledgments of a scholarly book. I wanted to get a sense of the writer's academic family tree and also, more voyeuristically, to see into his or her personal life. I came to realize that there is an art to writing acknowledgments, as I repeatedly saw scholars masterfully mold the topics of their books into a metaphor for talking about indebtedness. I suppose that I could rally a metaphor connecting either literary impersonality or the limits of vision to the many unseen friends and colleagues who have had a hand in writing this book—even though I am the only visible author. Instead, I'll simply admit that despite my fascination, I haven't mastered the genre of acknowledgments. My gratitude to those who have advised me or kept me sane as I wrote first my dissertation and then this book is, however, no less real for being expressed less artfully.

I was extremely fortunate to have mentors like Jed Esty, Joseph Valente, Julia Saville, and Jesse Matz as I was first developing this project. Jed and Joe not only challenged and encouraged me then but continued to do so as I took the dissertation apart and put it back together to form this book. No less crucial has been the feedback I received from Doug Mao, the series editor, and from the anonymous reader for Johns Hopkins University Press. Doug, the time and care you took with my manuscript is much appreciated.

I also owe great thanks to my wonderful colleagues and friends at the University of Maryland who generously read or discussed various parts of the manuscript, providing me with invaluable suggestions that led me in new directions and toward important connections: Kent Cartwright, William Cohen, Oliver Gaycken, Elizabeth Loizeaux, Peter Mallios, Sangeeta Ray, Brian Richardson, Jason Rudy, Martha Nell Smith, and Orrin Wang. Of my friends, special thanks are certainly due to Keguro Macharia, who is greatly

missed, and to Dana Carluccio. Dana, you probably have this book memo-
rized given the many times you discussed it with me, or read drafts of it, or
even simply heard me reading parts of it aloud as I was revising. The simple
truth is that this book wouldn't have been finished without you.

Beyond those who were directly involved with the book, I also want to
thank friends and colleagues whose conversations and encouragement have
kept me sane: Theresa Coletti, Melissa Girard, Katie King, Marilee Linde-
mann, Randy Ontiveros, Rochelle Rives, Tara Rodgers, Kathy-Ann Tan, Ves-
sela Valiavitcharska, and Mary Helen Washington. Moreover, though our
mutual pep talks are now years old, thank you to Tessa Oberg, who shared
the goal and is not forgotten. Tremendous thanks are also due to my parents, Michael and Marilyn Walter, for the many sacrifices they made and for
all the anxieties they assuaged. Thanks are due as well to my brother, Bryce,
who often had more faith in me than I had in myself. In addition, I thank my
extended family—the Edigers, the Kernohans, the Keltners, the Hoovers,
and the Walters—who never complained about the many, many family
events I've missed due to teaching, conferences, and research. I promise to
do better in the future.

Finally, I thank the Department of English and the Graduate College at
the University of Illinois for generously supporting research travel related
to this book. And I thank the University of Maryland for the Research and
Scholarship Award and the College of Arts and Humanities Publishing Sub-
vention, which together gave me time to revise and helped me to cover the
permissions costs associated with this volume's many images. In addition, I
thank *Textual Practice* and *Modern Fiction Studies* for allowing me to incorporate material from my articles published in those journals. Great thanks are
also due to my research assistant, Eleanor Simpson, for all her hard work in
helping me to secure permissions and to Isabella Moulton and Valerie Or-
lando for their translation work during that process. In addition, many thanks
to everyone at Johns Hopkins University Press for all their work in transforming my manuscript into a book.

**Optical
Impersonality**

Introduction: Eye Don't See
Embodied Vision, Ontology, and Modernist Impersonality

[T]here is here no problem of the *alter ego* because it is
not *I* who sees, not *he* who sees, because an anonymous
visibility inhabits both of us, a vision in general, in virtue
of that primordial property that belongs to the flesh, being
here and now, of radiating everywhere and forever, being
an individual, of being also a dimension and a universal.

Maurice Merleau-Ponty, *The Visible and the Invisible*

If it were the human personality in [a man] that was sacred
to me, I could easily put out his eyes. As a blind man he
would be exactly as much a human personality as before.
I should have destroyed nothing but his eyes.

Simone Weil, "Human Personality"

On 26 June 2006 the *New Yorker* ran a cartoon by Bruce Eric Kaplan showing
a nondescript, bespectacled office worker speaking on the telephone. The
caption read: "I'll take care of it impersonally." The joke of course is that the
caller, whether colleague or customer, is presumably looking for the personal touch and the worker nonchalantly reverses that service: to take care of
something "impersonally" is here to evacuate the personal. Moreover, a wry
paradox plays around the questions of whether an "I" could in fact do something "impersonally" and whether a cliché like "I'll take care of it personally"
could count as a personal expression in the first place. Finally, Kaplan's image
humorously ties the worker's insufficiency to a literal and metaphorical short-
sightedness through his defining feature: his large spectacles.

The basic structure of Kaplan's cartoon is also the assumed framework
that literary critics have brought to the study of modernist impersonality.

Scholars have read the modernist rejection of Romantic expressivity—the belief that literature announced its author's essential self or interiority—as both a complete evacuation of a writer's subjectivity and a denial of embodied specificity. The modernist interest in whether and how to write impersonally has been read as the apotheosis of this evacuation and denial. However, modernists didn't actually treat impersonality as a simple negation of personality. Instead, they took up the more fundamental question of what a personality is, as well as what more there is to the human subject than the person. The inadequacy of existing accounts of modernism's impersonal aesthetic is suggested by the fact that we have yet to grapple with its pervasive but largely unremarked concern with vision and its embodied limits—a connection that resurfaces even in Kaplan's cartoon, in those large spectacles. This book traces how modernist impersonality formulated and answered the question of what a person is specifically through its intervention into the intertwined histories of sight and reason, images and texts, and otherness and selfhood in Western thought.

Although these sets of concepts come from different locations—from scientific and philosophical studies of perception, from aesthetic theories, and from social systems—the central premise of this book is that for centuries these concepts have cascaded into and through each other. Before the nineteenth century, Western accounts of human vision tended to separate the eye that registered external forms from a rational mind that reflected upon and even perfected those forms. This visual model complemented a dominant aesthetic view in which images were associated with stable sensory information, and texts with objective reason. This latter division in turn supported a host of social binaries in which the dominant term enjoyed greater access to the space of rational thought, mobility, and development: male and female, professional and working class, non-raced (or white) self and racialized Other. Beginning around the middle of the nineteenth century, however, this longstanding model of vision lost ground to one in which the thinking subject, the perceiving body, the perceptual object, and the material world couldn't be so firmly separated. Although this new physiology of vision originated with scientific investigation, it opened a space for a new cultural collaboration between vision, the image, and subjectivity. This book is about how modernist writers intervened in and indeed even structured that collaboration, shaping what the science of vision meant for the modernist world.

Modernists did this work through *imagetexts*, or works that blend the re-

spective territories of the seeable and the sayable, such as a picture poem.[1]
Where science directly investigated the complex workings of sight and reason, imagetextuality translated these investigations into the complementary
register of images and texts. In both the scientific and aesthetic registers,
indivisibility was key. In the new model of vision, for example, a rational
subject no longer actively reflected upon visual percepts that passively recorded the physical world. Instead, the perceiving subject was itself part of
that physical world, and its embodied processes, structures, and defects
shaped perception, including the ocular apparatus, visual cognition, and
visual memory. Modern stylists of impersonality probed this idea by creating complementary amalgams of images (the supposed bearer of stable sensory information) and texts (the supposed bearer of objective reasoning). In
this way, modernists developed a vernacular science in aesthetic form, and
they used this form to consider how the new physiology of vision affected
notions of selfhood and identity. The attempt to interrogate these notions
and indeed to turn them into a social politics is the defining work of modernist impersonality.

A moment from Ford Madox Ford's tetralogy *Parade's End* (1924–28) can
help concretize this argument. On the surface *Parade's End* follows the protagonist, Christopher Tietjens, from his life as a government statistician and
landed gentleman to that of a soldier, watching as his interest in social and
social-scientific conventions yields to more intimate struggles with love
and the devastations of the Great War. Critics have commonly suggested that
the tetralogy stages a division between impersonality and emotion, which
it formally replicates by passing from realist objectivity at the start to modernist impressionism in its later sections.[2] That impressionism, meanwhile,
is assumed to exemplify modernism's commitment to a self-contained "I"
removed from social reality.[3]

Tietjens' visual perceptions on the front, however, challenge the basic
premises on which these views depend, namely, that modernists used impersonality to oppose embodied experience, including emotion, and that
modernism was solipsistically devoted to an autonomous, coherent "I."
While commanding a battalion near the front and recollecting both his last
argument with his estranged wife and a recent conversation with another
officer about her, Tietjens is overtaken by a visual phenomenon of great
interest to Ford's contemporaries. He has before him a reporting notebook,
in which he's recording "his own case" in a distanced, social-scientific fashion (355). His record nonetheless unfolds in a fragmentary and stream-of-

consciousness style and on top of that is layered with his visual memories from the two conversations he's recording. This complex palimpsest of thought, memory, and perception is abruptly interrupted when Tietjens is recalled to the present, initially by the cry of another soldier but then by his attention to a physiological experience. Looking down at the bright white sheets of his notebook in a state of physical exhaustion, Tietjens sees "thin films of reddish purple," which gradually become an ever "fainter" and wavering "luminous green," as they reach the darkness beyond the "right-hand top corner of the paper" (355). He sees float across the page, in other words, what scientists and philosophers refer to as *subjective color*. Color was long thought to be basically subjective because the human eye collapses objective manifold light mixtures into only a few fundamental colors.[4] But the term *subjective color* refers more narrowly to color phenomena that originate strictly in the eye and brain rather than in the object world—in other words, to color that has no external correlate. Tietjens' experience of subjective color draws specifically on contemporary studies of embodied ocular phenomena, specifically the study of color opponency, visual saturation, and microsaccades.[5] The human visual system interprets information about color by processing signals from the eyes' cones and rods in an opposing manner (e.g., red vs. green). Visual saturation, or the overstimulation of cone cells, leads one to see a color-opposite afterimage of the form that caused the overstimulation, because it results in the eyes' temporary inability to register the color of that form and the brain reads the resulting weak signal as the opposite color. Tietjens' experience roughly follows these principles: as he shifts his view from the bright white paper that frames the red blotches floating in his field of vision to the darkened room, his eyes record a negative (green) afterimage of those blotches. Technically, following Hering's contemporary theory of color opponency, we would expect Tietjens' afterimage to be the grey-black opposite of the white paper background rather than the green opposite of an already subjective visual phenomenon (the red blotches), but the scientific thread is nonetheless present. Indeed, it closely resembles an experiment that the biologist T. H. Huxley describes in *Lessons in Elementary Physiology* (1866; rpt. until 1930), which recommends gazing lengthily at a red dot on a piece of white paper and then at the white background itself, after which the reader should see a greenish dot (221). Ford's possible adaptation of Huxley is augmented by Tietjens' perception that the red/green blotches are actually floating across his field of vision. Such movements accurately reflect the effects of microsaccades, the small involuntary eye movements that result from fixating on an object. Ford thus displays a working if slightly flawed knowledge of the new physiology of vision in the later nineteenth century.

Beyond that, though, Tietjens himself also seems to understand that science, because he correctly registers his experience as "an effect of fatigue, operating on the retina." At first he feels indignant toward the materiality, incoherence, and uncontrollability of his optical experience, what he refers to as "his own weakness" (355). At the same time, though, he finds value in the experience, because it connects him to O Nine Morgan, the young soldier in his battalion who was recently killed. Tietjens believes that "his retina [is] presenting him with the glowing image of the fellow's blood" as a physiological-affective connection beyond "identity" that "join[s]" the two of them (356). The optical experience thus creates a space to entertain a specific model of selfhood and otherness: in place of discrete and self-possessed individuals, this model emphasizes elements of subjectivity that quite literally exceed and reorganize the boundaries of the person.

This episode in *Parade's End* exemplifies the modernist understanding of being and knowing within the impersonal aesthetic. Ford's deployment of optics both as a thematic interest and as part of his character's general knowledge shows us that he was engaging the broad, accelerating complication of vision that took place toward the end of the nineteenth century. The then new model of vision contested notions of an objective, rational observer that took in faithful representations of external objects in the world. Tietjens, as we see, is a *part* of the world, a highly embodied subject existing in a stream of physiologically mediated perceptual phenomena and having little control over himself or his surroundings. Though the new physiology of vision didn't simply replace the older model, it was enlarged upon in philosophical writings on ontology and epistemology, as well as in popular scientific images and writings on optical technologies and illusions and on visual defects and the care of one's vision. This modern scientific vernacular was the immediate context for literary modernism's burgeoning aesthetic of impersonality.[6] Thus, when Ford overwrites Tietjens' record of "his own case" with subjective visual images, he isn't weighing an impersonal social science against a personal impressionism; he's making optical science a window onto the impersonality that already resides within the human subject. This impersonality consists most basically in a material subjectivity, but it also includes that subjectivity's social implications, at which Ford just begins to gesture. Like Ford, modernists read the indivisibility of the perceiving subject and the perceptual world as a call for variously positioned subjects to renegotiate their relationships to each other within that world. This renegotiation took a range of political forms for modernists, but it always reckoned with new boundaries and power relations between social subjects, as (officer) Tietjens' nonidentitarian connection to (subaltern) O Nine Morgan registers. The combination of embodied subjectivity and its social consequences is what *optical impersonality* signifies in this study.

The case of Tietjens also demonstrates the final key element of optical impersonality: the fact that modernists used form to explore this subject, rather than leaving it only to the level of theme. Despite Tietjens' posture of social-scientific distance and authority, his experience and thus the narration flood the report with the fragmentary, temporally layered recollections and streams of consciousness that typify impressionist narrative technique. Ford thus renders Tietjens' layered *verbal* account inseparable from the partial, constructed, and unstable *images* that originate from his psyche and his sensorium.

> But that was as far as Tietjens got in uninterrupted reminiscence of that scene. He was sitting in his flea-bag digging idly with his pencil into the squared page of his note-book which had remained open on his knees, his eyes going over and over again the words with which his report on his own case had concluded—the words: *So the interview ended rather untidily.* Over the words went the image of the dark hillside with the lights of the town, now that the air-raid was finished, spreading high up into the sky below them . . .
>
> But at that point the doctor's batman had uttered, as if with a jocular, hoarse irony, the name:
>
> "Poor—O Nine Morgan! . . ." and over the whitish sheet of paper on a level with his nose Tietjens perceived thin films of reddish purple to be wavering, then a glutinous surface of gummy scarlet pigment. Moving! (355, ellipses and emphasis original)[7]

Between the words of the report and of the doctor's batman and the images of the remembered scene and of the subjective optical phenomena, Ford creates a formal amalgam of image and text that characterizes Tietjens' experience of optical impersonality. It makes basic sense that what I've called optical impersonality would intersect and reverberate with images as the objects of sight. But there are more specific historical reasons for optical impersonality to have taken up not just images but, more precisely, the relation of images and texts. The rational objectivity of the observer in old theories of vision was strongly associated with a divide between images and texts: in Anglo-American culture (and in Western European cultures more broadly) texts were presumed to capture an observer's interiority, active reason, and disembodiment, but images were treated as if they passively conveyed external objects of observation, along with their stable form and materiality. The physiology of vision that emerged in the nineteenth century instead proposed a materially mediated observer, along with an image that was unreliable at any particular moment and that was not an instantaneous record but instead unfolded over time. The new image, in other words, looked a lot like the old version of text, and modernists like Ford magnified this effect by creating blended visual and verbal representations. These imagetexts didn't just put image and text side by side; they highlighted the way the newly conceived image bore properties of temporality and conventionality that were presumed to be textual, because text unfolds over time and is composed of arbitrary symbols. These imagetexts thus broadly blurred the borders of the seeable and the sayable and at their strongest highlighted how the interaction of images and texts is in fact constitutive of all representation. I take the pursuit of this imagetextuality to be the formal signature of optical impersonality.

Reformulating modernist impersonality thus requires close attention to the three cultural sites that became the crucible for its development: the history of optical science, the history of image-text relations, and the history of personality. The significance of these histories and their intersections have been obscured in part by a lingering critical belief in the chasm separating modern science, on the one hand, and modernist literature, on the other. Though this "two cultures" narrative has been broadly challenged by recent accounts of popular science in the later nineteenth and early twentieth centuries, those that extend their accounts specifically to literature have tended (1) to focus on the rise of a new physiology of vision in the Victorian period; (2) to consider only science fiction rather than the high or avant-garde modernism concerned with impersonality; or (3) to be interested in some branch of science other than optics.[8] But the "two cultures" narrative is only one problem. Compounding it is the way that the very proliferation and popularization of optics in modern culture ironically obscure its role in impersonality. Optical technologies, illusions, and discourses that made clear the limitations of vision became thoroughly embedded in modern visual culture, from painting to psychoanalysis. Thus writers didn't always have to engage directly with scientific theories of the image and the observer in order to explore embodied vision. Only if we acknowledge the breadth of the visual-scientific vernacular can the full range of impersonalist authors and texts become clear. And only by registering the way this vernacular's image and observer intersected with the discourse of personality, and particularly with its late nineteenth and early twentieth-century reconceptualization as a performance or visual spectacle, can we appreciate how and why optics, imagetextuality, and personality came together in the impersonal aesthetic. By triangulating these histories and anchoring them with further examples from Virginia Woolf and again from Ford, I'll begin to demonstrate that modernists didn't use impersonality to cast themselves adrift in the midst of profound cultural change but instead undertook a fascinating attempt to bring key scientific, aesthetic, and social shifts together and indeed to push them in new directions.

The Visual Vernacular, Imagetextuality, and Modernism's Optical Unconscious

Two perhaps familiar images roughly schematize the differences between the new physiological paradigm in nineteenth-century ophthalmological science and what had come before. Figure I.1 is from an eighteenth-century edition of René Descartes' *Dioptrics* (1637), and figure I.2 is from the physician and physicist Hermann von Helmholtz's *Physiological Optics* (1856-66). In the first image, the line RST is the retina, which appears as a thin, transparent aperture. Descartes' homunculus observer substitutes for the brain behind the monocular eye and gazes out through that retina. This image suggests an enclosed, autonomous mind for which sight is a faithful record, immune to the vagaries of the body. Compare RST with the second image, which is Helmholtz's rendering of a cross section of the retina, thick with nerve fibers, ganglion cells, and nuclei. Not only do we register the material density of vision here but there's no distinction between the observer and this density. Indeed, accompanying this image is Helmholtz's claim that "*the human eye is not exactly centered,*" a challenge to the perfect geometry of Descartes' central line of sight, represented in line XS (*Physiological Optics* 1:116). In literally decentering vision and pointing to its material limits, Helmholtz's model also unmoors both being and knowledge.

This schematic maps nicely onto Jonathan Crary's largely Foucauldian divide between classical and modern, or objective and subjective, vision.[9] Crary has argued that in the first decades of the nineteenth century the truth of vision became grounded in the density and materiality of the body,

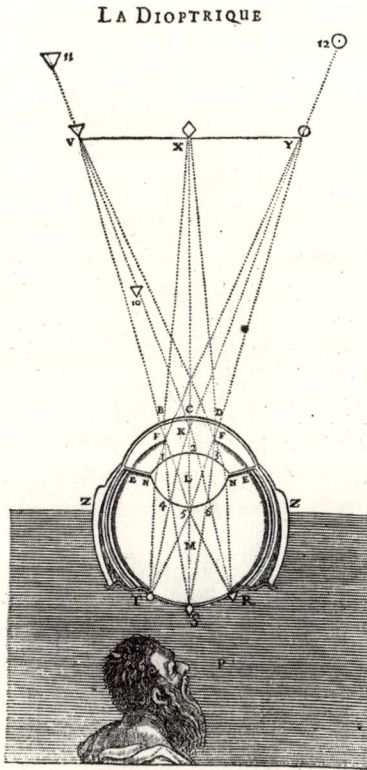

Fig. I.1. Engraving of a geometric model of the eye from Descartes' *Dioptrics,* following the *Discourse on Method* (1637), Bibliothèque de l'Académie de Médecine, Paris. Courtesy of Bibliothèque de l'Académie de Médecine / Archives Charmet / The Bridgeman Art Library.

an argument that is consistent with Foucault's larger claim that at this moment systems of thought no longer existed outside and beyond humanity but were instead subject to physiological conditions. This shorthand, however, oversimplifies the history of visual science, so it will be useful to fill in and complicate the sketch, especially with an eye to the complementary history of image-text relations. In 1604 Johannes Kepler's *The Optical Part of Astronomy* outlined the first accurate mathematical theory of the camera obscura, an optical device whose aperture lets rays of light into a darkened space in order to project images from outside onto an enclosed screen. Kepler used his calculations to explain the mechanics of image formation on the

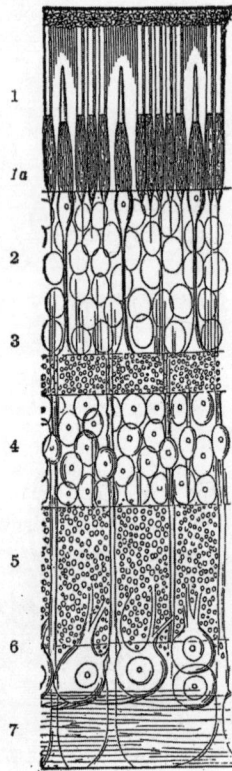

Fig. I.2. Diagram of a cross section of the retina from the 1924-25 English edition of Helmholtz's *Physiological Optics*.

eye's retina. His discovery of the retinal image made vision analyzable according to the abstract laws of mathematics and physics and also sharply distinguished between the subject and object of sight.[10] Building on a long-held ocularcentrism in Western philosophy, Descartes used Kepler's research to locate vision in a clear mental gaze through which we see and know objectively.[11] He posited that if the eye provides an image, as Kepler showed, then that image is made truthful by reason. More specifically, he argued that the "structure in the eye receives the figure impressed upon it by the light," and the figure conveyed is then passed to "the common sense, in the very same instance and without the passage of any real entity from one to the other." Common sense, or reason, in turn "impresses on the imagination those very figures which come uncontaminated and without bodily admixture from the external senses" (qtd. in Judovitz 75).[12] On this reading, and in keeping with figure I.1, the observer is figuratively enclosed within the camera obscura—an ahistorical, disinterested, disembodied self removed from the world it claims to know. Its mind's eye, like the lens of a camera obscura, is singular rather than binocular, and stable rather than subject to saccadic motion.

This camera obscura model of vision was formative, but it certainly didn't go uncontested until Helmholtz or even the nineteenth century. Indeed, it would be inaccurate to say that Descartes himself was unconcerned with the physiology of vision. He readily accepted the limits of the eye (as opposed to the clear mental gaze) and offered shrewd speculations about short- and long-sightedness as well as ocular accommodation. In addition, Descartes distinguished his clear mental gaze from sensation by routing the former through the pineal gland, in the brain, which he took to be the place where soul and body come together. While the pineal gland's role in visual perception was meant to secure the separation of mind and body, it points to an overlap rather than a border, attenuating Descartes' mental gaze.[13] Much more forcefully, though, David Hume emphasized in *A Treatise of Human Nature* (1740) that humans have knowledge of things only through their imperfect sensations and also that "we transfer the judgments and conclusions of the understanding to the senses," so that habit and weak memories of past impressions distort our processing of sensation (374-75). Moreover, Hume argued that because of the fragmented nature of memory, humans have in fact only a bundle of sensations associated with a self, rather than any coherent metaphysical self. Though Thomas Reid considered visionary images equally with visual ones (as I discuss in chapter 1), he also argued powerfully against the camera obscura model of vision in *An Inquiry into the Human Mind* (1764):

> There is not the least probability that there is any picture or image of the object either in the optic nerve or brain. . . . Nor is there any probability, that the mind perceives the pictures upon the *retina*. . . . There are other material organs, whose operation is necessary to seeing. . . . If ever we come to know the structure and use of the choroid membrane, the optic nerve, and the brain, . . . some more links of the chain may be brought within our view, and a more general law of vision discovered. (120-30)

Even by the later nineteenth century, when Helmholtz had theorized more "links of the chain," there was far from a consensus. Helmholtz himself made a summary of existing theorists in his *Physiological Optics,* dividing the sensationalists (including William Porterfield, Alfred Wilhelm Volkmann, Kaspar Theobald Tourtual, and Johannes Müller), who believed in an innate ability to sense depth, spatial location, form, and three-dimensionality, from the empiricists (such as Johann Friedrich Herbart, Ernst Wilhelm von Brücke, Johann Czermak, and Helmholtz himself), who thought that all knowledge of form in visual perception depended on experience.

Despite these qualifications, though, Descartes' broad model of vision gained influence by intersecting with widespread beliefs about the nature of the image and image-text relations. As W. J. T. Mitchell has argued, the image is a system of classification in the Foucauldian "order of things," meaning that it's "the general notion . . . that holds the world together with 'figures of knowledge'" (*Iconology* 11). Conflicts over the nature and use of images are thus cultural battles in disguise; they employ a seemingly neutral metalanguage to rationalize a social, ideological, or philosophical agenda. Such conflicts tend to unfold, whether implicitly or explicitly, in terms of the relation between images and texts as the two dominant representational modes. Beliefs about the nature of images and image-text relations are thus a kind of relay between science and philosophy, on the one hand, and art, on the other—a relay that proves crucial to the mechanics of modernism's impersonal aesthetic.

The initial complement to Cartesian philosophy in this image-textual relay is the Enlightenment shift toward an expressive model of language, the belief that linguistic signs are arbitrary rather than natural.[14] Following this shift, texts were increasingly distanced from sensory referents by their supposed conventionality and abstraction, while images were instead strongly associated with those referents by the contemporary science and philosophy of perception and memory. This development remade the *differences* between images and texts, in terms of their *materials* of representation and institutional tradition, into a seeming *opposition* at the level of their *effects.* Across the eighteenth and nineteenth centuries the perceived semantic superiority of image or text would fluctuate, as would literary efforts to compare the visual and verbal arts. The eighteenth century, for instance, saw the neoclassical return to Horace's tradition of *ut pictura poesis* (as painting, so poetry), which elevated and attempted to harness the representational power of the image in a literary pictorialism. In the Romantic period, by contrast, the word was elevated above the image because of its supposed fitness for representing an unfolding thought; the "sister arts" analogy and in turn pictorialism were correspondingly denounced.[15] In the scientific realm, the atlases that played a key role in representing nineteenth-century scientific consensus structured objectivity in two very different image-textual ways. Some emphasized mechanically produced images that were so committed to the object as it was seen that they (1) didn't correct scratches left by the photographic lens and (2) jettisoned the practice of using an ideally representative image in favor of offering numerous images that captured a range of observations. Other atlases, by contrast, omitted images altogether; their scientist-authors instead prioritized invariant structures and temporal sequences that functioned like the abstract signs of a language.[16] However, whether the image or the word dominated in scientific or aesthetic estimations, and whether literature imagined a "sister arts" relation or a *paragone* (a struggle between image and text for representational dominance), what would broadly hold across the eighteenth century and much of the nineteenth was the sense that the image is natural, stable, and mimetic, while text is conventional, temporal, and expressive. This image/text binary presumed an essential identity for each representational mode and thus came, not coincidentally, to naturalize the social binaries associated with a Cartesian self. Since the image was deemed natural and verisimilar, it was also linked with materiality, spatiality, and stasis and thus with exteriority, the object, and indeed the feminine or racially/ethnically Other. By contrast, since text was regarded as conventional and temporal, it came also to be coupled with interiority, active reason, disembodiment, the subject, and the *man*-made or masculine—all qualities presumed of the Cartesian observer.[17]

Mitchell has located the end of this rigid image/text binary's dominance only in what he calls postmodernism's "pictorial turn," a "postlinguistic, post-semiotic rediscovery of the picture as a complex interplay between visuality, apparatus, institutions, discourse, bodies, and figurality" (*Picture Theory* 16). He describes postmodernism as the period of the imagetext because it recognizes that complex interplay and thereby the fact that "the interaction of images and texts is constitutive of representation as such" (*Picture Theory* 5). Although I've retained Mitchell's notion of the imagetext, it's important to register how the spread of the new physiology of vision by the early twentieth century—roughly from the publication of Helmholtz's *Physiological Optics* to its translation into English in 1924—suggests a different history of the imagetext's appearance. In contrast to the Cartesian self, Helmholtz's and other physiologists' theories about the idiosyncrasies of the normal human eye and of optical processing in the brain suggested an embodied observer whose knowledge was mediated by the psychophysiological limits of vision and the density and partiality of visual memory.[18] Their topographical models of the eye highlighted that there was no stability or permanence in the content of the visual field and hence no means of identifying a focused center and peripheral background in the visual image. The observer, even in his or her most controlled attentive state, was vulnerable to uncontrollable visual distraction, and the image was a reminder of this uncertainty. It was unstable and temporal, and it blurred the distinction between internal sensation and external signs. Acceptance of this observer and image—which extended far beyond scientists like Helmholtz and deeply into popular culture—was what constituted the new physiology of vision. It undercut authority, identity, and universality and demanded a new conception of ontology and epistemology.

In addition to materializing in high- or middlebrow science magazines such as *Mind* and *Nature,* this new visuality appeared in popular discussions of new optical technologies, entertainments centered on optical illusions, and handbooks on the proper care of one's vision. These popular sites captured the broad characteristics of the new physiology of vision without detailing specialized debates or necessarily incorporating subsequent developments. As the Victorian science writer Alice Bodington explained, even where scientists were interested in communicating with the public, the growth of science and specialization meant that a lot of work wasn't reaching the popular press, and even specialized audiences had a difficult time keeping up due to a lack of synthesis in various fields (Lightman, *Victorian Popularizers* 465). Just as importantly, often only a certain number of basics were required for the educational and entertainment purposes of the vernacular. People wanted to know how the optical gadgets and illusions being introduced into their homes and sites of entertainment worked. In addition, amid concerns that the rapidity and environmental stresses of modern urban life were causing a broad decline in people's eyesight, they wanted to know how to maintain their vision. The expansive visual-scientific vernacular that resulted, as well as its further adaptation in, for instance, painting and psychoanalysis, make crucial appearances in the work of the various stylists of modernist impersonality in this study.

Many optical gadgets of this period—stereoscopes, kaleidoscopes, phenakistoscopes, kinoras, cinema—had in fact been developed by scientists for

Fig. I.3. Kinora, c. 1914. Perhaps less familiar than some of the other devices mentioned, the kinora was an early motion-picture device. It worked essentially like a flipbook. A sequential set of images were attached to a core that turned via a crank and was viewed through a magnifying viewer. Before World War I, it was the most popular device for home movie viewing in Britain. Laura Hayes Wileman and John Howard Wileman Collection, North Carolina School of Science and Mathematics, Durham. Photograph by Fred Hurteau.

the laboratory or were based on their research. These gadgets exploited the embodied limits of the eye in order to produce their effects and also offered an image that was fragmented and that unfolded temporally as those effects (fig. I.3).[19] In addition to countless articles, manuals, and lectures on the gadgets themselves, more direct discussions of the physiology of vision, such as Huxley's *Lessons in Elementary Physiology,* explained errors in visual judgment in terms of the illusions produced by these devices. The public was also keenly interested in specialized technologies such as x-rays or kymography.[20] X-rays made people aware of a portion of the light spectrum

Fig. I.4. Sherringon Starling recording drum for a kymograph by C. F. Palmer Ltd. (c. 1955). Science Museum, London.

beyond the eyes' range. The kymograph (also known as the wave *writer,* suggesting imagetextuality) was a revolving paper-wrapped drum on which a stylus moved back and forth recording bodily activity such as blood pressure. Figure I.4 illustrates how the kymograph's graphic recordings captured an autonomic materiality through a distinctly modern image that made no appeal to mimesis or a total view.[21]

The career of the inventor and illusionist John Henry Pepper perhaps best exemplifies how popular illusion shows similarly participated in the new visuality.[22] Seeking to draw large crowds to his public lectures, first at the Royal Polytechnic Institution in London in the 1860s and 1870s and then on tour in the United States and Canada, Pepper developed the photodrome, an optical apparatus that caused seeming phantoms to appear at will. He would stage a popular play or story, such as Charles Dickens' "The Haunted Man" (1848), with his ghost effects and then follow with a lecture

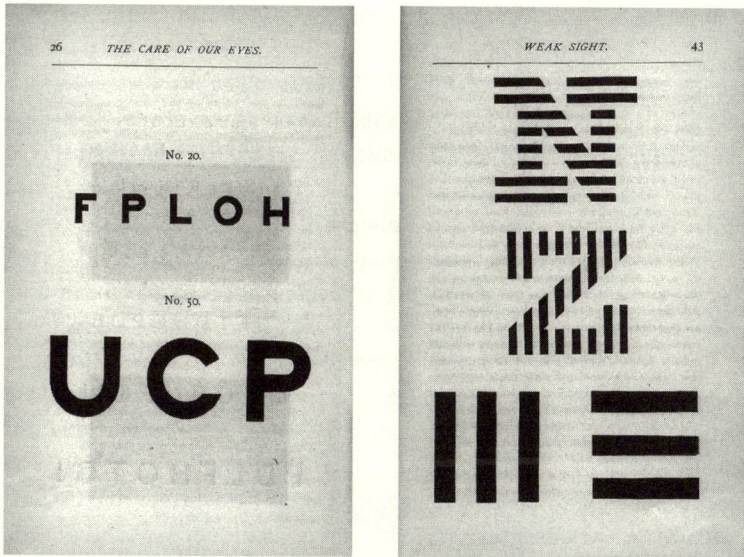

Fig. I.5. Test pages from Henry Angell's *How to Take Care of Our Eyes* (1878): *left,* sample of 20-point type to test for 20/20 vision; *right,* sample of hatched type to test for astigmatism. Cordell Collection, University of Maryland Health Sciences and Human Services Library.

in which he explained how the photodrome generated those effects. He also used similar optical principles to stage Shakespearean soliloquies delivered by the floating heads of Hamlet or King Lear. Both performances presciently connected literature, contemporary optics, and images that were in some way partial or fragmented and that couldn't be fully experienced in an instant.

Popular vision-care manuals, like George Harlan's *Eyesight, and How to Care for It* (1879), give perhaps the most extensive details about the anatomy and physiology of vision, starting as they did from the premise "that intelligent care of the eyesight requires some knowledge of the structure and functions of the organ of vision" (Harlan 10). These manuals explain the standard eye test for 20/20 vision (the ability to read 20-point type at 20 feet) and even include test type so that the reader can examine himself or herself for near- and far-sightedness and astigmatism (fig. I.5). They also describe and discuss treatment options for ocular defects, diseases, and injuries, right down to the very common *muscae volitantes,* or optical floaters.

Previous histories that considered this complex visual-scientific vernacular in relation to models of subjectivity and the political have read the intersection as a mechanism either for social regulation or, more recently, for a traditional liberalism rather than as a spur to a new ontology and epistemology.[23] Correspondingly, the few studies connecting these developments to aesthetic modernism have tended to argue that modernists acknowledged ocular science only to neutralize its implications.[24] By revealing how modernism's optical impersonality in both poetry and prose was instead part of this vernacular, this book joins work connecting optics to modern abstract and surrealist art (Krauss) and more recently French fictional modernism (Goulet), modernist film (Gaycken), and Edwardian genre fiction (Willis). In doing so, it also offers a new angle on literary modernism's attitude toward images. Critics have tended to assume either that modernist literature was solidly antivisual and anti-imagistic or, more commonly, that it epitomized an older attachment to a perfected image.[25] On the latter reading, modernists purportedly made their texts more like images in the hope of achieving the concreteness and immediacy images were traditionally thought to bear—even as they also held on to an interiority and transcendence traditionally linked to text. Such an effort contained text in its own world, sequestering both the work of art and the artist from shifting economic, political, or social pressures, both past and present. This reading renders modernism's engagement with the image a mere bid for the autonomy and individuality associated with the Cartesian observer. By contrast, I posit that as modernists became interested in the new physiology of vision, they avidly produced and consumed imagetexts, which belied not just the binary of image and text themselves but the many Cartesian hierarchies that followed. First, these modernists explore what their contemporary, Walter Benjamin, calls the "optical unconscious," the autonomic psychophysiology of the "image worlds" that condition all human subjects.[26] Second, their imagetexts showcase the qualities of image and text as media and explore how images and texts mutually implicate and interpenetrate each other, all in order to refuse the sense that any kind of art is a transparent window onto objects of representation. They thus occlude traditional ways of reading and seeing and intensify our awareness of the activity required in order for art, or even any percept, to *mean*. Third, they draw out the political implications of this optical unconscious—implications that generally weren't pursued by scientists or an entertainment-seeking public—and turn them to a range of political ends, both progressive and conservative.

Fig. I.6. William Hogarth's four-line drawing of a watchman and his dog going through a door. Reprinted from Ford Madox Ford, "On Impressionism."

We have already seen an example of this impersonal project in *Parade's End,* but Ford offers in his essay "On Impressionism" (1913) a still sharper crystallization of imagetextuality. In that essay, Ford analogizes his own method to a four-line drawing by the eighteenth-century printmaker and painter William Hogarth, who has been credited with pioneering Western sequential art, that is, the use of a sequence of images to tell a story. This drawing of a "watchman with the pike over his shoulder" and a "dog at his heels going in at a door" (37, 36) portrays only a vertical line for the door-frame, a curved line for the dog's tail, and two diagonal lines for the watch-man's pike (fig. I.6). It's clearly not a mimetic image, but it's nonetheless representative, both as a minimalist mode of reference to the objects it portrays and also as a partial and opaque representation of what so inter-ested Ford about human vision itself. Ford also emphasizes that "if you look at those lines for long enough, you will begin to *see* the watchman with his slouch hat, the handle of the pike coming well down into the cobblestones, the knee-breeches, the leathern garters strapped round his stocking, and the surly expression of the dog, which is bull-hound with a touch of mastiff in it" (37, emphasis added). Such a claim for visual extrapolation highlights the fact that Hogarth's image—really a graphic that evokes both textuality and imagistic visibility—is experienced temporally, inspires textual explana-tion, and is entirely unstable in its call upon the reader to fill in detail. Ford's example draws out the fundamental imagetextuality of all images, the fact that all images bear the supposed qualities of text. Moreover, it also presents an explicit imagetextuality as a way to explore timely questions of embodied visual perception, knowledge, and subjectivity.

A final example, from Virginia Woolf's last novel, *Between the Acts* (1941), showcases how the modernists used the imagetext that Ford describes to actively grapple with the fundamental categories of subjectivity that had long been both analogized to and naturalized by the image/text binary, categories like mind/body and male/female. Woolf uses the imagetextual form to work through and challenge some of these categories and also points overtly to the way that image-text relations had bolstered these categories in the past.

Between the Acts tells of a June 1939 day at the Olivers' English country home, where everyone is preparing for the village's annual pageant play. Early in the novel, readers are introduced to two paintings in the Oliver collection, paintings that stand as a lingering marker of both family and cultural history. The paintings hang next to each other, one featuring a lady leaning on a pillar and the other a man directing his horse. Woolf explains: "The Lady was a picture, bought by Oliver because he liked the picture; the man was an ancestor. He had a name. He had the rein in his hand. . . . He was a talk producer, that ancestor. But the lady was a picture" (25–26). Adding to this contrast, the ancestor's portrait was constructed by him, and he "seemed to [be] . . . addressing the company" from it. The unknown lady's picture, on the other hand, is "silence" (26). This silence spreads out into the room, which is itself "[e]mpty, empty, empty; silent, silent, silent," just like the vase beside the picture, which stands smooth and cold, "holding the still, distilled essence of emptiness, silence" (26).

This moment in Woolf's novel reads the history of the image in English culture through an image/text binary that bolsters several cultural values. Though both the lady and the ancestor are paintings, the ancestor "has a name," and he speaks, not only to the painter, with whom he arranges his own pose, but also through the centuries, as his painted likeness seems to address its viewer. He is thus the bearer of the word. The lady, by contrast, is repeatedly described as merely "a picture" with no name. The two paintings, whose subjects "never met," function to oppose image and text (26). Indeed, Woolf makes clear that this binary reaches deep into English history, for the almost metonymic relation she proposes between the lady and the vase beside her portrait evokes Keats' "Ode on a Grecian Urn" (1820), perhaps the most canonical Romantic reflection on the divide between the visual and the verbal. Woolf's lady, in other words, becomes the "still unravish'd bride of quietness" (line 1) that is Keats' urn, even as Woolf's two paintings visualize the image/text binary that Keats' poem announces. Just as importantly, Woolf's description delineates how this binary licensed others: the "picture" is feminine, silent, static, bodily, and empty, while the "talk producer" is masculine, active, self-determined, expressive, and interiorized.

The pageant play that organizes *Between the Acts,* and which features scenes from English history, signals a break from this image/text binary and its values. In the play's final act, meant to represent the modern moment, the actors return to the stage with all manner of reflective surfaces—cracked mirrors, tin cans, silver candlesticks, and glass jars. They turn these make-shift optical devices upon the audience. In their "[m]opping, mowing, whisk-ing, frisking," these reflectors serve as an "inquisitive insulting eye" that forces the members of a shocked audience to consider their materiality, visibility, and visuality (125, 126). The supposedly stable, verisimilar portraits of the Oliver ancestor and the unknown lady are gone. These devices in-stead show "[h]ere a nose . . . There a skirt . . . Then trousers only . . . Now perhaps a face" (125, ellipses original). Aligned with visual perception and optical gadgetry, the resulting images are fragmented and shifting. Their mirroring relation is neither mimetic nor whole but rather blatantly distort-ing. In turn, the self that these images represent isn't really a definable self at all. The devices catch not man and woman nor even male and female, but an imbricated "skirt," "trousers," and "face" of a fluctuating "our" (125). As these impersonal images accrue, a megaphone voice instructs the audience to participate by *"talk[ing] in words of one syllable"* and *"calmly consider[ing] ourselves"* and *"civilization,"* built as both are on *"orts, scraps and fragments"* (127). Words thus become just as compressed and incomplete and just as potentially puncturing as the pageant performers' caught images. Indeed, the actual inseparability of word and image is signaled by the simultaneity of the voice's *"orts, scraps and fragments"* and the narrator's description of the mirrors "flick[ing] and flash[ing]" (127).

Ultimately, Woolf's pageant play constructs an imagetext that refuses to oppose the verbal and the visual, expressive interiority and materiality, as the Oliver paintings had done. In challenging these binaries, it challenges what we have seen is an important basis for sociopolitical hierarchies of gender and class, both historically and in Woolf's novel. Moreover, Woolf shows that this work stems from a characteristically modernist interest— sometimes excited, at other times anxious—in registering a subjectivity that exceeds the personal and comprises unconscious and complexly interacting material, psychical, and social impulses. Thus far, then, we've seen that vi-sual and imagetextual concerns regarding subjectivity came to feed specifi-cally into a discourse of impersonality. The question of why it did so, how-ever, remains. And we'll find the answer by joining the history of optics and imagetext relations with the history of personality.

The Modern Image and Impersonality's Critique of Identity

From the fourteenth through the early nineteenth centuries the word *personality* meant "being a person as distinct from an animal, thing, or abstraction."[27] The principal basis for this distinction was the capacity for "consciousness and thought" (1a). By the early eighteenth century the term was also a marker of individuality, as in the philosopher Abraham Tucker's 1777 claim that "[p]ersonality is what makes a man to be himself, can never be divested . . . nor is interchangeable with that of any other creature" (4b). Here, to be a personality is to be a singular and distinctly male owner-agent (to "possess individual characteristics") and also to have "self-awareness" (3a). Such developments were supported by nineteenth-century legal discourse, in which *personality* began to mean "the subject of rights and duties recognized by law," signaling reason, action, and self-determination (7c). Personality was thus roughly analogous to citizenship and subjectivity. It was distinct from *personalty*, meaning objects that could be property (including any humans not considered persons). Compounding the term's link to individuality, the nineteenth century also extended *personality* to mean one who has "unusual or noteworthy" characteristics (4b).

By the early twentieth century, however, the bounded and singularizing nineteenth-century definition of personality, and indeed of personality *as* subjectivity, had wavered. Concepts like the "picture personality," formulated and popularized by Hollywood's star system, linked personality not only to fame but also to performance: to have personality meant to be *"fascinating, stunning, attractive,* [and] *magnetic,"* not only in the case of film stars but also for the broader public, both male and female.[28] Indeed, popular advice manuals of the period, like Henri Laurent's *Personality: How to Build It* (1915), prioritized a set of guidelines for breathing and grooming and a broad array of beauty aids rather than the moral interiority emphasized in Victorian manuals, in which personality was synonymous with character and closely linked to masculinity.[29] At this point, then, any idea of personality's stable, inalienable, and singularizing essence, not to mention its masculine privilege, became entangled with the belief that it was an ongoing spectacle. For men and women alike, personality was now relational and constructed rather than autonomous and given. It was effectively a fragmented and unstable image, just like the one imagined by the new physiology of vision.

Certain threads in the modern social and biological sciences bolstered this new notion of personality and put pressure on the implicit masculine privilege of older notions. In sociology, Marcel Mauss developed a social and ideological genealogy of the concept of personality that questioned the long link presumed in Western cultures between personality and consciousness, as well as the belief that the person is somehow sacred. Best captured in his 1938 lecture "The Notion of the Person; the Notion of the Self," Mauss' theory broadly influenced structural anthropologists like Claude Lévi-Strauss and particularly structural functionalists like Meyer Fortes. In perhaps more far-reaching ways, though, Freudian psychoanalysis denied that personality had a stable center in the ego and also refused the belief that subjects had substantial knowledge and control of themselves. Psychoanalysis proposed instead a massively incoherent subject, split across the ego, the id, and the superego. Even modern biochemists interested in a materialistic explanation of human behavior had a part to play. Studies like Charles Stockard's *The Physical Basis of Personality* (1931) emphasized the effects of autonomic systems, including the hormonal and nervous system, on personality, so that the fluctuating performance of identity was far from simply cosmetic, let alone willful. These proposals all hypothesized that there was no human subject like the imagined male personality with a perfectly rational self-control. Instead, human subjects were now universally and equally torn from the self-control that had previously been used to distinguish male "personalities" from objectified social inferiors (e.g., women, the working classes, or nonwhites).

These various resignifications of personality derived in part from the nineteenth-century science of memory in relation to chronic trance states and in particular to the extreme diagnosis of *dédoublement de la personnalité*, or double personality. As Ian Hacking has argued, prior to this moment psychological science had generally assumed a unique self that persisted apart from the diversity and transience of sensations, memories, and perceptions. Hacking cites the philosopher Théodule Ribot, and particularly his comments on *dédoublement* in *An Essay in the Positive Psychology* (1881), to characterize the shift away from a unique self. Ribot declares: "Let us first reject the idea of a *moi* as an entity distinct from states of consciousness. That is a useless and contradictory hypothesis; it is an explanation worthy of a psychology in its infancy. . . . I join in the opinion of contemporaries who see the conscious person as a compound, a resultant of very complex states." Ribot also goes on to note that members of the "old school . . . accuse the adherents of the new school of 'stealing their *moi*' " (qtd. in Hacking, *Rewriting the Soul* 207). Indeed, extreme cases of trance states, like *dédoublement,* questioned the unity and uniqueness that had characterized a *moi*. Sufferers, both men and women, functioned for extended periods of time with certain skills, affects, and physical ways of being, only to wake up with no memory of those periods and to occupy a different set of skills, affects, and physical ways of being. Often they moved unpredictably back and forth between these two distinct lives. This condition inspired doctors like Jean Martin Charcot and Pierre Janet (in France) and Morton Prince (in the United States) to understand personality increasingly as a mere "collection of present states of consciousness, comparable to a present visual field," and influenced by "its continuity with its past" in the form of "memory" (Hacking, *Rewriting the Soul* 206). The discourse of doubled personality, in other words, used collections of memories, thoughts, and bodily ailments to mark the boundaries between the now potentially multiple personalities of those who experienced chronic trance states. What Woolf would later call our *"orts, scraps and fragments"* had thus become personality itself. It was neither singular nor stable and was identified by visual observation rather than being strictly interior and nonbodily. Such incoherence, materiality, and performativity echoed in the new twentieth-century meanings of *personality* that I've detailed. Just as importantly, they were formative for a physiological optics. Jonathan Crary has described the way that scientists used research on trance states to gauge the embodied limits of visual attention, whether at the level of microsaccades, visual saturation, memory lapse, or cognitive focus.[30] Thus, at this epochal moment, reformulations of vision and of personality, both scientific and cultural, came together.

Despite this increasing complexity in the concept of personality, however, key lexicographical and literary reference works have understood *impersonality* very narrowly. The *OED's* brief entry for *impersonality* defines it merely as the "absence of personality" and glosses this absence as a lack of individual influence or consideration. Not surprisingly, the most recent citation is from 1897, prior to the real sedimentation of the modern personality I've described. The entry for *impersonality* in David Mikics' influential *New Handbook of Literary Terms* similarly focuses on an "escape from personality" and so emotion (154). Both of these reference works—one broadly cultural, the other specifically literary critical—presume an older formulation of personality as individuality, interiority, and agency and take the prefix *im-* in *impersonality* to indicate the "privation" or "negation" of those qualities.[31]

Until fairly recently such presumptions were also the norm in scholarship about modernism's impersonal aesthetic, especially scholarship focusing on

T. S. Eliot and Ezra Pound. The most frequently iterated claims were, first, that the aesthetic seeks but fails to eliminate personality in the form of subjective emotion, and second, that its underlying desire is really to value and protect a coherent authorial self.[32] Maud Ellmann has argued, for instance, that impersonality both gathers authority by announcing its emotionless objectivity and acts as a self-protective gesture through which modernists could disown any controversial material in their work. Ellmann thus sees the aesthetic as a prop for right-wing, multiply phobic politics and a protection from the prying eyes of psychologically minded critics. Along similar lines, Niels Buch-Jepsen has branded impersonality an effort to reassert authorial power in the face of a modern crisis of selfhood and representation that would later feed into New Criticism's "intentional fallacy." Impersonality, in other words, stages the author as a panoptic figure who claims the interpretive depriviling of the author as his own intention. Even less skeptical readings have agreed that impersonality is a kind of masking project for bolstering the self: it allowed modernists to distance themselves from those parts of their creative self-expression that they disliked (Albright) or to enlarge upon individual facets of the self without claiming them as representative expressions (Wilmer). Uniting all these readings of modernist impersonality are an interest in identity and identity politics and the related sense that modernism was all about the self rather than being culturally, ethically, or socially engaged. Both of these investments have aligned modernism with an old notion of personality regardless of how they judged an impersonal aesthetic in relation to it.

More recent work on impersonality, however, has pushed back against identity politics and its limits.[33] Without explicitly registering how modern resignifications of personality set the stage for impersonality, this new work usefully recognized two things: first, that modernists understood personality as merely a part and indeed not even the center of subjectivity, and second, that they saw personality as constructed rather than essential and relational rather than individual. In addition, these scholars usefully registered a positive political potential in the fact that impersonality not only deprivileged a longtime literary emphasis on self-expression but also worked to meet readers in a subjective space beyond the confines of the personal. Tim Dean and Rochelle Rives, for instance, have variously argued that impersonality represents an ethical practice of aesthetic "self-shattering," a literary ego rupture that "clear[s] a space for otherness at the expense of the writer's self" (Dean, "T. S. Eliot" 45). Similarly, Joyce Wexler has proposed that impersonality disrupts the way that language structures a gendered ego: it deploys contrary gender discourses to neutralize the writer's individuality and thus produce a nonidentitarian style through which to challenge social norms.

While this newer scholarly trend draws out the constructedness of personality in modernism, it has for the most part overlooked the role of the body in impersonality.[34] A couple of scholars, however, have begun the work of mapping the impersonal body. Charles Altieri has emphasized that the impersonal aesthetic sought to encourage new modes of feeling and sensation through the materiality of sound and structure. Similarly, Jewel Spears Brooker has shown that impersonality highlights the complex and shifting material relationships that connect people and the world. However, the most thoroughgoing example in this line can be found in Sharon Cameron's recent call for scholars to reconsider what the *im-* in *impersonality* really meant for modernists. Did they in fact hold personality and impersonality in a binary relation, Cameron asks, and did their *im-* entail a substance or characteristics rather than the lack of them? Cameron herself convincingly posits that modernists saw personality as simultaneously always already disintegrating *and* a social and experiential structure that one couldn't will oneself out of. Personality and impersonality, in other words, repeatedly intersect, and modernism's impersonal aesthetic centers on this intersection. It offers principally an attention to being that discerns the complex, inextricable relation between bodily sensation, feelings, mental states, and objects of the mind and also shows that these phenomena can't actually constitute individuality in constituting a personality.

This book develops Cameron's premise that modernist impersonality is a study of the nature of being, concerned with attending to the opaque, unwilled, and fluctuating systems of perception as well as to the making and unmaking of personality. It situates the impersonal aesthetic as part of the contemporary loss of faith in the sacred nature of personality that Marcel Mauss discerned and that also surfaced in the other popular and scientific notions of personality in the early twentieth century.[35] Modernist impersonality embraced and elaborated on what these new notions made possible. It seized on the image conceived by the science of memory and, more crucially, by a subsequent physiological optics. It placed this new visual image within aesthetic imagetexts and used these imagetexts to explore the subjective conditions of personality. These imagetexts, in other words, highlight personality's lack of essence or originality and also grasp at a decentered and shifting subjectivity that exceeds the personal. Thus, returning to etymology, the *im-* in *impersonality* signified for modernists not "negation" or "privation" but rather what goes "into" personality.[36]

Insofar as optical impersonality explores the making and unmaking of personality, it also fans the politics that were already sparking in other modern reformulations of personality. Chris Otter's recent discussion of the links between civil illumination systems and Victorian liberalism offers one way to register these politics and to see how modernist impersonality made its own contribution to disciplinary knowledge rather than simply reciting the contemporary science of embodied vision. Otter notes that vision and the subject of liberal humanism shared a common vocabulary: vision was long understood as volitional and distant, for example, while liberalism required visual actions like attention to detail and reading character. Municipal illumination programs marshaled the new physiology of vision to support liberal values. They aimed to create the ideal lighting conditions for the activities of the liberal subject—activities like learning and working independently. Yet if the new physiology of vision was politically rerouted to support the liberal subject, modernist impersonality showcases how that visuality might not actually comport with such a project and could indeed cut against it. Aesthetic impersonality, in other words, pushed the visual-scientific vernacular in a different direction. It did so by insistently asking how the new physiology of vision applied across the gender, racial, and class distinctions that had long distinguished a supposedly disembodied male subject from everyone else. The imagetexts that crop up in the impersonal aesthetic consistently move from making manifestations of impersonal subjectivity glancingly visible toward exploring the political implications of such a subjectivity for categories of social identity like gender and race. In some modernist writings, this exploration undermines the felt naturalness of these identities by highlighting the social and biological matrices within which they emerge. In others, such explorations end by rearticulating these identity categories in even firmer and stronger terms. Still other texts reflect a struggle between these two possibilities, for instance, where an effort to explore impersonal subjectivity yields to an impulse to preserve old identities within it but where those identities also continue to be haunted by impersonality's instabilities.

The following chapters, which cover roughly the 1880s through the 1950s, cut a broad swath across the modernist period. Moving between poetry, fiction, and criticism and between protomodernists, high modernists, avant-gardists, and antimodernists, these chapters suggest the real breadth of the impersonal aesthetic. In chapter 1, I begin by examining the origins of impersonality in the work of the Victorian aesthetic philosopher Walter Pater and two of his contemporaries, the collaborative poets Katharine Bradley and Edith Cooper, who wrote together under the pen name Michael Field. Pater's career demonstrates an important nexus in the new physiology of vision between a physiological optics and its philosophical extrapolation into new accounts of subjectivity. In his early study *The Renaissance* (1873) Pater used his familiarity with both fields to challenge the burgeoning art historical interest in promoting objective methods of attribution and in using them to stabilize artists' professional identities. Pitting contemporary optical science and philosophy against art historical dating methods, Pater refused to consolidate and winnow Renaissance painters' *oeuvres* and identities and instead took the groundbreaking position that the art image, the artist, and indeed more fundamentally the human subject were fluctuating imagetexts. Pater specifically adopted the term *impersonality* to describe his view in two later essays, "Style" (1888) and "Prosper Mérimée" (1890). He also adopted in work and life a continual performance of restraint that gestured at those parts of subjectivity that exceed simple "expression." Such a practice, intersecting as it did with the contemporary reformulation of personality as performance, was another tool in the arsenal of aesthetic impersonality's various stylists, another way for them to turn optics into social politics. Bradley and Cooper recognized that this extension had the potential to loosen Victorian gender and sexual norms. In addition, Michael Field points to the expanding and indirect ways in which writers could encounter and torque the visual-scientific propositions that Pater knew more directly and extensively as an Oxford don. *Sight and Song* (1890), Field's volume of ekphrases (or poems about paintings), draws on the contemporary conventions of mass-produced and richly illustrated museum guidebooks to point to a broad redefinition of all images as nonmimetic, fluctuating, and decentered. Bradley and Cooper were thus among the first to recognize in popular visual culture both a scene and a mode for turning the new physiology of vision into imagetextual models of an impersonal subjectivity.

In the remaining chapters I demonstrate that as the visual-scientific vernacular expanded in the early twentieth century, something akin to Field's approach became the dominant animating force for the impersonal aesthetic. From film and abstract art to advertising and psychoanalytic dream analysis, modern stylists of impersonality expanded the range of their imagetextual theorizations of embodied subjectivity even as they focused more persistently on the politics of those theorizations. In chapters 2 and 3, I offer detailed histories of two writers whose work scholars have actually opposed to modernist impersonality, H.D. and Mina Loy. I show that these writers not only produced and consumed the imagetexts that appear so regularly in the impersonal aesthetic but also worked with varying degrees of confidence to turn impersonality toward progressive political causes. One of the few modernists to explicitly embrace her relation to nineteenth-century figures like Pater, H.D. engaged with multiple versions of a vernacular visual science—including abstract painting and sculpture, cinema, and psychoanalysis—through her participation in two aesthetic communities: the imagists and POOL. H.D.'s career-long engagement of this vernacular reveals a complex evolution in thinking about impersonality's reformist politics. H.D.'s early imagist verse and her manifesto on visual experience use imagetextuality to outline an embodied subject who bears only blurred sexual and racial identities. Her later film production and criticism as part of POOL move beyond the contours of the individual subject to consider the melding of spectator and spectacle. In this melding, embodied identities are not individual possessions but the unstable product of a nexus of social and organic imperatives, a politically consequential notion that rejects both biological essentialist and social constructivist views of race and gender.

The writer-painter Mina Loy was much less confident than H.D. about impersonality's progressive implications, at least initially. She worried that the translation of optics into a new model of subjectivity would founder on the shoals of race and gender before it could rework them. Writers might use impersonality, in other words, to feed the contemporary social perception of women and racially marked subjects as incomplete personalities and thus second-class artists and citizens. Yet in a variety of midcareer works Loy increasingly used a visual vernacular, ranging from photography and television to x-rays and fluoroscopes, to represent the impersonal forces governing subjectivity. Her friendship with the artists Marcel Duchamp and Richard Oelze, who were affiliated to different degrees with surrealism, also likely led her to turn that visual discourse into the backbone of her eventual major endorsement of optical impersonality, her late novel *Insel* (1935–61). This work, which surreally details her friendship with Oelze, offers a significant adumbration of the logic of impersonality and also vindicates impersonality's gender and racial politics. By recognizing both Loy and H.D. as significant and previously unacknowledged stylists of an optical impersonality, these chapters enhance our sense of the centrality of this aesthetic to modernism.

Further charting the breadth of this aesthetic and its politics, in the final chapters I focus on two modernists who sought to balance their fascination with impersonality against their wariness of its application to progressive politics. The self-appointed antimodern modernist D. H. Lawrence developed the most ingenious of these balancing acts. As a teacher and reader of physics and evolutionary science, Lawrence viewed modern optics as a common denominator for those fields and adapted its model of embodied vision into what he called an "alert science." Yet where Loy worried that the implications of optics wouldn't alter gender and racial difference, Lawrence worried that they would. His response depended on a paradox. On the one hand, his alert science embraced imagetextuality as a genuine blow not only to a transcendent perception and observer but also to the social binaries of gender and race that applied to that observer. On the other hand, alert science also posited that if individuality, gender, and race were unmoored, that didn't mean they simply faded away; instead they inhabited a hazy and thus unassailable space without origins and contours. In other words, such identities existed but were impossible to pin down, so there was no approach for refuting them. I read Lawrence's career as a marshaling of genre after genre toward building his more conservative impersonal politics, from his poetic record of embodied visual acts to the paradoxical model of subjectivity expressed in his criticism on postimpressionist painting and psychoanalysis to his last and most controversial novel, *Lady Chatterley's Lover* (1928), in which he attempts to induct readers into his impersonal imperative.

If in the bulk of this book I trace the fullest radius of modernist impersonality by considering writers who either have often been actively dissociated from the impersonal aesthetic or simply remained invisible to scholars of it, I close by using this new history to resituate the modernist most associated with impersonality, T. S. Eliot. Eliot's impersonal project, like Pater's, originated in his academic studies of the science and philosophy of vision and subsequently in his exchanges with the science writer J. W. N. Sullivan. A close comparison of Sullivan's 1919 articles in the *Athenaeum* and Eliot's early essays on impersonality show that Eliot adapted Sullivan's ideas about the nature of science, his rhetorical gestures for discussing the relation between art and science, and even his use of optics as a source of scientific examples. In both *The Waste Land* (1922) and his verse play *The Family Reunion* (1939) Eliot then used visual philosophies and technologies as well as the performative space of the theater to develop imagetexts that reject what he saw as a widespread modern denial of impersonal subjectivity. Like Lawrence, though, Eliot harbored a persistent ambivalence toward the potential reformist implications of an optical impersonality. Where Lawrence managed actually to exploit impersonality for his conservative political ends, Eliot developed the very different strategy of simply containing impersonality's capacity to rewrite social relations. He weighted the destabilizing traits of impersonality toward gendered bodies in order to try to neutralize its progressive implications, though with uneven success.

To see the arc of optical impersonality bend from Walter Pater to T. S. Eliot, from Michael Field to D. H. Lawrence, is to recognize not only a new way of constellating modernists but also a fundamental connection between scientific and literary modernism, a connection that shows that the current vogue for life sciences in the arts and humanities is certainly not without precedent. But what might it mean to bring together modernist impersonality and that current interest more specifically? What might we gain, in other words, by recognizing modernist impersonality's afterimage in something like contemporary affect theory? I argue in the afterword that the fundamental structure of optical impersonality surfaces in the recent work of Brian Massumi and Eve Kosofsky Sedgwick, two influential but diverging theorists of affect, or those psychophysiological changes that we experience as emotion. Massumi has theorized an ineluctable material subjectivity in part through modern optics, notably the *Ganzfeld,* or "total field," experiments of the late 1920s and 1930s, which sought to isolate the elemental physical and physiological conditions of vision. Sedgwick, meanwhile, adapted her own affect theory into an imagetextual fabric art grounded in modern visual technologies and meant to produce a loss of self. Yet Massumi in particular also often resorts to a notion of the "*pre*personal," and the exclusions and linearity of this temporality have brought sharp criticism. I thus propose in the afterword not only that modernist *im*personality is a forebear of affect theory but also that it offers a useful conceptualization for some of the work this theory is trying to accomplish today. Reciprocally, I argue that affect theory's understanding of the political as a force that operates both within and beyond ideology may help to explain modernist impersonality's political nature and why its diverse politics have long been overlooked.

Although affect theory is one of the objects of analysis in this book, I want to note finally, as I move to consider those objects, that my method shares something with the spirit of affect theory, in particular with Massumi's notion of "radical empiricism" (*Parables* 16). Massumi argues that current empiricism is impoverished because it self-selects its objects of study in a way that ironically distorts the world around it: scientists decide what counts as a region of normative variation around a phenomenon and then study only what falls within that region as a way to characterize the phenomenon. This impoverished empiricism, to use Massumi's terms, takes a broad and shifting "potential" and artificially winnows it down to a predictable set of "possible" outcomes. By contrast, in this book I work to stay true to modernist impersonality's potential. Impersonality formally and thematically develops a visual-scientific vernacular whose complexity and drift are both open and piecemeal. To capture that openness, I've recorded not only those moments in which a particular writer deals directly with the new physiology of vision but also those moments in which a writer approaches this science in less obvious ways, such as through quantum physics or n-dimensional geometry. I've thus proceeded in a spirit of radical empiricism, consistently avoiding any trimming or simplification of a writer's impersonal style to make it neatly follow one pattern. By recognizing how a wide variety of modernists extrapolated the new physiology of vision into highly varied imagetextual experiments that explore and represent an impersonal subjectivity, we can understand the sources and nature of impersonality much better than we have done heretofore. The resulting account of modernist impersonality gives us both a new perspective on modernism and a new way to engage pressing theoretical questions in the humanities today.

1 A Protomodern Picture Impersonality

Walter Pater and Michael Field's Vision

> Gathering himself together from the complex world and
> standing back as it were to gaze upon it[,] the mind of man
> embraces the third great idea under which in turn he may
> figure to himself as the master of nature and akin to its
> creator[:] the idea of the mind itself[,] of the *ego* or of
> personality or will[,] or of the soul or spirit of man as it
> is variously named.
>
> Pater, "The History of Philosophy"

> "Open-gaze" at it. . . . Dutch-picture the little scene on the
> brain. *Do not hack or wear yourself.* Yield not to vanity, and
> refuse to *go out in the Sun.*
>
> Katharine Bradley to Edith Cooper, 8 August 1887

In a rare lecture delivered at the London Institution in November 1890, the philosophy scholar and art critic Walter Pater labeled the French dramatist Prosper Mérimée a too perfect impersonalist. Mérimée was so coldly self-effacing, Pater argued, that his style emphasized "transparen[cy]" over the "half-lights" of perception, and so cynical that he represented human materiality and its opaque workings only negatively, in terms of "maliciously active, hideous . . . bodies."[1] But though Pater condemns Mérimée's impersonality, his critique doesn't simply comport with scholarly accounts of his supposed investment in an individual personality, whether as the "father" of a subjectivist literary impressionism or of a modern homoerotic aesthetic anchored in identity politics.[2] "Prosper Mérimée" doesn't reject aesthetic impersonality in favor of personal expression. Instead, it proposes two models of impersonality, the second formulated for the most part as an *alterna-*

tive to Mérimée's. This other, distinctly positive impersonality concerns itself with the "half-lights" of perception and the opacity of materiality in which they originate, accepts the impossibility of transparent knowledge, and constructs the resulting opaque impersonality as the condition of personality rather than simply as its opposite. It thus participates in the turn-of-the-century redefinition of personality detailed in this book's introduction, a redefinition that located personality in a broad flux of memory, perception, and social performance rather than in an essential identity or selfhood.

Pater's presentation of this other impersonality marks a significant moment in the genealogy of an impersonal aesthetic. As a philosophy scholar, Pater had a much more direct and specialized knowledge of visual science than did many of the modernists, who gained their sense largely from a vernacular science that circulated in visual culture. Pater's knowledge makes his aesthetic an important window onto the scientific roots of modernist impersonality. The ingredients of his aesthetic date from his first and most controversial book-length work, *The Renaissance* (1873, 1877, 1888, 1893), where Pater situates his aesthetic project within the new physiology of vision that rejected the disembodied, objective observer of Cartesian optics and instead took vision as a complex process that is subject to the material limits of perception and the density and partiality of memory. Pater draws out the implications of this new visuality for being and knowing, thereby laying the groundwork for modernist impersonality and its intervention into vernacular visual science. Even more importantly, Pater's aesthetic crystallizes the formal role of the imagetext in this process. As I explained in the introduction, the relation between objective observer and transparent vision had long been complemented by an image/text binary in which text conveyed rational thought and the image was a static, mimetic record of external objects. A new model of vision could thus in theory be explored and even magnified by new image/text relations. *The Renaissance* transforms this theory into practice: where optics blurred the subject/object divide, it presents imagetexts that blur the image/text divide. It privileges, in both form and theme, an image that is conventional and unfolds over time—qualities traditionally reserved for text—rather than being natural, static, and mimetic. Pater uses this imagetext to interrogate the embodied observer of the science of vision and to theorize a material subjectivity that exceeds the self.

Pater's Prosper Mérimée lecture folds his early aesthetic into an explicit discourse of impersonality. The lecture uses the label "impersonal" to describe the subjectivity that Pater adapted from the new physiological optics.

It also declares that the work of accessing that subjectivity and exploring its effects are Pater's aesthetic goals. Finally, its warnings against the improper practice of impersonality gesture at the political potential of such an aesthetic. These explanations together prefigure the outlines of what optical impersonality means and does.

But Pater's lecture neither explicitly elaborates on impersonality's political potential nor identifies an artist who can serve as a positive foil for Mérimée. We do not have to look far, however, for artists who filled these gaps; Pater's friends the poets Katharine Bradley and Edith Cooper (alias Michael Field), did both. Bradley and Cooper, who were in the audience at Pater's Mérimée lecture, offer a more explicitly politicized formulation of his aesthetic both in their collaborative performance as Michael Field and in *Sight and Song* (1892), their volume of poems about paintings. As a complement to Pater's *Renaissance* and its participation in the burgeoning field of art history, *Sight and Song* clarifies impersonality's imagetextual appeal to contemporary visual culture. Its project harnesses the nineteenth-century reproduction and circulation of artwork through museum prints and guidebooks as a way of modeling the image and the observer proposed by vernacular visual science. Though Field today occupies a marginal position in the literary canon—a position that arguably points to the breadth of an impersonal aesthetic—Bradley and Cooper were well known to prominent modernists such as W. B. Yeats, H.D., and Roger Fry.[3] Indeed, the 1916 *Cambridge History of English Literature* includes an entry for Field, and "their" work was featured in the 1936 *Oxford Book of Modern Verse*.[4] This historical prominence makes Field an important touchstone in a genealogy of modernist impersonality.

Vision, *Anders-streben,* and Performance in *The Renaissance*

The Renaissance, first published in 1873 and variously revised and supplemented until 1893, intervened in the then new field of art history. In doing so, it offered not simply words about images but a play on the inseparability of word and image—in contrast to the longstanding artistic habit of treating the seeable and the sayable as fundamentally different and at their closest still mere analogies. The chapters of Pater's art history, each of which is organized around a different featured artist, range across poets like Joachim du Bellay and painters like Sandro Botticelli and even consider the poetry that Michelangelo wrote on his more famous sketches. *The Renaissance*'s imagetextual exploration consistently engages the new physiology of vision and the image and observer it hypothesizes, sometimes through the lives of the artists themselves and sometimes through commentary on the new science of dating and attributing their art. Its art history also goes beyond this engagement to develop an aesthetic that looks to the opacities of materiality, the embodied nature of perception, and the inseparability of observer and world in order to frame a new and growing model of subjectivity.[5]

In "Leonardo da Vinci," the earliest written of *The Renaissance*'s nine chapters, Pater uses the life of Leonardo to introduce the volume's concern with contemporary optics.[6] This use is rooted in Leonardo's nineteenth-century reputation, as launched by Jules Michelet's *The Renaissance* (1855) and Edgar Quinet's *The Revolutions of Italy* (1848), both of which Pater had read.[7] Such texts, as Barrie Bullen has argued, emphasized three key points about Leonardo that had often been elided in earlier histories: (1) that he intuited the ideas of modern science; (2) that he existed at a transitional moment in the history of science, between medieval religious scholasticism and the free intellectual inquiry of the Renaissance; and (3) that as both a painter and a scientist he considered the eyes the "chief organ" and was deeply interested in their mechanics.[8] Extrapolating from these three points, Pater's essay uses Leonardo's transitional position within the history of science to express *The Renaissance*'s own position as it negotiates a transition to the new physiology of vision. Drawing on the nineteenth-century belief that Leonardo was a forebear of modern science, as well as on his particular interest in the mechanics of vision, Pater describes Leonardo's project in terms of a physiological optics. At the same time, though, Pater also maintains Leonardo's connection to the visionary, which we might link not only to the older religious scholasticism of Leonardo's time but also to Descartes' transcendental, objective vision. Indeed, if Leonardo's anatomical study prefigured a modern focus on the physiology of perception, his discussions of graphic perspective explicitly compared the human eye to the mirroring mechanics of the camera obscura, thereby prefiguring the work Kepler would do to pave the way for a Cartesian visuality.[9] In Pater's hands, however, the overall weight of Leonardo's aesthetic falls on an embodied vision, just as the weight also falls in *The Renaissance*'s larger aesthetic.

Pater sets out the scientific context of "Leonardo da Vinci" with an epigraph from the Enlightenment scientist Francis Bacon's *Instauratio Magna* (1809-14) that declares man to be the "minister and interpreter of nature," while the passage it comes from characterizes circumscribed acts of observation as humans' only means of knowing the natural world. For Pater, Leonardo literally embodies the shift toward Bacon's observant interpreter. He notes that Leonardo's "perfection of the older Florentine style of miniature-painting," represented in his "lost picture of *Paradise*," "awoke in [him] some seed of discontent" that led him to an art that would use observation to explore the "meaning of nature and purpose of humanity" (*R* 81). The epigraph and biography together portray a kind of positive fall from a contained, metaphysical existence (suggested by the lost miniature of paradise) to the active observation of the physical forces driving humans and nature alike. Indeed, Pater pictures that fall as a "plunge . . . into the study of nature," after which Leonardo "brooded over the hidden virtues of plants and crystals, the lines traced by the stars as they moved in the sky, over the correspondences which exist between the different orders of living things" (*R* 81). A shifting conception of vision, moreover, is mixed up with the discontent at the root of this plunge. Pater describes the young Leonardo painting Florentine miniatures as "the cheerful, objective painter, through whose soul, as through clear glass, the bright figures of Florentine life passed . . . on to the white wall" (*R* 81). The objectivity and visual transparency of this neat formulation cast Leonardo's transformation as a dissatisfied turn from the camera obscura observer, whose mind's eye immediately registers the world. The mature Leonardo instead observes with his "eyes opened" to opacity, the byword of the physiological optics of Pater's own day: he learns "the art of going deep," of "tracking the sources of expression to their subtlest retreats," of attending to what is "hidden" in the natural world, and of catching "things of a peculiar atmosphere and mixed lights" (*R* 81, 81, 81, 83).

Pater favors the materiality of this visual shift in his discussion of what was thought to have been Leonardo's Uffizi *Medusa,* now known to be a sixteenth-century Flemish painting perhaps modeled on a lost Leonardo (see fig. 1.1). Pater uses terms of stark materiality to explain why Leonardo's portrayal of the Medusa stands out from those of other painters: "Leonardo alone cuts to its [the subject's] centre; he alone realises it as the head of a corpse, exercising its powers through all the circumstances of death" (*R* 83). Pater lingers over and seeks even to magnify those mortal circumstances in his own prose: "About the dainty lines of the cheek the bat flits unheeded. The delicate snakes seem literally strangling each other in terrified struggle to escape the Medusa brain. The hue which violent death always brings with it is in the features; features . . . like a great calm stone against which the wave of serpents breaks" (*R* 83). In addition, Pater argues that this painting rematerializes an earlier lost *Medusa* that Leonardo supposedly had painted

Fig. 1.1. Flemish artist, *Head of Medusa,* 1500s. Uffizi Gallery, Florence.

on a wooden shield. This hypothetical earlier piece underscores the embodied nature of vision in two respects. First, in the Greek myth Leonardo depicts, Perseus needs the shield if he is to have any hope of seeing Medusa
without turning to stone; that need for an intervening device symbolizes
the mediated nature of vision, the sense that the eye cannot directly and
completely capture the world. Second and similarly, the painting's existence
on a distinctly nonreflective wooden shield announces that pictures (and
indeed images more broadly) aren't simply mirrors of nature.

Though Pater clearly values Leonardo as a protomodern philosopher of
embodied vision, he tempers that portrayal by positing that Leonardo's "clair-
voyance" keeps the "mass of science" from "over-cloud[ing]" his art (*R* 83,
89, 84). Pater's appeal to the visionary in this and other moments distances
Leonardo from a physiological optics but is nonetheless consistent with
debates taking place in the nineteenth century between sensationalists and
empiricists. The philosopher Thomas Reid, whom Pater read in 1861 (Inman,
Pater's Reading 25), proposed a distinction between sensations, which derive from the immediate actions of the senses, and perceptions, which are
given by divine assistance and associated with objects that exist whether
perceived or not. Reid's optical experimentation encompassed both physiological conditions like double vision in people who squint and prophetic

second sight. Pater's claim that Leonardo's philosophy bears the "modern spirit" of observational science, while also retaining "the older alchemy . . . [of] double sight" is evocative of Reid (R 86, 84).

Still, despite such moments of hesitation, Pater's essay ultimately emphasizes that Leonardo came down on the side of materiality and physiology. Pater reads Leonardo's "return to nature" as an attempt "to satisfy . . . a microscopic sense" of that "*subtilitas naturae* which Bacon notices" (R 86), a sense that is "many times greater than the subtlety of the senses and the understanding."[10] Beyond the explicit reference to instruments of scientific visualization and Baconian empiricism, Pater also uses less obvious cues that, particularly when set against the conclusion to *The Renaissance,* deepen his verdict on Leonardo. For example, Pater notes that Leonardo was engaged in "a strange variation of the alchemist's dream, to discover the secret, not of an elixir to make man's natural life immortal, but of giving immortality to the subtlest and most delicate effects of painting" (R 84). This commentary suggests Pater's overwhelming insistence in the conclusion on the specifically material evanescence of human life and the relation of that evanescence to artistic perception. Because humans are made up of "natural elements . . . and elementary forces," Pater argues, we are but an interval in a constant flux that "rusts iron and ripens corn" and "leaves us all under sentence of death but with a sort of indefinite reprieve" (R 186, 186, 190). The only chance of "expanding that interval" is to get as many sensations or "pulsations as possible into the given time," and art enables that expansion because it promises "to give nothing but the highest quality to your moments as they pass" (R 190). Read against this argument from the conclusion, the description of Leonardo's anti-alchemical dream becomes a ringing endorsement of an artist of material limits. Indeed, Pater's absorption with the corpse in his reading of Leonardo's *Medusa* underlines these echoes across the two essays.

As this comparison suggests, while "Leonardo da Vinci" figures a choice between two visualities and hints at the goals of an aesthetic grounded in the new physiology of vision, the conclusion to *The Renaissance* more directly engages that science and explicates its refashioning of subjectivity. This final essay, which was actually drafted before any of *The Renaissance*'s main chapters, considers in detail the fragmentation both within and between complex mindbodily systems like memory, consciousness, sensation, and respiration.[11] Pater approaches what he calls a "continual vanishing away" across these systems through both the life sciences and skeptical philosophy

(*R* 188). From the life sciences, he highlights the common chemical elements that make up humans and the natural world, such as "phosphorus and lime," and also traces the eternal processes of "waste and repair" that drives both (*R* 186). From skeptical philosophy, he highlights consciousness as a stream of "momentary acts of sight and passion and thought" that have already "ceased to be" before we can even apprehend them (*R* 187, 188).

Crucially, Pater fills in both fields by appealing to embodied vision. Regarding the life sciences, he explains the "perpetual motion" of our "physical life" by describing "the passage of the blood, the waste and repairing of the lenses of the eye, the modification of the tissues of the brain under every ray of light and sound" (*R* 186). This description likely draws on Herbert Spencer's *The Principles of Biology* (1864-67), which proposes that "repair is everywhere and always making up for waste" and offers as illustration the circulatory system's regeneration of eye tissue (1:173). Likewise, Pater metaphorizes the ephemeral nature of physical life as "the gradual darkening of the eye, the gradual fading of colour from the wall" (*R* 187)—where that "wall" might be either a literal visual object or a figure for the eye's retina (as in Descartes' camera obscura model of vision). In either case, vision is dark and faded because it's distinctly embodied. The figure also again recalls important work in visual science, this time Johann von Goethe's *Theory of Colors* (1810), which offers an early account of colored shadows and chromatic aberration, processes that produce subjective color in perception.[12]

Pater fills in the study of consciousness with similar allusions to the bodily limits of vision. He figures himself and his reader as together observing the complex system of consciousness through a skeptical lens, an experience that's as temporal and partial as the new, modern image. He begins, "At first sight experience seems"; he then moves on to the qualification "But when reflexion begins to play upon those objects"; and he offers further instability with the additional qualifier "if we continue to dwell" (*R* 187). In addition to this observational evolution, Pater emphasizes that if the mind understands only a "dream of a world," then we must admit that our knowledge of mind and body alike is similarly limited (*R* 188). Highlighting the play of dreamlike images here, he argues that though perception records a "perpetual outline of face and limb," this outline or boundary is "but an image of ours" (*R* 186-87). Moreover, again evoking the camera obscura, he suggests that human "personality" is but a "wall" in the "narrow chamber of the individual mind" (*R* 187). It's a blank surface that receives perceptual images that are themselves shifting impressions rather than direct reflections of the outside world. By likening personality to the unstable, partial, and constructed image of the new physiology of vision, Pater recalls the philosopher Johann Fichte's *The Vocation of Man* (1800), which announces:

> There is nothing enduring, either out of me, or in me. . . . I know of no being, not even of my own. . . . Pictures are . . . the only things which exist, and they know of themselves after the fashion of pictures:—pictures which float past without there being anything past which they float; which, by means of like pictures, are connected with each other:—pictures without anything which is pictured in them, without significance and without aim. I myself am one of these pictures:—nay, I am not even this, but merely a confused picture of these pictures. (1:402)[13]

Pater's conclusion goes on to confirm that the subjectivity he theorizes throughout *The Renaissance* is in crucial dialogue with contemporary visual science in its professional and vernacular forms. If this vernacular offers the "image" of "losing even [one's] personality," then Pater's aesthetic refuses what it labels as a "grotesque individualism."[14] While critics have often read the conclusion's interest in perception as advocating a solipsistic hedonism, the essay instead demonstrates *The Renaissance*'s commitment to both accessing and exploring the implications of an autonomic or involuntary material subjectivity quite in tension with the self-containing gesture of solipsism.[15]

Just as importantly, though, Pater's scientific interests in *The Renaissance* aren't simply thematic. Rather, they give rise to an aesthetic project that emerges between "Leonardo" and the conclusion. This project has two key aims: to perceive the autonomic subjectivity of a physiological optics and, through art and life together, to represent that subjectivity and provoke an awareness of it in others. In formulating this aesthetic, Pater again leans heavily on Leonardo as a figure for his own work. He gravitates toward two principles that he at first associates somewhat ambivalently with Leonardo's project but then embraces across *The Renaissance* as a whole. These principles supply the scaffolding for Pater's critical analysis of the artists he has collected in the book, and this scaffolding allows him to elaborate more specific, and more specifically imagetextual, techniques for highlighting a material subjectivity distinct from "grotesque individualism," one that he will eventually recast as an optical impersonality.

Pater's first aesthetic principle is based on the fact that Leonardo, in both his art and his science, is continually "smitten with a love of the impossible" (*R* 82). His effort to register and represent the "unknown" places in a "temperament" is never fully attainable and for this reason is treated as a mode of perpetual, unconsummated desire (*R* 92). Pater suggests that Leonardo wishes to inspire a similar desire in his audience, a longing that would be directed at both art and artist. Early in his Leonardo chapter, Pater is rather anxious about the incompletion and imperfection inherent in Leonardo's "impossible" aesthetic, worrying that it sparks a highly uneven productivity. He vacillates over the "restless" periods in which Leonardo didn't work and the pieces he didn't finish or "endless[ly] retouch[ed]" (*R* 88). However, in *The Renaissance* as a whole, imperfection becomes a crucial principle of Pater's own artistic project.

Pater's second aesthetic principle allows the artist who has achieved a sense of incompletion to represent it and produce an awareness of it in others. This principle revolves around Leonardo's use of a "cryptic language" that can capture the density of perceptual experience and indeed of subjectivity (*R* 97). Pater suggests that this language, which amounts to a formal program, represents its object in a way that carries it "altogether beyond the range of its conventional associations" (*R* 94). Neither transparent nor smoothly conventional, such language can "plunge" into "human personality" and express "places far withdrawn" even from dreams (*R* 87). Leonardo's portraits, for instance, represent not selves but an opaque subjectivity beyond the personal. This subjectivity includes the flux of various hidden "element[s]" in Leonardo himself, like the uncontrollable "reflexes of things that had touched his brain in childhood" and the unconscious influence asserted by those around him (*R* 97, 82). Pater casts *La Gioconda* (c. 1503–6), Leonardo's most famous and most enigmatic portrait, as an example; she was at once a real woman and an "image" that "defin[ed] itself on the fabric of [Leonardo's] dreams." Extending beyond Leonardo and Lisa, this painting's cryptic language expresses what "in the ways of a thousand years men had come to desire," even without knowing it. Pater connects this cryptic quality to the complexity of new physiological models of subjectivity when he declares that *La Gioconda*'s beauty is "wrought out from within upon the flesh, the deposit . . . of strange thoughts and fantastic reveries" belonging to nature and humanity (*R* 98).

The principle of a cryptic language extends from Leonardo's portraits to his own public persona. Pater suggests that Leonardo courted a certain "fascinat[ion]" (*R* 77), not only in his "country and friends" but in subsequent generations, by making himself something "strange" and "secret" (*R* 78), like *La Gioconda* itself. According to Pater's reading, Leonardo's dramatization of a secret, whether in his art or in his own persona, activated in others Leonardo's own impossible desire to know what was opaque in the human sub-ject. Where incompletion captured the nature of subjectivity, cryptic lan-guage was a formal way to insist that viewers experience that persistent incompletion and thus further highlighted the impossibility of perceptual and representational transparency and of absolute knowledge.

Although Pater first derives the principles of incompletion and of cryptic language from Leonardo's life and work, he gives them greater form as he uses the subsequent artists in his collection to build his own aesthetic. Pater's last-drafted chapter, "The School of Giorgione," together with the preface and the conclusion, lays out with particular precision the way that optics and imagetextuality drive his achievement of these two principles. The call to see and represent subjectivity "with the finest senses," for example, bears out the principle of incompletion (R 188).[16] Using the "finest senses," Pater explains, means combating the "roughness of the eye," which loses a certain specificity of "persons, things, [and] situations" because of its material limits (R 189). This combat, though, must begin with an analysis of perception it-self. In other words, an artist must register that the project of seeing is an incomplete approximation by making his or her own perceptual operations and their material limits an object of study, rather than persisting in the hope of simply nullifying those limits. This prescription amends Pater's fellow Oxford scholar and critic Matthew Arnold's aesthetic directive "to see the object as in itself it really is"[17] by adding that the "first step" toward doing so "is to know one's own impression as it really is, to discriminate it, to re-alise it distinctly" (R xix). *The Renaissance* takes the compound perceptions of one's shaping perspective and the object perceived as the "primary data" of its aesthetic (R xx). It suggests that by acknowledging the material limits of perception, an aesthetic of incompletion can offer access to a "*vraie vé-rité*," a "truer truth," than even the objective reality that Arnold strives to know (R 121).

To achieve these compound perceptions, *The Renaissance* recommends what it calls a "susceptibility" to sensation (R xx). The notion of susceptibil-ity departs from a Cartesian understanding of knowledge as the product of an enclosed, objective observer and welcomes instead the vulnerable, dis-integrated workings of bodily sensation as a means of knowing. In fact, Pater characterizes this susceptibility as a "mortal disease," a condition that points to the ultimate material limit, the uncontrollable disintegration of death (R 190). Not only is Pater's aesthetic "quickened by the sense of death," it's even specifically "smitten" by it ("PWM" 309; R 190). The mortal disease of susceptibility thus amounts to a desire to explore the body's complex systems, opacities, and limits. Though Pater qualifies this "passion" as one for which "the outlets are sealed," he nonetheless proposes that it "begets a tension of nerve, in which the sensible world comes to one with a reinforced brilliance and relief—all redness . . . turned into blood, all water into tears" ("PWM" 303). This mortal illness, Pater suggests, offers an "open vision" that "at last apprehends a better daylight, but earthly, open only to the senses" ("PWM" 305).

Pater's focus on the shaping forces of perception and his focus on courting a susceptibility to sensation are thus strategies for living out Leonardo's first principle, his insistence on incompletion as the hallmark of perception and subjectivity alike. Pater believes that only after enacting these strategies can an artist reach the second stage of his aesthetic, in which he promotes a similar vision of subjectivity in his audience. It's in this second stage that Pater fleshes out Leonardo's second principle, his cryptic language, in two key formal practices: the pursuit of Anders-streben in art and the pursuit of a withholding self-presentation in life.

Anders-streben literally means "striving beyond," but it refers in Pater's text to a specifically formal program in which an artist's handling of one art can allow that art "to pass into the condition of some other art"; that is, it can allow a partial alienation from the representational limits of a given form, such as poetry or painting (R 105). This notion ultimately explains the thematic and formal role of imagetextuality in Pater's aesthetic. We have seen that across The Renaissance Pater thematizes a partial, unstable image that has both the temporality and the conventionality attributed exclusively to text under the traditional image/text binary. Recall, for instance, Pater's claim that the common understanding of the body as a "perpetual outline of face and limb is but an image of ours" (R 186–87). This claim reveals that the belief in a natural, mimetic image complemented a belief that the body was a boundary between self and world, interior and exterior. In place of that natural image, Pater substitutes a specifically constructed one—"an image of ours"—and analogizes the human subject to it. He suggests that the actual instability and constructedness of both the body and the imagetext characterize subjectivity as well. At the same time, The Renaissance also makes imagetextuality the model for its own form, as an art history that continually renegotiates and refuses to separate the seeable and the sayable. The notion of Anders-streben, outlined in Pater's essay on Giorgione, supplies the theoretical grounding for this thematic and formal imagetextuality, not only in Pater's aesthetic but also in the modernist impersonality that would follow on its heels. He ultimately suggests that *Anders-streben*, and by extension the imagetext, effectively does the work of Leonardo's cryptic language.

Pater in fact explains *Anders-streben* in relation to a famous formulation of the image/text binary: the eighteenth-century German philosopher and art critic Gotthold Ephraim Lessing's *Laokoön: Or, the Limits of Poetry and Painting* (1766). Lessing's binary associates images with the body and presumes that they are natural and static; it aligns texts with the mind and presumes they are conventional and temporal. In other words, Lessing's image/text binary complements a Cartesian mind/body dualism. Likewise, the qualities he attributes to the image support the belief that vision is instantaneous and transparent, that we see the world as "in itself it really is," to return to the later words of Matthew Arnold. Pater follows Lessing in defining each artistic medium in terms of its primary sensory material—a note, an image, a word. Like Lessing, he also initially emphasizes that the distinct nature of each artistic medium, deriving from its reliance on a distinct human sense, means that one art cannot be translated into another.

Their agreement stops, however, when Lessing's theory becomes a separate-spheres ideology of content, or a belief that certain topics are appropriate only to certain art forms. This approach appears to suggest that each art is a transparent window onto a certain subject matter and that opacity arises only when one moves across them. Pater instead argues that there is no transparency at all, so he sees no difference between the opacity within and across art forms. Just as the artist can study perceptual limits as a way to partially overcome them, one art's careful appeal to the sensory material of another art can allow for its "partial alienation from its own limitations," a qualified process of overcoming that Pater extends to perception as well (*R* 105). Pater names this process of partial alienation *Anders-streben* and exemplifies it principally through the "pictorial poetry" of Giorgione's paintings (*R* 117), in other words, with an imagetext. In addition, Pater links this imagetext to understandings of vision by labeling it "a fragment of Venetian glass" through which the viewer sees what is figured (*R* 104). This metaphor keeps the impossibility of representational and perceptual transparency central to Pater's aesthetic by evoking specifically colored, textured, or otherwise embellished glass; it does the same for representational and perceptual totality by evoking a fragment. Because the imagetext is opaque and fragmentary, Pater suggests, it functions as a form of Leonardo's cryptic language: it leaves behind both transparency and "conventional associations" in order to model the material opacity of the human subject (*R* 94). *Anders-streben* doesn't quite register—as the modernists would—that *all* images are imagetextual insofar as they "are not . . . static or permanent in any metaphysical sense," "are not perceived in the same way by viewers," and "involve multi-sensory interpretation" (Mitchell, *Iconology* 14). Yet Pater's formal aesthetic does expand the field of observation from what is highlighted in Lessing's theory and subsequently in Arnold's as well. It makes the opacity of the human subject an object of study without dissolving that opacity; it keeps the body that wants to see itself always shy of its achievement.

Anders-streben thus offers a compelling example of how an interest in vision could motivate a pursuit of aesthetic imagetextuality. Pater's richest example of a successful use of *Anders-streben* to study the nature of being appears in his commentary on Giorgione's art, and more broadly Giorgione's "veritable school" (*R* 116). Here, Pater not only casts Giorgione's canvases as imagetexts, or "painted idylls"; he also states that they are "like persons," announcing that Giorgione's *Anders-streben* includes a particular understanding of subjectivity (*R* 117, 111). Later, Pater maintains that Giorgione's art portrays "phases of subject . . . volatised almost to the vanishing point" of the eye, that is, to the material limits of vision.[18] According to Pater, Giorgione's imagetextual art creates the sense that "some messenger from the real soul of things must be on his way to one," but he never fully makes that opaque core visible.[19] He leaves the reader always desiring to know, and always faced with the limits of knowing.

Pater's emphasis on the "Giorgioneseque" moves this conscious imperfection beyond Giorgione himself. He takes the many copies of and variations on Giorgione's style made by students and later painters as part and parcel of Giorgione's *Anders-streben*. Such an approach dissents strongly from the professionalization of art history in the mid-nineteenth century, which replaced the common practice of attributing as many works as possible to artists of note with a "science" willing to overturn traditional attributions in the name of accuracy. Pater's Giorgionesque refuses this new science by proposing a model of art and authorship that comports instead with the new image of contemporary optics. Playing on the premises of an embodied vision, Pater questions the notion of originality with regard to both art and personality. He weaves his literary portrait of Giorgione from an amalgam of canvases in the painter's then agreed-upon canon, paintings of contested attribution, and many copies and variations that reincarnate Giorgione's work. In the process, Pater often discriminates very little among these categories and even makes inaccurate attributions. Moreover, as part of this amalgamation, he proposes that the images of Giorgione's "school" actually "fill out the original" (*R* 116). This claim posits a reciprocal circuit of influence that denies any essence to the original and indeed explodes the very meaning of that term. Pater suggests that there are no originals, no stable images that order knowledge and authorize a chain of paler representations; there are only unstable and proliferating imagetexts.

Applying this idea beyond art and to subjectivity, Pater locates a similar instability in Giorgione himself. On the one hand, he emphasizes that Giorgione "really makes himself felt" (*R* 122). On the other hand, he describes this "influence" as "a spirit or type in art" rather than a proof of individuality (*R* 116). Giorgione thus becomes an "impersonation of Venice itself, its projected reflex or ideal" (*R* 116-17). His status as an "impersonation" and a "project[ion]" effectively renders him an image. An intertextual reference solidifies this suggestion. J. A. Crowe and G. B. Cavalcaselle's *History of Painting in North Italy* (1871)—one of Pater's principal sources for *The Renaissance*— maintains that "it is perhaps to his [Giorgione's] early intercourse with aristocratic company that he owed the peculiar breadth of distinction which we find in all his impersonations," meaning all his paintings (123). Paired with Crowe and Cavalcaselle's conjecture, Pater's description of Giorgione as an "impersonation" makes the artist synonymous with his "painted idylls." Since Pater makes the tendencies of the paintings now apply to the painter as well, and since one of those tendencies is the paintings' imagetextuality, Giorgione is not simply an image but rather an imagetext.

As Pater extrapolates from art to artist in his discussion of the Giorgionesque, he also supplements *Anders-streben* with the second of his formal techniques for representing an "open vision" of subjectivity: a lived practice of withholding that duplicates Leonardo's efforts to fascinate. Pater's reading of Leonardo suggests that by representing the "most secret parts" of material things and "human personality," the painter ignited in his audience an impossible desire to know subjectivity and a willingness to embrace how that subjectivity "effac[ed] their own individuality" (*R* 86, 87, 92). Pater's discussion of Giorgione's impersonations renders him an example of Leonardo's project. It thus shows how performance is key to *The Renaissance*'s aesthetic. Indeed, the scientific dating techniques that Pater eschews not only seek to identify those paintings done by Giorgione but also promise to unmask the real Giorgione himself for full public consumption. Pater, by contrast, relishes the insurmountable barriers to fulfilling that promise. He notes that we know only one or two dates, one or two circumstances, in the "life and personality of the man" (*R* 115). He also directly rebukes the new science with the pointed observation that diminishing the number of works in a painter's *oeuvre* cannot increase knowledge of the painter himself. Pater supplements the few facts known of Giorgione's life with a list of the many questions that remain, and at the end of his essay he attributes Giorgione's "efficacy" precisely to these uncertainties, suggesting that Giorgione exists beyond the strictly ascertainable facts (*R* 122). Ultimately, in mingling Giorgione's works with those of many other painters, Pater insists on the mysterious relation between artist and public. His open quarrel with accurate attribution doesn't hide Giorgione from the reader where other art historians attempt to reveal him. Instead, Pater demands that readers experience a persistent wonder about when they are engaging with Giorgione and when they are not. He thus preserves the structure of mystery required between artist and public. Pater's deliberate efforts to incite this structure in his readers signal that *The Renaissance* doesn't remain simply a manual of artistic production and consumption but instead becomes an example of the aesthetic he values. Indeed, moving beyond the pages of *The Renaissance* itself, critics old and new have noted in Pater's own life the same "rare visib[ility]," "evanescence," and "mask" that he foregrounds in his literary portraits.[20]

At first glance the influence artists exert in Pater's aesthetic may seem to bolster their personal coherence and independence, just as their withholding themselves in public life may suggest a rich and contained interiority.[21] However, Pater's aesthetic practices repeatedly locate personality in performance, particularly a performance marked by partiality and unoriginality. Such practices do not set a coherent interior self against an exterior uncertainty; rather, they focus on the susceptibility of the supposed self to what it is imagined to exclude. They thereby participate in the turn-of-the-century resignification of personality described in the introduction. From popular advice manuals to celebrity culture, and across psychological, physiological, and sociological discourses, personality could no longer reliably be understood as an inalienable and controllable possession synonymous with the singularity and rich interiority of Cartesian dualism. Instead, just as Pater declares of Leonardo, these narratives suggest that to have personality is quite simply to be "*fascinating, stunning, attractive,* [and] *magnetic*" (Susman 217). Personality, in other words, is a spectacle, a transient but certainly material image, tied not to an essence but to the complex interaction of sensation, memory, and perception. Such a formulation departed sharply from Victorian notions of character, which believed in an inner authenticity and moral self-discipline that supported an older understanding of personality. By contesting this influential notion of character, *The Renaissance* highlights that the modern resignification of personality was the fulcrum on which an impersonal aesthetic depended.

Pater contra Mérimée: Toward an Imperfect Impersonality

Pater's Prosper Mérimée lecture, delivered more than twenty years after he began writing *The Renaissance,* confirms the connection between a reconceived understanding of personality and an impersonal aesthetic. In his 1888 essay "Style" Pater had already described his effort to represent a material subjectivity as "impersonal." "Style" describes Pater's own aesthetic principles as the "blood" that "nourish[es] the body" of desirable art, determining "its very contour and external aspect" (412). Underlining the materiality of the description, he notes that such art should represent "unconscious" systems (in this case the circulatory system), which Pater calls "soul-fact[s]" (405, 406). This representational project is "in a real sense 'impersonal,'" according to Pater, and the "plenary substance" of the soul-facts themselves finds "only one phase or facet" in "personal information" (412, 396, 406, 406).[22] The opaque subjectivity that *The Renaissance* traced thus now becomes a specifically impersonal subjectivity. "Prosper Mérimée" elaborates this explicit incorporation of impersonality into subjectivity by critiquing Mérimée for misunderstanding impersonality as instead objective, emotionless, and only negatively embodied. The lecture makes clear the precise relation that Pater sees between impersonality and personality and also ultimately hints at his belief that an impersonal aesthetic has a transformative political potential.

Like the conclusion to *The Renaissance,* "Prosper Mérimée" locates in the nineteenth century an increasing philosophical skepticism about the possibility of complete knowledge. It prefigures Foucault's famous claim that nineteenth-century philosophers realized that knowledge couldn't be dissociated from the "peculiar functioning" of the body and thus lost faith in objective understanding and representation (*Order of Things* 319). Pater emphasizes the nineteenth-century critique of the mind's "pretensions to pass beyond the limits of individual experience" and its increasingly "empirical science of nature and man" (11, 16); his more specific discussion of Mérimée also repeatedly points to "the blind and naked force of nature and circumstance" and to the "uncontrollable movements" they inspire (35, 35). Pater even suggests obliquely the role that the new physiology of vision played in deflating the mind's pretensions when he casts objectivity as a "great *outlook* [that] had lately been cut off" (11, emphasis added). This loss, Pater suggests, produced two types of aesthetic impersonality: a positive type, which embraces this state of affairs, and a negative type, practiced by Mérimée, which resists it. According to Pater, Mérimée's art strives for the "perfection of nobody's style": it uses impersonality to reassert an objective view evacuated of personal influence, but one that nonetheless supplies the interior space of the coherent, willful personality (36). Working toward such an art, Mérimée overlooks the secrets of "light and shade" that are the very conditions of sight (15). He thus expresses "none of those subjectivities, colourings, [and] peculiarities of mental refraction" that constitute Pater's soul-facts (37). Where materiality does enter Mérimée's art, it's simply to portray what is "rude" and "crude" in humanity (14), what Mérimée figures as "maliciously active" and "hideous" bodies (31). Finally, Mérimée's characters diverge sharply from Leonardo and Giorgione in having neither mystery nor fascination. They are "inevitable to sight," "[p]ainfully distinct," and without "atmosphere" (15). They stand, like solitary forms on "some hard, perfectly transparent day," trying to thwart rather than represent the opacity of the subject (15).

Pater returns to the values of *The Renaissance* to suggest an alternative to Mérimée's aesthetic and thereby a more positive model of impersonality. He advocates replacing the century's lost "great outlook" with an art of "queries, echoes, reactions, after-thoughts" (15)—an art that explores the unwilled "forces in human nature" that lie beyond the "apparent surface" (14). Correspondingly, he portrays these forces as a broader "genius of nature" rather than the "terrible" materiality that Mérimée assumes and that his aesthetic seeks to escape (29, 36). Pater's critique of Mérimée basically has him marshaling this positive model of impersonality to explain how Mérimée arrived at his negative one. Pater argues that just as some early experience imprinted itself on Leonardo's psychophysiology and eventually helped him produce *La Gioconda,* so some early injury was the cause of Mérimée's negativity toward materiality. It led him to guard too much "against his own instinctive movements" and to commit himself to the possibility of transparent knowledge (14). Where *The Renaissance* advocates an illusive performance that will dramatize the incompleteness of subjectivity in public view, Mérimée instead adopts a "mask," a protection against all injury to his pride (14). Ultimately, Pater proposes that Mérimée's aesthetic vindicates by its "very impersonality that much worn, but not untrue saying, that the style is the man" (36). In other words, effectively making impersonality the very condition for personality, Pater argues that Mérimée's impersonal aesthetic is "an effective personal trait . . . transferred to art" (37). This becomes Pater's answer to the question of "how much or how little of one's self one may put into one's work" (35). He implies that the utter absence of personality in perception is "as little possible as a strict realism," because impersonality is constitutive rather than exclusive of personality (36). With this answer, Pater again blasts Arnold's directive to see an "object as in itself it really is." Plus, he now effectively recasts *The Renaissance*'s challenge to that directive as an impersonal aesthetic.

While "Style" and "Prosper Mérimée" together confirm that the project of *The Renaissance* was to explore an impersonal subjectivity, these two later essays also hint at the political potential of such an impersonal aesthetic. "Style" proposes that impersonal art presents "new or old truth[s] about ourselves and our relation to the world" in order to "ennoble and fortify us in our sojourn here" (413). More specifically, it claims that these truths can support the "redemption of the oppressed" and the "enlargement of our sympathies with each other" (413). "Prosper Mérimée" draws this liberating potential out a bit further. Though Mérimée was both antidemocratic and the empress Eugénie's close friend, his irreligious and anticlerical attitudes made him fairly liberal for his time. Pater nonetheless emphasizes a more conservative view of Mérimée's political service. Separating Mérimée from the democratizing sympathy that Pater so valued, he portrays him not only as politically "indifferent" but also as pointedly manipulative and conventional rather than redemptive: Mérimée rose "to social, to political eminence," Pater claims, by offering a "reassuring spectacle" of the world's most "conventional attire" (14). Pater offers little detail on this staged conventionality beyond Mérimée's effort to preserve old Roman churches as relics of that great empire when he was inspector general of monuments. But regardless of this paucity of evidence, Pater's portrayal implicitly links Mérimée, along with his art's obsession with power, to "the tomb of the Revolution," permanently "seal[ed]" off by "Napoleon" (11). Pater then goes on to offer a foil to Mérimée in the "masters of French prose whose art" begins "where the art of Mérimée leaves off" (37). These vaguely defined impersonalists offer a new battlefield in a waylaid revolution. Their focus on embodied experience conquers objectivist claims, just as the divine rights of the "old French royalty" had been brought down (11). But while such language fairly well sings of liberation, "Prosper Mérimée" neither specifies who these French masters were nor elaborates on how they achieved this revolutionary end. How could exploring an impersonal subjectivity question social hierarchies? How could it redeem the oppressed or enlarge our sympathies toward one another?

Pater's lack of detail is perhaps the cause for the long-held critical belief that he dismissed the political. In addition, as scholars have more recently begun to discern his aesthetic politics, it's also perhaps the reason for the broad range of their readings. Following Pater's own cues, some critics have noted a revolutionary trajectory in his aesthetic. Richard Dellamora, for instance, has argued that Pater was staunchly "anti-phallogocentric," because his focus on individual sensation was consistent with an impressionistic homoeroticism ("Critical Impressionism" 127). By contrast, other scholars have seen in Pater's aesthetic a commitment to patriarchal social norms. Jesse Matz and Tamar Katz, for instance, both argue that Pater wielded social binaries of gender, age, and class in order to maintain a traditional mind/body dualism over and against a less stable notion of subjectivity premised upon impressionability. Hovering somewhere between these two poles, still other critics, like Heather Love and Jacques Khalip, have argued for Pater's politics of refusal. They propose that his aesthetic defers social engagement as a political response to the queer experience of social displacement. Pater's art, in other words, responds to his own alienation, as a gay man, from established cultural norms.

What unites these diverse readings of Pater's politics is their focus on individual identity. They don't recognize that Pater's aesthetic amounts to a critique of identity and that it's this critique that he finds politically liberating. In other words, Pater highlights an embodied, impersonal subjectivity that can't be squeezed into or stabilized by identity and can't be used to prioritize some subjects over others. He gestures toward the latter, political implications of this subjectivity when he pauses in "Style" to explain that while the impersonal artists he points to are male, it's not because his project is itself gendered but rather because he lives "under a system of education which still to so large an extent limits real scholarship to men" (397). By contrast, Pater presents our universal subjection to the automaticity and flux of impersonal subjectivity as the foundation for that all-important "enlargement of our sympathies with each other," suggesting a challenge to inequalities that organize social hierarchies. Pater's aesthetic politics thus raises a set of broad questions about subjectivity that implicate the very terms in which identities like gender and sexuality were conceived.

We can fill in Pater's fleeting critique of identity by returning briefly to the politics of image-text relations detailed in the introduction. The Cartesian model of vision that stood behind the image/text binary was itself a foundation for social difference, as certain subjects were believed to have greater access than others to the space of objective thought. Correspondingly, the image/text binary was itself used to map and indeed naturalize social difference. W. J. T. Mitchell has argued that Lessing—Pater's interlocutor in his elaboration of *Anders-streben*—secures the image/text binary in part by analogizing it to a culturally dominant gender binary. This analogy stabilizes both sides of the binary, for the seemingly neutral metalanguage of the means of representation naturalizes patriarchal norms. Lessing portrays painting, in its silence, stasis, and beauty, as feminine, while poetry's mindful eloquence and active expressivity make it masculine. Moreover, Lessing also casts the French tendency to blur visual and verbal genres as both a feminized refinement and a kind of illicit sexuality, while the English and German tendency to distinguish such genres indicates honesty, an appropriately restrained (hetero)sexuality, and manliness. If we read Pater's *Anders-streben* through Mitchell's history, we can see that it resists not only Lessing's image/text binary itself but also these related cultural politics. It repudiates naïve theories of mimetic representation and rejects the easy naturalism of the image/text divide, but in doing so it also punctures Lessing's gender, national, and racial essentialism.

Pater himself prompts us to read *Anders-streben* in this extended way. He insists in "Style" that because an impersonal writer is "a lover of words for their own sake," he will be "a minute and constant observer of their physiognomy . . . on the alert not only for obviously mixed metaphors . . . but for the metaphor that is mixed in all our speech, though a rapid use may involve no cognition of it" (402). He implies that the image/text binary is exactly such a metaphor and indeed is the ultimate proving ground of his call to attend to the values embedded in language. He explains that for the writer who's aware of these unconscious metaphors—who "liv[es] in the full sense of them"—"the elementary particles of language will be realized as colour and light and shade" (402). The image/text metaphor, in other words, will give over to a more fundamental blurring of the seeable and the sayable, powerfully characterized by Pater's appeal to a language become optics. What this discussion of style seems to indicate is that Pater's use of *Anders-*

streben to thematize an impersonal subjectivity draws out the metaphorical work that the image/text binary does in the hands of someone like Lessing and does something quite different. It presents an embodied impersonal subjectivity that negates the possibility of the disembodied reason that Lessing would associate with men and with Germans, as well as the possibility of a static, immediately perceptible image, which Lessing would associate with women and racial or national Others. By using imagetextuality to represent this impersonal subjectivity, *Anders-streben* stylistically performs impersonality's challenge to gender, sexual, and racial binaries.

Pater's related investment in the artist's withholding display of self and in the unattainable desire that such a display incites similarly enacts a challenge to essential identities, particularly to middle-class manliness. In the Victorian period, the hegemonic middle-class manliness was organized around the display of self-discipline as a badge of sociopolitical worth. However, it was equally committed to disavowing the necessity of that display in order to preserve the fiction of autonomous interiority. According to James Eli Adams, numerous *fin-de-siècle* male writers unintentionally exposed the tension inherent in that disavowal when they adopted the manner of the dandy, an earlier model of masculinity, as a way to unite their artistic or scholastic vocation with middle-class manliness. The dandy was interested in intellectual refinement and pursued self-discipline in the form of a displayed nonchalance. When late Victorian writers did the same, their performance highlighted contemporary masculinity's disavowed spectacular nature. Jessica Feldman has pushed Adams' argument even further, contending that dandified writers actually sought to construct a resistant masculinity. According to Feldman, these writers claimed embodiment and visibility over and against the logic of a Victorian manliness that deemed those traits feminine. Such writers thereby exposed the constructed nature of gender and also denied the gender binary on which manliness relied.

By advocating the artist's withholding display of self, Pater's impersonal aesthetic, like the dandy, highlights performativity and relationality. In exposing the mechanisms by which Victorian patriarchy worked to consolidate its sociopolitical force, he subtly questioned that force. Pater doesn't, however, aim to create in its place some other kind of masculinity, whether normative or resistant. His withholding performance instead displays an impersonal subjectivity that entirely exceeds gender or other forms of identity. It destabilizes the self, not least because it points to an incoherence and an automaticity inherent in all human beings, qualities that older notions of personality deny and that patriarchal structures displace onto various social Others. Pater's aesthetic thus surpasses the oppositional force that Feldman associates with the dandy by challenging the concept and structure of identity itself, not just particular norms of gender or sexuality.

It's important to bear this challenge in mind when considering Pater's aesthetic investment in a consuming desire for the unattainable. Scholars who read this investment as code for a socially impossible homosexual love draw the boundaries of Pater's politics too narrowly. Throughout *The Renaissance* and his later essays Pater suggests that being "smitten with a love of the impossible" signifies an ineluctable material subjectivity, an impersonality, and the self-consuming work of registering it (*R* 82). This "passion" manifests an "open vision" and a "tension of nerve, in which the sensible world comes to one with a reinforced brilliance and relief—all redness . . . turned into blood, all water into tears" ("PWM" 303). Such a passion is queer in the most radical sense of that term, since that desire is never capable of cohering into an identity. Pater's portrayal of this desire, which isn't even consistently sexualized, exceeds any specific object. It includes homosexual desire, for instance, in the tutelary relationships of the eighteenth-century German historian Johann Joachim Winckelmann, the subject of *The Renaissance*'s last chapter. However, it also incorporates Leonardo's longing for his mother, from whom he was separated in infancy, as well as Giorgione's ache for a woman who either left him for a pupil or died of the plague. It even includes Gustave Flaubert's incredible "love for literature," which "Style" construes as an insurmountable "pursuit" (406). In its inexhaustible range, this desire becomes a symbol for the need to perceive and represent impersonal subjectivity, while also acknowledging the impossibility of ever fully doing so. It involves dwelling in relentless effort and failure, and it finds success in registering that failure. Such work is liberating in the sense that it denies any social hegemony premised upon objectivity (like the patriarchy of Victorian manliness) and offers a broadly queer embrace of the flux of being.

Pater's friends Katharine Bradley and Edith Cooper developed this liberating potential in his impersonal aesthetic and its specific prescriptions for art and life. They did so in both their public performance of Michael Field and their volume of picture poems, *Sight and Song*, composed around the time of Pater's Prosper Mérimée lecture and modeled on the art historical work of *The Renaissance,* right down to its focus on the old Italian masters. The poets' life practice and their art together clarify the politics of Pater's impersonal aesthetic and point to its influence. They also underscore that aesthetic's visual origins. Indeed, because Field was actively publishing until 1913 (with posthumous collections appearing even thereafter), Bradley and Cooper act as a kind of bridge between Pater and modernist impersonality.

The Visual Field(s): Framing the Politics of Paterian Impersonality

The arc of Bradley and Cooper's shared intellectual and aesthetic life makes clear why this aunt and niece, and eventual romantic couple, so effectively translated Pater's aesthetic into more explicitly political terms. Both women studied philosophy at Bristol University College (with Cooper taking a first), suggesting that Pater's philosophical intertexts, from Thomas Reid to Eduard von Hartmann, were accessible and of interest to them. The women also read and indeed met with scientists, like Herbert Spencer, even as Bradley actively campaigned against vivisection practices.[23] Such pursuits point to their broad knowledge of the contemporary physiological studies that so intrigued Pater. Add to these interests the women's avid museumgoing (from the Grosvenor to the Louvre to the Uffizi), as well as their knowledge of art critics referenced by Pater, like Johann Joachim Winckelmann, Gotthold Ephraim Lessing, and John Ruskin, the latter of whom was in fact Bradley's mentor for a time, and it's not surprising that Bradley and Cooper became early and devoted readers of *The Renaissance*.[24] Indeed, as a crystallization of that devotion, Bradley returned from her 1880 trip to the Uffizi with a print of its supposed Leonardo *Medusa,* the painting so important to Pater's reading of Leonardo's scientific aesthetic. She gave the print to Cooper, along with a letter that used phrases from Pater's essay to describe both it and its painter (*F&P* 17).

By the time of this gift Bradley and Cooper had also begun to collaborate as poets, and the impersonal subjectivity that Pater first characterized in *The Renaissance* seems also to frame their compositional practice. Though scholars have sometimes read their collaboration as a blissful lesbian union, neither their similar upbringing nor their romance produced any such comfortable identity. Instead, Bradley and Cooper described their joint aesthetic as a painful process that forced them to confront the instabilities of selfhood that Pater's aesthetic emphasized. As Bradley explains in an 1886 letter to their friend the sexologist Havelock Ellis, "[I]f one [of us] begins a character, his companion seizes and possesses it; if one conceives a scene or situation, the other connects, completes or murderously cuts away" (qtd. in

Sturgeon 47). The vocabulary of both conception and violence stresses a self-shattering sort of expression, as well as human materiality.[25] Such a vocabulary recalls Pater's appeal to mortal illness in describing Leonardo's aesthetic efforts to grasp impersonal subjectivity. In addition, Bradley's longer explanation to Ellis expands on this point by variously naming as its subject "we," "he," "one," "other," "Edith," and the pair's more than pseudonym, "Michael Field." This plurality of unstable pronouns and relationships again suggests a subjectivity beyond a stable and singular personality and in its gender crossings even hints at a challenge to the essentialism of Victorian gender and sexual norms. Moreover, like Pater, Field emphasizes images as part of this process. Bradley's letter to Ellis figures their hard-won verse as "a perfect mosaic," a picture made of fragments, within which the two women complexly "cross and interlace" (qtd. in Sturgeon 47).[26] Not only partial and constructed but also a product of voluntary and involuntary processes, this mosaic aptly crystallizes the complexity of the visual image driving the new physiology of vision. Correspondingly, the fact that Bradley and Cooper's collaborative *text* creates this mosaic *image* recalls the imagetextual "striving beyond" of Pater's *Anders-streben*.

It's perhaps not surprising, then, that Bradley and Cooper solicited Pater's acquaintance in June 1889 by sending him a copy of *Long Ago,* their just-published collection of Sapphic verse, nor that by 1890 they were visiting his rooms every Monday and had fondly christened him "Tottie" (Emma Donoghue 55). Indeed, their joint journal, "Works and Days," records that in that same year the women not only excitedly attended Pater's Prosper Mérimée lecture but also paid him tribute in their verse play *The Tragic Mary,* whose title they took from his recent essay "Dante Gabriel Rossetti" (1889) (*W&D* 120). Four years later, upon Pater's death, the women memorialized him and reiterated their support of his aesthetic and its visual origins in a Petrarchan sonnet:

> The freshness of the light, its secrecy,
> Spices, or honey from sweet-smelling bower,
> The harmony of time, love's trembling hour
> Struck on thee with a new felicity.
> Standing, a child, by a red hawthorn-tree,
> Its perishing, small petals' flame had power
> To fill with masses of soft, ruddy flower
> A certain roadside in thy memory:

And haply when the tragic clouds of night
Were slowly wrapping round thee, in the cold
Of which men always die, a sense renewed
Of the things sweet to touch and breath and sight,
That thou didst touch and breathe and see of old
Stole on thee with the warmth of gratitude. ("Walter Pater (July 30, 1894)")

Field's elegy plays a bit with Petrarchan form, which tends to introduce a problem in the octave that it resolves in the sestet, thereby giving the poem a feeling of self-sufficiency. This sonnet's problem might seem to be the loss of a youthful perceptual sensitivity because of Pater's impending death. But Field refuses to label the limits of materiality a problem by reserving mention of Pater's approaching death for the volta, that is, the beginning of the sestet. In a sense, the sestet does go on to offer closure with respect to this problem that isn't one, because memories of Pater's perceptual sensitivity return as death looms. However, Field's focus doesn't secure the self-sufficiency implied by the closure of the Petrarchan form. To understand what it does instead, it's important to take in the poem's full thematic arc. Field's octave muddies any distinction between the emotional-sensational and the intellectual, the body and the mind, in its particular focus on light, both the condition for vision and the common figure for knowledge (or enlightenment). Field describes the "new felicity" through which "light" "[s]truck" Pater in youth and connects this felicity to his mindbodily awareness of light's hidden workings, its "secrecy." The encounter conjures the core of Pater's impersonal aesthetic, his awareness of the density and opacity of vision. We're guided to this suggestion not only by the focus on perceptual sensitivity but also by Field's further connection of this "new felicity" to "love's trembling hour." We have seen that both a heightened sensitivity and a perpetual desire are foundational to Pater's aesthetic. Indeed, in the closing sestet Field leaves open this "trembling" desire, refusing to specify its object or point to its consumption, so that Pater's attentiveness to impersonal subjectivity never results in self-presence or perceptual immediacy and therefore self-sufficiency. Rather, though Field emphasizes the comfort that Pater felt in his final moments, the re-membered sensations "[s]tole" over him. In other words, he neither recalls nor subsequently controls them; he can only feel "gratitude," even as the poem can only accept the inevitability of death. This acceptance that "men always die"—complete with the image of nature shrouding a fading Pater in clouds—echoes Pater's own appeal to the radical materiality of the corpse in characterizing impersonal subjectivity, including in his discussion of Leonardo's *Medusa,* the painting that so resonated with Bradley and Cooper. At the same time, the poem's focus on a shifting set of memories recalls Pater's portrayal of Leonardo's fragmented memories and dreams.

However, even though Bradley and Cooper were firmly committed to the impersonal aesthetic that Pater developed, they were not as certain of his own fidelity to its political implications. The two believed his aesthetic offered an alternative to "individual mannerisms," but they also thought his later work neutralized this alternative's political potential (*W&D* 10). Specifically, they came to see Pater as horribly "prudish," a judgment that cemented their dedication to adapting his aesthetic toward more starkly political ends (*W&D* 119). That dedication is particularly visible in the couple's public performance of Michael Field and in the imagetextuality of *Sight and Song.* These two creative sites draw on contemporary visual culture, particularly commodity spectacle, to adapt a Paterian impersonality that would more explicitly challenge Victorian gender and sexual norms.

Scholars have already explored how the female coauthorship behind the Michael Field signature troubled nineteenth-century formulations of a unified and presumably masculine lyric voice. In the early years of Bradley and Cooper's collaboration the women entreated friends to keep the secret of their identities, but by 1888 these identities were well known, and the pair continued to publish as Field—and even, strangely, to push for secrecy—until their deaths more than twenty years later. Some critics have used Bradley and Cooper's secrecy to read Field as a disguise that allowed the women to write more personally or gave them masculine credibility. However, the broader consensus has been that the couple openly deployed the Michael Field signature to highlight gender and sexual instability.[27] Robert Fletcher, for instance, has suggested that Michael Field pointedly mimics and confounds the nineteenth-century symbolics of poetic inspiration, because the signature imbued a male poet with the voices of two women whose collaboration made them neither themselves nor each other. The Field signature, in other words, belies the singular and masculine nature of the inspired poet and transforms the power dynamic typically imagined between that poet's verbal expression and a silent female muse. Thinking more broadly of both the lyric and subjectivity, Yopie Prins has asserted that Field "exploited and exploded" lyric authorship as the "solitary utterance of a single speaker" and did so to decenter the "personality of the poet" (75, 74). In this formulation, the lyric poet that Field models, acting as a metonym for subjectivity, allowed Bradley and Cooper to explore being beyond a self-contained notion of individual identity and to implicitly question the stable and essential nature of gender and sexuality.

To fully understand Field's political challenge, though, we need to recognize that Bradley and Cooper's performance of Field *outside* their poetry also enacted the performative aspects of Pater's impersonal aesthetic, and with an eye toward magnifying the emancipatory politics that critics have discerned in the Field signature. Bradley and Cooper's investment in performance is evident in the substance of their work, namely, in the large number of verse plays they wrote and in their efforts to see them produced.[28] This commitment to performance reaches its apotheosis, however, in their staging of Michael Field in their daily lives. The women included their pseudonym as part of a stable of publicly used pet names, Field being Cooper and Michael being either Bradley or Cooper.[29] They also often spoke of each other and of themselves together using the singular masculine pronoun, effectively announcing themselves as Field. In addition, the pair frequently used the monogram "MF" on items like luggage and jewelry, most notably on a surviving locket that contains a miniature of Cooper with the initials in the lower right corner and two interlocking Roman symbols each representing maleness located, significantly, just before Cooper's eyes (fig. 1.2). Similarly, in "Works and Days," which Bradley and Cooper intended for publication, the women alternate between diary entries, in which they refer to themselves as "I" or "we," and more theatrical narratives that describe daily events through dramatic dialogues, complete with stage directions, in which Michael and Field or "the Poet" are characters.

These idiosyncratic dramatizations, frequently enacted through commodity culture (like monograms and lockets), exist as word, picture, and theater and thus blur the boundaries between the seeable and the sayable. They also embrace the Paterian belief that personality exists only in performance. But Field extends Pater's point about personality to a point about the serial staging of gender. They insist that two people can become one, and one person two, or more precisely that two can become something more than persons. But they also insist that a woman can become male, and a man female, or perhaps that everyone is more broadly queer than those labels allow. Field's unceasing rotation of parts within this drama emphasizes the fundamentally performative nature of gender identity. And if cryptic language could point toward impersonality in art, then within Field's perfor-

Fig. 1.2. Locket by Carlo and Arthur Giuliano containing a miniature of Edith Cooper by Charles de Sousy Ricketts, 1901. Courtesy of the Syndics of The Fitzwilliam Museum, Cambridge.

mance in life impersonality could similarly be suggested by social confusion, such as the confusion of an observer noting that the monogram on Field's luggage announces a singular personality but appears identically on both Bradley's and Cooper's individual valises. Such confusion, and the impossibility of getting beyond it, shrugs off the norms of Victorian middle-class masculinity that readers would initially associate with a "Michael Field." More broadly, this performative withholding points toward a complex subjectivity that lies beyond the personality assumed for that or any name.

Such an assiduously displayed withholding or incompletion, so reminiscent of Pater, helps to explain the strangeness of Bradley and Cooper's effort to maintain the secrecy of Field as a pseudonym well after people actually knew their identities. By alternately obscuring their authorial status, hinting to various people about their *oeuvre,* and explicitly soliciting feedback on their work from writers they cared about, the pair fluctuated between distinguishing themselves from Field and promoting themselves as Field, even when their lack of anonymity would seem to make either gesture moot. They thus called attention to the perpetual incompletion of knowledge and to the play of selfhood, the way that it shifts through experience, performance, memory, and relationality. In other words, the secrecy that Bradley and Cooper entreated around the Field signature was not about maintaining its integrity but about staging the withholding that Pater advocated and drawing out its political potential.

Two incidents during an 1890 gathering at the American socialite and poet Louise Chandler Moulton's London salon confirm this reading. Early in the evening, Moulton went around presenting Bradley and Cooper "as a poet, as Michael Field," until Bradley pulled her aside and insisted that she "introduce us by our Christian names," as though there were a secret about Field to be kept (*W&D* 134). Later in the evening, though, while talking to Oscar Wilde about Pater's aesthetic, Bradley couldn't resist identifying herself as Field. She playfully handed Wilde a gift she had just received from Moulton, a book inscribed to Michael Field, believing that "he understood" the gesture (*W&D* 138). Taken together, these moments suggest that Bradley performed a contrived attempt to hide a secret that was already widely known in order to exploit the dynamic of a secret. Significantly, she pursued this work in the context of a laudatory discussion with Wilde about the value of Pater's impersonal aesthetic. In other words, she staged her peek-a-boo withholding for a trained audience, and with the cues to that training in place. Indeed, Bradley and Cooper go on to highlight Wilde's training in their journal's subsequent account of Pater's Mérimée lecture: Wilde, who also attended the lecture, evidently teased Pater about his withholding manner, joking that the audience hadn't so much heard him as overheard him when he spoke (*W&D* 121).

It's at just this moment, at the time of the Mérimée lecture, that Field's Paterian aesthetic takes a new turn with their ekphrastic collection *Sight and Song*. This volume of poems about paintings more directly highlights Field's concern with the nature of vision and images and thus extends their political reading of Pater to his notion of *Anders-streben*. Scholars have already identified *Sight and Song* as having a distinctly visual aesthetic. However, they have tended to conceptualize the volume's visuality exclusively in terms of a lesbian-feminist challenge to the male gaze. In addition, where they do register a broader epistemology of vision, they haven't considered how it riffs on contemporary optical science, particularly as mediated through Pater.[30] And yet, the embodied observer posited by the new physiology of vision was central to *Sight and Song,* and specifically to its imagetextual form. The volume's two epigraphs forecast its understanding of vision: they capture a turn away from the visionary image underwriting the symbolics of poetic inspiration and toward an embodied observer and visual image. The epigraphs also hint at how this turn resists politicized conventions about gender, identity, and social citizenship.

One of the epigraphs—"I see and sing by my own eyes inspired"—comes from Keats' "Ode to Psyche" (1819), which tells of how the goddess' beauty inspired the poet-speaker with the "loveliest vision" and in turn with song (lines 43, 24). In the quoted line, a sleeping Psyche is the unstated object of "see," suggesting the poem's larger masculine prerogative. But the line itself doesn't emphasize either that objectification or the poem's larger visionary arc. Instead, it highlights only the poet-speaker's "own eyes" and links saying to their actual rather than imagined seeing. By isolating this one line, Field refuses not only a visionary vision but also the gender hierarchy of poetic inspiration: a masculine speaker giving voice to a silent and feminine muse. *Sight and Song's* other epigraph clarifies the embodied limits of sight that Keats' line doesn't acknowledge. Recorded in the original Greek from Sophocles' *Oedipus at Colonus* (c. 406 BCE), the line is a declaration by the blind and dying Oedipus: "In all that I speak there will be vision" (line 74).[31] Though in this play the blinded Oedipus bears a prophecy and thereby a kind of authority from Apollo, he doesn't himself have visionary ability, and the main thrust of the play is his search for an auspicious place to die (as Apollo's prophecy is about the good fortune that his death will bring to those nearby). I thus suggest that Field's appeal to this line—and so to Oedipus' blind "vision" and mortality—is a figure for the embodied observer. Indeed, Field's citation of the line in Greek evokes the cryptic language that Pater associates with Leonardo and that he suggests should be the basis of impersonal art. Like Pater, then, Field negotiates in these two epigraphs both a disembodied, visionary model of sight and a physiological model and ultimately privileges the latter. Moreover, this negotiation announces that the volume will blur the seeable and the sayable—as does Oedipus' spoken vision—and that this blurring will explore the limits of knowledge and the opacity of subjectivity.

Sight and Song pursues this project in two ways: through the particular dynamic of its ekphrasis and through its play on the model of the museum

guidebook. In terms of the former, W. J. T. Mitchell has argued that ekphrasis—an extended description of a visual object or scene—may seem to advertise that image and text can do the same work, but in practice it actually
negotiates a deep ambivalence over just this possibility and often ends with
a fear of disrupting not only the image/text binary but also the various social
binaries related to it (*Picture Theory* 151-82). Ekphrasis is thus typically read
as a textual reinforcement of the male gaze, much like poetic inspiration:
the masculine text appropriates the properties of its visual supplement and
thereby supplants the feminine object on which it initially depended. If the
art historical work of *The Renaissance* is a kind of ekphrasis, however, it rewrites the tradition that Mitchell describes. As we've seen, Pater does negotiate an ambivalence about the relation between art forms: his focus on
the material particularities of each art suggests skepticism about the possibility of translating one art into another, while his notion of *Anders-streben*
preserves hope about the ability of one art to achieve the condition of another. However, Pater feels no ambivalence about this tension's social implications. On the contrary, he understands the imagetext as an invaluable way
to represent a subjectivity that exceeds gender difference. It offers a view
into the impersonal reaches of the subject by at once acknowledging bodily
limits and working to exceed them. In *Sight and Song* Field opts for a Paterian ekphrasis over and against the tradition of the form, urging readers to
view its ekphrases as (1) representing a modern image, (2) exploring the impersonal forces that shape vision, and (3) reflecting on the significance of an
impersonal subjectivity for categories of social identity.

Like Pater, Field frames *Sight and Song* as a kind of fluctuation between
ekphrastic hope and a qualification of such hope. On the one hand, their
preface describes an effort, "as far as may be, to translate into verse what
the lines and colours of certain chosen pictures sing in themselves" (v). Unlike traditional ekphrases, then, Field's picture poems evince a deep respect
for images' signifying power. In addition, the preface describes the effort to
understand that power in both imagetextual and visual perceptual terms:
not only do pictures both "see" and "sing"—just as the speakers of *Sight and
Song*'s epigraphs do—but Field's poems acknowledge that fact by working
to "see things from their own centre" rather than adhering to the "habitual
centralisation of the visible in ourselves" (vi). By blurring the distinction
between seeing and saying, the preface also begins to blur the human categories that these forms typically map onto. Thus, although the paintings
are "incarnate," or bodily, what they incarnate is in fact "poetry," or the form

traditionally mapped onto the mind (v). This complex visual and embodied relay between poetry and painting refuses the priority of the poet-observer and encourages empathy in the writer and the reader, just as Pater had suggested that impersonality could facilitate "the enlargement of our sympathies with each other" ("Style" 413).

But this visually anchored ekphrastic hope doesn't exist alone. The preface continually qualifies it, in part precisely because of vision's incomplete nature. Even a "patient, continuous sight" bears the "subjective" "fancies" of "the gazer," Field admits (v). Thus, the preface uses Gustave Flaubert, whom Pater briefly links to impersonality in "Prosper Mérimée" (36), to characterize a kind of dialectic that underwrites *Sight and Song*. Flaubert alternated between a conscious effort to "transport oneself into the characters and not to attract them to oneself" and having an inevitably "formative power in his work" (vi).[32] Adapted specifically to Field's ekphrastic project, this dialectic means that the women endeavored to comprehend the material limits of perception but also knew that such comprehension was constrained by those same limits. Nonetheless, Field emphasizes that by acknowledging materiality and thereby qualifying the ekphrastic hope, one still "obtain[s] an impression" of both subject and object that is "clearer, less passive, more intimate," thereby fulfilling some of that ekphrastic hope (vi). As with Pater's "open vision," then, materiality is simultaneously an incitement to and a constraint on Field's imagetextual project. Indeed, once again linking this image-textuality to a visual-impersonal ethic, Field's journal records a very similar formulation to open vision just a few years prior to *Sight and Song*. It commands the writers and the reader alike to "'Open-gaze' at it. . . . Dutch-picture the little scene on the brain. *Do not hack or wear yourself.* Yield not to vanity, and refuse to *go out in the Sun*" (*F&P* 193).

Ekphrastic innovation, then, is the first way in which Field carries out Pater's project. Their second technique draws on the much younger form of the illustrated museum guidebook or catalog. In the later nineteenth century such books not only armed a mass audience with knowledge of the art they could view in public museums; their entries describing the collections, artists, and paintings, as well as accompanying photomechanical reproductions of featured art, enabled armchair excursions that could substitute for visiting galleries altogether. Such books thus symbolized the increasingly explicit belief that pictures were reproducible and exchangeable and that they could circulate meanings and desires quite apart from their means of production.[33] W. B. Yeats' review of *Sight and Song* for the *Bookman* both recognized and misunderstood the volume's play on this genre: he condemned *Sight and Song* as an "unmitigated guide-book" rather than an original work of art, apparently overlooking the way that Field refused both the possibility and the value of originality (227). Indeed, although *Sight and Song's* preface emphasizes an investment in the art object, its guidebook conceit aligns the poems and paintings as equal links in a chain of images, neither re-creations nor entirely new. This conceit recalls Pater's Giorgionesque—the way it incorporated copies and appreciations of Giorgione's work along with his own paintings without distinguishing between them. Field, like Pater, thus suggests a modern understanding of the image as conventional and temporal and challenges the belief in both artistic and personal originality.

Field plays on museum guidebooks in two respects: in their means of producing *Sight and Song's* ekphrases and in the volume's arrangement. Bradley and Cooper's research for *Sight and Song* involved numerous museum excursions, and they used guidebooks, collection catalogs, and the like to prepare for their visits and to remind them of the paintings they had seen. For instance, in conjunction with their 1891 trip to the Dresden Gallery and the Städel Museum in Frankfurt, Bradley and Cooper purchased Giovanni Morelli's *Italian Painters* (1890), which guided them on a tour of the Borghese, Doria-Pamphili, Dresden, and Munich Galleries (*W&D* 48). As part of this tour, Morelli's book touted his own scientific theory of attribution for distinguishing art originals from copies.[34] Bradley and Cooper's willingness to work from the reproductions in Morelli's study twisted his influential investment in the artist's distinctive hand into just one more link in a chain of images. Field thus playfully subverts the same art historical commitment to originality that Pater had criticized in *The Renaissance*. Bradley and Cooper extended this subversion in a letter to their friend the art critic and "Morellian" Bernard Berenson, whom they challenged to guess which parts of *Sight and Song* each had written. Berenson recognized their jab at Morelli's method and perhaps even its implications not only for art but also for identity. He responded that guessing "simply does not enter into connoisseurship" and said that he would merely need "to know the work of each [woman] separately" in order to discern "what belongs to each" (qtd. in Fraser 561). Of course, this commitment to individual manner was exactly what Bradley and Cooper's impersonalizing collaboration refused.

In addition to using museum guidebooks to prepare for writing *Sight and Song*, Bradley and Cooper also arranged the volume itself with an eye toward

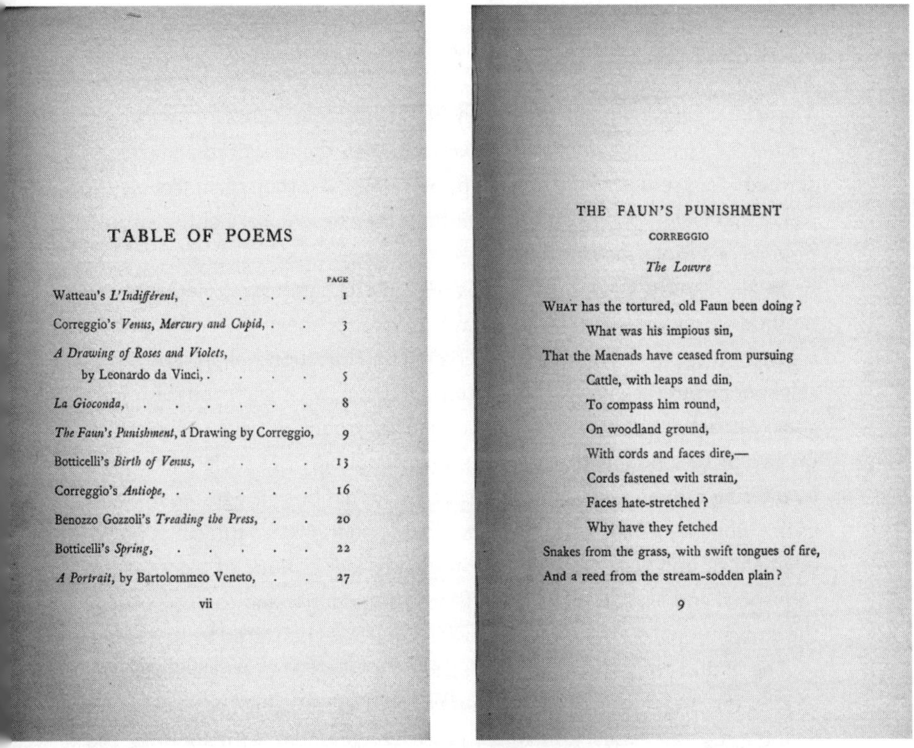

TABLE OF POEMS

vii

THE FAUN'S PUNISHMENT

CORREGGIO

The Louvre

WHAT has the tortured, old Faun been doing?
What was his impious sin,
That the Maenads have ceased from pursuing
Cattle, with leaps and din,
To compass him round,
On woodland ground,
With cords and faces dire,—
Cords fastened with strain,
Faces hate-stretched?
Why have they fetched
Snakes from the grass, with swift tongues of fire,
And a reed from the stream-sodden plain?

9

Fig. 1.3. Pages from Field's *Sight and Song: left,* opening page of its "Table of Poems"; *right,* sample heading from one of its ekphrases, in this case "Correggio's *The Faun's Punishment.*"

the average guidebook, which was organized around specific collections, schools, or artists and whose entries were accompanied by captioned illustrations that detailed title, artist, year of completion, and museum location. A prime example of such a guide is London's Grosvenor Gallery catalogs, which accompanied each season's exhibition and which Cooper mentions examining in an 1892 letter to her friend Mary Costelloe (qtd. in Fraser 558). Echoing this catalog, *Sight and Song*'s "Table of Poems" appears to be a list of art and artists, and the individual poems are similarly headed with information for identifying the versified art, including title, artist, and location (fig. 1.3). In the midst of this factual reporting, though, Field intermittently renames the versified paintings—for instance, Benozzo Gozzoli's *The Vin-*

tage and Drunkenness of Noah (1469–84) becomes "Benozzo Gozzoli's *Treading the Press*," and Antonio Correggio's *Madonna and Child with Saints Sebastian, Germinian, and Roche* (1524–25) becomes "Correggio's *Saint Sebastian*." These changes tend to occur where Field's ekphrasis focuses on a particular portion of a painting or drawing. Taken together, the new titles and circumscribed focus refuse a kind of guidebook objectivity: they again trouble the sense that Field's poems and the paintings they describe are either entirely original or simply copies.

In all of these ways, *Sight and Song*'s various paratextual elements and methods, from its epigraphs to its layout, advance the new visuality and its modern image and embodied observer. The collection's ekphrases themselves draw out the political implications of that new visuality and the impersonal aesthetic that Pater and Field organized around it. Let us concentrate on two picture poems that do more than simply rewrite social hierarchies by offering a feminist or lesbian perspective, as has been suggested by some critics (Ehnenn, White, Laird, Vadillo). These poems instead turn an acknowledgment of universal embodiment into a broader critique of a contemporary social and artistic focus on selfhood and identity and thereby expose the conventionality of the various social hierarchies bolstered by that focus.

The first of these two poems is Field's ekphrasis of Correggio's *Allegory of Vices* (fig. 1.4), a painting widely interpreted as restaging *Laocoön and His Sons* (fig. 1.5), a classical Roman sculpture by Agesander, Athenodoros, and Polydorus, and the piece on which Gotthold Ephraim Lessing later based his influential image/text binary.[35] Field's ekphrasis begins by cataloging the details of Correggio's painting, almost entirely without recourse to figurative devices like metaphor or simile. Field thus makes good on their promise to really attend to their chosen pictures, rather than to take them as a mere point of departure for lyric reflection. But their catalog also continually shifts between different compositional elements in the painting: the "Cattle" in the distance, the "Snakes from the grass," "the sun's and oak-leaves' flicker," "the old Faun's ear." (*Sight and Song* 9–12, lines 4, 11, 13, 16). These shifting details, along with the dilating and contracting length of the lines and marked enjambment, duplicate the unwilled saccadic jumps that are part of any act of vision and also emphasize vision's temporality. The following stanza is a particularly apt example because its initial focus on one of the maenad's "fanciful eyes" and then the object of her "glance" underscores Field's visuality, while a second maenad's "elat[ion]" feeds the verse's saccadic shift between objects and varying line lengths:

Fig. 1.4. Antonio Allegri da Correggio, *Allegory of Vices* (1528-30), Louvre Museum, Paris. Reproduced by permission of RMN-Grand Palais/Jean Schormans.

One sits with fanciful eyes beside him;
   Malice and wonder mix
In her glance at the victim—woe betide him,
   When once her snakes transfix
   His side! Ere they dart,
   With backward start
   She waits their rigid pause;
   And with comely stoop
   One maid, elate
   With horror, hate
And triumph, up from his ankle draws
The skin away in a clinging loop. (lines 25-36)

Fig. 1.5. Agesander, Athenodoros, and Polydorus, *Laocoön and His Sons,* c. 42–20 BCE. Vatican Museums, Vatican City.

Field's poem builds from its ranging catalog to a set of questions that underscore how embodied perception limits knowledge. Rather than offering a simple summary of the painted scene, the lyric voice loses itself in uncertainty: "What has the tortured, old Faun been doing?/What was his impious sin," and "What meaning is here, or what mystery,/What fate, and for what crime?" (lines 1–2, 49–50). The resulting dramatization of the image as neither semantically transparent nor immediate to the eye challenges the notion of the static, passive, and also culturally feminized image, just as Field's poem goes on to repudiate the broader patriarchal structures naturalized by the image/text binary. But to understand the richness of that repudiation, it's important to attend to Field's negotiation of Correggio's "intertext": the Roman sculpture *Laocoön and His Sons,* which in turn represents the fate ascribed to Laocoön in classical epic verse, from Virgil's *Aeneid* to Quintus Smyrnaeus' *Posthomerica.*

Although accounts vary, the gods punish Laocoön first by blinding him and then by sending sea snakes to consume him and his sons. Correggio's *Allegory of Vices* records only the latter punishment, and the snakes have become women who not only bear biting serpents in their hands but also resemble serpents in their roped hair ornaments and belts and even in the lines of their draperies. In addition, Correggio's women mirror in their poses Laocoön's sons in the Roman sculpture, so even as they are punishers, they are also implicated in "vice" itself. Indeed, numerous accounts claim that Laocoön was killed for making love to his wife before a sacred image, and Correggio capitalizes on that sense of illicit sex in the nudity and sensuality that constitute vice in his painting's central scene and involve both the male faun and the female maenads.

Field's ekphrasis departs from some of Correggio's interpretations in ways that highlight the imagetextuality of his painting, the fact that *Allegory of Vices* is a painting of a sculpture of a poem (or really of several poems). For instance, taken in the context of *Sight and Song*'s epigraphs, where Oedipus' blind vision seems to stand for the embodied materiality of sight, this poem's focus on embodied visual limits reciprocally hints at the ultimate limit of Laocoön's blinding, which disappears in Correggio's account. At the same time, moving from imagetextuality to political critique, Field has little use for the idea that Correggio's women are femmes fatales (as suggested by their sensuality) or even the instruments of a metaphysical hand (as suggested by epic accounts of Laocoön's fate). Instead, Field's poem speculates that the torturing maenads are revolting against the faun's judgmental male gaze. The faun had perhaps been watching, indeed laughing at, the maenads in their ecstasy, and the women refuse to be objectified:

> With fun the grey-bear shook
> At the Maenads' torn,
> Spread hair, their brave,
> Tumultuous wave
> Dancing; and women will never brook
> Mirth at their folly, O doomed, old Faun! (lines 55–60)

Although Field underscores the speculative nature of this causality, they still reinforce its critique of a scopic patriarchy by giving Correggio's title at the head of their poem not as *Allegory of Vices* but instead as *The Faun's Punishment*. The change casts the poem as part of a chain of mutually constitutive and always mutable images and texts that construct what we might call the

"Correggiesque," following on Pater's notion of the "Giorgionesque." Field thus links their skepticism of stable images and originality to their politicized critique of patriarchy.

This critique is slightly more complicated, though, for while Field offers an alternative account of the sources of the pictured scene, the poem doesn't use that account to deny Correggio's negative view of the women or even to let them stand as symbols for a feminist aesthetic. Rather, Field reinterprets what the women's possible vice consists in. Instead of highlighting the orgy that Correggio hints at, Field casts the maenads' potential vice as a failure to pursue the erotically coded restraint so central to a Paterian impersonal aesthetic. Field describes the faun laughing at the maenads for their specifically frenzied folly but, more importantly, offers a corrective to that folly in the poem's focus on the boy-faun in the foreground of Correggio's painting. This boy-faun is only partially visible, and his draped arm seems to rest on the painting's frame, pointing to the image's circumscribed and constructed view. He looks out with calm allure, his withholding inciting Field's desire to see and know. Correspondingly, Field's lyric gaze settles longest not on the tortured faun (whose pose and nudity are highly erotic), nor on the frenzied maenads (who have consummated their sadistic desire), but on this calm boy, entirely detached from the central scene. The poem's detailed description of the boy is increasingly tight and close, as if Field's eyes are progressively drawn to him rather than to the maenads' ecstasy. In addition, Field's description eroticizes the boy's comparative attention and restraint, effectively making him a new pictorial center:

> Grapes and stem at his chin,—
> Mouth of red the red grape-bunch enhances
>   Ere it is sucked within
>   By the juicy lips,
>   Free as the tips
>   Of tendrils in their curve;
>   And his flaccid cheek,
>   Mid mirthful heaves
>   And ripples, weaves
> A guiltless smile that might almost serve
> For the vines themselves in vintage-week. (lines 38–48)

Field's visual concentration on this boy-faun endorses his spectacular withholding and also suggests that having a heightened awareness of the painting's (and indeed any image's) partiality and conventionality yields a more fully reimagined male gaze than any simple identification with the women of the painting would do. The boy in fact peers outward to the viewer, offering a reciprocal circuit of observation that disturbs the underlying binaries and power dynamic of the male gaze. Ultimately, then, if Lessing looked to artistic representations of Laocoön's death as a means of arguing for an image/text binary, Field follows Pater's challenge to Lessing by using Correggio's rendition of *Laocoön and His Sons* to challenge that binary, replacing the disembodied objective observer that Lessing presumes with an embodied and fundamentally impersonal one that disturbs social identity.

Field's ekphrasis of Bartolomeo Veneto's *Idealized Portrait* offers a second example of how their concern to explore the embodied observer's social implications doesn't amount simply to their empowerment of the female or queer figures in the paintings under review, as is often argued (fig. 1.6). Somewhat akin to Field's portrayal of the offended and offending maenads in the previous poem, the Veneto ekphrasis alternately empowers and critiques the pictured woman's beliefs and actions. Field uses this dialectic to express both the method and the philosophical and political object of their impersonal aesthetic.

Veneto's painting presents the sitter as Flora, the Roman goddess of flowers and spring, through her bouquet, veil, and laurel crown. The painting thus exemplifies what was commonly termed a *fancy picture* in the eighteenth and nineteenth centuries: it shows an unknown young woman whose idealized costume and pose introduce elements of storytelling or myth, though her own beauty was likely the instigation for the piece's creation.[36] A fancy picture, in other words, falls somewhere between a portrait (a rendering of a person) and an allegory (a representation of an abstract ideal). Field's dialectical attitude toward Veneto's pictured woman plays on this duality of the fancy picture, particularly its imagetextual potential as a kind of narrative portrait.

Field's opening stanza details the woman's appearance and thus the painting, according to the qualities of the traditional image that were so often used to secure a male/female binary:

A crystal flawless beauty on the brows
Where neither love nor time has conquered space
On which to live; her leftward smile endows
The gazer with no tidings from the face;

Fig. 1.6. Bartolomeo Veneto, *Idealized Portrait of a Courtesan as Flora,* c. 1520–25. Städel Museum, Frankfurt am Main. Courtesy of U. Edelmann—Städel Museum/ ARTOTHEK.

> About the clear mounds of the lip it winds with silvery pace
>> And in the umber eyes it is a light
> Chill as a glowworm's when the moon embrowns an August night. (*Sight and*
>> *Song* 27–30, lines 1–7)

The woman's "crystal" beauty suggests the transparency of glass, while the fact that her face has yielded time no "space/On which to live" implies a static, atemporal spatiality. Moreover, the woman expresses no interiority, since the viewer receives "no tidings from the face." Just as importantly, following close on the heels of this traditional model of the image is a model of vision consistent with it. Field links the woman's "Chill" eyes both to the bioluminescent "glowworm," which emits a so-called cold light that lacks the sun's radiance, and to the moon, whose light is a mere reflection of the sun's. On the one hand, then, the woman is doubly separated from the sun, the bearer not only of radiant light but also, more figuratively, of enlightenment and reason. On the other hand, the moon's reflective and thereby passive nature links the woman's image to a model of vision that's comfortably mimetic.

Over and against this portrayal of femininity, the image, and vision, Field's subsequent stanzas relocate the painting within a modern imagetextuality largely by inventing beliefs and actions for the female sitter, who Field imagines has herself solicited her portrait. Field first announces this new direction by recording Veneto's title in their header not as *Idealized Portrait* but simply as *A Portrait*. This alteration broadcasts Field's effort to displace the idealism regarding women, images, and vision suggested in their poem's opening catalog. Taking a cue from the fancy picture's appeal to stories, Field's ekphrasis goes on to describe a courtesan who's used to being read and exploited as a passive body in line with the traditional image but who's also accustomed to recognizing and exploiting that reading herself, in part by manipulating the coding of her image:

> So was she painted and for centuries
> Has held the fading field-flowers in her hand
> Austerely as a sign. O fearful eyes
> And soft lips of the courtesan who planned
> To give her fragile shapeliness to art, whose reason spanned
> Her doom, who bade her beauty in its cold
> And vacant eminence persist for all men to behold! (lines 29-35)

The specific story that the courtesan elicits in her portrait is an empowering but highly ironic portrayal of herself as the virginal Flora, a construction that highlights the conventionality of Veneto's painting. In addition to the above-cited bouquet of "field-flowers," she selects a "well-bleachen white" veil and a "spiky wreath" of "immortal hue" and also coyly bares "one breast" (lines 30, 22, 25, 25, 27).

However, Field's ekphrastic alterations are once again more complicated than a feminist assertion of female agency. Despite the courtesan's sharp reasoning and her seemingly modern understanding of the image, Field critiques her imagined motivations, specifically the fact that she ultimately hopes to exploit Veneto's painting as a way of possessing her beauty for all time. In keeping with the traditional image that Field characterizes in their opening catalog, the courtesan wants to use her portrait to escape materiality and temporality. Gazing upon herself in the mirror, she decided to be painted, with the expectation that the painting would be a mirror to nature, a verisimilar image that would freeze the beauty she saw as her property:

> She saw her beauty often in the glass,
> Sharp on the dazzling surface, and she knew
> The haughty custom of her grace must pass:
> Though more persistent in all charm it grew
> As with a desperate joy her hair across her throat she drew
> In crinkled locks stiff as dead, yellow snakes . . .
> Until at last within her soul the resolution wakes
>
> She will be painted, she who is so strong
> In loveliness, so fugitive in years. (lines 8–16, ellipses original)

To some extent, Field sympathizes with the courtesan's decision to "give her fragile shapeliness to art," largely because it reverses the patriarchal norms of artistic production, according to which a male artist chooses a sitter in order to facilitate his own vision. However, Field's poem ultimately condemns the courtesan as prostituting her body for the pay of eternal youth: she bids her "beauty in its cold / And vacant eminence persist for all men to behold!" At no point does Field associate the courtesan's views of art, the image, or materiality with the eroticized allure of withholding so central to Pater's, and in turn *Sight and Song*'s, impersonal aesthetic. Indeed, contrary to a notion of impersonal subjectivity, the courtesan "had no memories save of herself / And her slow-fostered graces" (lines 36–37). Field emphasizes that this self-centeredness meant that the courtesan gave to art only "a fair, blank form, unverified by life" (line 42) rather than any awareness of subjectivity or the world.

Field's final stanza punctuates this conclusion and its connection to an imagetextual image:

> Thus has she conquered death: her eyes are fresh,
> Clear as her frontlet jewel, firm in shade
> And definite as on the linen mesh
> Of her white hood the box-tree's somber braid,
> That glitters leaf by leaf and with the year's waste will not fade.
> The small, close mouth, leaving no room for breath,
> In perfect, still pollution smiles—Lo, she has conquered death! (lines 43–49)

The stanza begins and ends with the declaration that the courtesan has "conquered death." The repetition does not, however, reinforce the truth of the statement. Instead, it cloaks it with uncertainty if not emptiness, a fact made clear by a reversal charted in the lines sandwiched between the two declarations. The first five lines speak of the courtesan's "fresh" "eyes," as well as a clarity that "will not fade," suggesting that she has accomplished the permanence she seeks. But the last two lines imply that the image she so carefully molded still includes mortality and therefore also time. Field describes the courtesan's "small, close mouth" not as always youthful but as suffocating: "leaving no room for breath." Likewise, from that mouth "still pollution" smiles; the connotation is embodied imperfection, contamination, and extinction. Thus the courtesan's image has not in fact "conquered death" and thereby rendered her body a controllable, self-determined possession. Instead, the poem's final phrase is deeply ironic, perhaps an echo of the irony in the courtesan's construction of herself as an always virginal Spring.

Ultimately, this ekphrasis, as well as *Sight and Song* as a whole, subtly announces a commitment to the ontological and visual-material grounding— and less subtly to the political consequences—of Pater's impersonal aesthetic. It's committed, first, to the modern image and observer circulated in the new scientific vernacular of vision; second, to the impersonal subjectivity engrained in this vernacular; and third, to the political capacity of that subjectivity to disrupt embodied identities and social hierarchies. *Sight and Song* suggests that Bradley and Cooper's desire to represent impersonal subjectivity was a key reason that they performed nonnormative identities and relations, both in poetry and in life. That this desire was not fully achievable is also an important part of their aesthetic. Field's commitment to incompletion and its significance can help us to see Pater's aesthetic as deeply political, even as it revises our understanding of what's more explicitly politicized in Field's work. Read in this light, the never-finished second volume of *Sight and Song* parallels Pater's Leonardo, with his endless retouching and intermittent unproductivity.[37] If Field's first volume aimed to register the idea that vision, knowledge, and representation are all partial and mediated and to showcase the politics of that fact, this unfulfilled second volume suggests that Bradley and Cooper viewed even their acknowledgment as incomplete.

This same principle of incompletion is also the frame through which we can understand those modernists who inherit Pater and Field's interest in an impersonal aesthetic. These modernists pursue aesthetic impersonality as a visual study of being that seeks to create imagetexts of a psychophysiological subjectivity that conditions personality—the *im* in *impersonality,* as it were—and also to explore the political implications of this subjectivity. Yet to locate the origins of modernist impersonality in Pater's and Field's responses to the new physiology of vision in the later nineteenth century is not to say that the aesthetic they adapted from it or the political potential they saw in it represents the exclusive trajectory of modernist impersonality. Modernists took up the impersonal project's necessarily loose ends and developed them in varying directions. Some modernists, such as H.D., drew out the liberating potential that Pater hinted at and Field elaborated upon. But other modernists, such as D. H. Lawrence, turned the opacity of impersonal subjectivity toward a more conservative potential. What all the modernists shared, though, was a belief in impersonality's political value, whether or not they were consistently able to tap into that value themselves. Moreover, in one respect the methods through which the modernists pursued an impersonal aesthetic did grow increasingly close to Field's project. Moving into the twentieth century, as the vernacular science of vision shaped visual culture in increasingly pervasive ways, modernists understood that they were grappling with the implications of that vernacular whenever they engaged visual culture. Like Field, then, the modernists looked increasingly to contemporary visual culture, such as psychoanalysis and film, to shape the imagetextual models of impersonal subjectivity that I examine in subsequent chapters.

2 Images of Incoherence

The Visual Body of H.D.

Impersonaliste

[N]ot a woman, not a goddess even, but . . . [a] song, a
spirit, a white star that moves across the heaven . . . Yet
she is embodied— . . . a personality as the most impersonal
become when they confront their fellow beings.

H.D., "The Wise Sappho"

In April 1949, Norman Holmes Pearson sent his friend the writer-actress
H.D. a manuscript of an essay entitled "The American Poet in Relation to
Science," in which he discusses her work along with that of other prominent
modernists, including Pound, Eliot, and Rukeyser. In this essay, which soon
appeared in *American Quarterly*, we see the modern fruition of what circulates diffusely through Pater's and Field's work: the sense, among modernist
writers and critics alike, that "the world as we know it today . . . has been
defined by science," by the "mystery of functions" and "changing matter"
that science points to and by the challenges that these scientific principles
pose to the "dignity and freedom" that have long distinguished human "personality" (1, 1, 2, 1, 14). Yet while Pearson's characterization of science's importance and even some of its premises was shared by Pater and Field—and
as we'll soon see, H.D.—his ultimate focus on science's almost totalizing
power over social, economic, and cultural structures is much more simplis-
tic than their aesthetics suggest. Pearson argues darkly that Renaissance
science "gave us the free world . . . and the apparent dignity and freedom of
man," while today "it is science which seems to have taken them from us"
(1). But Pater, Field, and H.D. didn't see science as something to be either
grateful for or fearful of, depending on the moment. Instead, they took an
active role in shaping what the "new vista of knowledge" in science would
mean within and for modernism (1). I'll return to Pearson's essay and its

actual argument about H.D.'s poetry momentarily. But first, let me put in play an example of how H.D. shaped modernism's scientific "vista" by turning to a moment in her novella *The Usual Star* (1934). This understudied novella was part of a projected but never completed "Borderline cycle" in the 1920s, indicating its connection to H.D.'s involvement with avant-garde film, including *Borderline* (1930), discussed in the final section of this chapter.[1]

The Usual Star encapsulates H.D.'s broader attitude toward the science of embodied vision by describing the experience of her alter ego, the protagonist Raymonde Ransome, as she strolls through London. Raymonde feels as though she's "set in" some "throbbing" and "vibrant body" and that from within it she and her friend "were one pin-point, one star-point, to let some sort of out-light into this cumbrous city consciousness. 'We see beyond this, but we must be in it, to see it.' . . . They had projected London, made it, pin-point of imperfection, blight on material surface. 'We have made this thing, as people make screen vision. We have projected London'" (20). Raymonde perceives London as both a complex physiological body capable of sight and a perceptual image. Moreover, she casts herself as a pupil or aperture that simultaneously allows "out-light" into the consciousness of London as body and also constructs a previously unseen view of London as image. Such a complex formulation entirely reworks the classical philosophical representation of the seeing subject as a camera obscura. That representation had modeled an enclosed, objective observer with a transparent mind's eye capable of perfectly registering the world. Like Pater before her, H.D. draws out how a modern physiological optics undid this camera obscura model. Not only does she emphasize the unwilled material body charted in modern optics but the body she describes is also simultaneously her own and the external world of London, a multiplicity that stages how this optics collapses the classical division of interior from exterior. In addition, H.D.'s description gives not simply Raymonde but her and her friend together, the aperture function of the camera obscura. This change reasserts the mechanics of binocular vision and shows that its embodied complexities— and the "pin-point of *im*perfection" they offer—belie the autonomous, singular individual and transparent knowledge imagined by the camera obscura model.

Moreover, H.D.'s description and the image she imagines also show that modernists' negotiation of optics extended to a vernacular science formed from modern visual technologies like cinema. Raymonde's sense that she's at once a film camera (she "made this thing" as people make "screen vision") and a projector (she "has projected London") implies a visual perception that creates the world rather than knowing it immediately and whose images are thereby constructed rather than natural or transparent. Furthermore, the name Ray-monde (or "world light") makes not only London but also Raymonde herself the light image she projects, once again muddying interior/exterior and subject/object. Just as importantly, H.D. also suggests that Raymonde dimly grasps and represents those systems within the human subject that shape vision but exceed personality, including the "throb" of circulating blood and the periphery of "consciousness." H.D. thus doesn't simply restate the claims of contemporary optics; she launches an aesthetic project from the "new vista" of that optics. By positioning Raymonde as a new visual technology, H.D. announces her own aesthetic effort to visualize the *im-* of impersonal subjectivity, to grasp and represent what goes into the person. Her effort plumbs what Walter Benjamin, also interrogating subjectivity through modern visual technologies, would call the "optical unconscious" just a few years later.

While Pearson's essay appeals to H.D.'s work to make the case for science's importance to modernist poetry, he misses her adaptation of modern optics, as well as her particular formulation of modernist impersonality. This is principally because he argues that while modern poetry draws on current scientific methods, it also recovers and preserves the certainty of an earlier "Renaissance heritage." Pearson maintains, in other words, that while modern science has "erased" "personality" by "reduc[ing]" the "area of reality," the modern poet stands for and reasserts "the dignity and freedom of the individual" (14).

Though written more than sixty years ago, Pearson's argument still captures two major trends in H.D. scholarship. First, though scholars have frequently identified H.D.'s modernism with her negotiation of images, they hesitate to elaborate her sustained investment in science and to consider the link between these two interests.[2] Joining Pearson, critics like Charlotte Mandel and Adalaide Morris have acknowledged that H.D.'s desire to probe subjectivity has scientific ties, but they dilute those ties in their particular arguments. Mandel suggests that although H.D. drew on scientific technologies like the microscope, the telescope, and the cinema projector, she ultimately refused scientific epistemology, as exemplified by the "scrutinizing gaze" of her botanist grandfather and her astronomer father (309).[3] Mandel concludes specifically that H.D.'s art turns away from a visual image and toward a transcendent, visionary one, a conclusion broadly seconded, for instance, by Rachel Connor and Helen Sword. Morris, on the other hand, maintains that H.D. engaged continuously with scientific epistemology but nonetheless aligns her interest in the embodied observer somewhat ahistorically with later twentieth-century concepts like chaos theory, making her dialogue with science at times more theoretical than timely.

Pearson's portrayal of H.D. as a champion of personality, and in particular an outdated formulation of it, prefigures a second trend in recent criticism. Where H.D. scholars consider modernist impersonality, they generally gloss it as the pursuit of "objective truth about reality" and counterpose it to H.D.'s "personal," "feminine" aesthetic.[4] Even Susan Stanford Friedman's suggestion that H.D. revisits personal experiences in her prose in order to be impersonal in her poetry still maintains the sense that impersonality is a negation of personality and thus limits H.D.'s practice of that aesthetic (*Penelope's Web* 5-6). Similarly, though Joyce Wexler notes that the scholarly focus on personal lives has obscured women writers' pursuit of impersonality, she nonetheless understands impersonality as an escape from subjectivity.[5]

However, as was true of Pater and Field, whose work she knew well, H.D.'s investments in optics, images, and impersonality were in dialogue.[6] Her effort to record a "presence" in the human subject that "has vanished or is just now departing" was a distinctly visual and scientific project rather than a visionary one (Morris 98). She saw the optical unconscious as a way to approach a subjectivity beyond personality—what she called the *personal-impersonal*—and indeed to explore a new locus and meaning for embodied identity.[7] Like Field, H.D. believed that this always incomplete exploration would challenge hegemonic social hierarchies pertaining not only to gender and sexuality but also to race. She marshaled an expanded scientific vernacular in a range of modern sites—including abstract art, avant-garde cinema, and Freudian psychoanalysis—in order to develop a more sophisticated account of impersonal subjectivity and to rally that account into the liberating politics of her aesthetic. The new forms of imagetextuality that H.D. created to achieve this work are in fact part of the modern scientific vernacular of vision.

From H.D.'s imagist verse in *Sea Garden* (1916), through her experiential manifesto *Notes on Thought and Vision* (1919), to her film essay "Cinema and the Classics" (1927) and her exegetical pamphlet for *Borderline,* one of several films in which she starred, her aesthetic projects together suggest two broad phases in her impersonality. Early on, she focused on the particular embodiment of the human subject and on the way that gender, sexual, and racial identities are muddied when the privilege of objectivity underwriting key social hierarchies comes unhinged. She appealed to the imagist school of poetry, in particular its adaptation of both contemporary science and abstract art, to emphasize a seeing subject that was circumscribed by its material limits and whose embodied identity was both constructed and constraining. Later, though, she turned to newly developed cinematic and psychoanalytic images, which emphasized a melding of spectator and spectacle, in order to insist on the unbounded nature of the seeing subject and to posit a complex nexus of social and organic imperatives within which identities acquire shape and continually fluctuate. By advancing this view, H.D. took an important step toward rejecting both purely biological essentialist and social constructivist views of race and gender. Across her career, then, far from distancing herself from science and impersonality in favor of subjectivity, H.D. sought new and politically consequential forms of subjectivity in the marriage of science and aesthetics.

Mixing an Imagist Pigment: Modern Art, Science, and Materiality in *Sea Garden*

At the close of his manifesto "VORTEX" (1914) Ezra Pound illustrates his declaration that "the primary pigment of poetry is the IMAGE" with the following pairing: "In painting Kandinski [*sic*], Picasso. In poetry this ['Oread'], by 'H.D.'" (154). Such a pairing calls for reading H.D.'s early poetry in relation to modern art's non-verisimilar or abstract image, which was so foundational to the theory and techniques of poetic imagism and vorticism. However, Pound's gender politics—and in particular the way he rechristened his former fiancé, Hilda Doolittle, as "H.D. Imagiste"—has overshadowed such an exploration of *Sea Garden*, her first volume of verse. Critics have often sought to distance H.D.'s aesthetic from Pound's influence, and specifically the concerns of imagism, including impersonality and visuality, both of which are mistakenly cast in terms of objectivity. The common premise for approaching *Sea Garden*, and H.D.'s early interest in painting and sculpture more broadly, is that her goal was to "endow personality" over and against an imagist project of "impersonality" (Camboni 40, 58).

Let me point more specifically, though, to a couple of important readings along these lines. Cassandra Laity has distanced *Sea Garden*'s frequently floral poems from imagism by linking them instead to a subjective and decadent *fin-de-siècle* symbolics. She argues that by describing flowers in extreme conditions of geography, weather, and decay, *Sea Garden* traffics in a *fin-de-siècle* necrophilia that's utterly at odds with the objectivity valued by imagism. By contrast, Mandel has actually accepted that *Sea Garden* has a residue of imagism; she reads the floral poems as zooming in, detailing botanical bodies, and mimicking a practice of flaying, all of which enact a positivist visuality that she associates with imagism. But Mandel has also emphasized that H.D. would quickly abandon this visuality—and even does so in certain ways in *Sea Garden*. What's most interesting about these particular efforts to distinguish H.D. from Pound's impersonality and visuality is their focus on the eroticized, corpselike materiality discernible throughout *Sea Garden*. Such a materiality actually comports quite well with what Daniel Tiffany has described as the basic nature of Pound's imagist image. I want to build on Tiffany's work, which I detail below, by exploring this image, along with its connections to modern art and optics, as a central formal and thematic concern in *Sea Garden*. I argue that from this early moment H.D. began to turn the modern scientific vernacular of vision negotiated in imagism toward an impersonal aesthetic capable of imagining and sustaining modern forms of subjectivity.

Pound's early association of "Oread" with Picasso and Kandinsky is part and parcel of his larger appeal to abstract experimentation in the visual arts to formulate his imagist and then vorticist aesthetic. Though "VORTEX" cites one of Pater's most-remembered examples of *Anders-streben* as an "ancestor" of imagism and vorticism, it also departs sharply from the Renaissance art that had so interested Pater and Field (153).[8] "VORTEX" instead aligns Pound's work with those modern painters and sculptors who refused a long-dominant perspectivalism and naturalism in trying to visualize the unseen. Art critics have often characterized modern abstraction as an effort to purify the visual arts of narrative and thereby to distinguish image from text. But as W. J. T. Mitchell has argued, abstract art's oddly familiar obscurity compels textualization or theorization by artists, critics, and viewers alike (*Picture Theory* 231-40). Thus, Pound's appeal to an abstract art image isn't a departure from the imagetext that was so formally and thematically central to Pater and Field and in turn to modernist impersonality. Rather, both the abstract image and the appeal are themselves a kind of imagetextuality. By offering deceptively simple images that are recognizable but make no mimetic claims, these artists produce a kind of opaque immediacy that appealed to Pound. They continually frustrate the desire to see or possess the image, gesturing persistently at what remains just beyond the threshold of the visual field. By associating his poetic project with such artists, Pound

makes imagism revolve around an abstract image that simulates the visible
and suggests a visuality continually defaced by the invisible.[9]

Both Jonathan Crary and Rosalind Krauss have directly linked modern
art's opaque immediacy (as broadly ranging as Cezanne's postimpressionism, Picasso's cubism, and Duchamp's dadaism) to a physiological optics,
showing that art and science alike explored how "human vision" is "less than
a master of all it surveys" (Krauss 178). Krauss documents, for example, how
Max Ernst's surrealist collage novels fragmented and recategorized images
and even optical experiments and technologies from the French popular
science magazine *La Nature* in order to stage a mindbodily unconscious that
structures but is also just beyond the threshold of vision. By negotiating
such abstract art, Pound's imagism thus taps not only into a version of imagetextuality but also into the modern scientific vernacular of vision. Like this
art, imagism in turn participates in that vernacular's effort to understand
perception, images, and indeed subjectivity as an effect of complex psychophysiological processes.

The scientific thrust driving imagism is perhaps most apparent in Pound's
recasting of imagism as vorticism beginning in mid-1914. His new moniker
drew on the concept of a "vortex," introduced into physics by none other
than Hermann von Helmholtz, a major force in the later nineteenth century's
new physiology of vision.[10] Pound not only used the unusual pseudonyms
Bastien von Helmholtz and Baptiste von Helmholtz at this transitional moment[11] but explicitly positioned his poetic vortex in a "boundless ether"
("Wisdom of Poetry" 501) and emphasized the artist's role in "DIRECTING a
certain fluid force" ("VORTEX" 153) in the universe through art's "vibration"
and "intensities" (*Spirit of Romance* 94). Such terms echoed those turn-of-
the-century physicists who had extrapolated from Helmholtz's vortex in
order to investigate the fundamental construction of matter.[12] Even a minimal knowledge of Helmholtz's influence within physics would have meant
that Pound was broadly familiar with optics as another major site of Helmholtz's materialism. The etiology of vorticism thus eventually arrives at optics as an inciting vocabulary for imagism and vorticism alike.

Indeed, Poundian imagism and vorticism are perhaps best understood in
terms of a dichotomy typical of a physiological optics. This science and even
its related vernacular anchored vision in an opaque body but nonetheless
strove to visualize that opacity by creating measurements of hidden bodily
workings. Likewise, Pound hoped that the body's unwilled processes could
guarantee access to the world, but he continually had to confront the recal-

citrant opacity of the images the body produces. A major component of Tiffany's account of imagism is that Pound frequently staged this dichotomy and resulting incompletion as an impersonalizing process of "transgress[ing] the bounds of gender and . . . identity" (137). In other words, Tiffany argues that imagism negotiates a masculinized desire for an autonomous, objective image that continually surrenders to a frank admission of the image's inescapable materiality, represented by a feminized haunting in dreams, memories, and visionary experiences. Tiffany argues further that Pound aligns this materiality of both the image and the observer with an impersonal corpse that he must continually re-member. Imagist poetry, Tiffany concludes, works according to the logic of that corpse: it offers the "possibility of resemblance" and familiarity but ultimately is neither the thing represented nor some other thing, just as the dead body is "neither the same as the one who was alive . . . nor another thing" (8).

During this period in which Pound was developing imagism and then vorticism, he was an important interlocutor for H.D. as she forged her own early aesthetic. Though her scientific reading at this particular moment is unknown, her library at her death points to a lifelong commitment to the scientific underpinnings of imagism. It includes numerous popular works on physics and materiality, such as the British physicist Sir James Jeans' *The Mysterious Universe* (1930) and *The Stars in Their Courses* (1931), issues of *Proteus: A Journal of the Science, Philosophy, and Therapy of Nature,* and reviews of the Russian physiologist Ivan Pavlov's work on conditioned reflexes. H.D.'s reading gives us reason to take seriously Pound's claims in "VORTEX" that in her early poetry she pursued a version of imagism. *Sea Garden* incorporates a visual art image in order to draw out the fundamentally impersonal nature of subjectivity implied by contemporary visual science. In H.D.'s case, she saw in classical sculpture the kind of imagetext that Pater discerned in modern abstract art—an image that bore opaque immediacy, was associated with radical materiality, and tried to visualize the unseen.[13] Indeed, H.D.'s appeal to classicism echoes T. E. Hulme's 1908 lecture to the Poets' Club: "The [modern] classical poet . . . remembers always that he is mixed up with earth. He may jump, but he always returns back; he never flies away into the circumambient gas" (62). Soon after that lecture, Hulme would in fact reframe his classicism in terms of modern abstraction, a shift that influenced Pound's vorticism. We can map H.D.'s classical version of the opaque imagist image—and her remaking of the gender dynamic that

Pound uses to mark it—through a close consideration of four poems from *Sea Garden*.

The first of these poems, "The Contest," styles itself as an ekphrasis of a work of art, recalling Field's *Sight and Song*. The poem begins by minutely describing a male athlete in competition: "Your stature is modelled/with straight tool-edge," "you are chiselled like rocks," and in "your wrist" "there is a glint like worn brass."[14] Although this description evokes classical sculpture, H.D. turns this potentially static mass into the vehicle for a second metaphor for complex and shifting natural processes: to have a "stature modelled/with straight tool-edge" is actually to be "like rocks/that are eaten into by the sea" (lines 3-4); similarly, the "white" color that initially suggests marble becomes instead "a limb of cypress/bent under a weight of snow" (lines 20-21). Where the traditional image/text binary tightly associates the image with the body and text with the rational mind, here H.D.'s layered metaphorical movement across body, sculpture, and slow but inevitable natural cycles precludes both the image and the body from being stable or atemporal, as that binary would have it. In fact, the processes that both create and erode the statue are part of the simultaneously willful and unwilled kinesis of the athlete's body as well. H.D.'s depiction underscores the athlete's physiology and movement, from the "chords' stretch" in his wrist to the "clenched muscles/of [his] slender hips" (lines 6, 10-11).

Despite the repeated "you" that structures every stanza and conjures a stable, coherent figure being addressed, the poem's kinetic depiction insists that the athlete is anything but autonomous and self-contained. Instead, he occupies a liminal space—the transformation and undoing of a boundary—like the line between land and sea to which he's analogized; more deeply, he occupies a space between art object, human subject, and external world. Indeed, "the contest" that this poem names but never describes seems to be attached, if anything, to this pivot between the poem's mode of address to its subject and its depiction of the nature of that subject. On the one hand, we have the autonomy suggested by the athlete's strength, attention, and control; on the other hand, we have the powerful automaticity suggested by the shifting material elements that compose both him and the world.

Part 3 of the poem draws out how the contest contained in this image-textual athlete might implicate gender politics, though it imagines those implications differently than does Pound's imagism. At the close of part 2 the speaker suggests, "you have entered the hill-straits—/a sea treads upon the hill-slopes" (lines 24-25), and part 3 continues, "Myrtle is about your head,/you have bent and caught the spray" (lines 26-27). If the poem's interlocutor was previously a statuesque male athlete, it now seems to be an icon upon the prow of a ship, tossed up and down in the spray as the ship sails upon the sea. Such a figurehead, again connected to a liminal space between solid and liquid environs, was typically feminine. Correspondingly, the natural elements used to describe the image-object have now become flowers rather than rocks, for example, "your feet are citron-flowers" (line 32). As Tiffany has argued, Pound's imagism stages a dialectical division between knowledge and limitation through acts of gender transgression: knowledge-desiring men are continually haunted by feminized figures of the body's opaque and mediated images. In "The Contest," however, while materiality yields gender instability, that materiality isn't tied exclusively to femininity, nor is the poem anxious about this process. Indeed, lest the now-female carving appear solely passive, driven by ship and sea, the poem closes with the claim that "your shoulders" "have melted rare silver/for their breadth" (lines 37, 38-39). In other words, the female body has actively contributed to its own form, and gender doesn't therefore simply map the contest between self-control and a potential positivism, on the one hand, and mediumistic impressionability, on the other. Rather, H.D.'s contest cuts across socially constructed gender identities even as her imagism still bears the dissident pleasure that Tiffany locates in the more limited gender transgression of Pound's imagism. Indeed, H.D.'s speaker effectively courts the image in both its masculine and feminine forms, suggesting that her close attention to the contest between control and material embodiment yields a queer eroticism beyond gender.

In the second poem, "Loss," H.D. draws out this dissident pleasure and explicitly connects it, as does Pound, to the absent presence of a corpse. Here the speaker is explicitly part of the poem, a comrade of "you," who is again lovingly observed and described:

> And I wondered as you clasped
> your shoulder-strap
> at the strength of your wrist
> and the turn of your young fingers,
> and the lift of your shorn locks,
> and the bronze
> of your sun-burnt neck. (*CP* 21-23, lines 42-48)

While this description recalls the athlete figured in "The Contest," the "bronze" statuesque imagetext of this poem is a visual memory of a love object, now drowned. The speaker is the final survivor of a group whose fallen members form a "ghastly host" that haunt the speaker's memory (line 19). Preparing to meet death as well, "chok[ing] with each breath," the speaker re-members those comrades' demise, particularly the bronze beloved's (line 7). The beloved's corpse, claimed by the sea, is "alone untouched," its "white flesh" preserved by "salt" (lines 20, 21). These qualities of the corpse symbolize the paradox of the imagist image: it aspires to an "untouched" or perfect resemblance, but its inescapable materiality points nonetheless to both bodily limits and a constitutive unknowability. H.D. underscores these qualities not only in the speaker's haunted and partial memory—"I wonder if you knew how I watched" (line 56)—but also in the implication of the speaker's own impending death.

This same dialectic between transparency and material opacity appears in the impressions that the beloved's "feet cut . . . on the paths," impressions that the dying speaker ironically "followed for the strength / of life and grasp" (lines 33, 34-35). The footprint is an indexical image: the object or thing it signifies has been there to make it but is not itself available. To trace this absence, and so to re-member the corpse, suggests the illicit pleasure of union with the lost beloved. This union is an undoing of a stable and singularizing selfhood: it's fatal (as the speaker is stumbling toward death) and it's queer (as neither the speaker nor the beloved has a gender). This encounter, which figures an engagement with the imagist image, points to the remaking of subjectivity in its struggle to grasp the impersonal contours of perception but also to acknowledge the inevitable short-sightedness of that grasp.

H.D. further schematizes imagism's desirous tracing of an absence in another poem, "Pursuit." In this poem as in "Loss," the speaker is searching for an unseen "you" by following "the print of your foot" across the sand, grass, wood-path, and ledge slope (*CP* 11-12, line 4). Quite differently from in "Loss," however, the seeking speaker is not correspondingly flooded with memory images. Instead, the speaker begins in a rather positivist mode, attentively and seemingly objectively tracking the pursued: examining "where your heel pressed" on the purple hyacinth buds, and discerning how "a dead leafspine, / split across, / show[s] where you passed" (lines 15, 22-24). By the third stanza, however, the speaker's passion surges, undermining this willful, self-possessed model of perception: "You were swift, swift!" and ". . . you climbed

yet further!" (lines 25, 34). The speaker, who began the poem with an indifferent "What do I care" (line 1), now acquires more of an embodied presence with this impassioned declaration, which also, significantly, tangles the
speaker up with the material movements of the pursued. This response
evokes the affective and materialist side of the imagist image. In keeping
with this turn, even as the speaker enters a kind of hallucinatory shared
memory with the pursued, perceptions become crucially just out of reach:
the speaker "can almost," but not quite, "follow the note [of a snapping
root]/where it touched this slender tree/and the next answered" (lines
30-32). These limits become more firmly marked as the poem then lapses
into a series of questions: "Did your head, bent back,/search further—";
"Did you clutch,/stammer with short breath and gasp" (lines 42-43, 46-47).
Unlike Field's "The Faun's Punishment," which pushes against the unan-
swered questions it has for its painted interlocutor, H.D.'s poem ends with
the speaker's resigned statement, "some wood-daemon/has lightened your
steps./I can find no trace of you/in the larch-cones and the underbrush"
(lines 50-53). The reader, who has felt some anxiety for the hotly pursued
and apparently frightened interlocutor, is unlikely to register the speaker's
failed pursuit in the negative terms that often characterize a materially limited knowledge for Pound. In other words, the poem ends, for speaker and
reader alike, with an acceptance of the embodied limits of perception and
of the incomplete knowledge that results from those limits. Just as importantly, the entire trajectory of the poem makes one stark departure from its
source text, the classical myth of Daphne's pursuit by Apollo. Like Daphne,
H.D.'s interlocutor is chased, prays, and is saved through disappearance
or transformation. But the interlocutor is not clearly a woman, nor is the
speaker clearly a man. Such a departure—the poem's lack of clear gender
markings—belies or at least exceeds the heteroerotics that Tiffany traces in
imagism.

   "Cities," the final poem of *Sea Garden,* brings Poundian imagism's appeal
to modern abstract art to the fore as a means of expressing H.D.'s ambivalence about that imagism. This poem's speaker repeatedly questions the
value of abstract art and thus seemingly of the Poundian image. While the
poem reflects explicitly on two cities, one ancient and one modern, and on
the intentions of their maker, the speaker characterizes each city essentially
as an image that's structured according to the maker's shifting aesthetic.
The ancient city image features:

. . . the beauty of temple,
and space before temple,
arch upon perfect arch,
of pillars and corridors that led out
to strange court-yards and porches
where sun-light stamped
hyacinth-shadows . . . (*CP* 39-42, lines 14-20)

In contrast to this detailed and varied classical image—which throughout *Sea Garden* has been H.D.'s own imagist touchstone—the modern-city image suggests a rigid honeycomb of spare, geometric cells:

street after street,
each patterned alike,
no grace to lighten
a single house of the hundred
crowded into one garden-space. (lines 5-9)

The restrained lines, simple shapes, and dark cell-like houses offer an opaque immediacy that resists visuality and thus suggests at least some forms of the abstract art that Pound deemed so foundational to imagism. And yet, in H.D.'s hands the modern city's honeycomb appearance suggests that while it may be able to collect the pollen that brought to life the old city and its beauty, it's not in itself a clear form of art.

Indeed, as in the searching speculations that close "Pursuit," H.D. frames this poem with an agonizing question: "can we believe" that the modern-city image wasn't created in dissatisfaction—that its maker instead meant to frame a "new splendor" and that its geometric spareness will enable people to "grasp" the "beauty [that] was over them,/through them, about them" (lines 10, 38, 31, 32-33)? The speaker hopes that the experiment of the "new city," and in turn the modern-art image of Poundian imagism, will "construc[t] new people" and so "a beauty unrivalled yet" (lines 36, 39, 41). But in survey-ing the scene, the speaker sees only "larvae," "hideous first, hideous now," "disfigured" and "defaced" (lines 44, 43, 49, 49). Though *larva* is Latin for *ghost,* these grotesquely "disfigured" young bees are hyperembodied rather than metaphysical; they in fact follow the logic of the corpse, being "neither the same as the one who was alive . . . nor another thing." H.D.'s distinctly negative description thus seems to condemn Poundian imagism through the radical materiality of the corpse that's so central to its understanding of impersonality, even though H.D. herself has otherwise appealed to this formulation. Correspondingly, where the speaker looks negatively on this image, the modern city's "dark cells" become a mass mentality, an impersonal race pursuing a eugenic project against the "few old cells" who re-member the past (lines 46, 52). "We protect our strong race," these dark, larvae-filled cells exclaim (line 64). "You are useless./Your cell takes the place/of our young future strength" (lines 65-67).

The poem doesn't end on this negative note, though. While the speaker resists the dark cells' eugenic proclamation, it doesn't more broadly counter impersonality with an individualist aesthetic. In fact, the speaker comes to discern a positive message in the modern-city image, essentially channeling its maker in a way that recalls the dynamic of possession in Poundian imagism. The closing stanzas, whose italics indicate that the speaker has shifted to the maker of cities, respond to the "few old cells" with the declaration:

> *The city is peopled*
> *with spirits, not ghosts, O my love:*
>
> *Though they crowded between*
> *and usurped the kiss of my mouth*
> *their breath was your gift,*
> *their beauty, your life.* (lines 78-83)

Here the larvae are now distinguished from "ghosts" beyond the end of life. They are instead "spirits" poised at life's origins, the swirl of material elements on whom the old cells' existence and memory in fact depend. While these new cells are still "usurpers," destabilizing a coherent self, their usurpation is not now a eugenic cleansing but rather the presentation of a "gift": the gift of "their breath," which in turn becomes "your life." This polymorphously perverse kiss of the maker, the spirits, and the old cells stages an alluring impersonality, one without a stable or coherent gender.

Ultimately, then, while H.D. questions aspects of Poundian imagism, she nonetheless begins to work with its ingredients, including a focus on visual art, materiality, and opacity, and she begins to outline a kind of liberating potential in those ingredients, particularly with regard to gender and sexuality. In *Notes on Thought and Vision*, written a few years later, H.D. would commit to these beginnings by more thoroughly schematizing material opacity and how it structures the visual field. She would also address the related function of an impersonal aesthetic that attends to such an opacity. In developing this scheme, H.D. continues to appeal to the visual art that so shaped her early imagism and to its understanding of the embodied image and observer. However, her increasingly specific treatment also more firmly positions her imagetexts as part of a scientific vernacular of vision that mixes psychology, physiology, and optics.

"Sign-posting" Impersonality in *Notes on Thought and Vision*

H.D. wrote *Notes on Thought and Vision,* a pastiche of experiential record, aphorism, myth, and manifesto, as "psychological data" for her friend the sexologist Havelock Ellis (H.D., *Tribute* 130). The initial spark for *Notes* was H.D.'s extraordinary visual experience during a July 1919 trip, just after the birth of her daughter, Perdita. *Notes* folds the data of H.D.'s experience, in which a series of subjective images and colors seemed to float before her eyes, into an impersonal aesthetic that extends *Sea Garden*'s imagist understanding of the embodied image and observer. Thus, if *Notes* "interrogate[s] the social and aesthetic implications of the new sciences," as Robin Pappas has argued (152), it does so by developing an aesthetic impersonality that adapts the scientific study of vision as a psychophysiological process into an exploration of the impersonal nature of being and the sociopolitical function of art.

Notes characterizes what H.D. calls "over-mind vision," which is essentially an extended proprioception—the then new scientific term for one's awareness of the parts and movements of one's perceiving body (21).[15] H.D. takes this over-mind vision as the basis for artistic production. Using her own experience as a model, she offers two possible "sign-posts" into "over-mind consciousness" (24, 23), both of which are visual artworks: Leonardo's *Virgin of the Rocks* and the ancient Greek sculpture *Delphic Charioteer* (see fig. 2.1). H.D. emphasizes that by gazing on these and other signposts she has become a "receiving centre" for their "definite message," the experience of which is a "hypnotic effect" that registers the embodied limits of visual attention (26, 24, 26). She also explains that she has recorded these messages of autonomic materiality in her own art. *Notes'* account of over-mind thus retains H.D.'s imagist appeal to the visual arts, and even to abstract representation, because those signposts' messages come in the coded form of "dots and dashes" (26). At the same time, though, her interest in visual attention documents that *Notes* turns more directly on optics and observation than *Sea Garden.* Her new imagetextual language works to remap the

Fig. 2.1. Collage from H.D.'s scrapbook of the 1920s. Recalling Field's play on museum guidebooks in *Sight and Song,* this collage features a guidebook photograph of the *Delphic Charioteer*'s bust, with identifying caption, upon which H.D. layered a photograph of herself, likewise a profile bust and with a similar hairstyle. The collage underscores the importance of the *Delphic Charioteer* as a creative signpost for H.D. and also draws out the centrality of imagetextuality in her impersonal aesthetic. Yale Collection of American Literature, Beinecke Rare Book and Manuscript Library. © The Schaffner Family Foundation; used by permission of New Directions Publishing Corporation, agents.

human subject in terms of impersonality, to offer a program for achieving an incompletely extended proprioception, and to explain how to produce and appreciate an impersonal art that assimilates that achievement and reflects on its sociopolitical value.

H.D. defines over-mind consciousness, through her own visual encounter, as both a limitation and an expansion of sight. She describes feeling as though "a cap of consciousness" were affecting her eyes, so that "things . . . appear[ed] slightly blurred" (18), but she also records that through a "physical effort," and despite a "grinding discomfort of mental agony," she was able to refocus her vision with new clarity (18, 19). Emphasizing the bodily nature of this visual shift, H.D. suggests that the cap of consciousness then became like a "jelly-fish" that reached its "long feelers" down her body, through the

"nervous system," manifesting a set of "super-feelings" not materially different from the "physical arms and legs" (19). She experienced a similar set of
"feelers float" from the "love-region" of her body "up towards the brain"
(20). These new feelings and clarity of sight together dislodged her sense of
self and self-control and allowed her to perceive her thoughts as themselves
embodied, passing in and out, "visible like fish swimming under clear water"
(19). Ultimately, then, H.D. portrays over-mind vision as an extended proprioception marked by a now impersonal awareness of the complex psychophysiology of vision and visual cognition and of the unstable outline of both
the body and consciousness.

H.D. draws out the implications of such an awareness by replacing the
mind/body dualism of the camera obscura model of vision with a simultaneously monistic and tripartite subjectivity. She denotes not two but three
subjective components—"body, mind, [and] over-mind" (17)—and figures
their ideal relation as a circle, with each component properly balanced and
"run[ning] into" the next (46). H.D. links this balance, and so her model of
the human subject, to the binocular and stereoscopic mechanics of embodied vision. She diagrams two over-mind centers in the body—one in
the head, the other in the "love-region"—and suggests that these centers,
like the lenses of an "opera-glass," each produce a visual alteration (23). For
those with the correct balance of subjective components, these lenses may
be "properly . . . focused" to "bring the world of vision into consciousness"
(23). H.D.'s extended proprioception thus draws on the thoroughly material
and partial nature of vision to replace the autonomous, self-contained Cartesian subject with an embodied subject who must continually strive to
grasp its limited knowledge of and control over both self and world. Indeed,
H.D. places value on those who strive for such awareness.

She goes on to offer two further analogies for her over-mind vision, which
together suggest the basis for that value by turning ultimately to identity
formation. First, she states that when over-mind is in the head, it possesses
and melds with mind, and mind possesses and melds with body. This complex system signals the proper balance, integration, and awareness of the
subjective components, even as H.D.'s appeal to possession—to being decentered or diffused by another agency—points to a persistent automaticity
and unknowability in the subject. H.D. casts this combination of heightened
intelligibility and stubborn opacity endemic to over-mind as the very substance of the "eternal, changeless ideas" that "beget" not only "all drama,
idea, music, . . . or song" but, significantly, all "science" as well (23). The no-

tion of a creative and shared begetting across art and science introduces H.D.'s second analogy: procreation. Emphasizing the necessity of "certain definite physical relationships" for achieving this vision, H.D. proposes that when over-mind is in the "love-region," it's "placed like a foetus in the body," which itself takes on the "character of mind" (17, 17, 19, 22). Similarly, she describes the visual alterations offered by the dual over-mind centers as "two forms of seed" that together allow one to be "born again" into a new world of vision (50).

Havelock Ellis, being H.D.'s initially intended reader, may have influenced her procreative simile here. However, she takes the simile in two contrary directions that together show that her scientific understanding of the embodied image and observer reconfigures the basis of identity formation, away from the essentialisms presumed in most contemporary sexology.[16] On the one hand, H.D.'s analogy of over-mind to "a foetus in the body" leads her to stipulate a compulsory heterosexuality within her aesthetic, one that comports with much sexological discourse: "[i]t takes a man and a woman to create another life," she concedes (50). On the other hand, though, H.D. argues that a lover wanting to encourage the growth and awareness of being that is over-mind vision "must choose one of the same type of mind as himself, a musician, a musician, a scientist, a scientist, a general, a young man also interested in the theory and practice of arms and armies" (22). The example of a productive martial pederasty not only promotes relations of sameness through a homoerotics, it suggests a paradoxically (pro)creative homosexuality. This sexual paradox is in fact doubled, as H.D. later likens the impersonal systems that create over-mind to the "oyster [that] makes the pearl" (51), implying a (pro)creative process that similarly refuses a gender binary but is nonetheless neither autonomous nor self-contained, because a pearl begins when a bit of grit is somehow introduced into the oyster.

The latter aspect of H.D.'s procreative analogy suggests her desire that the embodied observer posited by a physiological optics might suspend a socially constructed gender and sexual difference without canceling the materiality of the body. But as the analogy moves back and forth across bodily organs and social relations, H.D. also implies that such identities are the product of an entangled circuit of both social and biological imperatives, making a suspension of gender and sexual difference more complicated. She suggests that an aesthetic impersonality stemming from over-mind vision follows both these directions of vaunting hope and more complex limitation:

it records the give and take of trying to grasp impersonal subjectivity while still being subject to it, even as it also draws out the sociopolitical implications of impersonal subjectivity that H.D. imagines for identity.

Notes surveys the work of such an impersonal aesthetic by presenting a genealogy of over-mind artists encapsulated in three principal representatives: Leonardo (the painter of one of H.D.'s own signposts), the ancient Chinese poet Lo-fu, and the ancient Syrian poet Meleager. This genealogy extends backward by many centuries the history of (proto)impersonal art that Pater had sketched in *The Renaissance.* Indeed, H.D.'s brief discussion of Leonardo, like Pater's, heralds her investment in optics and in the project of bringing that science to bear on art. Leonardo's *Note-Books,* a copy of which H.D. owned, famously described the principle behind the camera obscura and identified it with the anatomy and function of the human eye.[17] As part of this description, Leonardo notes that "the eye . . . receives . . . into itself" "all the objects that are in front of it," "that is to say on its surface, whence they are taken in by the common sense, which considers them and if they are pleasing commits them to the memory."[18] Much more than Leonardo, H.D. highlights the mediating role of memory by characterizing Leonardo as a refractor of images whose observational mode of being allows him to represent a subjectivity beyond the personality. She argues first that Leonardo "went mad if he saw a boy's face" or "a child with yellow hair . . . like the goldsmith work he had learned" as an apprentice, because these sights and memories were his signposts into over-mind vision (26). She then explains that through this "mad" amalgam of memory and perception Leonardo's "brain was Leonardo, the personality," but he "saw the faces" of those he painted "with his over-mind" (18). In other words, Leonardo was not simply a self and a mind; he was simultaneously an embodied impersonal subjectivity and an awareness of that subjectivity and its limits. In addition, recalling the camera obscura mechanism that was so important to Leonardo's optics, H.D. argues further that his resulting paintings are genuine "window[s]," not strictly on the world, but on "over-mind" itself, a fact that accounts for their artistic greatness (18). Building on these claims, H.D.'s discussions of Lo-fu and Meleager extend the question of an impersonal aesthetic to a social terrain, specifically to the constitution of embodied identities that had shaped her remapping of subjectivity. At the same time, these discussions also detail the imagetextual style of the aesthetic she has in mind.

    H.D.'s portrayal of Lo-fu bears a double valence that allows her to reimagine the traditional gender and sexual dynamic of creative inspiration, much in the way that Field had before her. On the surface, Lo-fu's experience typifies that of a male poet inspired by a female muse. After gazing lengthily at an apple branch, Lo-fu's "conscious mind ceased wondering," and he entered a hypnotic over-mind state in which he began to see the branch as "continents to be explored"—a metaphor of unknown territory frequently attached not only to an opaque unconscious but also to female sexuality (43, 44).[19] Drawing out this latter association, H.D. explains Lo-fu's over-mind vision as a heteroerotic response to a feminine, bodily image: he felt that "his apple branch, his beautiful subtle mistress, was his" (45).

And yet, two facts provide a contrasting subtext for this history of Lo-fu and suggest that H.D.'s commitment to the embodied image and observer of contemporary optics actually transforms the retrograde gender attributions of his musings and the ultimately objective view they seem to support. First, though H.D. describes Lo-fu as a male poet from the Ming dynasty, the only known ancient Chinese poet by that name is a legendary woman poet of the Han dynasty. H.D. is likely to have had that female poet in mind, as a *yüeh-fu* (folk song) about her was among Pound's Chinese translations.[20] Assuming that this is the case, H.D. has chosen to refer to a female poet with male pronouns. This practice produces a kind of gender dissonance through layering or multiplicity and thereby parodies the traditional masculinist and heteronormative myth of creativity. Indeed, H.D. goes on to explain that "[t]he body of a *man*" (46, emphasis added) can just as readily function as a sight of inspiration, a claim that refuses to grant a singular power structure to the creativity myth.

Building on this idea, H.D. anchors her tale of Lo-fu to the common mythological identification of the human body with a tree, leading the weight of her tale to fall ultimately on the idea of a universal embodiment. Taking as her basic premise that the "body . . . was as impersonal a thing as a tree," H.D. introduces another branch, a "white pear-branch," among a list of material and decaying or deathly versions of otherwise metaphysical entities: "Zeus Melios, God in the black earth, death, disruption, disintegration; Dionysius Zagreus, the flower torn, broken by chemical process of death" (47, 33, 32). This list identifies the pear branch with an impersonal "mystery greater than beauty and that [mystery] is death" (33). Such a coding reasserts imagism's corpselike image in all its radical materiality and opacity (33).[21] Juxtaposing Lo-fu's apple branch with this similar pear branch shows that his erotic union is really an "approach to something else": to a realization that humans are universally and inescapably embodied over and against the cultural projection of embodiment solely onto women (45). H.D. also emphasizes a reciprocal gaze instead of the one-way dynamic of inspiration and the stable subject/object binary it imagines. She does so by describing how Zeus destroyed the pear branch for fear that it was "more white against the sky than the passion of his shaft"—in other words, more alluring than the (phallic) lightning bolts he wielded (33). This act makes plain that the male subject wants not only to see but to be seen and thereby that subjectivity is not opposed to but caught up with objecthood.

Notes' discussion of Meleager, known for compiling the first anthology of Greek verse, in the first century BCE, turns this consideration of identity formation toward race, while also concretizing the particular imagetextual style that H.D. believes can best capture impersonal subjectivity. Meleager's anthology, which includes the epigrams of forty-seven predecessors and several of his own, begins with a prefatory poem describing each contribution as a particular flower, together constituting *Stephanos* (garland), the title of the anthology. This prefatory poem effectively presents the collection as an imagetext, an image accruing figuratively through the progression of a significantly multiperspectival text. Not only that, but individual epigrams in the collection were themselves imagetexts in the form of *technopaegnia,* or figure poetry. The epigram of Simias of Rhodes, for instance, not only is shaped like an egg but has to be read in an egglike order: not linearly, but from the outside shell in, moving back and forth from beginning to end, until the center, or yoke, is finally reached.[22] In H.D.'s portrayal this imagetextual style is a product of over-mind vision. She ventriloquizes Meleager contriving *Stephanos* in honor of Christ, through whom he had achieved such vision: ". . . I would plait the red violet to the white violet. . . . I would bind the stem of the crocus to the stem of the wild-hyacinth, that each might show less lovely about your brow" (37). H.D. explains Meleager's interest in a "less lovely" tribute through a discussion of materiality. She begins by noting that "[o]ne must understand a lower wisdom before one understands a higher" and then deliberately tries to reorient what *lower* and *higher* mean: "[T]o understand dung chemically and spiritually and with the earth sense, one must first understand the texture, spiritual and chemical and earthy, of the rose that grows from it" (31–32). In other words, she posits that the rose is the lower wisdom and the dung the higher and indeed then asks, "Is the earth greater or less than the white rose it brings forth? Is the dung greater or less than the rose?" (32). This discussion emphasizes that the "beauty" of *Stephanos*—and so the imagetext more broadly—comes "chemically and spiritually" from materiality (32). Indeed, it relies on a proprioceptive awareness of bodily workings and limits, what H.D. calls the higher "wisdom of ugliness," garnered through over-mind vision (32). H.D. attaches this higher wisdom to blurred racial and gender identities in the figures of both Meleager and Christ. Meleager's over-mind vision of Christ offers him a knowledge of materiality that both enables his poetry and changes his attitude toward his own racial identity.

More specifically, in H.D.'s account Meleager initially bemoans what he understands as his miscegenated race, his "Jew[ish] father" and "Greek mother" (33). He seeks to displace all connections to his Jewishness, to forget the Hebrew script and tongue and to free himself from his merchant father's rotting goods. He wants instead to study the "divine" script of the "golden Plato" (i.e., the Greek language of his mother) and to "live with a poet's mind" (34, 35, 34).[23] In this quest Meleager effectively refuses materiality and takes shelter in a transcendental notion of art and intellect. H.D. suggests, however, that these desires are transmuted when Meleager witnesses Christ's arrival in Gadara (detailed in the Christian Bible, Mark 5:10-20), a sight that allows him to achieve over-mind consciousness. In this altered state, Meleager abandons his distrust of the body and elevates Christ as one who's able to do two things: to receive the message inherent in "the priest-like body of the [Delphic] charioteer" (one of H.D.'s own signposts to over-mind vision) and to fall "in love with things as well as people" by "look[ing] at" them (27, 28). Significantly, the bodily erotics of this description suggest no fixed object choice and thus lend no specific gender or sexual identity to the observer.

Complementing this lack of a singularizing essence, Meleager's vision also nullifies his disgust with his own mixed identity, because he recognizes Christ as having both a Jewish father and a Greek body and speech. H.D. draws out the implied mixed racial identity by noting that behind the religion of Christ is the Greek goddess Demeter. The fact that both God and Christ reinstantiate that Greek figure also creates an amalgamated gender identity: "Christ and his father, or as [Demeter's] Eleusinian mystic would have said, his mother, were one" (53).[24] In this proposed unity Christ is descended from a Jewish-Greek mother-father and thus becomes an even earlier node in an over-mind genealogy that questions individual identities organized around cleanly binarized notions of gender and race.

From this new perspective, Meleager comes to value over-mind vision as a voice "more portent," or more momentous, "than the script of the golden Plato," a script associated with his earlier desire for disembodiment and a transcendental art (35). Meleager makes this speaking vision the basis for a new art exemplified by the imagetext of *Stephanos*. Significantly, this new aesthetic shifts Meleager's project from one of forgetting both materiality and the Hebrew speech and tongue to one of remembering—gathering and voicing the songs of his predecessors—much in line with the material re-membering of imagism. Indeed, Meleager's over-mind aesthetic once again identifies the "wisdom of ugliness," a new understanding of materiality and identity alike, as the principal concern of H.D.'s now evolving impersonal art (32).

Ultimately, then, *Notes'* analysis of visual perception concretizes the connection between a contemporary optics and the development of modernism's impersonal aesthetic. H.D. expands upon the imagist image she developed in *Sea Garden* by pointedly embodying the process of creative inspiration and also by outlining how embodied impersonal subjectivity might reconceive embodied identities. At its most hopeful, *Notes* imagines that these identities are actually undone. In its more pragmatic moments it suggests that impersonal subjectivity offers an incomplete record of the fluctuating nexus of social and biological imperatives that produce these identities. Taking these directions together, H.D. begins to represent the impersonal artist as a social diagnostician, who may not explode sexism or racism but nonetheless exposes the specifically modern problems that these biases generate.

As H.D.'s career evolved, she would turn to two new sites in the scientific vernacular of vision—avant-garde film and Freudian psychoanalysis—to further develop her impersonal aesthetic and reflect on the problems of embodied identity. In her later formulations she focused extensively on the mutual construction of spectator and spectacle; granted a larger role to the dialectic between representing impersonal subjectivity and being subject to its limits; and explicated more forcefully the social implications of her aesthetic for the racial body. By mobilizing the optical infrastructure of film and psychoanalysis to develop these formulations, and by focusing on how the structures of vision shape questions of gender and race, H.D. worked at the very origins of contemporary film criticism.

Close Up and Impersonal: Subjectivity through the Camera Lens and the Talking Cure

After *Notes on Thought and Vision,* H.D. wrote several *romans à clef* about her early efforts to derive "an image no matter . . . how inchoate" that would capture the material limits of perception and thereby the instability of subjectivity (*HERmione* 5). The first of these novels, *Paint It Today* (1921), formulates this effort in the familiar terms of painting: a young H.D. must chart her course between the "rapt" formula of yesterday's Pre-Raphaelites and the "jagged, geometric prismatic" of tomorrow's modern abstract art (3). However, by 1927's *HERmione,* the last of these *romans à clef,* H.D. signals her departure from her early aesthetic by adopting two newly available visual discourses for marking subjectivity. She bemoans that in her early years there was "no sign to show you 'Oedipus complex' [or] . . . 'mother complex' " (47). Nor was there a "cinematographic conscience" to allow you to see "form superimposed on thought," or things both "magnified" and "shrunk" "out of proportion" (60). In pointing to this earlier lack, H.D. suggests that recent film techniques, from closeup and panorama to the layered and depth effects produced by splicing or superimposing negatives, were now offering her a new language for approaching the subject's incoherence. Likewise, by appealing to Freud's Oedipal narrative of ego formation and sexual development, H.D. underscores that the impersonal subjectivity she had so thoroughly embodied in *Notes* was no less psychical in form and function. Indeed, in linking the cinematic and psychoanalytic through her "cinematographic conscience," H.D. follows Freud's own tendency to use visual technologies and effects to analogize unconscious psychical processes, as well as some of the dynamics of his talking cure. Freud's tome *The Interpretation of Dreams* (1899), for instance, models the "mental apparatus" in terms of both a microscope and a telescope (575, 576n2), while the earlier *Studies in Hysteria* (1895) debates whether perception works like a telescope or a photographic plate.

Critics have richly documented H.D.'s joint appeal to film and analysis, particularly in the 1920s through the 1940s. They have focused chiefly on H.D.'s involvement in POOL, the film production company run by H.D.'s partner, Bryher, and by Bryher's nominal husband, the writer-director Kenneth Macpherson, with whom H.D. was also romantically involved in the late twenties. POOL's feature-length silent film *Borderline,* in which H.D. starred, employed Hanns Sachs, a member of Freud's inner circle, as a consulting analyst. Likewise, POOL's film journal *Close Up,* which was the first of its kind in English and ran from 1927 to 1933, strongly espoused the view that film was an apt mode for representing psychical states. Sachs not only wrote essays along these lines for *Close Up,* as did H.D. herself, but also served as Bryher's and briefly H.D.'s own analyst.[25] It was in fact through Sachs that H.D. became Freud's patient, first in 1933 and again in 1934.[26] In other words, cinema and psychoanalysis multiply intersected in H.D.'s personal and professional milieu.

I want to suggest that the scientific—and specifically the physiological—roots of film and even psychoanalysis help to account for H.D.'s interest in combining these two visual discourses to further develop her impersonal aesthetic. It's become a critical commonplace to note film's formal and technological origins in later nineteenth-century physiological science, but the typical narrative holds that by the turn of the twentieth century scientific and popular cinema had diverged. However, Lisa Cartwright and, more peripherally, Jonathan Auerbach have traced the continued importance of scientific cinema in the early twentieth century, especially for defining life in terms of a dynamic body. Cartwright and more recently Oliver Gaycken have also argued that this understanding of life and the particular image techniques used to produce it had a lingering influence on modernist avant-garde film.[27] Indeed, *Close Up* variously showcased film's origins in and importance to physiological science, and the impact of this context on H.D. surfaces particularly in "Cinema and the Classics," a three-part essay on film technique that was her first contribution to the journal.[28] Three aspects of turn-of-the-century physiology's film motion studies and their cultural influence are pertinent here.

First, physiological cinema was consistently committed to foregrounding the filmic apparatus, even as popular cinema began masking its technologies to produce the illusion of a continuous moving image. Indeed, the public attended viewings of scientific films, whether at society meetings or exhibitions, with a distinctly "machine interest": they came to see the workings of the apparatus as much as the images it was producing (Cartwright 5). Second, physiological films most often recorded movement by developing a "graphic method" of inscription that was more concerned with capturing duration than with depicting objects.[29] This method eschewed a verisimilar or representational image in favor of a nonmimetic one. Because its graphic image functioned as a kind of language (with conventionality and temporality), the method promoted imagetextual ways of seeing that drained the

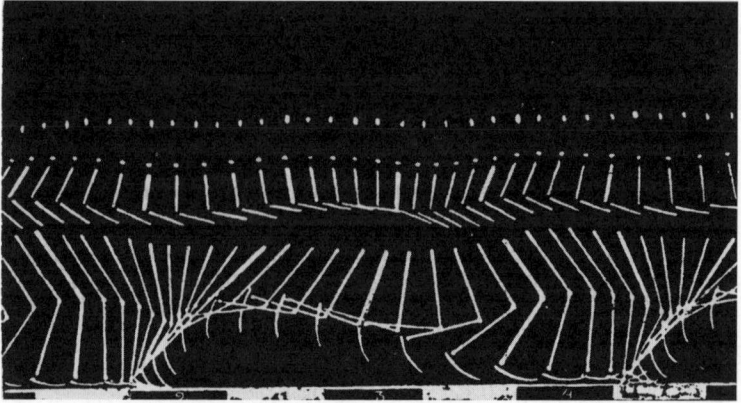

Fig. 2.2. Étienne-Jules Marey, film motion diagram of the human gait. In order to produce the film from which this diagram was made, Marey had his subject don a black suit and hood with white markings to indicate the appendages, and then to walk against a black background. The study shows duration and movement without mimetically representing the object. Reprinted from Marey, *Le mouvement* 61.

cultural content from the traditionally stable, verisimilar image (see fig. 2.2). Physiological films' conjoined emphasis on apparatus and use of a graphic image to capture life led to a third pertinent characteristic: the dynamic body they depicted revolved around a profoundly unwilled set of interlocking mechanisms, from muscular reflex to blood flow, that underwrite apparently voluntary acts, such as lifting one's leg. Indeed, in some cases these films demoted the body to being merely the site rather than the agent of physiological events, for example, in shots of the diffusion of oxygen from the lungs.

While these modern physiological films were certainly familiar to Freud— because many found their subjects among the neurotic patients he would invent psychoanalysis to explain and treat—scholars have emphasized his rejection of the scientific visualization of mental illness and biological explanation more broadly.[30] Instead of training a scientific gaze on the physiological symptoms of disorder, Freud attended to the meaning of those symptoms by talking with his patients. Yet, as much as this method may seem to prioritize the verbal over the visual, visualization and indeed a kind of imagetextuality continued to be important to Freud's model of the psyche. He often drew on an expanded set of visual technologies that raised questions about optics, agency, and knowledge similar to those posed by physiological films. In "A Note on the Unconscious" (1912), for example, he made the relation between a photographic negative and print into his model for the crucial relation between unconscious and preconscious thought. He explained that all thoughts, like all photographs, begin as negatives, but only some are admitted to the positive (printing) process (264). As Sarah Kofman has pointed out, this analogy's implicit reference to the camera obscura—the device at the heart of modern photography and cinema alike—transforms the traditional philosophical symbol of a transparent disembodied sight, one that faithfully reproduces everything in the field of vision, into a sign of opacity and thereby of limited agency and knowledge, including self-knowledge (25-26). Thus, the characteristics of the human subject promoted by physiological films were also central to the talking cure; both Freud and these films were participating in an extended science of embodied vision. In addition, film was itself firmly embedded in the vocabulary of psychoanalysis, whose formulations, such as *screen memory, projection,* and the *dream scene,* took filmic devices and characteristics completely for granted as a credible model of the invisible mechanisms of the human mind. Just as importantly, Freud offers his own imagetextual visualization of these mechanisms in a key moment in *The Interpretation of Dreams* when he seeks to describe the relation between perception, memory, the unconscious, and the preconscious. Echoing the graphic method of physiological film, he incorporates three diagrams into this discussion of the "mental apparatus," each of which is temporal, schematic, and nonpictorial (fig. 2.3). Indeed, Freud himself emphasizes these aspects of his imagetextual images by stating that "[s]trictly speaking, there is no need for the hypothesis that the psychical systems are actually arranged in a *spatial* order. It would be sufficient if a fixed order were established by the fact that in a given psychical process the excitation passes through the systems in a particular *temporal* sequence" (575).

"Cinema and the Classics" exemplifies how these particular aspects of the visual-scientific vernacular—of Freudian psychoanalysis and early physiological film—shaped H.D.'s evolving impersonal aesthetic. The essay revisits what H.D. had long characterized as a problematic modern "dissociation" of "body and soul," a binary that she casts not as granting a panoptic objectivity but rather as a distinctly limited "point of view."[31] In particular, H.D. considers this dissociation, or desired dissociation, the primary source of a widespread modern failure to recognize impersonal subjectivity. She thus sets out in "Cinema and the Classics" to outline a modernist film and, more

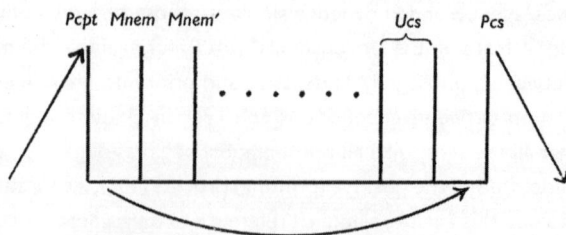

Fig. 2.3. The third of three diagrams of psychical function in Freud's *Interpretation of Dreams*. *Pcpt* stands for perception; *Mnem,* for the memory systems; *Ucs,* for the unconscious; and *Pcs,* for the preconscious. Central here are the arrows Freud uses to highlight temporality and duration rather than an object, just as in film motion studies of the day.

broadly, an aesthetic that would promote this model of human subjectivity made available in contemporary optics and in its related scientific vernacular of vision.

Emphasizing the mutual construction of spectator and spectacle, H.D. begins her outline of such a film by describing its ideal viewer: an "advance guard" that exhibits a "microscopic mind" and is simultaneously a "microbe" "prod[ding]" its way toward "understanding" ("CC" 105). By tying the mind to a microscope, and perhaps even to the microcinematography of modern science films, H.D. isn't so much suggesting that the ideal spectator has a prosthetically augmented vision, but rather that this spectator attends to the apparatus of visualization itself. As early physiological films trained viewers to do, H.D.'s advance guard pays concentrated attention to the filmic apparatus—to the sets, costumes, and camera shots that mold the image. It thus regards that image as a mediated creation and projection rather than a transparent mirror of reality. Moreover, H.D. aligns her advance guard with the moving microbes that often populated modern physiological films, like those of the Swiss biologist Julius Ries, and that taught audiences a fascination with life as a dynamic process.[32] Suggesting that this connection is in fact part of the ideal spectator's frame of understanding, H.D. argues that such spectators not only attend to film apparatus but also concentrate on their own perceptual experience in the theater as part of the film. In particular, recognizing that their experience is subject to unconscious mechanisms—precisely those mechanisms traced in scientific motion studies—this audience accepts a kind of lulled hypnotic state as one product of film viewing. Indeed, H.D. describes this automaticity or limit to visual attention as a crucial window onto the impersonal systems that structure vision, knowledge, and subjectivity: "[W]e were hypnotized by cross cur-rents and interacting shades of light and darkness and maybe cigarette smoke. Our censors, intellectually off guard, permitted our minds to rest. We sank into this pulse and warmth and were recreated . . . watching sym-bols of things that matter . . . [symbols] of some super-normal or some sub-normal layer of consciousness" ("CC" 116). Ultimately, then, H.D. links her advance guard to both a conscious, willed effort to know and an uncon-scious affective drift toward knowing.

However, it's also crucial to H.D.'s film aesthetic that only certain films could create such a layered experience. Just as her ideal spectator parallels the viewer trained by a scientific cinema, H.D.'s ideal film itself privileges the qualities of the physiological film image in two ways. First, H.D. advocates a proportionate image, one that "merges" the "naturalistic" with an equal measure of "formalis[ation]" or abstraction ("CC" 111, 111, 112). Such a depar-ture from mimesis overlaps with the physiologists' graphic method of visu-alization. Thus, for example, H.D. advocates representing a tree through a branch set against the "wall of an empty room, with suitable cross-effect of shadow" ("CC" 111). And even as this branch recalls *Notes'* tale of Lo-fu, its placement against a blank wall evokes a scientific scene: that wall repeats the carefully constructed blank backgrounds against which physiological films framed their subjects.[33] Similarly, her recommendation to substitute a branch for the tree evokes the synecdochal tendencies of physiological film, in which the rough marks of the appendages stand for the whole human body (see fig. 2.2) or an isolated pulsing vein stands for the whole circula-tory system. Like physiological film itself, the resulting portrayal draws at-tention to the mechanics of film projection, that is, to light and shadow on a blank wall. Likewise, this combination of naturalism and formalization highlights the fact that naturalism is itself mechanical and conventional.

The second quality of H.D.'s ideal film revolves around cinematic sound, what she calls the *movietone,* or more specifically around the film image in relation to burgeoning sound technologies ("CC" 114). H.D. distinguishes popular Hollywood from the European avant-garde, which drew its style from earlier physiological films, by pointing to their differing attitudes to-ward the movietone. She champions avant-garde cinema for continuing to pursue silent film even after Hollywood unanimously adopted sound. And she anchors the value of the avant-garde's silent films in the fact that they

draw attention to the cinematic apparatus. In other words, like physiological films, avant-garde films don't camouflage their images as verisimilar or
imbue them with a sense of being "real"; they instead present the screen
image as a stylized "mask," devoid of a voice that mimics self-presence ("CC"
115, 114). H.D.'s characterization of her ideal film strikingly prefigures Benjamin's "Work of Art in the Age of Mechanical Reproduction" (1936), in which
he calls for a cinema that would "introduce us to unconscious optics" rather
than offering "an aspect of reality which is free of all equipment" (234).
Indeed, Benjamin similarly characterizes this optical unconscious and the
film that would represent it by pointing to early motion studies, particularly
Marey's already mentioned study of the human gait: "Even if one has a general knowledge of the way people walk, one knows nothing of a person's
posture during the fractional second of a stride. . . . Here the camera intervenes" (237). Significantly, though, Benjamin adds, again in keeping with
H.D., that if film "extends our comprehension of the necessities which rule
our lives," it does so only by pointing to "an immense and unexpected field
of action" rather than by making that field fully appear (236).

Another way in which H.D. scoops Benjamin relates to his sense, in "Little History of Photography" (1931), that modern visual technologies and the
optical unconscious they lay bare open onto "the instinctual unconscious"
of "psychoanalysis," revealing what is "meaningful yet covert enough to find
a hiding place in waking dreams" (512). H.D.'s ideal film not only embraces
the qualities of physiological films, it pointedly carries their investigation
of dynamic bodily systems into a more direct exploration of the psyche,
thereby reinforcing the rejection of Cartesian dualism with which "Cinema
and the Classics" began. H.D. explains that formally and thematically her
ideal film produces a situation in which spectators can access and negotiate
images of unconscious desire that exceed but condition personal experience,
thereby opening themselves up to impersonality. She argues, for instance,
that the mechanics of film projection—so consistently highlighted in her
ideal cinema—symbolically mark "some super-normal . . . layer of consciousness," making film the "medium" most able to represent the unconscious
and preconscious "psychic phenomena" that Freud describes ("CC" 116, 112,
112). Indeed, the simultaneous formalization and naturalism of H.D.'s proportionate image correspond with Freud's notion of the dream image as a
product of those psychical phenomena. The Freudian dream image is a kind
of imagetextual cryptogram: it portrays in opaque form ideas and desires
relocated to the unconscious but seeking expression. H.D.'s proportionate

image echoes the effects of displacement and condensation, processes through which these unconscious messages are coded and thereby become expressible in dreams. The proportionate image, informed by both physio- logical film and psychoanalysis, is thus conducive to registering the imper- sonal psychophysiological matrix that is the human subject.

A brief return to H.D.'s dislike of the movietone should help to concret- ize these claims. H.D. argues that when accompanied by sound, the "screen projection is not a mask, it is a person, a personality." The mask is more valuable because it "presented life but so crudely" that it could become part of that "super-normal or sub-normal layer of consciousness" that shapes personality. By moving from the mask to the personality, film departs from "this layer of self" that houses the psychophysiological processes of imper- sonal subjectivity ("CC" 116). Both the screen image and the audience are short-changed in this departure. The former is "robbed of the thing behind the thing that had grown to matter so much to the picture adept" ("CC" 115); at the same time, the audience literally has nothing to attend to—it "can't *help* this show; [it is] completely out of it" ("CC" 116)—and thus is locked away from both a conscious effort and an unconscious drift toward knowing impersonally ("CC" 116). Interestingly, whereas in *Notes* H.D. had tried to reconceive the sources of creative inspiration for the single artist or viewer, here she appeals to cinema and psychoanalysis in order to consider the mass image and collective fantasy. Her reconceived impersonal aesthetic is thus pushing her to think in less individualistic and also more distinctly social terms. Also key is the way in which H.D.'s ideal film not only supports the spectator's attentive effort to register the mediated nature of perception but also promotes the kind of hypnotic state that marks the limits of vision and functions similarly to the dream state. The attentive and uncontrolled layers of knowing in this combination point to the complex relay among the various mechanisms and desires that make up human subjectivity. In fact, the combination parallels the workings of film projection itself. The human eye holds its impression of a movement a fraction of a second after that movement has ceased. This *persistence of vision,* as it's called, makes cinema possible by blurring the edges of images of successive movements into a coalescing sequence. Thus, film projection objectifies the temporality and instability of embodied vision but is also subject to it. This dynamic of acknowledging and overcoming is much more precise now that H.D. has shifted her visual technology from the opera glasses of *Notes on Thought and Vision* to the film camera and projector.

However, H.D.'s newly cinematic impersonality is not merely an update of her aesthetic's methods; the increased social rootedness of her impersonality translates into increasingly explicit social stakes as well. In this development H.D. actually differs from the physiological films whose qualities she so valued. Such films' graphic techniques generally purged the familiar cultural signifiers of corporeality: they presented a lung or the shape of a leg more often than they pictured, for instance, a male body or a white body. They therefore relieved themselves of any responsibility for addressing issues of history, subjectivity, and identity.[34] "Cinema and the Classics," however, takes on that responsibility. Its lengthy classification of avant-garde and Hollywood cinema unfolds through a complex reshuffling of the hegemonic terms of three racial, or rather racist, discourses: eugenic Nordicism, the myth of the black rapist, and Freud's account of the totem-driven primal horde. This reshuffling doesn't really manage to get outside of these discourses, but it does make visible the oscillating cultural and biological imperatives that inform embodied identity. Such a strategy reframes competing scholarly claims that H.D. was either actively racist or overwhelmingly antiracist by showing that she positioned herself as a diagnostician of the production of race as a category, but a category that couldn't simply be diagnosed away.[35]

The question of race emerges most clearly in H.D.'s discussion of Greta Garbo's avant-garde and Hollywood careers, which she maps by juxtaposing a European "Nordic beauty," on the one hand, and an American audience figured as "African tribesm[e]n," on the other ("CC" 106). The reference to Nordic beauty recalls early twentieth-century efforts, undertaken most notably by the political economist William Z. Ripley and the anthropologist Madison Grant, to distinguish the United States' older, northern European immigrants from the new influx of southern and eastern European immigrants. Grant's *The Passing of the Great Race* (1916) and Ripley's *The Races of Europe* (1899) put the Nordics—a race of "rulers and aristocrats . . . self-reliant and jealous of their personal freedom" (Grant 227–28)—at the apex of a hierarchy of European races, which in turn were all superior to the African race.

H.D. both plays on and refuses this conclusion by arguing that in the United States, Hollywood has merely managed to pollute the "nordic ice-flower" that Garbo was in her early avant-garde films in Europe, turning her instead into "the most blatant of obvious, crepe, tissue-paper orchids" ("CC" 107). Translated into the terms of H.D.'s ideal film, this pollution means that not only has Hollywood severed Garbo's connection to materiality (by transforming her from a "nordic" and a "flower" to skimpy "tissue-paper") but the "obvious[ness]" of her new form has disallowed the impersonal work of spectatorship. These changes together obliterate the effects of Garbo's early European form. On the one hand, then, H.D.'s racial idiom values racial purity and affirms Nordic superiority even as it turns an American racial discourse against the United States itself (because America is the racial polluter). On the other hand, H.D.'s "ice-flower" label cuts against the essentialism of such purity by blending the naturalism and formalization that's been an important part of her writing on film; this label joins two natural objects to characterize a formal concept (a nonexistent ice-flower). More importantly, H.D. explicitly notes that "'nordic' [is] another word they [Americans] fall for," part of the commodification of the star "thudded into his [the specta- tor's] senses for some months" before entering the theater ("CC" 106). This mocking announcement makes clear that H.D. deploys her Nordicism ironi- cally to criticize a form of cinema that won't acknowledge its own racial logic and whose bluntly realistic aesthetic robs its icons of their iconicity.

H.D. continues to specify this robbery, and indeed this pollution, by ap- pealing to a further American discourse of miscegenation, this one anchored in sexual violence. H.D. portrays the Nordic Garbo as a pure white woman, a flower from the North who's "swiftly cut and grafted in America into a more sturdy . . . rootstock" ("CC" 105). This act of horticultural hybridiza- tion is achieved through apparent sexual violence when Garbo, a "captured Innocent," is "deflowered, deracinated, [and] devitalized," leaving her a "pho- togenetic guise," a term that suggests a racialized corruption of the star's photogenic beauty ("CC" 107, 106, 107, emphasis added). H.D. reinforces the sense of sexual violence when she codes the ideal film viewer's dissatisfac- tion with Hollywood in terms of the need to rescue a threatened woman: it's "the duty of every sincere intellectual to work for the better understanding of the cinema . . . [to play] Perseus, in other words, [to] the chained Virgin." H.D. then reinforces the miscegenative connotations of this violence by suggesting that it leaves Garbo blackened—"black-eyed" and "dark," with a "black-dyed wig, obscuring her own nordic nimbus" ("CC" 107). This new "photogenetic guise" can't help but align itself with H.D.'s simultaneous claim that American filmgoers are like "African tribesm[e]n" who "accept" only the "flat-faced . . . effigies" that have "so long been imposed" on them ("CC" 106). In all, then, H.D.'s deployment of the intertwined strands of miscegenation and sexual violence, coupled with her analogy of the Ameri- can audience to an African tribe, plays around the edges of one of the most volatile components of U.S. racial history, one that she would just a few years later engage more directly in *Borderline:* the myth of the black rapist.[36]

H.D.'s rhetoric seems to register in this myth questions of embodiment much later theorized by Robyn Wiegman, who argues that what motivated both the myth and the lynching it supported was not only white men's desire to control their lineage by controlling white women's bodies but also their effort to achieve a sense of disembodiment by violently disciplining black flesh. H.D.'s description compresses the two male roles that Wiegman identifies in the myth by depicting the white male controller of bodies, Hollywood, as itself also a figure of embodiment, the deflowering black male body. She posits not only that Hollywood is responsible for raping Garbo but also that Hollywood requires "a reel or in some cases an artist or a producer [to be] . . . gelded" ("CC" 106). Such compression doesn't actually reject the desire for disembodiment underwriting the myth, but it does present Hollywood's racialized body as an unstable referent. In other words, race isn't a clear biological essence that H.D. simply names; it's instead the effect of an act on a victim.

While H.D.'s discussion of eugenic Nordicism, miscegenation, and sexual violence establishes the overall pattern through which she exposes the accrual of racial identity, that pattern is given its most extended development in her engagement of *Totem and Taboo.* In *Totem and Taboo* Freud links modern black "savages" to a much older "primitive man," claiming that both are a kind of "atavistic image," being transparent in motivation (because they lack repression) and frozen in time (because they aren't evolving toward civility).[37] Freud also claims that the totem functions as primitive man's image of "horde," or group, identity (*Totem* 156). Following from these notions, H.D. characterizes Hollywood as a primitive African "medicine man" who "dupe[s]" or "dope[s]" his "horde," the now uncivilized American audience, with only a single familiar "totem" of beauty ("CC" 106).[38] In this manipulative casting the totemic Hollywood Garbo doesn't offer images of spectators' unconscious mechanisms or desires, as H.D.'s ideal film can do. Instead, she's an obstacle to accessing such images, a nationalist sublimation or "race fixation" that means that the audience "doesn't in the least know, in fact would be incapable . . . of saying what [it] does want" ("CC" 106).

Not only that, but when read alongside the myth of the black rapist this totem doubly condemns American cinema. According to Freud, the totem anchored primitive law against incest: a man could not copulate with a woman of his own totem. Yet, according to H.D., the Hollywood Garbo is both a totem and a product of sexual violation. Hollywood thus effectively rapes its totem to produce it, a paradoxical breach of totemic law. This paradox is then compounded by H.D.'s depiction of Garbo's rape as both an act that produces the racial body and an act of miscegenation that blurs racial distinction. These moments suggest that the doing—the constitution of racial embodiment—is simultaneously an undoing that signals the shifting nature of identity. While H.D. repeatedly voices her critique through racist discourses, perhaps even lending them some force, she not only interweaves these discourses in ways that call attention to their repetitions but mockingly reassigns the roles within them. Such strategies lay bare the mechanisms of the production of race in order to record the fluctuating social and biological imperatives that shape embodied identity and indeed impersonal subjectivity.

H.D. further registers the force and breadth of these circulating imperatives—and also softens some of her own problematic binaries—by using Freud's racial discourse when characterizing her ideal cinema and spectator as well. In *The Interpretation of Dreams* Freud likens dream images to a "pictographic script" (312), prefiguring *Totem and Taboo*'s definition of totemism as the "primitive technique of writing [in] . . . pictograph" (137). Freud draws out this racialization of dream work in *Totem and Taboo* by aligning savages with civilized dreamers, whose hidden investments, "concealed behind the manifest personality," have partially evaded repression while they slept (117). H.D. redeploys this link between savages and the impersonal imagetexts of the unconscious to blur the binaries inherent in her own racial metaphors. While she portrays her ideal spectator as having a more developed consciousness than that of a racialized Hollywood viewer, she also champions her ideal film as the bearer of art "since the days of the stone-writers" and as specifically akin to the hieroglyphs in "the temple of Karnak" ("CC" 105, 108). By contrast, she denigrates Hollywood as a modern "circus" complete with "crowds" and "pink lemonade" ("CC" 105). At this moment, then, Hollywood is a civilized, commodified spectacle, and the avant-garde are latter-day primitives, now applauded for a picture writing that resembles the totemic image that H.D. had condemned in her discussion of Garbo.

H.D. extends this complex (re)negotiation of totemism while critiquing the movietone. She proposes that sound interferes with the theater's proper function as a "temple" in which we commune with "our dolls, our masks, our gods" ("CC" 108, 116). In addition, she links this communion to the hypnotic state through which her advance guard can become "far enough removed" from a "censor[ious]" consciousness to be "recreated," and she casts this transformation as a return to the "primitive beginning" ("CC" 116). Such a function for the theater now depicts totemism as a positive mass fantasy rather than simply a negative national sublimation. Ultimately, then, H.D.'s appeal to *Totem and Taboo* exposes the varying and even conflicting threads of racial embodiment in Freud's discourse and in her own aesthetic. The complexity of her portrayal shows how impersonality destabilizes the social binaries that construct race, but racial discourses also continue to supply the vocabulary through which she explains impersonal subjectivity. In other words, H.D. stages a continual circling back into some of the same conventions against which she began. By undertaking this staging—and thereby acknowledging that she doesn't escape race—H.D. encodes the inevitable limits of any effort to see beyond an identitarian self or person.

In all, then, "Cinema and the Classics" offers a rigorous update of H.D.'s impersonal aesthetic, showing that she has adapted new avenues in the scientific vernacular of vision to her own creative purposes and is steadfastly probing the social reach of that adaptive work. H.D.'s revised aesthetic is bold in its embrace of a taut balance between concentrated attention on the apparatus of vision and images and an experience of the embodied limits of attention. She also freshly situates this balance within the mass spectatorship of a film-watching audience rather than within the individual subject-object circuit of inspiration. Just as importantly, this aesthetic cues a forthright appreciation of the difficulties of exceeding identity and of activating the liberatory social potential of impersonal subjectivity. The real testing ground for H.D.'s proclamations, though, was her contemporaneous involvement with actual filmmaking.

Borderline's Aesthetic of Identity Dis-order

In an unpublished essay on *Wing Beat,* the 1927 POOL short in which she made her acting debut, H.D. recounts "the personal impersonal experience" of "seeing its [the film's] fragments" projected in a "way-side cinema" ("*Wing Beat*" 1). An announcement for the film, also likely written by H.D., calls *Wing Beat* a "study . . . not of persons" but rather of the complex workings of "telepathy," "the chemistry of actual attraction," and the subjective recesses beyond the "frail, too-high, too inaccessible brink" of the "*will*" (*Wing Beat* announcement). These two statements together suggest that H.D. saw her participation in POOL productions as an extension of her impersonal aesthetic and its attempt to represent those unconscious psychophysiological forces within the subject that condition perception and indeed personality. POOL's subsequent film *Borderline* represents H.D.'s most expansive involvement with its productions. In addition to starring as Astrid and writing the film's accompanying explanatory pamphlet, she also was involved with film publicity and participated in developing a potential playlist for the jazz band that was to accompany the otherwise silent film during screenings.[39] Moreover, H.D. helped to complete many of the montage sequences for *Borderline* when its writer-director, Kenneth Macpherson, became ill during postproduction ("Autobiographical Notes"). Indeed, her responses to a 1929 questionnaire in the *Little Review* suggest that she may even have shot some of the film's scenes.[40]

H.D. was perhaps so expansively involved with *Borderline* because the film was POOL's first (and ultimately only) feature-length production, and the only one of its films ever to have public screenings. Likewise, the fact that Macpherson first began working on his filmscript in early 1929, at the peak of H.D.'s romantic relationship with him, may have been a factor. However, beyond these personal motivations, I would suggest that H.D.'s heightened interest stemmed from the fact that *Borderline* was the POOL film most representative of her evolved impersonal aesthetic and the social implications that she attributes to it in "Cinema and the Classics."

A few years after making *Borderline,* Macpherson recounted in Nancy Cunard's *Negro: An Anthology* (1934) that he had originally imagined the film as a critique of the "captivating ways of lynch-made farmers and their victims" in the modern American South ("Negro Film Union" 206). He further explained that he'd had to compromise on his original vision because the film "would have been banned and its maker declared insane" (206).[41] Macpherson's comments, coupled with *The Story,* a leaflet distributed at screenings that notes the film's dealings with the "racial borderline," have set critics searching for a key to bypass *Borderline*'s formal and situational opacities.[42] In other words, imagining the film as a cipher, they have looked for a way to directly access its critique of race, or more broadly identity, including gender and sexuality as well. Some of these scholars have discerned a fairly successful antiracist platform in the film, whether through its representation of the "machinery of white racism" or its "substantial inter-racial collaboration" (Debo 372). Others, however, have pointed to H.D.'s costar Paul Robeson's primitivized and monumentalized character as stereotyped and therefore limited.[43]

It's not hard to see this racial content in *Borderline* and to connect it to

H.D.'s own writing on race in "Cinema and the Classics." *Borderline* charts the volatile conflict that emerges as two sexually and emotionally intertwined couples, one black and one white, converge on a remote European town. The white couple, Astrid (H.D.) and Thorne (Gavin Arthur), have come to town with a "mulatta," Adah (Eslanda Robeson), with whom Thorne is having an affair. In an effort to end that affair, Astrid notifies Adah's estranged black husband, Pete (Paul Robeson), who happens to be working in the bar of a nearby hotel, of Adah's presence, and the two temporarily reunite. In an ensuing quarrel between Thorne and Astrid over her actions, Thorne kills Astrid. While he's quickly exonerated, the black couple find themselves blamed and are driven from town and from one another by the aggressions of a moblike townspeople. This plot effectively remediates H.D.'s own mocking recirculation of an American discourse of miscegenation and sexual violence in "Cinema and the Classics." More explicitly than that essay, *Borderline* offers a sort of funhouse mirror of the myth of the black rapist. A white man, rather than a black man, is having an affair with a woman who's not simply black but a "mulatta"—that is, one whose body already concretizes the white fear of miscegenation. Moreover, to this refraction we might add that Astrid, the white woman, manipulates rather than being exploited and that Thorne is violent toward Astrid, rather than Pete, the black man. Perhaps most importantly, Annette Debo has also pointed to a clatter montage sequence during the film's bar fight between Pete and a white townsperson (played by Macpherson himself) over Astrid's murder. In this scene, shots of the bar patrons' angry faces are intercut with imagery suggestive of lynching: flames, white fists, and an advertisement featuring a black male body. For Debo, this scene is a rebus for Macpherson's racial intentions, namely, his effort to expose the psychology of racism.

However, connecting these points to the racial symbolics of "Cinema and the Classics" also situates *Borderline* in a framework that isn't strictly racial or even identitarian. Most fundamentally, "Cinema and the Classics" details an aesthetic that traces an opaque, impersonal subjectivity and also shows that this subjectivity puts embodied identities like race in an uncertain light. Impersonality focuses on the social and biological matrix that structures identity, a matrix that exceeds any firm model of racial identification and thus leads to race's perpetual making and unmaking. In *Borderline* the plot likewise promotes a psychophysiological experience and awareness of impersonal subjectivity even as it also draws out the implications of that subjectivity for embodied identities like race. As J.S., an early reviewer for the *Manchester Guardian,* wrote, *Borderline* "subordinate[s] and sometimes obliterate[s] . . . the appeal of individuality" or "personality." To call this goal more primary than the film's racial politics is to return to Macpherson's claim that *Borderline* forces "white man" to confront his own "instability" instead of displacing it onto a "race-problem" ("Negro Film Union" 206). In "Cinema and the Classics" H.D. attributes such an instability to both the fact of human embodiment and the contrary modern desire to "dissociat[e]" "body and soul" ("CC" 108). Thus, while Macpherson suggests that *Border-line* "goes into the labyrinth of the human mind," leading critics to focus on psychological instability, it's crucial to recognize that the film records a dense and automatic subjectivity wherein the psychical and physiological are inseparable ("As Is" 236). Macpherson himself suggests such a psycho-physiological focus for *Borderline* by linking the film's principal confronta-tion to both vision and emotion. Responding to British critics who panned the film for its opacity, Macpherson proposes that their critique stemmed from *Borderline*'s alienating tendency to see things "through a window or a keyhole," coupled with its related representation of "emotional being," be-cause Englishmen were embarrassed when brought face to face with that seeing and being ("As Is" 238). Macpherson's response diagnoses an anxiety in modern humanity that's organized around two conjoined concerns: the category of emotion, which crucially works across the supposed mind-body separation that H.D. claims modernity is keen to police; and a fragmented way of looking that enacts the limits of vision. Macpherson's connection of these two concerns reminds us once again that a monistic model of subjec-tivity is part and parcel of an embodied model of vision.

Judith Brown has recently registered *Borderline*'s crucial relation to sen-sation and thus to materiality and also recognized that the film maps a kind of unstable subjectivity through which identity shifts, proliferates, and frac-tures. However, perhaps because Brown doesn't frame her reading in terms of modernist impersonality, she doesn't register two important aspects of *Borderline,* aspects that capture its significant connections to H.D.'s aes-thetic: its imagetextuality and its dual incitement of conscious attention and unconscious affective drift in the viewer. In terms of the former, Brown sees *Borderline*'s splicing and spatial recombinations of images as a visualization of the fractures of subjectivity that escape from the film's silent plot. How-ever, this return-of-the-repressed reading, wherein the nature of subjectiv-ity unfolds in the triumph of *Borderline*'s pictures over its narrative, doesn't quite account for the film's structure. *Borderline* is an entirely imagetextual

experience: its silent images are inseparable from its placards detailing dialogue and plot points, its screening leaflet, and even H.D.'s accompanying
exegetical pamphlet. Macpherson's clatter montages do indeed present images in a jarring sequence that refuses a coalescing picture in favor of a hectic
juxtaposition that shifts and signifies. But in doing so, these montages challenge, rather than reinforce, an opposition of image and text. Like physiological film—and in turn like the impersonal film that H.D. advocates—the
montage technique makes the cinematic machinery visible, disabling any
sense that the film image is a complete and unmediated view of the world.
It thus calls attention to the textual qualities of all images, to their conventionality and temporality. But Macpherson's use of this technique takes a
further step in this direction by using sequences that demand a rapid reading of the relationships among the montages' images in order to understand
the film's broader plot—like the sequence of flames, fists, and a black body
that announces the townspeople's move toward racial violence. In these
multiple ways *Borderline*'s montages begin from and reflect the sense that
the seeable and the sayable are inseparable. Macpherson himself links this
work to the film's ability to excite in spectators a "special nervous reflexive
response," distinct from all "individual attractions," that would deepen their
understanding of unconscious mindbodily phenomena and processes.[44] Imagetextuality thus becomes an analogy for and a gateway to impersonal
subjectivity.

This "special . . . response" that Macpherson refers to opens onto the
second aspect of *Borderline*'s optical impersonality: its dual incitement of
attention and distraction. Brown has argued that the leaflet *The Story,* and
by extension H.D.'s longer pamphlet, worked to suspend the audience's intellectual engagement so that they would be passive, entranced recipients of
a strictly sensational experience. In other words, explaining the plot kept *Borderline*'s spectators from thinking about the film and pushed them instead
to submit to the images playing on their senses. And yet Macpherson himself emphasized that film should lay bare the embodied nature of thought
by deepening it, not simply suspending it: "Simplicity is for tired people.
And everything in life is done for them. . . . And the result is we stand quite
still and our minds lie fallow and soggy with traditions. . . . But the film [*Borderline*] to me and to anybody who bothers to think twice, is *life,* and breathes
with the breath of life, and life is not simple" ("As Is" 237). Macpherson's
words—his appeal to thought and breath alike—evoke the dynamic life-in-
movement so central to early physiological films. They suggest that he in-

tended *Borderline* to be a rigorous mental and physical experience even as that conscious attention would inevitably give over to the affectively charged hypnotic drift that Brown notes. This dual effect on spectators, which H.D. had so lauded in "Cinema and the Classics," captures the complex embodied reality of life—and as Macpherson puts it, "[L]ife is not simple."

But rather than continue to marshal the terms of "Cinema and the Classics" to read *Borderline,* I want to close this chapter by considering H.D.'s own pamphlet *Borderline: A POOL Film with Paul Robeson* as exactly such a reading of her film. H.D. uses the pamphlet to promote *Borderline* as a successful translation of her impersonal film theory into practice. She does this not only by establishing how the film employs her unique style but also by arguing that it thereby mobilizes the liberating implications of impersonality for embodied identities like race.

H.D. begins by emphasizing the imagetextuality of both her pamphlet and the film, as well as their relation to each other. First, her essay doesn't simply offer words about images; instead, it intersperses pages of film stills within the text without necessarily making any effort to refer to or describe those images. This opaque relation turns aside any expectation that word and image will have clearly distinguished and complementary roles and thus insists that H.D.'s imagetextual practice isn't about simply putting visual and verbal modes of representation together but about doing so in a way that troubles the division between the seeable and the sayable. Second, H.D. creates a complex collage of fragmented stills from *Borderline* for the cover of her pamphlet (fig. 2.4). These fragments, which are cropped, rotated, and overlapped, show characters from the film at different distances and looking in different directions, all interspersed with images of the characters' eyes. One particular area (in the upper left quadrant) brings these strands together by showing a kneeling Thorne gazing into Pete's closed eyes. The overwhelming effect of this cover is to highlight the fact that the eyes are far from a transparent window, whether on the world or on the soul. This combination of fragmentation and opacity recalls H.D.'s use of the same collage techniques in her 1920s scrapbook (see fig. 2.1), likely created jointly with Macpherson.[45] It also echoes the clatter montages that Macpherson uses in *Borderline* itself, setting up the imagetextual connections between the two artists' work.

H.D. also showcases *Borderline*'s imagetextual status by turning her attention to Macpherson's script for the film. She notes that this script contains "some 1000 pictures," as well as directions that "read like captions."[46] Her

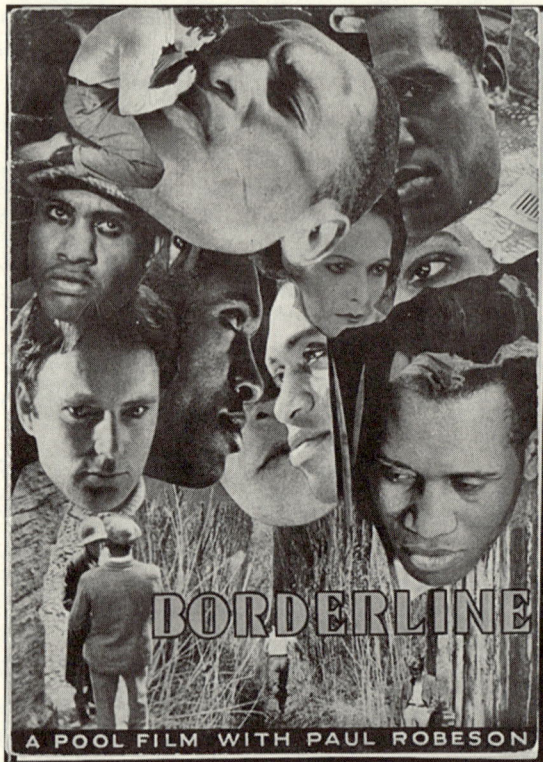

Fig. 2.4. Cover of H.D.'s *Borderline: A POOL Film with Paul Robeson.* Yale Collection of American Literature, Beinecke Rare Book and Manuscript Library. © The Schaffner Family Foundation; used by permission of New Directions Publishing Corporation, agents.

portrayal melds script and film, with the script glossing the film and some of its shot directions actually becoming *Borderline*'s textual placards. In addition, H.D.'s own imagetextuality in citing six of the shot directions and describing images from Macpherson's script reinforces both the script's and the film's imagetextuality. Indeed, this reinforcement is arguably reciprocal, thereby melding Macpherson's *Borderline* and H.D.'s pamphlet. Ultimately, both the pamphlet's citations from the script and its melding with the film draw attention to the apparatus of the film's production, including the pamphlet as part of that apparatus. They thus highlight the constructedness of *Borderline*'s imagetextual images—which is, according to "Cinema and the Classics," a key function of an impersonal film aesthetic.

It's not surprising, then, that H.D. takes this focus on apparatus one step further. Her pamphlet uses an unexpected combination of present, future, and past tenses to narrate not only *Borderline*'s dramatic action and the experience of watching it but also the process of making and even naming the film. "*Borderline* is chosen as the name of this new film; clarid [*sic*] sequence of ideas will show why," the essay opens (*BP* 221). And it continues: "Light flows over a face. That means nothing or little to you. There is a bronze forehead and the eye sockets are gouged out just this way; there is a concentration of shadow here, a plane of light here. . . . [T]hose lights have been arranged, re-arranged, deliberately focused. . . . He [Macpherson] gouges, he reveals, he conceals" (*BP* 227). This rhetorical choice gives readers the sense that they are watching the film and its production as they read the pamphlet and also potentially that they are reading an interpretation of the film as they watch it. Such a sense suggests that *Borderline* is still being made and re-made not only through H.D.'s interpretation but through the viewer/reader's screening as well. Overall, this rhetorical choice extends the film into its perceptual experience, blurring the chronological, representational, and qualitative distinctions between the two. If H.D.'s pamphlet created a mutually constitutive resonance between the imagetextuality of her writing and that of Macpherson's film, this new blurring of film and experience continues that process to similar effect. It captures the constructedness and flux, and also the "personal impersonal experience," of artistic production and consumption, as viewers, actors, director, critic, and readers all come together through perception.

While H.D.'s focus on a resonating imagetextuality has thus far implicitly linked Macpherson to her impersonal aesthetic, her pamphlet also makes an explicit connection by positioning him as a member (like herself) of the meager band of modern impersonalists that she championed in *Notes*. H.D. argues that the visuality of Macpherson's aesthetic brings the "vibrations" of past art into "line with modernity" by creating "portraiture in movement" (*BP* 228). Such meaning-filled vibrations recall the coded "dots and dashes" of impersonal art that H.D. emphasized in *Notes*. Correspondingly, she analogizes Macpherson to one of her own "sign-post" artists, Leonardo da Vinci, and in a way that strikingly brings together all of the visual and scientific discourses that have shaped her impersonal aesthetic: optics, painting and sculpture, cinema, and psychoanalysis. H.D.'s portrayal of Macpherson as Leonardo works by marshaling two aspects of Freud's essay "Leonardo da Vinci and a Memory of His Childhood" (1910), which her "Writing on the Wall" notebook (1944) shows was not only important to her but actually a gift from Freud.[47] Freud's essay characterizes Leonardo as an artist-scientist who was both dedicated to observation and connected to a primitive past and who was thereby in tune with a subjectivity that exceeded personality. H.D.'s aesthetic would presumably have attracted her to this characterization, perhaps leading her to draw out these same qualities in her pamphlet's discussion of Leonardo and Macpherson.

Like Pater, who was indeed one of his sources, Freud champions Leonardo as the "first modern natural scientist" owing to his particular "scopophilic instinct," in which he "forgets his own insignificant self" and which allowed him to grasp at the complex "secrets of nature."[48] Freud implies that Leonardo's view of these systems led him "to abandon [art] in an unfinished state or to declare that it was incomplete" ("LM" 77). More specifically, while Freud doesn't quite make this fragmentary state a positive quality in the way Pater had, he nonetheless presents it as a sign that Leonardo the scientist was interested in a problem behind which "he saw countless other problems," so that he was "no longer able . . . to see the work of art in isolation and to tear it from the wide context to which he knew it belonged" ("LM" 77).

Freud's portrayal of Leonardo echoes the visual-impersonal art and artist that H.D. imagines, right down to the effort to see into an impersonal materiality that blurs the isolation of subject and object and also the need to record the fragmented results of that effort due to embodied seeing and being itself. H.D. thus follows Freud by emphasizing Macpherson's "Leonardo-like curiosity" and aligning his work on that "renaissance miracle," the film camera, with Leonardo's scientific dissections (*BP* 225). She figures Leonardo as the "*steel* blade" and Macpherson, with his "grey-*steel* eyes," as meticulously clipping and piecing together fragmentary shots, so that both men alike "discover by its hidden valve formation, why the human heart should beat so" (*BP* 224, 225, 225, emphasis added). In addition, H.D. maintains that the "Leonardo-esque modernism" of Macpherson's clatter montages offer the "lightning" effect of seeing a scene, or indeed seeing the human subject, from multiple angles simultaneously (*BP* 225, 228). These "various stops, different focuses, [and] indeterminate 'pans' up and down" suggest at once a kind of visual immediacy and the impossibility of such an immediacy (*BP* 225). H.D. captures this condensed relation by embodying Macpherson's camera—it's not only "all steel," it's also "all sinew"—and by comparing it to the "one human EYE" shared by the three Gorgons in classical mythology (*BP* 226). Her description cumulatively structures Macpherson's impersonal art as a mode of scientific observation centered on embodied subjectivity, and one that works specifically through fragmentary images that objectify the limits of its observation.

H.D.'s second borrowing from Freud's portrayal allows her to emphasize that Macpherson's impersonal art also mobilizes the liberating implications of impersonal subjectivity for embodied identities in the way that "Cinema and the Classics" outlines. Freud's essay interprets Leonardo's commitment to scientific investigation as a sublimation of "infantile sexual researches" that never gave way to sexual maturity ("LM" 78). Moreover, the essay uses a racial discourse of recapitulation to code Leonardo's perpetuation of "child[hood] for the whole of his life" as a connection to the primitive and even to the exotically Eastern ("LM" 127). Freud explains that recapitulation, in a psychological context, is the idea that "the individual's mental development repeats the course of human development in an abbreviated form" and that "to understand the mental life of children we [therefore] require analogies from primitive times" ("LM" 97, 96). Although this theory arose as an account of the development of the human species, it was also prominent as an account of distinct races; indeed, that distinctiveness was imagined to be one hallmark of species development, as Freud's above-cited remarks from *Totem and Taboo* suggest.

Freud offers two examples to elucidate Leonardo's suspended recapitulation. The first relates to the "*unconscious picture-puzzle*" of Leonardo's childhood memory in which a kite's tail whipped against his mouth ("LM" 115n). While Leonardo uses the memory to explain his scientific interest in investigating flight, Freud follows a chain of linguistic associations back to the ancient Egyptian hieroglyph for *mother,* who was a "figure without any personal character" ("LM" 115n, 93).[49] These associations become Freud's evidence that Leonardo's memory and in turn the scientific interest that Leonardo associates with this memory "contain survivals" from "primeval" belief ("LM" 97). Freud's second example of Leonardo's childlike science returns to the East and to its primitivization. Freud discusses a set of letters addressed to the "Diodario of Sorio (Syria), Viceroy of the Holy Sultan of Babylonia," in which Leonardo describes imaginary travels to Asia Minor and even conversion to Islam among engineering plans and accounts of contemporary natural phenomena ("LM" 128). By making these letters evidence of Leonardo's childlike investigations, Freud again links Leonardo's primeval belief to the East, though now to a contemporary rather than ancient Egypt, Syria, and Armenia. This link returns to a recapitulatory logic that takes cultural difference in the present and rewrites it as differing degrees of racial distance from the primitive past. Freud's analysis of Leonardo thus subtly but persistently racializes the unconscious driving both his science and his art. While such a racialization draws on racist discourses, it also works against the social dynamic that concerns *Borderline,* namely, white men's displacement of their own subjective embodiment onto the racial Other. Freud's racialization remains *within* the human subject, not to be disavowed. And H.D. both relies on and multiplies this tension in order to expose the social and biological matrix within which identity accrues.

Much like "Cinema and the Classics," H.D.'s *Borderline* pamphlet plays on Freud's primitive account of Leonardo's latent memory to establish the connection between Macpherson's impersonal film aesthetic and the racial politics he expresses in *Borderline.* H.D. observes that "the film as Macpherson directs it" is like a dream in its "process of remembering" (*BP* 233). More specifically, she suggests that *Borderline* is "a personal dream, gone further into the race dream" and is written in a "dynamic picture-writing" that "permeates our consciousness" and imparts "soul secrets," though "we may not know what it is or why" (*BP* 233, 234, 233, 235, 225). Like the theory of recapitulation on which Freud trades, H.D.'s description is suggestive of both the universal human race and race as a category that organizes social difference. This double coding persists as H.D. explains that the film dream is based in, surpasses, and returns to racial difference. *Borderline* charts a "dream in . . . Pete and Adah" that "permeates our consciousness" as humans. It begins with Pete's "great negro head," which "like a dream . . . looms disproportionate, [with] water and cloud and rock and sky all subsidiary to its being"; goes on to let the viewers "see (with Pete) hill and cloud as, on that first day created"; and yet still insists that this day precedes "the time of white man's beginning" (*BP* 233). The continual sifting of both the universal and particular senses of race in this analysis suggests—as in Freud's portrayal of Leonardo's memory—that race figures a density or opacity within the human subject rather than supplying an external site for displacing such opacity, as it had in the myth of the black rapist. H.D.'s description of *Borderline* thus captures and confounds the stakes of lynching and suggests that Macpherson's film does the same. Continuing along this line, and in a way that's evocative of Freud's image of Leonardo as a (primitive) Egyptian, H.D. also proposes that *Borderline* constructs the "high spaces of the Karnak temple" and that in this temple "Egyptian bronze and Greek marble [are] . . . allied and welded" (*BP* 227). She thus implies that Macpherson's hieroglyphic or imagetextual film materially unites black and white, bronze and marble, and abstracts them from any stable racial essence.

In addition, echoing Freud's demystification of Leonardo's dream, H.D. both explains and refuses to explain the latent social content of specific hieroglyphs in Macpherson's film. On the one hand, she points to an early scene in which Astrid is angry with Thorne over his affair with Adah and notes that Macpherson's montage at this moment contains rapid shots of a noose and Thorne's feet dangling in the air interspersed with shots of his face. She proposes that this montage, barely perceptible "but bound to have subconscious significance," poses a shocking reversal of violence meant to undermine lynching (*BP* 234). More specifically, she explains that this montage's condensed imagery implicitly asks, "If a black man is hanged for loving a white woman, why should not a white man be likewise lynched for loving a black one?" (*BP* 234).

On the other hand, and to a much larger extent, H.D.'s exegesis tends to veer away from interpreting single scenes or montages in favor of reflecting on the notion of a borderline itself. Such a strategy forces viewers to actively grapple with their own fragmented experiences of *Borderline*'s impersonal imagetexts and also provides a kind of framework for this grappling. A borderline polices an inherently tenuous division: it signals a delineation of difference (a marker of the bounds or borders of a space) precisely at a meeting place where the sense of difference is hard to maintain (and to be a borderline is to exist in precisely such an interstitial space). For H.D., the concept suggests the simultaneous sameness and difference characterizing human subjectivity—the inseparable psychophysiological systems of the body, on the one hand, and the fact that those systems' opacity gives rise to an incoherent and thus divided self. She highlights the pervasiveness of borderlines in the production of Macpherson's film: the cast is and is not a "troop of players," because several members aren't professionals; the film's setting in a remote border town is and is not part of the "social"; and Macpherson, as a director, isn't "allied with the ultra-modern abstract school," but neither is he "out of sympathy with realistic cinema" (*BP* 225, 221, 223, 223). H.D. argues that within this simultaneously under- and overdetermined environment the racial borderline that the film negotiates both is and is not. The film's symbolics position racially white and black characters as alike both dark and light. Pete is "oil and heat," signifying his "dark brow," while Astrid is "hail and a stuffed sea-gull," signifying her rigid figure encased in a white Victorian shawl (*BP* 223). And yet Pete is also "white cumulous cloud banks," while "his white fellow-men"—being the "shadows" of his whiteness—are all "dark" (*BP* 224). Moreover, the white characters, as shadows, are merely images of the cloudlike Pete that are cast upon the earth below. But because Pete is himself also the earth "under all their feet" and because the film's "theme flowed toward him," he seems to be as well the (white) screen on which their (dark) images are projected (*BP* 224). In this way, H.D. argues, the film explores the workings of embodied identity, implicitly asking, "[W]hen is white not white and when is black white and when is white black?" (*BP* 223).

In all, H.D.'s *Borderline* pamphlet concretizes her evolution toward more social models of impersonality: she has moved from simply developing and theorizing her own aesthetic to championing the impersonal work of her fellow modernists. The constitutive relationship between her pamphlet and *Borderline* suggests that aesthetic impersonality was achieved not only artist by artist but at the level of circulation across artists and artworks. H.D.'s efforts to call attention to this cultural circulation should instruct scholars in the current need to trace aesthetic impersonality across a wider range of modernists than has so far been attempted. In subsequent chapters, such a tracing will reveal that not all modern stylists of impersonality shared the confidence or indeed the enthusiasm that Pater, Field, and H.D. had in impersonality's liberating potential. Modernists took the same scientific vernacular of vision in different directions, pointing to the varied cultural meanings and political purchase that an impersonal understanding of subjectivity could support.

Getting Impersonal
Body Politics and Mina Loy's
"Anti-Thesis of Self-Expression"

> We're all pervaded by a consciousness that goes beyond
> while intensifying the personal.
>
> Loy to Carl Van Vechten, [1915]

A 1917 *New York Evening Sun* profile crowned the writer, painter, and inventor Mina Loy the quintessential "modern woman" ("Do You Strive" 10). Her particular qualification for this title, so the profile went, was that her art endeavored "to express her personality" and did so by crystallizing into symbols "the images that fl[ew] through her brain" (10). Years later, the News and Gossip columnist for *Creative Art* magazine would second this emphasis on Loy's personality in an announcement for her 1933 New York exhibition: "Mina Loy, who is having her American premiere at Julien Levy's Gallery, is in Europe as distinguished as a person as she is as a painter." Harriet Monroe, the editor of *Poetry* magazine, reported more disparagingly of her 1923 meeting with Loy, "I may never have fallen very hard for this lady's poetry, but her personality is irresistible. . . . Yes, poetry is in this lady whether she writes it or not" (96). Even Loy's friend the writer Natalie Barney, when introducing Loy's poetry reading at a meeting of her Académie des Femmes in May 1927, said that the event was designed to "enhance the personality of [the poet]" (158), which she compared to that of "a somnambulist" who has "gazed upon the Gorgon" and so gained "some perception of a fourth dimension" (160).

Given such appreciations of Loy's personality, which were at times over and above appreciations of her work, it shouldn't be surprising that she exhibited a fraught relationship to personality and in turn to modernism's aesthetic of impersonality, at times embracing or eschewing both terms. With a couple of recent exceptions, however, this complexity has gone un-

recognized by scholars. Instead, critics have duplicated the trend I pointed
to in H.D. scholarship: they have assumed that impersonality was a masculinist bid for "authorial invisibility" and have categorized Loy's work as a
clear rejection of that bid, a distinctly personal expression "borne [*sic*] not of
cultural transcendence but of cultural disenfranchisement" (Gilmore, "Imna,
Ova" 271, 276). Critics have supposed, in other words, that Loy's feminist
project was fundamentally incompatible with modernism's impersonal project.[1] Even when recent critics have begun to chip away at this view of Loy's
exclusive investment in the personal, they still haven't captured the full
contours or stakes of impersonality. Charles Altieri takes Loy's work to exemplify modernist impersonality, and specifically to show that it resists the
"cultural vanities" supported by having the "lyric express individual personality" (53). But he nonetheless persists in defining impersonality as an "apparent objectivity" (54). Jessica Burstein too sees Loy as part of a modernist
effort to move beyond the personal and even links that effort to an interest
in human materiality that departs from Altieri's objectivity. But Burstein
doesn't consider how materiality, especially in the scientific discourse of the
day, insists on the density and opacity of the subject. Indeed, she sees in
human materiality the possibility of perceptual transparency and immediacy, privileges that are ruled out by the physiological optics that I've described.[2] Yet if we return even to those contemporaries of Loy who lauded
her personality, we can see hints that her aesthetic was actually much in line
with the impersonal style I've thus far traced through the work of Pater,
Field, and H.D. Loy's project presumes an autonomic subjectivity in excess
of the personality and endeavors to use a scientific vernacular of vision in
order to grasp the opaque psychophysiological forces that constitute that
excess and condition knowledge.

The *Evening Sun* article with which I began in fact weds Loy's personality
to the fluctuating perceptual images, both current and remembered, that
"fl[ew] through her brain." This language, whether intentionally or not, points
to a distinctly modern definition of personality as the product of unwilled
psychophysiological systems rather than an internal, controllable possession. In addition, the reporter extends this understanding of personality to
Loy and to her aesthetic. Barney's comparison of Loy to a "somnambulist"
similarly suggests the nineteenth-century scientific origins of this understanding of personality in the study of trance states like somnambulism and
dédoublement de la personnalité, or doubled personality. *Dédoublement* was

interpreted as a kind of extreme somnambulism in which a sufferer alternated between two exclusive webs of memory and perception—what were deemed two distinct personalities. Such a diagnosis belied the notion of a persistent and singular identity separate from memories, images, ideas, and perceptions; it defined personality as nothing more than a collection of present states of consciousness conditioned by forgotten or never known thoughts and material processes. Barney's added claim that the entranced Loy had "gazed upon the Gorgon" hints at the connection between such an incoherent subjectivity and a mediating perceptual system. In mythology, Perseus can only gaze upon Medusa through the mediating intervention of an image—the reflection in Perseus' shield—a fact that Walter Pater famously took as a figure for embodied seeing and being in *The Renaissance*. Even Barney's further belief that Loy's gaze allowed her "some perception of the fourth dimension" taps into and indeed links Loy's aesthetic with an additional node in the scientific vernacular of vision, namely, popular discussions of relativity and of higher-dimensional space, including Einstein's fourth dimension of spacetime. As I discuss in more detail below and also in the following chapter, the notions of a fourth dimension and of relativity captured the artistic imagination as potent symbols of the smallness and indeed distortions of the human scale for grasping "the mysterious universe," to quote the title of the English astrophysicist Sir James Jeans' popular 1930 account of modern physics.[3]

Loy's belief that "we're all pervaded by a consciousness that goes beyond while intensifying the personal" and her use of imagetexts to mark the contingent nature of perceptual images and so of knowledge developed haltingly. This slow process and Loy's lingering uncertainty about the social implications of an impersonal project have likely contributed to critics' tendency to misapprehend the connection between modernist impersonality and Loy's aesthetic appeal to images and embodiment.[4] That ambivalence certainly shapes her early and perhaps best-known essay, the "Feminist Manifesto" (1914), as well as her contemporaneous advertising pamphlet *Auto-Facial-Construction* (1919), in which her explicit anxiety over modern gender roles tempers her interest in impersonality. However, a variety of midcareer works demonstrate that Loy subsequently developed an aesthetic dedicated to the impersonal forces of the embodied observer. Indeed, she herself provides a remarkable account of this development in her later novel *Insel* (1935-61), which fictionalizes her real-life friendship with the surrealist painter Richard Oelze in order to stage a reflection on aesthetic impersonality. *Insel* dubs surrealism impersonal and taps its particular scientific vernacular in order to revisit Loy's initial concerns about the aesthetic and to record her gradual resolution of her ambivalence.

Feminism and Faces: Staving Off the Threat of Impersonal Negation

Loy's early anxiety about impersonality stems principally from her concern about the social subjugation of women, what she calls in the "Feminist Manifesto" the cultural production of woman as a "**relative impersonality**," meaningful only relative to men and impersonal when compared with men's individuality (154). In this formulation, impersonality marks women's subjection to a cultural model of universality that privileges men by presuming that the individual is male. Susan Gilmore has extrapolated this diagnosis of chauvinism into Loy's supposed repudiation of aesthetic impersonality. And yet Loy's rejection of impersonality in a social context doesn't map as neatly onto a definition of impersonality in an aesthetic context. This rejection does help explain, though, why Loy would worry about aesthetic impersonality: if an impersonal art emphasizes the instability and unknowability of the expressive subject, whether male or female, then it could run counter to women's nascent efforts to assert a norm of female autonomy over and against the passivity generally ascribed to them. To represent an impersonal subjectivity—and so belie the possibility of autonomy—might be to sacrifice a still anticipated female independence and thereby undo the ongoing feminist process of "becoming modern."[5] Thus, while Loy had no reason to view aesthetic impersonality as automatically suspect, she might indeed have been wary of its potential effects. In the "Feminist Manifesto," which Loy drafted in Florence in November 1914 and sent to the writer and patron Mabel Dodge Luhan, she handles this wariness by arranging a set of dialogues and collisions between competing ideologies, allowing her to insist on women's selfhood—as opposed to their relative impersonality—while nonetheless documenting her unease with notions of the self, or of the human subject as simply a self.

The "Feminist Manifesto" seeks to establish a specifically female selfhood first by joining futurism's antisocial, singularizing tendencies with the collectivist goals of feminism.[6] Loy plays what she considers the positive aspects of each discourse against the politically destructive aspects of the other. Drawing on futurist ideology, she exhorts women to "be **Brave** & deny at the outset" feminism's "pathetic clap-trap war cry **Woman is the**

equal of man" (153). Yet she also chafes at futurism's advocacy of a separate-spheres ideology, bemoaning in fine feminist rhetoric that "[a]s conditions are at present constituted—you [women] have the choice between **Parasitism, & Prostitution—or Negation**" (154). In other words, women can agree to become either wives (what Loy calls "parasites") or prostitutes; their only other option is to forgo any relation to men and thus be viewed, in the most severe version of women's social impersonality, as nothing at all. As Loy splices together such contradictory elements of futurism and feminism, her arguments in favor of female agency also seize upon these ideologies' unacknowledged agreements, at times disturbingly so. For instance, she echoes both the platform of the feminist birth-control movement and futurism's hygienic-eugenic ideals when she attempts to remove the stigma from discussions of sex and reproduction—"there is nothing impure in sex" (156)—and offers the unsavory contention that "[e]very woman of superior intelligence should realize her race-responsibility" of "producing children in adequate proportion to the unfit" (155).

The general neutralization of bodies inherent in this ideological hybridity ultimately takes more explicit and forceful forms in Loy's argument. In fact, her fear that any challenge to the subject's autonomy might block women's ability to become modern leads her to attack the body *along with* impersonality, rather than to oppose the two, as Gilmore has argued. With influential modern thinkers like Otto Weininger and Georg Simmel relegating women to an egoless, bodily impressionism—in a sense excluding them from full subjectivity and so from artistic and social institutions—Loy finds herself inclined to view the (female) body as fatal to women's social power.[7] She thus closes the "Feminist Manifesto" by recommending the "unconditional surgical destruction of virginity . . . at puberty" as a means of inspiring "psychic development" (155). In other words, she violates the body in the hopes of controlling anatomy and thereby challenging the cultural and biological imperatives that make up female gender identity.

Ultimately, Loy intensifies this disciplining of the body by introducing another, divergent ideology into her mix: the largely outdated Victorian ideal of character that Pater had so contested in his impersonal aesthetic. Loy uses this discourse to frame her de-virginization project as the conscious (female) self's ability to instrumentalize the body, or at least as the starting point for that ability. This framing begins with the premise that the current "value of woman" depends on her trading her "physical purity" to a man in exchange for his taking the "life-long responsibility of her" (155, 155,

154). Such a "manoeuvering [*sic*]" centers on woman's cosmetic and mannerly project of making herself becoming (155). The Victorian notion of character, by contrast, posited a (male) individual whose method of self-development hinged on a dialectic of working on the body to overcome it and whose economic labor and independence were the proving ground of that dialectic and his value to the community. Loy reroutes this masculine discourse into a strategy by which women could become modern rather than simply be becoming. She condemns a collectivist feminism as "**Inadequate**" to address women's social and economic subservience and characterizes her alternative method, the destruction of virtue, as a gesture of bodily control meant to force women out of the "letharg[y]" of marriage and onto a path of self-discipline that would lead to the "intrinsic merits of character" and a "concrete value" (153, 153, 154). This appeal to character contrasts sharply with the more unstable and socially mediated notion of personality that had largely eclipsed it by the early twentieth century. That later notion of personality emphasized complexes and conditioning over and against the individual will and was therefore consonant with an impersonal understanding of subjectivity. Loy marshals character in order to fold personality, and in turn impersonality, back into a disembodied autonomy, making an older model of manhood meaningful for modern womanhood. This effect then culminates in a final instrumentalization of the female body: reproduction. Loy argues that the "devastating psychological upheaval" of de-virginization will create a self-conscious woman who "express[es] herself through all her functions," including maternity (153, 154). The children of such a woman will stem from "a definite period of psychic development" and manifest the "individual lines" of her "personal evolution" (155). Maternity thus becomes merely a biological "faculty" of personal expression and a self-assertive gesture of bodily control (154).

Although the "Feminist Manifesto" ends with this apparent commitment to the self and self-expression, Loy's framing correspondence with Luhan suggests that she was aware not only of her doctrine's overweening attachment to individualist modes of social protest and artistic creation but also of the limits of such an attachment. Luhan's known interests in futurism, feminism, and personality made her a natural first reader for the "Feminist Manifesto." Her enthusiasm for Loy's earlier essay "Aphorisms on Futurism" (1914) had led her to pursue its publication in Alfred Stieglitz's photographic journal *Camera Work,* and she'd sent Loy a copy of the parapsychologist Frederic W. H. Myers' *Human Personality and its Survival of Bodily Death* (1903) as a work of interest.[8] In addition, Luhan's New York salon was then host to numerous feminist and birth-control reformers, including Margaret Sanger, Frances Perkins, and Mary Heaton Vorse.[9] And yet, despite Luhan's constellation of interests, in Loy's 1914 letter accompanying her draft of the "Feminist Manifesto" she jokes that this "absolute resubstantiation of the feminist question" is "easily to be proved fallacious—There is no truth—anywhere." Even assuming a sympathetic reader, then, Loy distances herself from the "Feminist Manifesto." Indeed, though it's today frequently cast as one of her most representative works, she never revised the draft or tried to have it published, a further suggestion of her hesitancy.

In a second letter, written a few months later, Loy in fact continues her distancing strategy by describing the manifesto as a mere "fragment of Feminist tirade." More interestingly, she also declares, in reference to its final proposition: "I find the destruction of virginity—so daring don't you think—had been suggested by some other woman years ago—see Havelock Ellis" (letter to Luhan, [1915]). This declaration registers Loy's awareness of the manifesto's sensationalism and acknowledges its ideas as borrowed. Not only that, but its reference to Ellis points to Loy's interest in contemporary psychology and physiology and suggests shared intertexts between Loy and her fellow modernist H.D., who would shortly dedicate her impersonal manifesto, *Notes on Thought and Vision,* to Ellis.[10] Loy's acknowledgment thus variously diverges from the autonomous, self-disciplined model of identity and intellectual production advocated in the manifesto itself. Packed amid eulogies for friends who, like Luhan, had left Loy's expatriate community in Florence, these comments instead suggest a far less insular, more relational notion of personality and creativity.

At the same time, though, these letters to Luhan don't mark Loy's final departure from the disembodied identity on which she had centered her gender politics in the "Feminist Manifesto." Such a departure would be a long time in the making. Thus, a few years later Loy would develop an exercise regime for (re)training the face to express the personality.[11] Though all that remains of that regime is her advertising pamphlet *Auto-Facial-Construction,* this pamphlet displays Loy's continued concern with subduing the body in the service of an internal, essential personality and offers her politicized reconfiguration of the feminine desire to be becoming. At the same time, though, the pamphlet also registers another small step toward the alternative framework of optical impersonality. True to its participation in the distinctly visual cultural world of advertising, what's new in this slightly later piece is a more explicit acknowledgment of a performative, relational personality, even as Loy tries to inoculate against the implications of this personality. In addition, we also see a broader grappling with physiological science and with embodied identity beyond gender.

The spark for *Auto-Facial-Construction,* or rather for the lost method it describes, seems to have been Loy's discovery and practice of Bess M. Mensendieck's system of functional movement beginning around 1910.[12] Mensendieck began her career studying sculpture but ultimately left art school to attend the Medical College in Paris and eventually the University of Zurich.[13] While in Paris, she worked on the neurologist Guillaume B. Duchenne de Boulogne's "Physiology of Motion" project, which sought to map the function of individual human muscles. After finishing her medical degree, Mensendieck used her understanding of muscular, skeletal, and neurological systems to create a distinctly physiological form of modern body culture. She advocated training the body and mind to work together to make self-conscious muscle placement and movement into learned automatic habit, a method she referred to as "sculpt[ing] in flesh" (*Look Better, Feel Better* 5). True to this appeal to her early art training, Mensendieck felt that the written word alone was insufficient for instruction and relied on a specifically visual pedagogy that included illustrated textbooks and classes led by certified teachers.[14] In fact, Robin Veder has pointed to two aspects of Mensendieck's visual pedagogy that are important elements of the modern scientific vernacular of vision. First, Mensendieck's books focused on didactic sequences of images (fig. 3.1). Following the structure established by earlier photographic motion studies (significantly the same studies that H.D. engaged in her film criticism), these sequences were printed from left to right to show a chronological progression. In other words, the images have a narrative; they are imagetexts. In the case of figure 3.1, in which Mensendieck is herself the model, the narrative is: follow my system and this is progressively how you will look. Second, Mensendieck also pursued a kind of "eye training" that Veder calls "x-ray vision," pointing to the logic it shares with that modern visual technology ("Seeing Your Way to Health" 1344). Whether through cutaway illustrations that reveal the muscle and bone beneath the models' nude flesh or through exercise sequences performed naked before a full-length mirror, Mensendieck trained students to see changes in their underlying musculature and skeletal frame and even the flush that

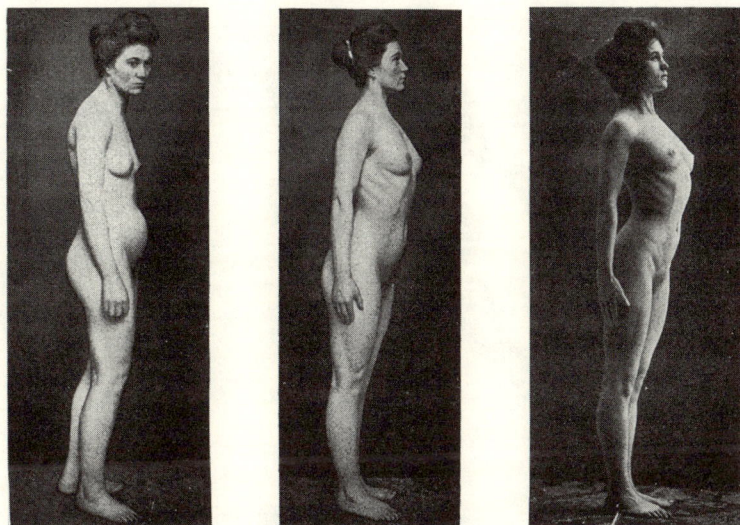

Fig. 3.1. Photographic sequence detailing improved functional movement. Bess Mensendieck uses her own body to display what a student will look like on the first day of instruction, then after one month, then after three months. Reprinted from Mensendieck, *Körperkultur der Frau*, plates 1-3.

marked increased circulation (figs. 3.2 and 3.3). The goal of all this training, both visual and physiological, was full-bodied and individual expression. As Mensendieck explained, "[T]he power of the soul . . . permeates the entire body. . . . The personality is expressed by the individual as a whole" (*"It's Up to You"* 32). Mensendieck's system thus managed to turn her physiological training into a body culture of art, images, personality, and self-expression.

In *Auto-Facial-Construction* Loy adapts Mensendieck's ideas to the face, seeking to secure the autonomous singular self against not only the natural aging process but also what she understands as the modern condition. Loy's pamphlet argues that while historically the face offered a perfect visualiza-tion, a mirror image, of the personality, now the "new interests and activities of modern life" had disrupted this natural relation.[15] Loy rallies her potential clients against this disruption with the cry that they have an "inherent right not only to 'be ourselves' but to 'look like ourselves'" (*AFC* 165). She thus folds Mensendieck's artistic discourse of self-expression into a more urgent appeal to a liberal discourse of rights, one that has long presumed an autono-mous, disembodied self.[16] Just as Mensendieck tries to harness the auto-

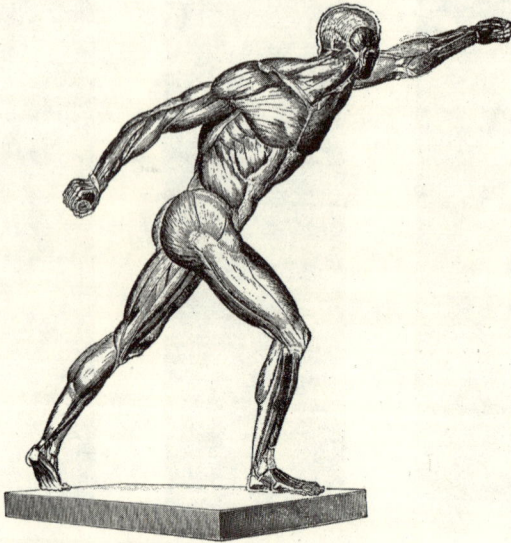

Fig. 3.2. Cutaway diagram of the underlying muscular structures of a moving body. Reprinted from Mensendieck, *Körperkultur der Frau,* 16.

nomic systems of a physiological body to a regime of willful self-fashioning, Loy aims to unite an essential, autonomous personality, the impersonal forces of culture and materiality, and a (facial) image that fluctuates but mustn't seem to do so.

Loy's method, or really her advertisement of it, pursues this unification first by reversing a typical Marxist logic, which supposes that commodity culture alienates products from the bodies that created them. Loy claims instead to redress modern life's alienation of personality from the face precisely through the commodity in the form of her method. But the resulting commodified facial image of personality is quite distinct from the natural mimesis that she hopes to recuperate. Indeed, its constructedness suggests that the personality to which it's welded is also constructed, relational, and unstable. Seeming to understand these implications, Loy offers a sleight-of-hand substitution. She emphasizes that through her production process one manifests, paradoxically, a "constant and natural resource" of beauty, a kind of raw material rather than a manufactured good (*AFC* 166). This return to raw material refuses the implications of the commodity by making the production process circle back on itself to create a "natural resource" that was

Fig. 3.3. Preston Duncan, *Class Receiving Mensendieck Instruction at Yale University.* Though publication of this photograph in Mensendieck's book postdates Loy's initial involvement with Mensendieck's system, the photograph nonetheless shows what a class Loy could have taken would look like. Reprinted from Mensendieck, *Mensendieck System of Functional Movement,* xiii.

always already there rather than some kind of manufactured or constructed product.

Auto-Facial-Construction continues this sometimes dizzying effort to stabilize personality by equating two opposing notions of it: Hollywood's "picture personality" and Myers' metaphysical "larger Self." Right from her initial premise that "the face is our most potent symbol of personality," Loy aligns her method with Hollywood's production of what she would later call, in a poem about the actress Marie Dressler, the "Film-Face" (c. 1934). Starting in the mid-teens, American film companies began not only to reveal the names of their previously anonymous players but also to publicize particular actors using headshots. As H.D. would sense in her analysis of Garbo's Hollywood career, a star's face quickly became a kind of paradox: an individuated product. Pursuing a singularizing course through films, magazines, and publicity posters, the celebrity face took on a set of personality traits, promoting the sense that personality was itself a performative accrual rather than a natural essence.[17] This face, and in turn the personality more broadly, was in a very pointed way an imagetext. However, as Roland Barthes famously noted, the star's status as both a person and an institution allowed fans either to acknowledge or wholly ignore the imagetextual system that produced him or her (deCordova 9). Loy's pamphlet does both. On the one hand, she explicitly links her method to the star system by claiming that her exercises offer a "renascence," or rebirth, for actors and actresses, a way to "reconstruct" their image (*AFC* 166, 165). On the other hand, Loy repeats the elision that Barthes diagnoses, because she denies that the resulting image is either a product or a sign of an inevitable material flux. She not only claims that in her method "the original facial contours are permanently preserved as a structure which can be relied upon without anxiety as to the ravages of time," she also posits that achieving this structure brings the "facial contours in harmony with the conditions of [the] soul" (*AFC* 166, 165). I want to suggest that this and other appeals to the "soul" in *Auto-Facial-Construction* work to tame the picture personality with Myers' contrary notion of a "larger Self," or extended personality, that is the essential human soul.[18]

A poet and philologist, Myers was better known as one of the founders and early researchers for the London-based Society for Psychical Research, which sought to bridge the gap between psychology and psychiatry, on the one hand, and spiritualism, on the other. *Human Personality and its Survival of Bodily Death,* the compendium of Myers' work that Luhan sent to Loy, argues for a singular personality or soul that precedes and exceeds the body—and even the forces of heredity and evolution—rather than being limited by them. This personality's effects included autonomic physiological processes, unconscious states like dreams or trance, and supernormal perception like telepathy (1:15). According to Myers, this extended and distinctly unified personality and the particular vision it enabled accounted for embodied phenomena like afterimages and also gestured toward a "metetherial world" of images accessible only through second sight (1:xix).[19]

A February 1920 letter to Luhan about *Auto-Facial-Construction*'s method makes Loy's engagement of Myers clear. In it, she critiques his parapsychological efforts as "lack[ing] the element of taking risks that art and life have," implying that her pamphlet approaches the same goal, namely, proving that personality transcends the body, but from a better angle. This better angle notwithstanding, *Auto-Facial-Construction* repeats Myers' sense that personality is an interiorized essence that enjoys a greater longevity than does the body. More importantly, it also echoes a key paradox in his method. While

Myers presumes a stable, dualistic subject in whom willful self-expression takes precedence over a distinct body, in his focus on telepathic media, from automatic writing to vocal possession, he depicts personality as fully dependent on a body to express it. As Myers admits, the personality "selects what parts of the brain-machinery he will use, but he cannot get out of that machinery more than it is constructed to perform" (2:190–91). Likewise, Loy claims that her exercises can produce an "identity of your conscious will" with the "three interconnected zones of energy" housed in the skull's "muscular sheath," implying an autonomous, self-assertive personality (*AFC* 166, 166, 165). But she also admits that people are at the mercy of these centers—at the mercy of the body and its structures—for "the power to communicate" their "personalities" (*AFC* 165).

A second letter to Luhan, this time from July 1920, reinforces that Loy was aware that her method was ultimately hemmed in by bodily limits. Taking for granted that she was herself an advertisement for her method, Loy notes with regret that she had recently been "too ill to make my facial discovery convincing." The point here isn't that Loy's illness hadn't allowed her the time to market the method; rather, it's that her illness had shown in her face and thus rendered the method's merits less "convincing." In other words, Loy's regret is an admission that her method doesn't actually make people "masters of their facial destiny" or offer a way to sustain their faces as an ever-stable image of the "prolong[ed] youth of our souls" (*AFC* 166). On the contrary, a slight and momentary illness is enough to disrupt the supposed control of Loy's will over her body. This disruption not only marks the results of Loy's method as exaggerated, it also suggests that the theory on which her method is based—the theory that personality is reducible to the will—is itself flawed.

While Loy's acknowledgment of these points is both brief and subtle, her February 1920 letter to Luhan includes an anecdote that indicates that she was already becoming interested in a more complex model of personality and that this evolution was tangled up with the shifting scope of her thoughts on embodied identity. While the "Feminist Manifesto" seeks to refashion only the female body, *Auto-Facial-Construction*'s method, like Mensendieck's, applies equally to men and women and doesn't exhibit the same violence in neutralizing materiality. In other words, Loy's focus is no longer simply waging war against women's social inequality; it's grappling directly with the nature of personality, and not just with regard to gender. The anecdote that Loy shares with Luhan—which is about a group of Japanese rice pickers that she had seen on a boat to Chile—continues this shift by characterizing personality equally in terms of race and ethnicity. Loy explains that these workers exhibited the mutually constitutive relation between "souls and bodies and clothes and customs" that people didn't manage to "show over here." While she's struck by the rice pickers' apparent unity, she doesn't applaud them for successfully exercising their will over their bodies to achieve it. Instead, she replaces the dyad of will and body with a broader range of factors. And the reference to "customs" in particular suggests that these factors are always at least partly beyond the control of the individual that Loy's pamphlet itself privileges. With these shifts, Loy gestures toward an impersonal subjectivity in the form of a social and biological matrix that structures personality. She even implies that her new facial method will inaugurate the needed "show" of this subjectivity in the West. Underscoring her investment, Loy explicitly argues, contrary to claims in *Auto-Facial-Construction* itself, that these workers would "lose all significance," all coherence of personhood, if the relationship among interior and exterior, self and culture, and body and commodity were "disturbed."

Taken together, then, the "Feminist Manifesto" and *Auto-Facial-Construction* make clear that Loy's ambivalence toward the social implications of a modern notion of personality, and in turn of impersonality, was formative in her early career, whether those implications related to feminism, to the autonomy of the liberal human subject, or to the social and biological forces informing race. Where the "Feminist Manifesto" turns a disembodied conception of character emphatically against impersonality in a way that only Loy's letters undercut, the text of *Auto-Facial-Construction* grapples directly with the ingredients of modernist impersonality—including a modern notion of personality—if only to control them. It engages a notion of personality as unstable, produced by embodied systems, and inevitably compromised; and it does so with notable influence from physiology, modern visual culture, and the scientific vernacular of vision. Loy's letters about the pamphlet confirm its allusions and point to the moment when Loy first began to perceive modern personality and impersonality not as threats to her primary political goals but rather as concepts that could fuel her politicized art. As her project continued to evolve, she came to believe that the image and the observer proposed by the scientific vernacular of vision could provide her with an adequate framework for capturing a modern subjectivity that was neither fully transparent nor fully opaque to itself. Indeed, Loy came to embrace the idea that personality was itself a fragmented and mediated image. This embrace was in fact the first step in her development of an impersonal aesthetic. It's in her midcareer work—notably her poem "The Ceiling" (1945), her memoir "The Child and the Parent" (c. later 1920s), and her essay "Gertrude Stein" (1924)—that she really forms the contours of this aesthetic.[20]

Optical Experiments and a Poetics "Beyond the Personal"

Loy's longtime friend Marcel Duchamp advocated the playful practice of painting the first thing one saw each morning. Inspired by this practice, the writer Robert Carleton Brown composed a series of "optical poems" for Duchamp and Henri-Pierre Roché's aptly named dada magazine the *Blindman* (1917), for which Loy also wrote. The label "optical poem" captures Loy's much later project in "The Ceiling," in which a newly awake speaker stares up at the ceiling and describes a series of resulting subjective visual phenomena. As Ford had done in *Parade's End,* Loy in "The Ceiling" uses this experience to reflect on the impersonal nature of subjectivity and on the limits of knowledge, including self-knowledge. Loy's literary executor, Roger Conover, included one of several extant versions of this poem (never published in Loy's lifetime) in *The Last Lunar Baedeker* under the title "Ceiling at Dawn." However, in the absence of any dating or direction on the manuscripts, I take another version of the poem as more complete because of its inclusion of a lengthy final stanza that reframes its experiential record in philosophical terms. As this version isn't otherwise available, I reproduce it here in full:

> floating in oval of unclosing eye
> the white-washed shadow-drifts
> of indoor dawn
> film optic clouds
>
> the cinema-nirvana
> shifts
> palid [*sic*] ideograms
> and epitaphs of dreams
> upon a white slab slanted
> visual echoes
> in blanched rows
> —the dissolved, derouted,
> traffic of slumber.

An arid air-flower
In etiolate tents
Of our arousing

As the droning day
dilates
in early lights—
a spectral acre

and under a sunless artifice
of a four-cornered sky
lingering flies
convolve their slim-winged circles.

A blanched domesticated sky—
maps out the dawn and dusk—
The white rectangular plane
whereon parade the fancies of
the turned up eye—
Blank page on which I puzzle
out the featureless
the façade of the blind oracle
of destiny of whom we most inquire
the sufficiency of evil for a particular day—
Calcium lake which the
waking soul plunges its queries—
the virgin platform of
inattainable [sic] gestures
the untreadable elysses [sic]—
Stretched for the angels ascending
from the skies—
the passionate air ball
tug from the unperceptable [sic]
suction of your desire
towards the passionate
air ball—

"The Ceiling" opens, in its first two stanzas, by characterizing a fluctuating scene in the speaker's field of vision. This scene comprises not simply
the objective world (the play of morning light streaming into the room,

throwing shadows of the objects it meets upon the ceiling) but also the subjective markers of what Walter Benjamin had by now labeled the optical unconscious. "[F]loating in" rather than simply before the speaker's "unclosing eye" are pale "shadow-drifts" subsequently labeled "film optic clouds." Like Tietjens in Ford's *Parade's End,* Loy's speaker is sensing subjective optical phenomena, specifically either retinal afterimages or optical floaters, both of which render visible the embodied mechanics of vision. Afterimages are shadows that appear when the eyes' photoreceptors temporarily lose sensitivity due to overstimulation, such as staring at bright sunlight coming through a window. Optical floaters are shadows projected onto the retina by cell debris trapped in the vitreous humor, or optical film, and are particularly noticeable when one is lying on one's back, as the debris concentrates near the center of the eye. The "film optic" that accrues before the speaker's eyes—perhaps even a product of both of these phenomena—plays on the anatomy of the eye (the optical film) and the imagetextuality of cinema. Loy also piles dream images onto these physiological effects. Such fantasies can seem to linger and fade before one's eyes after waking, caused by a lag in the brain's processing of new visual stimuli with the opening of one's eyes and the onset of conscious awareness. The speaker's "cinema-nirvana" includes the "dissolved" and "derouted" "traffic of slumber," which the speaker experiences as so many "epitaphs of dreams" upon engraved headstones "in blanched rows." Loy's imagetextual invocation of death and decay through these "slabs" recalls the role that the corpse plays in imagism; it indicates the opacity and inescapability of embodied materiality, in particular the limits to perceiving and knowing that stem from such visual phenomena. Loy's reference to "palid ideograms" reinforces these limits and links her visual discourse back to the imagetextual cryptograms of Freudian psychoanalysis that were so important to H.D.

The next three stanzas of "The Ceiling" act as further ideograms in the speaker's heightened and shifting awareness of the optical unconscious. The visual images are now "air-flowers" grown in the "etiolate tents" of the bedclothes, forming a "spectral acre" as the day "dilates," like the pupils of the eyes in dim "early lights." They are also "lingering flies" that "convolve . . . slim-winged circles" in a "sunless . . . sky," mimicking and inverting the optical halos that can seem to appear around luminous objects because of fatigue or migraine. These two ideograms evoke the materiality of the optical unconscious, linking it to an oscillation of growth and decay and a spectrum of light and darkness. The form of these stanzas—and of the first two as well—heightens this sense of flux and multiplicity. Loy's minimal inclusion of capitalization and verbs, coupled with her extensive use of sonic devices like alliteration and consonance, as in "white-*washed* shadow-*drifts*," and of compounds like "air-flower," creates a flow that blurs images, one into another. On the other hand, the terseness of the stanzas, particularly the third and fourth, coupled with their overwhelming use of enjambment and highly irregular rhythm, stresses fragmentation and incompletion and so a certain opacity.

The closing stanza of "The Ceiling" turns to speculate on the nature of subjectivity and knowing indicated by the optical unconscious. The speculative tone is suggested in the greater length and number of lines in this stanza and in its halting punctuation in the form of numerous dashes. In addition, the "eye" of the first stanzas now becomes an "I," but only once and only in connection with the verb "puzzle," accentuating that the speaker's very state of being is cryptic and opaque. This "I" produces, though not entirely willfully, the poem itself, written in and by "the fancies of/the turned up eye" on the "[b]lank page" of the ceiling. The speaker "puzzle[s]/out" the epistemological and ontological contours of this "blind oracle/of destiny," which delivers not the transcendental clarity of second sight but instead "queries," "inattainable gestures," "the untreadable," and "the unperceptable" as markers of the embodied limits of vision and knowledge. Loy's grammatical errors, or what we might instead call near words, reinforce the imperfections that arise from these limits. Rather than dismissing the oracle as inaccurate, however, Loy instead concludes her poem by offering two further ideograms that implicitly frame its worth: a "Calcium lake" and a "blanched" or "sunless" "sky." The former ideogram for the room's white ceiling substitutes one of the most basic components of human bone (calcium) for clear waters, suggesting that a partial view into the optical unconscious taps into the basic elements of human materiality, even if it isn't the key to transparency or self-presence. The latter ideogram draws out the philosophical implications of such a knowledge for a Cartesian model of the human subject: by characterizing the interior space of the ceiling as a sky, complete with "film optic clouds" and "dawn and dusk," she blurs a Cartesian separation of interior and exterior, including not simply the room and the outdoors beyond the window but also self and world, as well as subjective and objective percepts. In other words, Loy precludes any construction of the room as Descartes' camera obscura of the mind and thereby refuses the disembodied, autonomous observer of Cartesian optics.

If "The Ceiling" thus hints at an impersonal aesthetic that adapts the image and the observer of a physiological optics, Loy's memoir of her earliest years, "The Child and the Parent," directly explains the contours of this aesthetic and its relation to a scientific vernacular of vision. Though now only partially extant, Loy's memoir is fascinating for its thorough dissatisfaction with the expressive personality that she had earlier so valued and for the clear connection it establishes between her burgeoning effort to develop an alternative model of subjectivity and her scientifically inflected understanding of vision and embodiment. The memoir both mythologizes Loy's early visual development and elaborates its centrality to what she calls her aesthetic of the "inconceivable," meaning that which can't be fully visualized about the human subject (chap. 4).[21] Mirroring H.D.'s appeal to the filmic image in her aesthetic, Loy's outline for "The Child and the Parent" begins with the thesis that personality is "like a roll of negative film," bearing images of things "already taken place" and requiring "a camera to project it" and a "surface to throw it upon" (fig. 3.4). This analogy establishes a crucial point: like cinema, which collects a sequence of stills into one moving picture by relying on the embodied limits of vision, personality comprises a collection of partial, mediated perceptual images, both present and remembered, and not an autonomous singularizing essence.

"The Child and the Parent" elaborates on this thesis, loosely compiling experiential memories and intuitions, as well as stories heard and overheard, to represent Loy's halting accrual of embodied identity from conception to early childhood. In the process, the memoir establishes three principles of being. The first is that the fundamentally embodied subject is "interpenetrated by intangible dimensions of concentrated distance to which our intellect has no access, except by the aid of the instruments of our sciences" (chap. 8). Most broadly, this notion of interpenetration refuses key binaries grounding a Cartesian optics: subject/object and interior/exterior. More specifically, though, the terms of this refusal echo a particular discourse on the limits of vision in non-Euclidean geometry and modern physics. Loy's idea that people are unable to visualize the dimensions of an uncontained subjectivity, at least without modern science, taps into debates in physics over visualizing the higher dimensions of curved space. Scientists questioned whether it was useful or even possible to cast such mathematically discerned phenomena in visually observable terms, whether those terms were "idea-images," like the analogy of formless energy to a particle and a wave, or actual built models of non-Euclidean shapes.[22] Regardless of their answers,

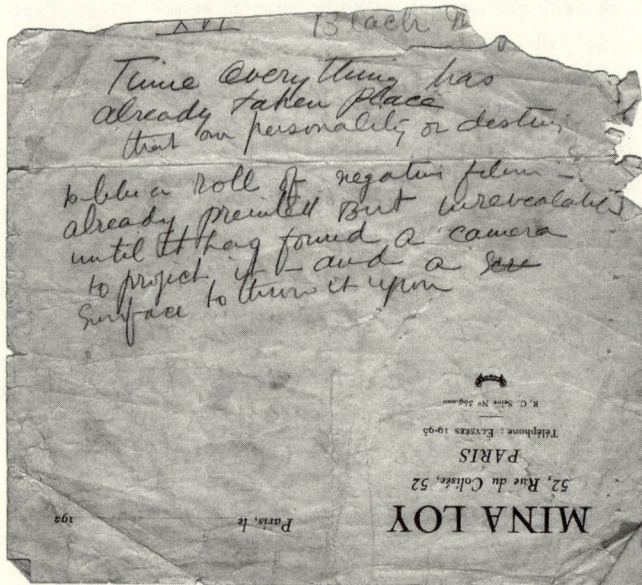

Fig. 3.4. Detail from Mina Loy's outline of "The Child and the Parent." The organizing thesis pictured reads: "Time everything has already taken place that our personality or destiny is like a roll of negative film—already printed But unrevealable until it has found a camera to project it—and a surface to throw it upon." Yale Collection of American Literature, Beinecke Rare Book and Manuscript Library. Courtesy of Roger L. Conover.

the curvature of space posited by non-Euclidean geometry and formalized as space-time by Einstein's theory of relativity discredited the notion of a Cartesian observer who bears an absolute and objective vision. Loy's second principle of being repeats this challenge by affirming that we aren't "transcendental observer[s]" but are in fact blind to the host of psychophysiological systems determining us—the fleshly "routes" bearing in us the "litter of ideas" held by "infintissimal [sic] races"; "the ceaseless signaling of the cerebellum," reporting "commands from an unknown control"; and the "currents of our life," "receiving and expelling their pouring velocities through ivory aorta and arteries" (chap. 8). Loy's third principle again echoes modern physics, or more particularly a vernacular version expressed in modern surrealism. André Breton famously held that ideas derived from the new physics might be applied to ontological problems and asked whether the "fragmentation" of time announced that mankind was preparing "someday to escape the principle of identity" (qtd. in Parkinson 56). Despite her rather mixed friendship with Breton, Loy similarly argues that the unseen cognitive, nervous, and circulatory systems delineated in her second principle in fact constitute a subjectivity that exceeds personality. She posits that the "apparent person, which marks the confines of the ego, though seemingly what each must be in his entirety, is actually where each 'leaves off'" (chap. 12).[23] "The Child and the Parent" ultimately draws out the implications of these three principles. It proposes that "[m]an is little else than a vehicle for forces whose inherence to himself he cannot explain" and also therefore questions "the existence of any personality" to begin with (chap. 8).

The conclusion that opaque psychophysiological forces bear on subjectivity becomes the lodestar of Loy's mature work. It defines her model of a monistic subject that's neither fully willful nor self-present, and it frames the goal of her aesthetic: to bring these opaque forces, as far as may be, into the reader's line of sight. "The Child and the Parent" announces this goal by grounding Loy's art in her early "infant vision," which resulted from her then merely "conditional" state of being (chap. 4). This mode of vision, Loy suggests, made her a "core of consciousness" so physical that she could actually "impact" and indeed meld with that place where "*the subconscious is more present than the person*" (chap. 4). Having experienced this impact early in life, Loy believes that she has subsequently been able to achieve in art an "antithesis . . . of self-expression," whereby she conveys a sense of the "subliminal selves" embedded in the "entrails" of those around her (chap. 4). In other words, by attending to the psychophysiological subjectivity signaled by the scientific vernacular of vision, Loy gained a view into those complex impersonal systems that structure both vision and personality.

By investing in visual perception as the grounds for an impersonal aesthetic, "The Child and the Parent" transforms Loy's earlier attempts to neutralize the body in the "Feminist Manifesto" and to a lesser extent in *Auto-Facial-Construction*. In "Gertrude Stein," her two-part letter to the *Transatlantic Review*, Loy clarifies that the goals and techniques of her newly impersonal aesthetic have a positive political potential, rather than posing a threat to social liberation, as she had earlier worried. Loy's portrait of her friend fronts this political potential, as it surfaces in Stein's complementary aesthetic, in two intertwined ways. First, rather than portraying Stein as being as autonomous as any man—her strategy for liberating women in the "Feminist Manifesto"—Loy points to a universal human embodiment that denies autonomy to anyone as the core of Stein's art. Autonomy, in other words, is no longer Loy's weapon against social hierarchy; it is a bulwark of social hierarchy that she attacks. Second, delving into Stein's Jewishness and also her own, Loy posits the popular model of the "Cosmopolitan Jew" as the ideal modernist observer. Lara Vetter has already pointed to the ways in which Loy was drawn to the racialized figure of the "Cosmopolitan Jew" for its "instability of identity" and "transnational blood," developed from "wandering so long in exile" ("Theories of Spiritual Evolution" 55, 54). Vetter has also suggested that Loy saw this instability—this consummate border crossing—as a challenge to various social and philosophical binaries.[24] I want to suggest that in "Gertrude Stein" Loy exchanges the disembodied human subject presumed by a Cartesian optics for an embodied, racialized observer modeled on this Jewish type. She signals that such an observer—as a figure for *all* subjects—is both modern (consonant with the contemporary scientific vernacular) and modernist (central to contemporary aesthetics). Loy proposes that Stein's exile point of view allows her to grasp the fallacy of a coherent and autonomous self and to see through the screen of the ego to the social and biological imperatives that structure identity. Stein thus illustrates an observational practice that, in Loy's estimate, supports a liberatory politics.

Loy forges the connection between Stein's racialized exile aesthetic and her own impersonal aesthetic in the playful poem that opens her letter:

Curie
of the laboratory
of vocabulary
    she crushed
the tonnage
of consciousness
congealed to phrases
    to extract
a radium of the word (305)

This poem compares Stein to the Nobel Prize-winning physicist Marie Curie, who studied the subatomic forces of matter, and more implicitly to the goal of modernism that Loy described in her early essay "Aphorisms on Futurism." In that essay Loy championed modernism for going "beyond the synopsis of vision" and also figured the effort of this new visuality as deforming "material to derive its essence," which exactly describes Curie's work of processing pitchblende to discover a new chemical element: radium (13). In the poem, Loy suggests that Stein, as "Curie/of the laboratory/of vocabulary," can process the distinctly materialized consciousness that adheres to language and extract and represent its most basic unconscious but still material elements.[25] The formal aspects of Loy's poem duplicate this project. The atomicity and enjambment of its lines suggest compression, while the off-rhyme and repeated syntax of lines 2 and 3, as well as the consonance in lines 4-6, bring materialized elements of sound into view, blurring the distinctions between words and distancing them from their meanings. In addition, the indentation of lines 4 and 8 constructs two interrelated four-line units that the poem processes into the "radium of the word," that is, into the closing extra line and the discovery made possible by the prior units' work. In its form and conceit, then, Loy's poem links Stein's aesthetic to the contemporary sciences of matter, to an awareness that vision is a "synopsis" rather than a full view, and to an embodied, opaque model of subjectivity—the basic contours, in other words, of Loy's own aesthetic of the "inconceivable."

Loy's appeal to Curie also announces her investment in Stein's status as a racialized exile observer. It was widely known in 1924 that Curie had immigrated to France to evade Russian czarist rule, which suppressed Polish nationalism. In addition, Curie elicited highly publicized xenophobic responses in France in 1911, the year she won her second Nobel Prize. First, the right-wing French press falsely claimed that Curie was Jewish, not truly French, and thereby kept her from winning a seat in the French Academy of Sciences. The press then reported on a rumored affair between the widowed Curie and the married French physicist Paul Langevin, portraying Curie as a foreign, Jewish homewrecker and causing her to flee briefly to England.[26] These aspects of Curie's life associate Stein's cosmopolitanism, alluded to in the opening prose of "Gertrude Stein," with exile. In addition, they make Stein's Jewishness—as contested as Curie's, though in very different terms—integral to that exile and to the observational perspective gained by it.[27]

Loy goes on to confirm the importance of Stein's Jewish exile perspective to her impersonal art. Loy describes her friend's poetry as a kind of cubism that echoes the stylistic tendencies of the Hebrew scriptures, including the syntactical circularity of Ecclesiastes and the paratactic verse of Job.[28] She reads Stein's *Tender Buttons* (1914) in particular as a paratactic lesson in the partiality and temporality of embodied vision, suggesting that Stein "associat[es] a subject with a verb which does not in fact belong to it, but which visually, is instantaneously connected" (308). Loy proposes that this technique portrays what is merely the "semi-honesty of the oval eye" and marks "a continuous flux of Being" rather than an individuality (308, 305).

Moreover, Loy's reading of Stein's "Italians" (1922) clarifies that she links this visual understanding of impersonal subjectivity quite powerfully to an anti-essentialist body politics. She registers in Stein's art a complex social and biological matrix within which identity shifts and accrues. Stein's exile view grasps the "plasm of life" that "spreads tenuous and vibrational between each of its human exteriorisations" (306). And Stein sees within this matrix the Italians' particular "biological insignia," which is at once cultural (what they say and how) and bodily ("sprouting hair," "a longer finger nail," a "sound," a "smell") (306). The particular passages that Loy cites suggest that this insignia is a challenge to racial essentialism. Stein notes, for instance, that

> [t]hey [the Italians] have something growing on them, some of them, and certainly many others would not be wanting such things to be growing . . . on them. . . . [H]aving such things makes them elegant and charming, makes them ugly and disgusting, makes them clean looking and sleek and rich and dark, makes them dirty looking and fierce looking. (qtd. on 306)

This description begins by suggesting something material about Italians, that they "have something growing on them," but immediately qualifies that identifying trait by adding, "some of them." Then, in describing those who have the characteristic, Stein suggests a set of widely varying and often mutually exclusive effects: it "makes them elegant and charming" but also "ugly and disgusting"; it "makes them clean looking" but also "dirty looking." For Loy, such language "exposes . . . our standardized biology" and yields instead a "racial consistency" that's actually "infinitesimally varied in detail" (306). These suggestions supply the framework for Loy's final passage from "Italians," this time Stein's wordplay with the idea of "the natural":

> They [the Italians] seem to be, and *that is natural* . . . They are talking, often talking and . . . they are then sounding in a way *that is a natural way* for them to be sounding, they are having noise come out of them *in a natural way* for them to have noise come out of them. (qtd. on 306-7, emphasis added)

In this passage, Stein's repetition produces what Loy calls the "very pulse of duration," or the "flux of Being," as the basic "core of a 'Being'" (305). In other words, the version of natural insisted upon here is an "infinitesimally varied" "consistency" rather than some stable essence. According to Loy,

Stein's challenge to such an essence—her playful refusal to see it as natural—amounts to a liberatory aesthetic politics. And by approving of Stein's aesthetic, Loy tests out her sense that her own burgeoning impersonal aesthetic has a similar positive political potential as well. "Gertrude Stein," "The Child and the Parent," and "The Ceiling" together demonstrate that as early as the 1920s Loy was deducing a theory of impersonal subjectivity out of her own visual experience and the scientific vernacular of vision that surrounded her. She was also filtering her own art, as well as the art of her contemporaries, through this theory, imagining a politically inflected modernist project devoted to observing and representing a subjectivity in excess of the personal. Loy's novel *Insel*, begun a decade later, in 1935, and intermittently revised until 1961, combines theory and art and serves as her longest and last word on an impersonal aesthetic. This novel, only published in 1991, shows that Loy harbored a nagging uncertainty about the political value of impersonality for much of her career but also that she used *Insel* to finally resolve her ambivalence and deliver her verdict.

"*Insel* in the Air": Weighing the Politics of Impersonality

In "The Child and the Parent" Loy captures an embodied, unstable, and automatically conditioned subjectivity by figuring the "flesh" as "islands in the air, whose routes bear the rush of infintissimal [*sic*] races" (8). *Insel* is the German word for "island," and in Loy's novel by that name she fictionalizes her fraught 1935-36 friendship with the German surrealist painter Richard Oelze in order to trace surrealism's aesthetic and lived investment in such a subjectivity. If "Gertrude Stein" positioned Stein's aesthetic as one form of modernist impersonality, employing it to consider the politics of Loy's own burgeoning impersonal aesthetic, *Insel* takes surrealism as another form and uses it to finally resolve Loy's ambivalence regarding the political value of impersonality. Surrealism's gender politics—the way it fetishizes women as a sign of the opaque subjectivity it explores—made it an ideal instantiation of Loy's early anxiety regarding impersonality for women and, more broadly, for a liberatory politics. Following "The Child and the Parent" and its aesthetic of the inconceivable, Loy's protagonist and alter ego in *Insel*, Mrs. Jones, proposes to write her friend and fellow artist Insel/Oelze's biography as a visual record not so much of his "individuality" as of its very "frontier" (65). She believes that such a record requires her to indulge in the impersonalizing process of inhabiting Insel's surrealist "ethic," which is fundamentally "congenital" and tied to both his art and his mode of being (74, 63). From the moment Jones resolves to write this biography to her decided break from Insel and their conciliatory final meeting, Loy puts surrealism on trial, and not simply through the gendered dimension of the Jones-Insel dynamic. She also returns to the familiar racial terms of "Gertrude Stein" in that Jones positively codes Insel as a racialized exile but also suspects him of racism. The symbolic devices Loy uses to chart Jones' alternating enthusiasm for and aversion to Insel's impersonality—devices that mine surrealism as a visual-scientific vernacular—clarify both the social potential and the social limits of an impersonal style as Loy sees it. *Insel*'s narrative structure finally endorses the politics of impersonality, providing a conclusion to the debate that Loy had waged with herself starting with the "Feminist Manifesto."

It's not difficult to appreciate how Loy settled on surrealism as a modern impersonal aesthetic. The work of her friend Marcel Duchamp, notably his behemoth project the *Large Glass* (1915-23; fig. 3.5), was a touchstone for the surrealists, and he openly admired the movement for refusing "visual productions that stop at the retina" rather than proceeding into the gray matter of the brain (qtd. in Krauss 123). Duchamp's art not only adapted a physiological optics but also developed an imagetextuality through which it explored opaque subjectivity as both a creative resource and a philosophical challenge to Cartesian absolutes. Jean-François Lyotard wrote of the *Large Glass* that "what the viewer sees is the eye and even the brain in the processes of forming its objects; he sees the images of these imprinting the retina and the cortex according to the laws of (de)formation that are inherent to each" (qtd. in Krauss 119). Elaborating on these complex visual mediations, Rosalind Krauss has argued that both the *Large Glass* and surrealism proper offer an image whose visual field isn't waiting emptily to mirror reality but is instead always already filled by habit and the mechanics of vision, not to mention the psychophysiological conditions of dreaming, fantasizing, hallucinating, and remembering. Linda Henderson, in *Duchamp in Context,* has specified the imagetextual nature of this image by examining the *Large Glass*' adaptation of optics in both its structure—particularly the segment titled "Oculist Witnesses"—and its accompanying notes. Henderson points to the ways in which Duchamp modeled the *Large Glass*' multimodal project and what he called its "Playful Physics" on Leonardo da Vinci's notebooks, with their blend of artistic and scientific work, particularly their concern with optics and perspective and their view of the body's mechanical functioning.

If Duchamp pointed Loy to surrealism's interest in optics, imagetextuality, and an opaque subjectivity, she would have found it equally important

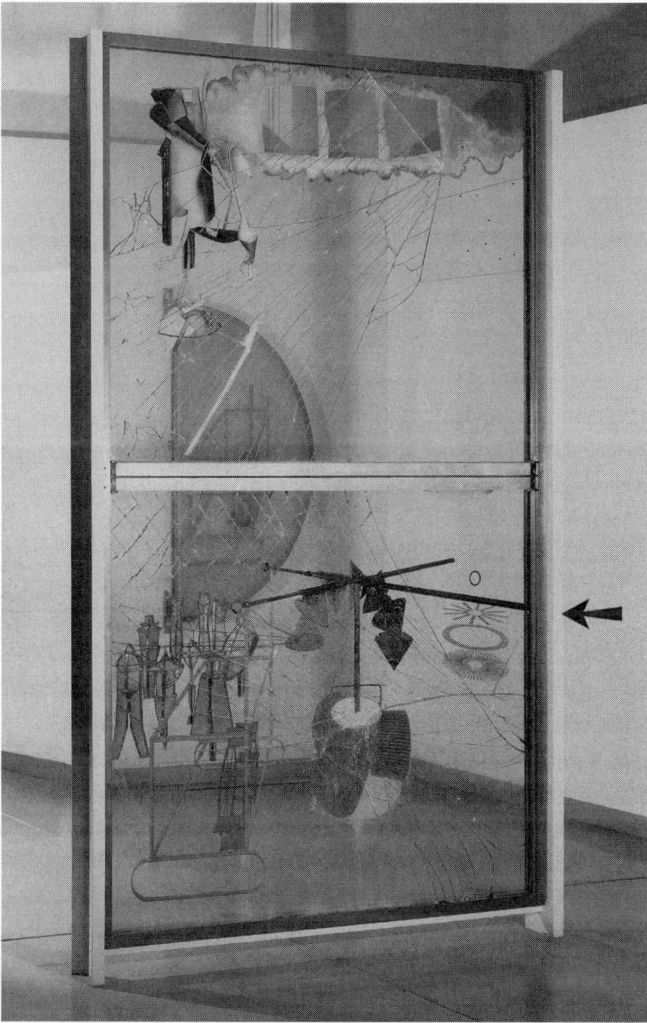

Fig. 3.5. Marcel Duchamp, *The Bride Stripped Bare by Her Bachelors, Even (Large Glass)*, 1915–23. Note in particular the arrow-marked portion on the right side of the bottom panel, where there is a vertical series of circular patterns. This segment is titled "Oculist Witnesses," and its circular patterns are based on opticians' tests for astigmatism. In addition, the *Large Glass* as a whole uses visual interference and exhaustion, as well as the mechanics of refraction, reflection, and polarization, to define *looking* as "the physiological registering of an optical experiment" (Henderson, *Duchamp in Context* 207). Philadelphia Museum of Art, Bequest of Katherine S. Dreier, 1952. Courtesy of the Philadelphia Museum of Art / Succession Marcel Duchamp / ADAGP, Paris / Artists Rights Society (ARS), New York.

that surrealists connected these interests to female bodies. Whitney Chadwick and Susan Suleiman in particular have shown that surrealists used fetishized female bodies as the condensed sign of the movement's threat to an autonomous self. Despite the sexism of this association, Katharine Conley has argued that surrealism's "automatic woman" figure was ultimately more invigorating than marginalizing for women artists in the movement. These artists, Conley maintains, threw themselves even more completely into surrealism's depersonalizing strategies, like collaborative creation or efforts to measure the unconscious through the body's jerks, excretions, growth, and decay. If Conley's study assesses the value of surrealism for women artists and for a feminist project—assuming that the movement posed both hindrances and support—*Insel* uses surrealism to perform essentially the same work for modernist impersonality. Loy prefigures and also exemplifies Conley's conclusions by ultimately approving of *Insel's* surrealist ethic and also portraying Jones collaborating with Insel in surreally embodied and impersonalizing ways in the process.

Jones' most approving impressions of Insel—and so of surrealism—hearken back to "Gertrude Stein": they correspond with Loy's multifaceted figuration of Insel as a racialized exile, grounded first in his literal exile from Germany. In 1933 the Nazi Party labeled Oelze's surreal art degenerate to the race, forcing him to flee to France, where he found himself increasingly exiled as a German in a country preparing for war with Germany.[29] It was during this tenuous period in Paris that Loy and Oelze met, and her novel highlights the importance of Insel's double exile to the visual perspective that Jones associates with his creative and lived surrealism. For instance, on one occasion Insel describes to Jones his condition of "forever fleeing," illustrating his marginal view by holding up a plate symbolic of society and suggesting that he's always "on the outside—peeping over the edge" (25, 59). The sound of airplanes, possibly German bombers, overhead punctuates his description, causing Insel to "shrink into himself" and Jones to realize that for him "war was not only imminent—he was already ripped open by its plough of anguish" (60). In sympathizing with Insel's position, Jones recognizes the importance of his racialized exile to his particular perspective in art and life and silently connects that status to her own: "One thing about Insel that had struck me was this sporadic distinction I had often been 'accused' of which I had always been eager to discover in anyone else who, like myself had 'popped up' from nowhere at all—as if all my life I had lacked a crony of my 'own class'" (59).

This connection between Loy's alter ego and Insel perhaps explains Loy's choice to deepen Insel's position as a racialized exile-observer by fancifully coding him as Jewish and thereby aligning him with her portrayal of Stein (and implicitly herself) as a "Cosmopolitan Jew." This coding appears from the earliest moments of the novel, for instance, in Insel's belief that he's "found a foreshadowing of [his] hounded existence" in Franz Kafka's *The Trial* (1925), a novel publicly burned by the Nazis because of its author's Jewishness (34). Slanted aspects of *The Trial*, which tells of a wrongfully prosecuted man, surface in Insel's experiences, reinforcing this comparison. For instance, Insel recounts a time when he was squatting in an abandoned apartment building and heard someone going from door to door knocking. Opening his door, Insel came face to face with a policeman and was hauled into court on trespassing charges, an incident that recalls *Trial* protagonist Josef K's door-to-door search for the location of his first court interrogation in a rundown apartment building. Amused by this and other similarities, Jones teases Insel, "You atrocious fake—you have no life to write—you're *acting* Kafka" (35). This claim, and its reverberation in Jones' characterization of Insel as playing a "part in a film" (30), connects his fanciful Jewishness to the organizing thesis of "The Child and the Parent," the idea that personality is like "a roll of negative film." As both Kafka and Josef K. (and so simultaneously writer, character, and actor), Insel represents not a singularizing essence but a complex imagetextual performance, and one linked to the long persecuted "Cosmopolitan Jew."

Loy's characterization of Insel as also a *clochard*, or tramp, broadens the terms of his exclusion from the body politic and comments more specifically and positively on his lived and creative surrealism. In "A Hard Luck Story" (n.d.), an unpublished fragment that repeats episodes from *Insel* and thus was likely once part of the novel, Loy describes *clochards* as having been "disinherited" by "sane society" (1, 2). They represent the "psychological frontiers of [its] unvisited region," what Loy refers to in significantly visual terms as "the blind spot in the civil eye" (8, 6). The blind spot, or *punctum caecum*, is the place in each eye's visual field where the lack of light-detecting photoreceptor cells in the retina means that we can't see, but because the brain fills in data from the other eye, we don't notice. Loy suggests that *clochards'* intimacy with this blind spot surfaces in the grit of "primeval clay" that's in their eyes (5). This reference to the "impersonal dirt" from which we're all formed exceeds any one nation or ethnicity and thereby posits both a universal visual embodiment and an impersonal inheritance (1). Further specifying that inheritance, as well as the value of the *clochards'* particular perspective, Loy goes on to suggest that their meager existence on the margins and in the dirt allows them to make visible those places in the "human psyche" where "individual auras" merge with the "collective aura" and are modified by the "tenuous coherence" of the "race" (5).

This unpublished source material helps us to see that *Insel* itself includes these same biopolitical sentiments in a more elliptical form. Jones elaborates on Insel's *clochard* status by describing him as a "primordial soft-machine without the protective overall of the daily job" (23). This appeal to the "primordial" recalls Loy's claim that a *clochard*'s meager existence links him to the primeval clay from which the human race evolved (23). In addition, recalling the blind spot that *clochards* embody, Jones suggests that Insel's *clochard* status rendered him the "blind back" possessed but infrequently recognized by all (54). This "blind back" refers most basically to our inability to see what's behind us—to the limited field of vision differently suggested by the blind spot. Loy hints at these scientific underpinnings of the blind back in yet another story, her dialogue "Mi and Lo" (c. 1930s). In that story she invokes modern visual technologies and the higher dimensions of modern physics to explain that the "blind back of man is the shutter on the fourth dimension": "it is the arresting plane on which the universe like a cinema on the screen, through the medium of the senses, projects itself."[30] Here the blind back is the threshold of an unseen higher-dimensional universe and indeed the screen on which we can see projections from that universe, produced through the medium of our senses. Insel offers a surreal embodiment of the human race's blind back that allows him and his art to serve as a screen on which to view the nature of the material universe, including the materiality of the subject. More specifically, Jones sees Insel as a projected image of the eponymous hero of *My Man Godfrey*, a 1936 film that the two watch together, in which a tramp opens people's eyes to two things: the vagaries of social identity and the fact that one doesn't control matter by throwing things away.[31]

Jones' approval of Insel's aesthetic in these various moments of his subtle racialization supplies the frame for her excited appreciation of her experiential and aesthetic collaboration with him. Indeed, the complex visuality of Insel's racialization provides the language in which Jones expresses that appreciation. She imagines that her "one point of contact" with Insel is their "eye-caves," the "boney structure around the eye" behind and within which she believes impersonal subjectivity resides: "Quite apparently to my subconscious the bit of my skull encaving the fragile area flew off me, crashed

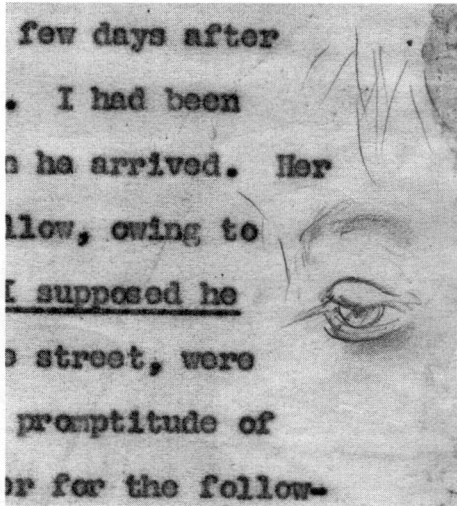

Fig. 3.6. Mina Loy. Marginal sketch of Insel's "eye-cave" on draft 2 of *Insel*. This sketch is one of many such illustrations on the *Insel* drafts, reinforcing the novel's imagetextuality. Yale Collection of American Literature, Beinecke Rare Book and Manuscript Library. Courtesy of Roger L. Conover.

onto his and stuck there. On the spur of this subvoluntary cohesion . . . I definitely penetrated (into) his mediumistic world where . . . whispered pictures took on a fair degree of resemblance to three-dimensional concretion" (66; see fig. 3.6).[32] Jones takes this embodied visual connection as an "impersonal responsibility" to record Insel's projections of subjectivity, understanding that this responsibility requires her to "giv[e] in to a dislocation of my identity" (69, 68). She commits to write Insel's life as that of a "person melted from view," a kind of impersonal biography (68). She also places this impersonalizing collaboration in line with her own aesthetic trajectory by comparing paintings from her recent exhibition with Insel's and noting their common attempt to "visualize the mists of chaos" (68, 37). She even suspects that it's this common visuality that allows her to perceive Insel's surreal projections of that chaos.[33]

One of Loy's own paintings from this period, a painting from the exhibition that just preceded her first meeting Oelze, offers a provocative glimpse of what Jones means by her shared visuality with Insel. *Teasing a Butterfly,* which Loy displayed in her 1933 Levy Gallery exhibition, features a background and faces that evoke a transcendent, celestial scene complete with

Fig. 3.7. Mina Loy, *Teasing a Butterfly*, c. 1933. Though this painting is dated 1902, it was likely done much later, around the time of Loy's 1933 Levy Gallery exhibition, of which it was a part. Burke notes that numerous paintings from this exhibition are misdated and that Levy may have encouraged Loy to use the earlier dates 1902 and 1903 in order to fetch higher prices (*BM* 379n). Private collection, Newtown, CT.

immortal cherubs. This surface scene, however, is sharply resituated within an embodied visual experience (fig. 3.7). The cherubs' empty eyes deflate their supposedly transcendent perspective, turning them into mere objects of the teased butterfly's field of vision—which is the actual focus of Loy's depiction. The proliferation of the cherubs' faces within circles of light represents not a sacred and omniscient immortality but rather the unique physiology of a butterfly's appositional compound eyes, each of which forms multiple images.[34] Loy plays with and denies a traditional linear perspective in painting this multiplicity and in her corresponding refusal of an exact center. Much like Duchamp's *Large Glass,* her painting replaces an older Cartesian perspectivalism with a physiological optics represented by the butterfly's nonmimetic, embodied vision. *Teasing a Butterfly* thus pictures the "chaos" of vision that Loy's alter ego, Mrs. Jones, describes and that she links with Insel's surreal impersonality.

Despite this shared visuality, though, Jones' sense of her sympathy with

Insel coexists with periods during which she wavers in her connection and responsibility to him, moments that dramatize Loy's hesitation over the politics of impersonality. At times, Jones fears and even loathes her collaboration with Insel, portraying him as a sort of archmodernist fiend, exploitative in his affiliations with both white and black women. These frequently sensational judgments exaggerate Loy's own early ambivalence about impersonality and mark her residual concern about the political efficacy of her subsequent formulations of it. Jones' sensationalism suggests that Loy felt that she had to indulge the worst critique imaginable of modernism's impersonal aesthetic before delivering her verdict.

Loy tellingly marks the shifts in Jones' appraisal of Insel's surrealism by transforming her visual metaphors for their collaboration, metaphors that nonetheless continue to signal the visual-scientific vernacular of both surrealism and Loy's own impersonal aesthetic. Jones initially understands Insel's material dependence on women as an accidental by-product of his process of *Entwicklung,* or development, through which he creates an identity akin to an endlessly reproducible photographic image rather than a singular coherent self. Jones notes that this process could just as readily support a reverse gender dynamic. For instance, while Insel has indulged his own development by leaning on women financially, Jones records his desire to marry her daughter—or rather, more surreally, her daughter's photograph—and to *"watch* her evolve": "It would be a very wonderful thing indeed to take part in [her] *Entwicklung,"* Insel declares (146). This desire shows Insel's willingness to switch roles, to support a woman's development as he's been supported. And it suggests that he sees Jones' daughter's subjectivity in the same terms as his own. Indeed, his focus on her photograph casts her as a similarly reproducible image rather than a coherent self, while his sense that her photo can evolve is a sharp departure from the traditionally feminine static image.

When Jones begins to fear that Insel's relationships with women are actually parasitic and that her spectatorial role in their collaboration does little more than objectify her, Loy resorts to a very different metaphor of instrumentation. In a fragment from draft 1, Jones analogizes Insel's aesthetic to a search for an optical instrument that will "contract diffused distance" and so bring "the unprecedented patterns" of the "cosmic obviousness he faces" within "view." Such a search dovetails with a 1942 interview in which Loy calls for an instrument that "would reduce to our focus the forms of entities hitherto visually illimitable" ("Towards the Unknown" 10). And yet in the published novel Jones decries the fact that Insel makes her into this desired instrument by positioning her in multiple passive roles—a visual object, a spectator, and a work of art. She feels that through his "wracking attentive-ness" to her and his simultaneous constitution of her as his audience, Insel finds in her "a reduction of focus to penetrate into the real world," and in the process "churn[s] me with his eyes into the colorless vapors of his cre-ation" (57, 56, 57). In Jones' view, this instrumentation cancels her own sta-tus as a fellow painter and writer and demotes her to the status of a passive element of Insel's surrealism. That passivity takes its ultimate form in the idea that she would be the actual material of Insel's art, one of the "vapors of his creation." Jones goes on to cast this transformation in terms that draw out its gendered visuality. She imagines that she has become, not just a spectator to Insel's art, but a spectator "encumbered with an enormous shell white as plaster" that "trailed to an end in a sail of mist" (66).[35] This descrip-tion can't help but evoke Sandro Botticelli's famous *Birth of Venus* (c. 1485), wherein that goddess of love and beauty is shown rising from the waves on a large scallop shell. Jones feels, in other words, that she has been reduced to Insel's surreal take on that painting and on its iconic femininity.

Jones' attitude toward Insel's relationship with several black prostitutes inflects these unstable gender politics of his impersonality with a negative racial politics. Insel repeatedly brags about his sexual relationships with these "negresses" but at the same time implies their inferiority by lamenting that he can't get rid of them (40). Jones rebukes him for his rough handling of these women (his attempt to push them off when they try to share his cigarettes), as well as his material reliance on them (the fact that they buy him meals). She declares that his own great suffering as an exile can't excuse his poor treatment of "a race whose ostracism 'debunks' humanity's osten-sible belief in its soul"—a race, in other words, similarly exiled (79). More-over, by imagining that Insel "look[s] very Simon Legree" (89), Jones hyper-bolically inflates his treatment of these prostitutes to match Legree's sexual abuse of his slaves Emmeline and Casey in Harriet Beecher Stowe's *Uncle Tom's Cabin* (1852). She later connects Insel's exploitation—his belief that that was the "way to handle negresses"—to his conduct toward her, claim-ing that he "has notions as to how white women should be handled, too" (89, 170).

Jones punctuates the menace of such handling by repeatedly associating Insel and his art with the excessive materiality of the corpse. If the corpse marked a kind of ambivalence in Pound's imagism, it similarly expresses here

Fig. 3.8. Mina Loy, marginal sketch of Insel's detritus projections on draft 2 of *Insel*. Yale Collection of American Literature, Beinecke Rare Book and Manuscript Library. Courtesy of Roger L. Conover.

Loy's lingering fear that an impersonal aesthetic might extinguish the force of the self without there being any corresponding release from socially constraining notions of identity. In her moments of uncertainty Jones resists Insel's surreal projections of impersonality—expressed in his art, his pronouncements, and even his mode of being—as the detritus of a corpse. She suggests that these "infinitesimal currents ran out of him" and "grew longer and longer as the hair of the dead, it is maintained, will leisurely fill a coffin" (50; see fig. 3.8). She likewise registers the messages carried on these currents as frightening inevitabilities, recoiling, for instance, from Insel's proclamation "*Sterben—Man Muß*" (Die, one must) and from his sense that memory "come[s] to life when fed on the same sort of stuff as that which formed it" (73, 69). In addition, contemplating Insel's painting *Die Irma*, which of course means "The Irma" in German but looks more like the imperative "Die, Irma" in English, she connects the eponymous figure with a menacing mode of heightened vision. Irma's eyes "illuminate" "an inner and outer darkness," a fundamental opacity in the human subject (132). Jones even punctuates the threat of this vision by imagining that the painting is "formed . . . of pus" from Irma's decaying body (132), seeming to allude to Oelze's drawing *Frieda*, which was acquired by the Museum of Modern Art, likely with Loy's assistance, for its 1936 *Fantastic Art, Dada and Surrealism* exhibit (fig. 3.9).[36]

Fig. 3.9. Richard Oelze, *Frieda,* 1936. Museum of Modern Art, New York. *Frieda* is strikingly similar to *Die Irma.* She stands "knee-deep" on the canvas and has hands that "ju[t] out from her body" as "if nailed to her hips like crossed swords." These hands "hardly ma[k]e a pair," because the one has "the bones on the back marked all of equal length" and "the other" has "one finger" that is "too long with an unmodeled edge which curved like paper against the background" (*Insel* 130, 131). Courtesy of Hans Brockstedt and of the Museum of Modern Art/Licensed by SCALA/Art Resource, NY.

Jones' similarly anxious response to another Insel painting—this one untitled, but a fictional counterpart to Oelze's *Expectation*—further underscores her intermittent suspicion of Insel's visuality (fig. 3.10). *Expectation* features a group of people gazing at an ominous sky and is quite possibly an allusion to the famous June 1926 cover of *La Révolution Surréaliste* magazine (fig. 3.11). This art magazine, which was published from 1924 to 1929, styled itself after scientific journals of the period, like *La Nature,* and this particular cover features a 1912 Eugène Atget photograph of a group of people staring at a

Fig. 3.10. Richard Oelze, *Expectation,* 1935-36. Museum of Modern Art, New York. Courtesy of Hans Brockstedt and of the Museum of Modern Art/Licensed by SCALA/ Art Resource, NY.

solar eclipse with the aid of pinhole projectors.[37] *La Révolution Surréaliste* playfully retitles Atget's photograph *The Last Conversions,* melding the phys-ical universe of astronomy (represented by the eclipse and its conversion of light to darkness) with the metaphysical universe of Judeo-Christian religion (the conversion of darkness to light, as in the biblical proclamation "and there was light" in Genesis 1:3). Oelze's title, *Expectation,* implies that the conversion, whether in the form of a solstice or a new and committed belief, is yet to come for his gazers.

This implication aptly fits Jones' attitude toward Insel's similar painting. Just as Loy, acting as an agent for the Levy Gallery, had shipped *Expectation* to the United States, Jones is preparing to send Insel's unnamed painting there. In a letter to a friend that mirrors one that Loy sent to her daughter Fabienne about *Expectation,* Jones describes the painting as "a gigantic back of a commonplace woman looking at the sky" and admits warily that she catches herself "staring at that sky waiting, oblivious of time, for whatever

No 7 — Deuxième année   15 Juin 1926

LA RÉVOLUTION
SURRÉALISTE

LES DERNIÈRES CONVERSIONS

SOMMAIRE

L'enclume des forces : Antonin Artaud
Le surréalisme et la peinture : André Breton.
RÊVES
Marcel Noll, Michel Leiris.
POÈMES :
Robert Desnos, Philippe Soupault, Paul Eluard,
Antonin Artaud, Michel Leiris.
TEXTES SURRÉALISTES :
Louis Aragon, Arp.
A la fenêtre : Paul Eluard.
Derniers efforts et mort du prévôt :
Pierre de Massot.

La dernière nuit du condamné à mort :
Benjamin Péret.
Le Pont de la mort : René Crevel.
CHRONIQUES :
L'opportunisme impuissant : Marcel Fourrier.
Liberté, liberté chérie : Maxime Alexandre.
Protestation : L. Aragon, A. Breton.
Georgia : Louis Aragon.
Correspondance. Notes.
ILLUSTRATIONS :
Arp, Giorgio de Chirico, Georges Malkine,
André Masson, Picasso, Man Ray, Pierre Roy,
Dédé Sunbeam, Yves Tanguy, etc.

Fig. 3.11. Cover of *La Révolution Surréaliste* 7 (June 1926). The photograph, by Eugène Atget, documents Parisians using protective viewers to witness the solar eclipse of 1912.

is about to appear in it" (20, 21).[38] Of course, *Expectation* features a group of people rather than a single woman, and Jones' partial perception implies that she's so thoroughly identified herself with one of those figures that she doesn't actually see the rest of the painting. Indeed, her description of waiting as "oblivious[ness]" suggests that what she finds "[m]ost eerie" in the painting is precisely its looming sense of partiality or incompletion—an inevitability in any act of vision (21).

While Atget's photograph registers the limits of vision in the fact that the crowd must use a pinhole projector to protect their eyes from the sun, *Expectation* records these limits instead through the fact that almost everyone is turned away from the viewer's gaze and those whose faces are partially unobstructed have no eyes. This partiality, if not outright opacity, is matched by the threat of a perpetually uncompleted act, the unarrival of whatever is to appear in the sky, and the fact that Jones continually catches herself staring at it. Incompletion in both forms suggests the way that a subjectivity organized around opaque limits undoes self-determination, including not only the ability to know what's going on in the world but even the ability to know one's own feelings and actions. Jones' resulting anxiety about incompletion, which recalls Pater's apprehension about Leonardo's unfinished works, is the foil for her positive impressions of Insel's program of *Entwicklung*. These two notions—incompletion and development—together neatly summarize the poles of her shifting responses to Insel's surrealism, poles that I have shown map Loy's ambivalence regarding the politics of impersonality. Given that each of these notions proposes a trajectory and that the novel is driven by the oscillating positions that Jones takes, the one she finally chooses determines the shape and meaning of Loy's map: whether she harbors her original skepticism about impersonality or leaves it behind. While Roger Conover and Elizabeth Arnold have read Jones as eventually rejecting the "disintegrated self" (Arnold 180) that Insel's vision offers, Andrew Gaedtke's more recent examination uncovers the novel's commitment to the opaque subjectivity of Freudian psychoanalysis, a discourse that saturated surrealism and participated in the modern scientific vernacular of vision.[39] I argue similarly that Jones finally endorses the political potential of Insel's surrealism, and so of modernist impersonality, by reasserting the commonalities between her aesthetic and Insel's, not at the level of the action but at the level of the narrative itself. This affinity suggests that *Insel* embraces the embodied limits of perception traced in the scientific vernacular of vision and figured in the imagetextuality of modernist impersonality rather than seeking to "overthrow" those limits or to create an "intertransparency of word and image," as Tyrus Miller has argued (217).

At the novel's close, Jones and Insel are estranged. Their impersonal collaboration has ceased with some amount of scorn, and each is leaving Paris because of the approaching war. As an offhand gesture, Jones has invited Insel to a café with the thought of a parting truce. Her disingenuous friendliness and Insel's clear annoyance about it, coupled with the real sensationalism of her negative impressions of him, seem to weight the novel finally against his aesthetic. However, two aspects of this meeting shift that balance. First, Insel's projections once again allow Jones to register those aspects of the human subject that exceed the personal. She feels her embodied status as a "reductive perceiver" and one for whom concepts "become gnarled . . . through restriction to the brain's capacity." But she also feels "magnifie[d] and enlarged" and that "time seemed, like light, to arrive in rays focusing on the brain at a minimum akin to images on retinas; and the further one projected one's being to meet it, the *broader* one found it to be" (173). On the one hand, then, Jones realizes that the eyes and the brain are alike governed by material limits; but on the other hand, and in tune with the mechanics of vision and the relative rather than absolute nature of time, she feels that she's partially exceeded her perceptual limits by exceeding her prior sense of being. She prizes this awareness of embodied subjectivity and of the limits of knowledge, gathered from what she calls her "communicative impersonality [with Insel], the final relationship of distinct similars confronting the same phenomenon" (174). With this approval and sense of similarity, Jones again reinvests in her collaboration with Insel even though she also criticizes his aesthetic during this same encounter.

The second aspect of this final scene that affirms Insel's surrealism, and so an impersonal aesthetic, depends on our alertness to the temporal split between Jones the character in the café and Jones the narrator looking back on her. If the former persists in questioning Insel's values, the latter fully endorses them. When Insel asks Jones how her impersonal biography (which, significantly, she's now writing alone) is coming, she exclaims, "[W]onderfully," and adds, "*Man muß reif sein*—One must be ripe" (177). Such an exclamation is clearly meant to displace Insel's impersonal message, "*Sterben—Man Muß.*" It's not surprising, then, that Jones' thoughts at this moment condemn the perpetual incompleteness of Insel's *Expectation* painting, suggesting that the woman in it will have lost patience and left by the time the signs she's waiting for appear. Jones imagines that "that commonplace back of a woman watching for signs on his painted firmament turned in anonymous patience to his chart of unarrival" but adds that "[t]he curtain of the sky came down and she was not there" (176). The narrative, however, contains this rejection of Insel by emphasizing the gap between this Jones experiencing the narrative events and the one recounting them. When the former states that her book is "going wonderfully," the latter explains: "I was feeling exceptionally 'good' about my work just then, *vainly imagining I had criticized my last incompletion*" (177, emphasis added). Thus, while the character Jones felt that she was successfully pursuing an aesthetic counter to Insel's, the narrator Jones retrospectively recognizes that feeling's falsity and places the principle of incompletion at the center of their shared project.

In other words, although incompletion has been a negative symbol of Insel's surrealism to this point, the novel acts finally to revalue it as a central gesture of an impersonality that no longer triggers Loy's political concerns and that may even bear political potential. While Jones does bemoan that the final "destination" of "the thousand directions" in Insel's aesthetic is "Nothingness," she also expresses what is in fact the novel's final word on the incompletion these directions signal and on their significance for embodied identity (176). Describing his fragmented impersonality and the awareness it inspires, Jones explains, "It was not black as night nor white as day; nor gray as death—only a nonexistent irritation as to what purposed inconsequence has led us into the illusion of ever having come into being" (176). This explanation positions Insel's incompletion as a sign of the impossibility of self-presence and a challenge to any stable, identitarian notion of being, because it announces that we are but an "illusion." In addition, by associating this challenge with a "nonexistent irritation" rather the "gray [of] death," Jones also refuses to equate impersonality with extinction, as she had previously done in her negative characterizations of Insel as a corpse. Thus Loy's persistent concern that "Nothingness" represents a unique threat for women—a concern repeatedly reflected in Jones' responses to Insel—appears to have receded. Moreover, Jones' language in fact suggests a reason for this withdrawal. Loy had earlier praised Stein for recording how the "flux of Being" produces the Italians' complex racialization, and here she takes this idea one step further by suggesting that being is itself illusory. This more radical notion of impersonality displaces the very terms according to which her various concerns about social hierarchies have been organized. We see such a displacement in Jones' reference to Insel's aesthetic as being neither "black . . . nor white." Jones has consistently expressed concerns about impersonality in terms of racialized gender, and the coding of black and white in racial terms has been a stark and important aspect of her evaluation of Insel's aesthetic. Thus, when she uses these terms to convey that Insel's aesthetic eludes the categories into which she has tried to place it, she implies that racial aspect of the text as well. Insel's projections blur black and white, eliding embodied identities and even the coherence of being, but without announcing an utter ontological end.

This interpretation of the novel's close gains force and historical depth not only in the light of Loy's many theorizations and performances of the impersonal mode, from "The Ceiling" to "Gertrude Stein," but also in light of Insel's own complex textual history. Like Jones, who realizes that she can't get beyond her last incompletion, Loy repeatedly revised *Insel* from 1935 until at least 1961, variously reordering, supplementing, and subtracting from its surreal map of the very "frontier of . . . individuality" (65). Her extensive reworking of the novel underscores the fact that incompletion was finally key to the potential she registered in its aesthetic and to the particular understanding of (visual) embodiment that anchored that aesthetic. If Loy had been grappling with the shape of subjectivity through questions of vision and embodiment across her career, the principle of incompletion offered a nuanced take on both that effort and that shape. As Pater had registered before her, to recognize the incomplete nature of seeing and being is to gain a partial view into the body's opacity, even as that opacity can't simply be overcome. Loy's attempt to publish *Insel* in 1961 suggests that in her own estimate her protracted acknowledgment of impersonal subjectivity had finally afforded her a limited but valuable sense of its contours.

Given Loy's longstanding pains to resolve modernist impersonality for herself and others, it seems fitting to close with one last imagetextual image from the end of her career—one that again signals the importance of embodied vision to her aesthetic. Figure 3.12 shows the author photograph that Loy organized for the dust jacket of *Lunar Baedeker & Time-Tables* (1958), a re-release of some of her earlier poetry and the last collection published in her lifetime. Loy asked her publisher, Jonathan Williams, to crop the photograph to show only her darkened eyes (*BM*, photo caption). This image replaces the stable and mimetic picture personality of *Auto-Facial-Construction* with a fragment that gazes out in a kind of opaque resistance to self-expression. Such a refiguring of the author function stands by *Insel*'s final commitment to modernism's optical impersonality and thus becomes a key for the "Baedeker" of impersonal subjectivity offered in many of the volume's poems. Indeed, the impressive jacket blurbs over which Loy's impersonal eyes preside point to the way that her poetry teaches lessons similar to those of H.D. (Edward Dahlberg) and was somehow beneath, behind, and beyond Pound's imagism (Alfred Kreymborg). Walter Lowenfels even registers Loy's own "playful physics," to return to Duchamp's phrase, in his claim that she "broke the sound barrier with words long before the Dog Star did, and still gives that feeling of panic that hits you when a poem arrives." Lowenfels' metaphor renders Loy's "lunar Baedeker" brighter than the brightest star seen from Earth. Its words are visual. They travel at the speed of light, which is faster than the speed of sound; and they hit upon your perception with the shock wave of breaking the sound barrier. According to this reading,

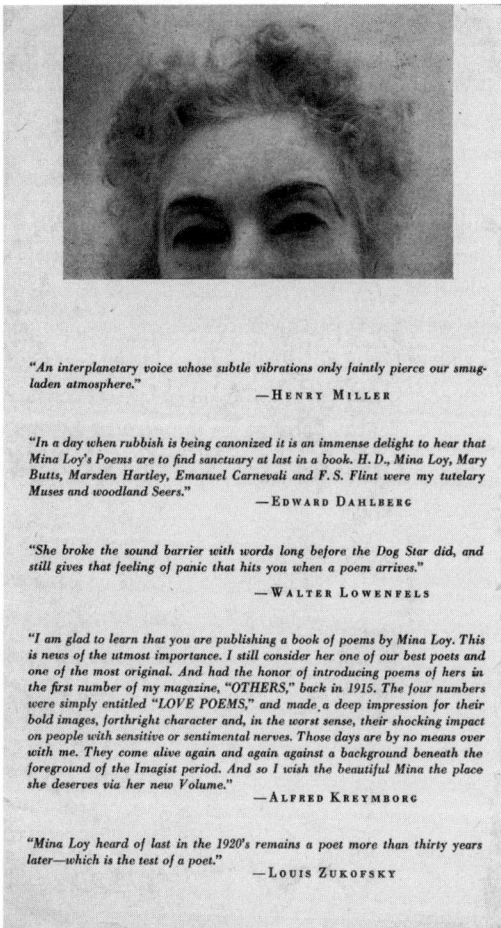

"*An interplanetary voice whose subtle vibrations only faintly pierce our smug-laden atmosphere.*"
—HENRY MILLER

"*In a day when rubbish is being canonized it is an immense delight to hear that Mina Loy's Poems are to find sanctuary at last in a book. H. D., Mina Loy, Mary Butts, Marsden Hartley, Emanuel Carnevali and F. S. Flint were my tutelary Muses and woodland Seers.*"
—EDWARD DAHLBERG

"*She broke the sound barrier with words long before the Dog Star did, and still gives that feeling of panic that hits you when a poem arrives.*"
—WALTER LOWENFELS

"*I am glad to learn that you are publishing a book of poems by Mina Loy. This is news of the utmost importance. I still consider her one of our best poets and one of the most original. And had the honor of introducing poems of hers in the first number of my magazine, "OTHERS," back in 1915. The four numbers were simply entitled "LOVE POEMS," and made a deep impression for their bold images, forthright character and, in the worst sense, their shocking impact on people with sensitive or sentimental nerves. Those days are by no means over with me. They come alive again and again against a background beneath the foreground of the Imagist period. And so I wish the beautiful Mina the place she deserves via her new Volume.*"
—ALFRED KREYMBORG

"*Mina Loy heard of last in the 1920's remains a poet more than thirty years later—which is the test of a poet.*"
—LOUIS ZUKOFSKY

Fig. 3.12. Back of dust jacket of Mina Loy's *Lunar Baedeker & Time-Tables,* 1958. Courtesy of the Black Mountain College Museum + Arts Center, Black Mountain, NC.

Loy offers an imagetextual view of the phenomenon perpetually promised in the darkened sky of Insel/Oelze's *Expectation,* a view of an impersonal materiality.

The rigor and indeed multiplicity of Loy's imagetextual account of impersonality across her career introduces us to new facets of this modernist aesthetic. From her marshaling of physics' concern with visualization to her appeal to body culture and surrealism as part of a modern scientific vernacular of vision, Loy shows how impersonality adapted a physiological optics and drew out its epistemological, ontological, and social implications. Even in her ultimate acceptance of the liberatory potential of impersonality, Loy doesn't simply second the political certainties offered by Pater, Field, and H.D. Her greater ambivalence moves us toward registering the broad sociopolitical spectrum along which modernists situated an impersonal aesthetic. She poses the question whether a writer who commits to the embodied image and observer of the modern scientific vernacular of vision inevitably rethinks embodied identity from the ground up and in a liberating way. In the next chapter we'll see D. H. Lawrence's answer to this question, aspects of which mark precisely the possibilities that shaped Loy's anxieties.[40] Not only did Lawrence see a way to retain and even bolster conservative formulations of embodied identity through an impersonal aesthetic, he did so with consistently more confidence than Loy mustered.

4 D. H. Lawrence's Impersonal Imperative
Vision, Bodies, and the Recovery of Identity

> I am sick and tired of personality in every way. Let us be
> easy and impersonal, not forever fingering over our own
> souls, and the souls of our acquaintances, but trying to
> create a new life, a new common life, a new complete tree
> of life from the roots that are within us.
>
> Lawrence to Katherine Mansfield, 12 December 1915

> [W]e are none of us more than a cell in the eye-tissue . . . of
> the macrocosm, the universe.
>
> Lawrence, draft fragment of "John Galsworthy"

Perhaps no modernist is so thoroughly associated with a concern to perceive and know through the body and the material world as D. H. Lawrence. In addition, perhaps no modernist has been read in such multitudinous and polemical ways with regard to this concern. Kate Millett, for instance, famously condemned Lawrence's investment in embodiment as the shell for an essentializing patriarchy, while Gilles Deleuze and Félix Guattari just as famously championed his model of flows, vibrations, and circuits for refusing both a mind/body split and any notion of fixed essences. Anne Fernihough has explained this wide range of critical responses by pointing to Lawrence's simultaneous use of conflicting notions of the organic, arguing that he effectively advances a protofascistic nativism and faith in semantic totality, on the one hand, and a canceling pluralistic belief in dynamism, material opacity, and rich polysemy, on the other. I posit here a slightly different economy for the aesthetic and ideological slipperiness of Lawrence's understanding of materiality, even as I trace the key role that this slipperiness played in his related formulation of modernist impersonality. Lawrence's adaptation of modern science and intervention in a scientific vernacular of vision moved strategically both toward and against political conservatism, so that his writing highlights the spectrum of political possibilities Loy recognized in impersonality. Indeed, Lawrence uses the indeterminacy that marks impersonal subjectivity in the liberatory formulations of that aesthetic in order to keep more conservative notions of individuality and identity in play; he portrays these conservative notions as themselves part of indeterminacy and therefore of the shift and flux of subjectivity. Pushing this strategy to its limit, Lawrence intermittently recovers individuality and various forms of embodied identity after destabilizing the social and biological bases for their existence. He even seems, paradoxically, to render such notions all the more unassailable for having no firm origins or contours, effectively creating a bulwark against the aesthetic politics of Pater, Field, H.D., and Loy.

Despite Lawrence's exhortation to "be easy and impersonal" and his belief that we are but "a cell in the eye-tissue" of the "universe," scholars have rarely linked his brand of individualism with modernist impersonality or with the physiological optics that impersonality draws out. Michael Bell, Michèle Hita, and, much earlier, F. R. Leavis have all pointed to Lawrence's focus on the "noumenal elusiveness" of true feeling, often falsified in personal consciousness (Bell 144). But they also oppose this focus to the "impersonality that the techniques of modernism sought to achieve" (Bell 133). Similarly, Daniel Albright has argued that Lawrence displayed not so much a "search for impersonality" as a kind of retro-Romantic "expression of enormous personalness" (9).

For a long time, critics likewise distanced Lawrence's aesthetic from modern science, directed not least by his own dismissive claim that science was "wretched in its treatment of the human body as a sort of complex . . . machine" and, more vehemently, that "scientists are liars."[1] Fernihough maintains, for example, that if there's any core to Lawrence's work, it's his dislike of scientific method (156–57); and Eliseo Vivas (45) and Michael Black (90) both argue that Lawrence refused all scientific vocabulary and explanation as debilitating mental abstractions. Lawrence's vitriol against modern science, however, didn't actually purify his work of terms, analogies, and even methods that adapt science into aesthetic form. Recent scholarship has begun to grapple with this fact, focusing mainly on contradiction—the sense that Lawrence often disagreed on the surface with scientists and scientific philosophers only to commit to them at a more fundamental level (Craig Gordon; Granofsky). We might further nuance this analysis, though, by recognizing that Lawrence's disagreements were quite consistently with positivism and that he was less resistant to modern science as a whole. A one-time student and teacher of science, Lawrence in fact consistently endorsed what he called a provisional "alert science" ("Introduction to These Paintings" 208).[2]

The ingredients of this alert science include the evolutionary theory, psychoanalysis, and physics that recent scholarship has begun to connect to Lawrence's work.[3] But what unites his adaption of these disciplines is the embodied image and observer that anchors the visual-scientific vernacular and an impersonal subjectivity that follows from it. Lawrence's engagement of this vernacular leads to the most radical moments in his writing, such as the posthumanism that Jeff Wallace has identified. Here, Lawrence refuses to think of the human as a transcendent category; attacks Cartesian dualism's separation of the mind from materiality and its presumption of self-presence; and rejects the idea that science (or any other epistemology) is an objective mode of knowing. At other moments, though, Lawrence adapts his science to recuperate an individuality and fixed sense of difference long caught up with the Cartesian subject, leading scholars like Jonathan Dollimore to condemn his commitment to a "self which is a law unto itself" (269).

The role of the visual-scientific vernacular in Lawrence's work reframes the more substantial critical attention paid to his investment in modern visual culture.[4] Despite his ideological differences from some stylists of impersonality, Lawrence's aesthetic marshals multiple forms of visual culture—sometimes positively, as with postimpressionist painting, and sometimes negatively, as with popular photography. Lawrence adapted a physiological optics precisely through these visual appeals and attempted to piece together what he saw as the epistemological, ontological, and sociopolitical implications of a corresponding impersonal subjectivity. Lawrence described his poetry, for example, as bodily "act[s] of attention" and his critical writing as provisional attempts to "abstract some definite conclusions" from the resulting percepts.[5] An examination of several of his often neglected poems and essays about poetry shows that they attend to an embodied subjectivity in excess of the person and develop an imagetextual form for representing it with increasing insistence and detail. Lawrence's critical writing in two areas, painting and psychoanalysis, transforms his poetic acts of attention into an alert science of the psychophysiology of vision that works both toward and against individuality and embodied identities like gender and race. Ultimately, though, Lawrence believed that the novel, more than any other genre, records and "affect[s] the whole man-alive."[6] His last novel, *Lady Chatterley's Lover* (1929), stages his alert science and its slippery ideological and aesthetic economy by serving as a scientific experiment in survival. This experiment uses an embodied model of vision to instruct readers in two areas: first, in the limits of an exclusively personal and an improperly impersonal view of being, and second, in the adaptive value of accepting one's embodied impersonal imperatives. Lawrence wields these imperatives to simultaneously refuse and carve out a niche for individuality and identity.

"Chaos Lit Up by Visions": Poetic Attention and Its Material Limits

In his preface to the American edition of *New Poems* (1920) Lawrence explains that there are two kinds of poetry, deriving from two understandings of "Time": the poetry of "the beginning and . . . the end" and the poetry of the "at hand."[7] He warns against the former type, which *seems* to offer the great satisfaction of "the infinite or the eternal" and of a "crystalline" or transparent "ideal" (*CP* 616, 616, 618). He also explains that the latter type—which has "no perfection, no consummation, nothing finished" (*CP* 616)—actually offers a truer view of "all the universe" (*CP* 618). This schematic, with its displacement of an absolute temporality and situated view of the universe, broadly echoes the thrust of Einstein's theory of relativity.[8] Relativity is the idea that space and time are interwoven in a single continuum—a fourth dimension of space-time—that can be experienced differently by different observers based on the observers' velocity and on the distorting effects of gravitation, which cause a curvature in space. Lawrence's schematic also speaks more directly to the complex systems of physiology and indeed against "biologists," who he believes "fix the living tissue . . . with formation" (*CP* 616). At-hand poetry, within which Lawrence locates his own work, records "the incarnate disclosure of the flux": the "emerging and flowing off" of "living tissue" and "plasm," "always open in their transit" (*CP* 616) and always "seething" with the "confusion" of "the soul and the mind and the body surging at once" (*CP* 616, 617, 617). Such a vocabulary, wherein "the quick of the universe is the *pulsating, carnal self*," folds relativity and its uprooting of absolute space and time into a psychophysiological science of movement and function that uproots the sharp divides of Cartesian dualism (*CP* 617).

A few years later, Lawrence's essay "Chaos in Poetry" (1929), also published as his introduction to Harry Crosby's poetry volume *Chariot of the*

Sun (1931), uses human vision to elaborate on this macrocosmic physiology, which encompasses the universe and the human mindbody in a living and distinctly open system. This later essay suggests that good poetry "makes a new effort of attention" toward the "for ever surging chaos" of the macrocosmic physiology and that this effort is sometimes—though indeed only sometimes—"lit up by visions, . . . [j]ust as the rainbow may or may not light up the storm" (*P* 255). Poetic attention in this analogy is not only distinctly visual; it's also thereby fleeting and material, like the refractions and reflections that produce a rainbow, that is, a visible spectrum of light. Lawrence argues that because people don't want chaos or opacity or invisible light, they paper over these material fluctuations and limits with images of "stability, fixity," and "apparent form" (*P* 255). He figures this compensatory effort as the act of holding up an umbrella against the storm and painting a picture of a clear sky on the inside. He suggests that his brand of poetic attention works against this desire for immediacy, order, and stability by variously slicing through the umbrella's images to give a view of the "chaos *alive*" beyond: "Then comes a poet, enemy of convention, and makes a slit in the umbrella; and lo! The glimpse of chaos is a vision" (*P* 258, 255). Lawrence reinforces the incomplete nature of this vision by emphasizing that the "act of attention" is a "groping" effort rather than a total discarding of the umbrella; but he also notes that "failure is [itself] part of the living chaos," not a barrier to it (*P* 261). Just as importantly, Lawrence explicitly casts a melding of image and text as a formal marker of this "groping" and the physiology that it works to perceive. He criticizes the idea that poetry is merely "a matter of words" as "pictures are a matter of paint," arguing instead that "poetry is a stringing together of words into a ripple . . . of colors[,] . . . an interplay of images," and that this "interplay" of words and images "'discovers' a new world within the known world" (*P* 255). Lawrence's poetic commitment to representing material opacity and the limits to knowledge, coupled with his belief that this work is distinctly visual and imagetextual, signals that the modern scientific vernacular of vision offered an important context for his thinking about subjectivity. His poetic attention and this visual vernacular share an insistence on the embodied and incoherent nature of the observer and the fragmented, temporal, and fluctuating nature of the image.

One way to concretize this connection between a visual-scientific vernacular and Lawrence's poetics is to juxtapose his rather odd formulation of an umbrella covered with slits to popular optical toys like the anorthoscope, the zoetrope, and the zoopraxiscope, all of which first appeared as part of

Fig. 4.1. Anorthoscope, c. 1840s. In this photograph, the outer, slit disc has been removed to show the inner, figural disc. Collection of François Binétruy.

the new physiology of vision in the nineteenth century. Invented by the Belgian physicist Joseph Plateau, the anorthoscope is particularly meaningful in this context because Helmholtz used it as part of his optical research on form perception, and it had a long afterlife among a modern public interested in optical illusions (fig. 4.1).[9] The device includes two circular discs mounted one behind the other, each capable of rotating at varying speeds in different directions; the outer disc contains a series of slits through which a viewer sees fragments of the stretched forms printed on the inner disc. While these discs were spinning, observers looking through the slits could recognize the underlying form—despite, or indeed because of, the limits placed upon their view. Lawrence's odd figure of a slit umbrella (with its similar circular shape) likewise reveals only small portions of the chaos beyond. But Lawrence has faith that the poetic acts of attention that make the slits in the umbrella can also sense the contours of chaos, in part precisely through their failure to render its complete form. A similar visuality—one focused on encounters and interferences over the absolutes of Cartesian perspective— thus underwrites both Lawrence's poetics and a scientific vernacular of embodied vision.[10]

Lawrence's poem "Virgin Youth" (1916), particularly his utter rewriting of it for inclusion in his *Collected Poems* (1928), aptly plays out this visuality and does so significantly through an experiential record of an opaque, unwilled subjectivity that's thoroughly embodied. Lawrence makes clear in his prefatory note to *Collected Poems* that he was dissatisfied with "Virgin Youth" as it appeared in his early volume *Amores* (1916), because he had allowed his mental-rational self to "interfer[e] with his demon" (*CP* 619-20 at 620). The revised "Virgin Youth," by contrast, "trie[s] to let the demon say his say" (*CP* 620). As the poem's title suggests, this "demon" is most explicitly the sexual impulses that overwhelm the virginal Lawrentian speaker. More fundamentally, though, the term signifies a subjectivity beyond the person, which the poem registers in terms of a break from habitual perception and an awareness of materiality and which it describes through a visual-scientific vernacular.

The early version of "Virgin Youth" outlines two modes of being—one personal, the other impersonal—by appealing to the characteristics of light waves and of electromagnetic radiation more broadly. Because such waves are polarized, their vibrations are restricted to a particular directional flow. "Virgin Youth" equates the speaker's shift away from personal being with a release from this polarization: "the life that is polarized in my eyes" suddenly "[f]lies like a wild thing across my body," awakening "passionate waves" in that body and "[l]eaving my eyes half-empty" (lines 3, 5, 9, 6). Drained of their "flame," or radiant energy, the speaker's eyes go vacant, and he gives in to the chaotic and autonomic "flood of life" in his body (lines 7, 20). Eventually, though, the polarization "reasserts itself," and the speaker's impersonal state passes (line 19). In effect, "Virgin Youth" mediates between a conventional, circumscribed vision that corresponds to the painted-umbrella perspective that Lawrence denigrates—here the "relentless nodality of my vision" (line 19)—and a "wild," "knotted" physiology that corresponds with the chaos beyond that umbrella (line 14). Written four years before Lawrence's preface to *New Poems* and twelve years before he developed his umbrella analogy, "Virgin Youth" shows that he's already formulating aspects of his macrocosmic physiology and warning against the restrictive presumptions of a habitual visual perspective. He's also already appealing to a scientific vernacular to develop these ideas.

The particular visuality of "Virgin Youth," however, is also less consistent than in Lawrence's later essays. While the depolarizing release of the speaker's radiant waves throughout the body troubles the mental ascendancy of Cartesian dualism, the poem nonetheless follows a Cartesian visuality by linking the eye strictly to the mind and staging a temporary evacuation of that mind's eye rather than the rise of an embodied vision. In addition, the poem figures the speaker's turn to an unwilled bodily state rather ambivalently by describing it as both "beautiful" and "tyrann[ical]" (lines 21, 17). Moreover, the poem ends without either mode of being—the visual-mental or the bodily—offering fulfillment: the "relentless nodality of [the speaker's] eyes reasserts itself," and he's left both "[t]ired and unsatisfied" (lines 19, 22). There's no clear sense of whether the dissatisfaction and exhaustion come from the return to a visual-mental being, from the body's "bursten flood of life," or both (line 20). Even the poem's form suggests ambivalence: it doesn't display fragmented acts of attention, as Lawrence would soon frame his at-hand poetics, but instead unfolds in two prosaic sentences that chart a thoughtful, withdrawn meditation, more mental than complexly experiential.

Lawrence's 1928 revision of "Virgin Youth" sheds this ambivalence and embraces the scientific visuality of his essays. The life that "looks through [the speaker's] eyes" and "behaves like the rest of men" still "slips away," but it's now replaced by a continued act of visual attention to what the speaker labels his "lower me" rather than simply an uncontrolled radiation in the body (*CP* 6-8, lines 2, 2, 4, 15):

> How beautiful he is! without sound,
> Without eyes, without hands;
> Yet, flame of the living ground
> He stands, the column of fire by night.
> And he knows from the depths; he quite
> Alone understands. (lines 24-29)

This stanza, the fifth of the poem, describes the speaker's visual attention, but its structure also gets at Lawrence's major changes to the poem's form from the 1916 version and the way that these changes likewise mark visual attention and its specifically embodied nature. In place of the two prosaic sentences of the original—sentences that unfolded in a single stanza of free verse—this stanza is one of thirteen that offer a highly parsed level of detail from continually shifting visual foci. The at-hand nature of the present-tense description is heightened by tersely phrased lines and a complex, irregular rhyme scheme that suggests an attunement to the dynamic bodily rhythms underwriting the speaker's experience.

Another stanza, from later in the poem, illustrates how further formal changes continue to mark this embodied experience. The speaker declares:

Traveller, column of fire,
It is vain.
The glow of thy full desire
Becomes pain. (lines 43–46)

In this ninth stanza we can see that as the poem goes on—and the speaker's virgin youth still ultimately leads him to refuse the material imperatives of his "lower me"—the lines become skimpier and the rhyme schemes, while still shifting, fall into a more limited range of *ab* patterns, indicating the narrow conventions that keep the speaker from the macrocosmic physiology of chaos. Lawrence's recasting of the poem's form thus records his now decidedly positive attitude toward the reinvigorating potential of impersonal subjectivity.

As a complement to this new form, the substance of the revised "Virgin Youth" makes clear that material opacity is central to this impersonal potential and in a way that recalls the visuality promoted by Lawrence's umbrella analogy. Prior to refusing the material imperatives of an impersonal subjectivity, the speaker announces that his attentiveness has revealed paradoxical and distinctly partial visions, such as a "light" that is "darkness" and a "know[ing]" that is "unknown" and "nowhere" (lines 37, 38, 31, 32, 33). These visions, corresponding as they do to the physiology of chaos seen through the scattered slits in Lawrence's umbrella, embed incompleteness and opacity in any perceptual and epistemological advances. The poem's celebration of opaque materiality culminates in its ironic deployment of a homunculus as a figure for embodied subjectivity. In classical accounts of vision, the homunculus was a tiny man housed in the brain that explained how the mind could see the optical images projected on the retina; he was a kind of escape hatch to avoid confronting the complex psychophysiology of visual perception. This homunculus thus became the ultimate symbol of an objective, disembodied self—as we saw in figure I.1. By contrast, in "Virgin Youth," as the speaker's mode of being shifts from personality to impersonality, he uses the term "[h]omunculus" to refer to a "lower me [that] gets up and greets me" with all the "[r]hythm," "[r]ipples," and "[q]uivering" of materiality (lines 16, 15, 10, 9, 13). Thus, whereas the first "Virgin Youth" took Cartesian visuality somewhat for granted, Lawrence's revision recasts both the homunculus and the impersonal vision through which the speaker perceives him as part of an embodied process, thereby refusing Cartesian visuality.

Lawrence reinforces this embodiment in a way that bleeds into the unstable gender and sexual politics that surface in modernist impersonality. First, he pictures the homunculus as the speaker's erect penis, who "stirs from his roots" and "stands," thus rendering him a bodily organ subject to autonomic impulses (lines 16, 18). Second, he figures this penis as also the newborn infant of the virgin youth, who seems to give birth following a "[r]hythm" in his "soft, slumbering belly" and the awakening of his "unknown breasts" (lines 10, 12, 7). The poem bears out this suggestion of pregnancy and virgin birth by likening the "[r]isen" and "wordless" homunculus to Christ (lines 17, 20), who is the "risen" "Lord" and the "Word . . . made flesh" (Luke 24:34; John 1:14). Together, these images don't just embody the homunculus, they do so with an exuberance that crosses and recrosses both male and female versions of a sexually differentiated body. "Virgin Youth" in fact abounds in examples of this androgyny, applied both to impersonal subjectivity and to the speaker. For instance, Lawrence overwhelmingly codes impersonal subjectivity as masculine until the final stanza, when the speaker apologizes for being unable to fulfill the impersonal imperatives of desire. At this point, he tells the homunculus, "I salute thee, / But to deflower thee," implying that though the speaker acknowledges the force of the homunculus (through his "salute"), he must "deflower" or violate the homunculus, not by having sex, but refusing to do so (lines 60–61). Though Lawrence's structure of deflowering is humorously reversed, what doesn't really change is the way the metaphor feminizes impersonal subjectivity. We see a similar process at work when the speaker describes the social conventions that constrain him. He begs the homunculus:

> Dark ruddy pillar, forgive me! I
> Am helplessly bound
> To the rock of virginity.
>
> . . . .
> I
> Would worship thee, letting my buttocks prance.
> But the hosts of men with one voice deny
> Me the chance. (lines 47–58)

These lines' mythological allusions depict the speaker in simultaneously masculine and feminine terms. First, he's a modern Prometheus who is "bound /

To the rock of virginity," not by the gods, but by "the hosts of men" themselves. His crime is that he would bring the "flame of the living ground" (line 26)—one of Lawrence's metaphors for the erect penis and also for impersonal subjectivity—to others. Second, though, the speaker is just as readily a modern Andromeda, the virgin princess who was "helplessly bound/To the rock" as a sacrifice to the sea monster Cetus. The multiple directions of Lawrence's description mark an instability in impersonal subjectivity itself, but not necessarily one he fully values. The speaker closes the poem by observing that the homunculus "impinges/On nothingness" (lines 61-62). This final appeal to a void seems to construe the poem's androgyny as an uneasy absence of a stable social and embodied identity.

In the year after Lawrence's *Collected Poems* appeared—and indeed the last year of his life—he released *Pansies* (1929), a collection of what he punningly referred to in his introduction as poetic *"penseés"* for "heartsease," fragmented thoughts to soothe a modern ailment, namely, the abstraction from the body bemoaned in "Virgin Youth" (*CP* 624-27 at 624). Lawrence explains that these thoughts "come as much from the heart and the genitals as from the head" and "run through" them all with their "own blood of emotion," as though part of the circulatory system (*CP* 624). Not surprisingly, then, two little flowers from this "bunch" of *Pansies*, "Climb Down, O Lordly Mind" and "Know Deeply, Know Thyself More Deeply," continue to develop Lawrence's belief that any mental detachment from bodily imperatives is destructive to one's awareness of and relation to impersonal subjectivity. The latter poem also offers further insight into the complex gender and sexual politics of Lawrence's poetic understanding of impersonality.

"Climb Down, O Lordly Mind" calls directly for a modern return to materiality and does so in distinctly visual terms. It exhorts the mind to "[c]limb down" to its rightful embodiment, recapitulating the critique of the homunculus in "Virgin Youth," but now in even sharper terms (*CP* 388-89, line 1). "Climb Down" invokes Descartes' famous "Cogito, ergo sum" but transforms it decisively, as the speaker declares, "Non cogito, ergo sum/I am, I do not think I am" (lines 40-41). Here acts of abstract thought are replaced with the certainty of lived bodily experience—what "exists . . . in my blood," an echo of the circulatory imagery of Lawrence's introduction (line 39). The poem then extends this challenge to Cartesian dualism by rewriting the Christianity of its underlying metaphysics. Where "Virgin Youth" playfully embodies the homunculus through references to Christ, "Climb Down" confronts Christian discourse more directly. The poem is full of biblical diction and imagery, from the apostrophe of its title ("O Lordly Mind") to archaic forms like "thyself" and "thou art," all of which recall the popular King James text (line 14). These devices aid Lawrence in reversing the story of Moses ascending the mountain to receive the Ten Commandments: in his version the main commandment is to climb back down to the body rather than to seek an ethereal voice.

Lawrence casts this counterphilosophy in specifically visual terms by likening the lordly mind to an "eagle" eye but then revoking that description with the rebuke, "alas, you are more like a buzzard" (line 2). This change replaces the soaring eagle and the all-encompassing objectivity of its bird's-eye view with a carrion bird that must seek and live on bodies. This replacement eliminates an easy mind/body dualism as well as the possibility of a complete or panoptic perception. Lawrence builds upon these points by arguing that humanity "is cerebral, intellectual, mental, spiritual" but also "instinctive, intuitive, and in touch" (lines 9, 10) and by concluding that the mind must therefore forfeit its supposed objectivity and transcendence: "The mind that needs to know all things / must needs at last come to know its own limits," including the fact "that thou art mortal" and thus "forever unknowable" (lines 11-12, 14, 15). More specifically, if what the mind presently believes is merely "a kind of fiction," Lawrence points instead to the "alternating consciousness" of some bodily subject beyond the self that, paradoxically, knows a fundamental not-knowing (lines 34, 35). The poem's farthest-reaching descriptions of this consciousness suggest that it will ultimately challenge the very "unique[ness]" of the mind and perhaps even of the self. As the speaker puts it, the mind's "unique day is over. / Absolutism is finished, in the human consciousness too" (lines 5-6). These lines connect this loss of uniqueness with the loss of absolutes that Lawrence elsewhere associated with the advances of modern science.

Lawrence returns to this loss of absolutes and, correspondingly, to this paradoxical knowledge of not-knowing in "Know Deeply, Know Thyself More Deeply." This poem delivers advice to those who have moved beyond the stage of "Virgin Youth" but must now confront the fact that love (not simply virginity) can also destroy a lived connection to impersonal subjectivity. If the mind knows only a "fiction"—or, more visually, the picture on the inside of the umbrella—then "Know Deeply" places love among those fictions, arguing that it brings with it certain negative trappings of selfhood. The poem clarifies Lawrence's belief that relationships exist most genuinely as an interaction between two impersonalities, or rather in the shared recognition of an already existing unity at that level of impersonal subjectivity. Just as importantly, the poem's critique of love plays out through the gender and sexual politics of a traditional image/text binary, showing the relevance of images not only to Lawrence's version of impersonality but to its political implications as well.

The speaker of "Know Deeply" begins by urging his female interlocutor to "go deeper than love"—to get beyond the ideal to the "heart" as a "living" organ (*CP* 392-93, line 8). Emphasizing the dynamic flux of energy that Lawrence associates with embodied life, the speaker analogizes this depth of affect to a geological substrate (a "wild rock" that's "molten" and "dense"), suggesting a materiality that's unwilled, shifting, and opaque (lines 2, 3, 3). The speaker evaluates the heat and pressure of his shared "experience" with the woman in terms of this autonomic and uncontained materiality, wondering whether there is indeed "a gem, which came into being between" them (lines 20, 10). Shifting the science of this conceit to a visual vernacular, the speaker explains that having this "gemmed" relation requires the woman to "lose sight of [her]self,/And lose sight of [him]," and also requires that he do the same (lines 20, 4-5). The couple must, in other words, *not* know the very idea of a self.

Lawrence goes on to link this forfeited vision and self-centeredness to the stable, mimetic image of a Cartesian visuality. The speaker argues that his interlocutor is unable to participate fully in an impersonal relation because she's overly invested in the mere "appearances of love" (line 14). Her entire lived relation to her body is an effort to stop time, to freeze an image of herself as one of romantic love's visual trappings. She "sit[s] with a mirror in [her] hand . . ./posing on and on as a lover" (lines 24-25), much in the way of the courtesan in Field's ekphrasis of Veneto's *Idealized Portrait of a Woman*. Even more than Field, Lawrence's speaker soundly rejects this self-absorption, remarking in the poem's final lines, "I do not want a woman whom age cannot wither./She is a made-up lie, a dyed immortelle/of infinite staleness" (lines 29-31). By using "ma[k]e-up" and "dye" to mask the signs of aging, to exist in an "infinite" stasis, the speaker's lover is reproducing the gender and sexual politics of the image/text binary: her mirror gazing and posing are in stark contrast to her lover's production of text in the form of the poem, reinforcing the idea that images are the timeless, feminine counterpart to temporal, rational, and so masculine texts. But the speaker's poetic harangue attacks both this traditional image and the femininity and sexuality ordered on it. "Know Deeply" thus refuses not only the image/text binary but also, effectively, its social politics, which would paralyze and silence women.

These poetic acts of attention, together with Lawrence's essays on poetics, show that he consistently worked to record imagetextual fragments of a physiology of chaos that he believed pervaded and exceeded the self. He glimpsed different angles of the ontological, epistemological, and sociopolitical questions posed by this chaos and built an account of impersonal subjectivity from these glimpses. In what does impersonality consist, and can we know (or not know) it? Can we—and should we—have a lived relation to impersonality? How does such a relation influence our connections with others and the world? In raising these questions and groping for provisional answers, Lawrence's poetry and poetics persistently adapt a modern scientific vernacular of vision. Though he sometimes appeals to a loss of sight in breaking from the absolutes of a Cartesian visuality, he nonetheless turns to the imagetextual image of a physiological optics to register the potentially liberating instability of a lost objectivity, selfhood, and social conventionality. Still, as we'll begin to see in Lawrence's criticism on painting and psychoanalysis, he ultimately turns this instability to very different political ends than do the modernists we've considered thus far. Like the observer of an anorthoscope, this criticism pieces together a theory of impersonality from the fragmented answers of Lawrence's poetry and the bodily visuality they model. This theory bends the instabilities of impersonality toward recuperating and even strengthening some sense of individuality and identity, sometimes but not always accompanied by quite conservative notions of gender, sexuality, and race.

From Impersonality to "Creative Identity": A Critical Sleight of Hand

Lawrence often dismissed the nonrepresentational modern art that was so important to Pound's and Loy's impersonality, describing it, for instance, in his essay "Introduction to These Paintings" (1929) as "lumps, tubes, cubes, [and] planes."[11] He nonetheless valued a postimpressionist art that Jonathan Crary and others have shown similarly adapted modern optics, in this case by representing the fleeting moment of observation as a blur of light, color, and motion rather than a faithful likeness of the world.[12] In his essay "Art and Morality" (1925) Lawrence passionately defends Paul Cézanne's postimpressionist still lifes from charges of immorality, largely in terms of the modern scientific vernacular of vision in which postimpressionism participated.

Fig. 4.2. Paul Cézanne, *Apples*, 1878–79. Metropolitan Museum of Art, New York, The Mr. and Mrs. Henry Ittleson Jr. Purchase Fund, 1961. Courtesy of the Metropolitan Museum of Art.

Focusing on Cézanne's apple still lifes, like the one shown in figure 4.2, Lawrence argues that their intensity, color, and texture over any actual verisimilitude get at a "fourth dimension" that's in "your blood and your bones . . . [and] your eyes."[13] In addition, though he suggests that "even . . . a Freudian" couldn't uncover what animates charges of impropriety directed against such objects, he nonetheless identifies their sources using a Freudian logic of repression and primitivism, which points to the additional role of psychoanalysis in Lawrence's visual-scientific vernacular ("AM" 163).

Lawrence blames the charges of impropriety on a "slowly-formed habit of seeing" in "civilised man," a habit that disavows a "dim eye-vision" once acknowledged by "primitive" cultures like that of ancient Egypt ("AM" 164, 164, 167, 164). More specifically, he explains that ancient "Greece . . . broke the spell of 'darkness'" and developed modern man's supposedly "All-Seeing Eyes," whereas "previously, even in Egypt, men had not learned to *see straight*. They fumbled in the dark, and . . . only *felt* their existence surging in the darkness of other existences" ("AM" 167). For Lawrence, these "All-Seeing Eyes," and their remove from a primal, "surging" materiality, have forced a civilized disavowal of the fact that vision is embodied and therefore limited. Cezanne gets at these material realities of vision, and the charge that he's immoral is merely a symptom of this civilized repression. Lawrence's interwoven engagement with postimpressionism and psychoanalysis—key sites of a modern scientific vernacular of vision—shows that this vernacular was the scene for his effort to theorize impersonality.

"Art and Morality" effectively announces this scene by applying the label "kodak-vision" to the disavowing "habit of seeing" that's censorious of Cézanne (168, 164). This label repositions Lawrence's poetic critique of Cartesian visuality as a direct account of modern visual culture. Kodak cameras, so popular in the early twentieth century, were modeled on the anatomy of the human eye—just like the camera obscura, which was so important to Descartes. This modeling made vision seem like a form of photography, a mimetic record of the world. Lawrence offers a three-pronged attack against kodak-vision's mimetic model. First, he argues that even if the eye produces a truly "photographic . . . image on the retina"—which he doubts—such an image is nonetheless not what the mind "take[s] in" (164). Second, he complains that contemporary art culture often feeds the false belief in objective perception by still privileging mimetic art and marginalizing forms that refuse to inflate our sense of the faithfulness of perception. He concludes that these twin values, the belief in photographic perception and the elevation of photographic art, have allowed man to "mak[e] himself in his own image," much like the mirror-loving female interlocutor in "Know Deeply": "The kodak bears witness . . . with the universal vision. And we are what is seen: each man to himself an identity, an isolated absolute, corresponding with a universe of isolated absolutes" (165; see fig. 4.3). Lawrence argues that such a "complete" self-perception, where all else is mere "background," makes humans into a frozen, sterile idea ("AM" 165), one that forsakes "the feeling of physical flesh-and-blood kinship" ("ITP" 190).

This denunciation of contemporary photography (which Lawrence also extends to the kaleidoscope and even the cinema) introduces some of the complications that characterize his theory of impersonal subjectivity and mark his departure from those modernists we've considered to this point. For example, while his denunciation embraces the embodied vision and relationality described in his poetry and even condemns identity as a mode of being, it also begins to yoke materiality to a conservative politics. Lawrence laments that kodak-vision has "substitut[ed]" for the forsaken "flesh-and-blood kinship" a democratic "ideal of social or political oneness" ("ITP" 190).

Fig. 4.3. Kodak advertisement for its self-timer, published in the *Saturday Evening Post* on 29 April 1921. Appearing just a few years before Lawrence's essay, this ad shows how Lawrence's complaints about "kodak-vision" intersect with the company's own visual discourse, specifically the way it models a stable and self-determined identity. Note the imperative "Kodak yourself" and the way that the man "catch[es]" not only his fish but effectively himself with the Kodak camera and self-timer in the top right photograph. Note as well the reference to persons: "If there are several persons along, they may *all* be in the picture." The claim is effectively that Kodak aids persons in making themselves and in seeming to see themselves completely.

This lament echoes his earlier essay "Democracy" (1919), in which he doomed present democracies for functioning on the principle of "Individualism, Personalism, or Identity" at the expense of a "single, incommutable, and unique" "creative identity" that's "inscrutable."[14] Such an appraisal simultaneously condemns and valorizes "identity" and also confuses its dismissal of individualism by simultaneously applauding what's "single" or "unique"—perhaps the most common descriptors for an individual. In other words, Lawrence practices a sleight of hand in which what seems to have disappeared in one place suddenly reappears in another. He gets away with this sleight of hand in part by invoking "inscrutab[ility]," which suggests that whatever distinguishes "identity" from "creative identity" simply can't be explained. Both rhetorical moves keep in play concepts that seem to have been rejected by the very notion of impersonality, including Lawrence's own poetic representations of it.

But "Art and Morality" and "Introduction to These Paintings" don't simply perform this conservative sleight of hand and move on; they continue to applaud dim eye-vision, with its challenge to identity, even as they also try to resuscitate individuality. This less conservative track reasserts a more destabilizing model of impersonality and also adds to Lawrence's visual-scientific vernacular by depicting as promising the contemporary intersections of modern art and optics with modern physics. Lawrence links dim eye-vision to a consciousness that's neither the "mind alone, [n]or merely the body" and that's not "transfus[ed] . . . with personal emotion" ("ITP" 207, 201). He suggests that this dim eye-vision continually resurfaces, despite the repressive force of kodak-vision, and he identifies two records of these re-surfacings: Cézanne's already noted apple still lifes and what Lawrence calls the "alert science" of modern physics ("ITP" 208). According to Lawrence, both of these records capture the "fourth dimension" by showing, first, that "we move and move for ever, in no discernible direction, [so] there is no center to the movement, to us," and second, that all matter and energy exist in relative relations rather than fixed forms ("AM" 167). Indeed, so united are Cézanne's apples and alert science that Lawrence's description of Cézanne's approach bleeds into a statement of Cézanne's knowledge (sometimes ahistorical) of modern physics, geometry, and optics:

> He knew . . . about the value of planes, the value of the angle in planes, the different values of the same colour on different planes: all about edges, visible edges, tangible edges, intangible edges: all about the nodality of form-groups, the constellating of mass-centres: all about the relativity of mass, the gravitation and the centrifugal force of mass, the resultant complex impinging of masses, the isolation of a mass in the line of vision . . . : also which is the aesthetic centre of the canvas, the dynamic centre, the effulgent centre, the kinetic centre, the mathematical centre . . . : all about spotting, what you spot, which spot, on the spot,

how many spots, balance of spots, recedence of spots, spots on the explosive vision and spots on the co-ordinative vision. ("ITP" 215-16)

Lawrence suggests that with this fusion of modern art and science—a fusion that speaks to the material instability of vision and knowledge, and even of being—Cézanne's apples come to exceed two prior apple absolutes: the original "sin" of Satan's apple and the "knock on the head" of Sir Isaac Newton's gravity-driven apple ("AM" 166). Through this hierarchy, Lawrence converts the critique that his poetry offered of Christian rhetoric and a mechanistic universe of absolutes into a more definitely modern scientific vernacular of vision. Indeed the many "spots" that Lawrence points to in Cézanne's art evoke blind spots, afterimages, and optical floaters, not to mention the invisible matter and dimensions, in the embodied field of vision.

"Introduction to These Paintings" adapts this fusion of art and science, as well as the impersonality it implies, into a specific aesthetic, notably one that confirms the role that imagetextuality plays in the embodied vision Lawrence imagines. He translates his rejection of mimetic images as frozen, sterile forms in "Know Deeply" into a critique of the art critic Roger Fry's notion of "Significant Form" in modern art ("ITP" 199).[15] Lawrence complains that whether mimetic or not, a great deal of modern art is "merely optical," meaning that it's visual without having any grounding in the materiality of seeing and being ("ITP" 194). He then casts Fry's significant form as the hallmark of this problematic opticality. He proposes that although Fry discusses a nonmimetic art whose lack of verisimilitude departs from the traditional image/text binary, he also privileges an image that's both frozen and transcendent and thus still clings to that binary and belies the dynamic embodiment of vision and subjectivity alike ("ITP" 200). In other words, Lawrence posits that the rigidity and idealism of Fry's significant form makes the modern art he advocates, not a departure from the disembodied, objective observer, but just "another apotheosis of personal conceit" ("ITP" 200).

Lawrence condemns this "personal conceit" first by caricaturing Fry as a false prophet who preaches, "Purify yourselves of all base hankering for a tale that is told, and of all low lust for likenesses. Purify yourselves, and know the one supreme way, the way of Significant Form . . . I am the revelation of Spiritual Life" ("ITP" 199). Fry's imperative to refuse any "hankering for a tale that is told" and his invocation of a "spiritual" rather than a material life marks his remove from imagetextuality. Lawrence's second strategy for condemning Fry is his appeal to Cézanne: while Fry's influential study *Cé-*

zanne (1927) takes the eponymous painter as the ultimate stylist of significant form, Lawrence instead argues that Cézanne favored a contrary imagetextuality and by extension refused all that was merely personal. Recalling
some of the tendencies that Pater associated with Leonardo, Lawrence emphasizes that Cézanne used both incompletion (or "leaving gaps") and also
failures of likeness through bad drawing (what Lawrence meaningfully calls
"insignificant form") to produce a sense of materiality and temporal change
in his paintings ("ITP" 205, 210). The result is that Cézanne's imagetextual
images—his apples, in particular—are impersonal, an expression of the "existence of matter" rather than of the "enclosed ego" or the "self-conscious I"
("ITP" 202, 201, 202). Indeed, "appleyness" becomes a cipher for this impersonality to the point that even when Cézanne isn't painting apples, but instead a woman, he's still somehow painting "the appley part of her" rather
than "her personality" ("ITP" 212). Moreover, emphasizing the way that impersonality crosses and thus disregards gender identity, Lawrence goes so
far as to declare that this impersonal quality of appleyness surpasses "even
her [the woman's] very sex" ("ITP" 212). As the "even" of this declaration
registers, Lawrence considers sex to be one of the more ineradicable features
of individuality, so it isn't surprising that his remarks here contrast sharply
with his slightly earlier essay "Democracy." There he champions a political
state that, unlike a democracy, would refuse "the enemy incarnate . . . personality" and so also any "question of equality or inequality" and instead
allow "each man [to be] himself, each woman herself" (*P* 711, 716, 716). Not
only does this impersonal politics retain gender, it becomes rather conservative by offering no means of redressing gender-based social relations;
"there can be no comparison" among citizens and no "public good," so there
is no social guarantee of rights (*P* 715, 711).

But if "Introduction to These Paintings" and indeed "Art and Morality"
don't finally emphasize this conservative side of Lawrence's impersonality,
his twin essays *Psychoanalysis and the Unconscious* and *Fantasia of the Unconscious* are more adept at wielding his sleight-of-hand rhetoric, wherein
individuality or identity disappears in one place only to reappear in another.
These psychoanalytic essays take the characteristics of alert science from
his writings on Cézanne—including a non-mimetic visualization and a vernacular physics, physiology, and optics—and turn them toward the unconscious.[16] In Lawrence's estimate, these anti-Freudian essays present a "theory of human relativity" that will "[r]ip the veil of the old vision across" and
help us "not *to know*, but *to be*" (*PF* 72, 65, 105). Lawrence's basic (and rather

slanted) premise is that Freud extends a Cartesian scientific tradition that works to make man the "undisputed master of his own fate" (*PF* 15).[17] Freud does this, Lawrence argues, by treating dream images as meaningful psychical expressions rather than as part of the physiology of our "tissue removing or arranging the dead body of our past day" (*PF* 15, 177). For Lawrence, this treatment casts the unconscious as an "inverted reflection" of conscious ideas, a readily intelligible secret agent. Lawrence claims that his own science "abandons" this dematerializing "intellectualist position," which would "order" the "unconscious," as well as the deathly stasis through which that position unfolds (*PF* 18). He suggests that his essays offer a kind of nonmimetic visualization of the opacity and flux of impersonal subjectivity by mixing "living experience" with the "first terms of a forgotten knowledge," or "science[,] that was universal over the earth" (*PF* 62, 64, 63). Moving between a modern physics, physiology, and psychoanalysis and a pseudoscientific mysticism, Lawrence creates a broad palette that allows him to perfect the slipperiness of his impersonality, only hinted at in his art essays. It formalizes the disorder of impersonal subjectivity, but that disorder then helps Lawrence to cancel individuality and identity in one place and to bring them back with all the more force in another.

Psychoanalysis and *Fantasia* begin by laying out a familiar psychophysiological scheme that brushes aside dualism and the related autonomy and individuality of the self. These essays argue that the unconscious is in fact the "first nucleus" of the body and that the subdivisions of this nucleus produce the "organs, glands, [and] nerve-centers of the human organism," including the brain (*PF* 33). This monistic evolution results ultimately in a set of four dynamic centers anatomized from a hodge-podge of physiology and mysticism: the solar plexus, the lumbar ganglion, the thoracic plexus, and the cardiac plexus. These four centers are supplemented at puberty by four more: the hypogastric plexus, the sacral ganglion, the cervical plexuses, and the ganglia of the neck. According to Lawrence, the eight centers together contain "nothing ideal" and so "nothing in the least personal" (*PF* 28). They are instead what Lawrence's friend and interlocutor the Jungian psychoanalyst Trigant Burrow called "the matrix of personality."[18] *Psychoanalysis* and *Fantasia* extend this matrix far further than Burrow by claiming that the "impersonal" "circuit" of the unconscious centers is in fact multiply and materially "extra-individual" (*PF* 28, 25, 25). First, Lawrence maintains that the parent nuclei that produce the initial cell of the unconscious live on, circulating dark currents of "vital activity" that influence the subject's psychophysiology and make it impossible to sever the parental bond (*PF* 75). In addition, Lawrence proposes that bodily cells store "dynamic content" from our impressions of people and objects as part of their everyday waste and repair and that the unconscious then creates bodily tissue from this content (*PF* 29). He even extends this cycle of influence to both astronomical bodies and local geographies. He claims that the chemical "element[s]" of the sun and moon are dynamically connected to and unavoidably affect our tissue, just as habitat is responsible for what people call tradition: the "inhabitants who live at the foot of Etna," for instance, "will always have a certain pitch of life-vibration," and their "tradition" is simply the inevitable "continuing of [that] . . . pitch" (*PF* 170, 154).

As Lawrence moves from outlining this complex and diffuse impersonal subjectivity to proposing an ethic for its functioning, he relies heavily on the visuality he developed in his poetry and his art criticism. *Psychoanalysis* and *Fantasia* actually operate quite like H.D.'s contemporaneous *Notes on Thought and Vision,* perhaps because all three essays were written soon after 1918, when Lawrence's close friendship with H.D. lapsed.[19] Lawrence echoes *Notes* by locating the precise meaning of impersonal subjectivity in a correct balance among the four main centers of the unconscious and exemplifies this balance through a proper equilibrium among four corresponding types of vision. Vision should be "manifold," Lawrence explains, which means that it should operate from all four impersonal centers (*PF* 122). And yet, "vision in us . . . proceed[s] too much in one mode" of sight, specifically the mode of "objective curiosity" (*PF* 102, 103). Returning to his familiar figure from "Climb Down," Lawrence thus exhorts readers to "*Descendez, cher Moïse. Vous voyez trop loin*" (Descend, dear Moses. You are seeing too far) (*PF* 71). In addition, he instructs them in what such a descent should look like, namely, the recovery of "root-vision"—his new label for the dim eye-vision of "Art and Morality"—whose embodiment and corresponding limits he emphasizes by comparing it to both the "*narrowed* vision of the cat" and the "*single point* of vision of the hawk" (*PF* 33, 102, emphasis added). Although the animals Lawrence chooses are known for a sight that's variously superior to humans', his focus on the weaknesses of such sight showcases that visual acuity is no antidote to embodied limits, because this acuity is itself limited to particular domains. For example, cats can see better at night but less well in the day as compared with humans.

Lawrence goes on to cast the difference between objective curiosity and root-vision in imagistic terms by turning, as H.D. does in *Notes,* to painting.

Keeping with his focus on animals, he relates objective curiosity to the veri-similar cows painted by the seventeenth-century Dutch landscape artist Aelbert Cuyp. And he relates root-vision to the more abstracted and dynamic cows of a contemporary children's toy based on Noah's Ark. Lawrence's comparison implies that Cuyp's cow image is stable and mimetic and feeds a vision restricted to objective curiosity, while the Ark toy's cow image departs from the traditional image/text binary by refusing verisimilitude and having a temporality derived from its being literally in play. In other words, the Ark cow's "dynamic abstraction" means that, like Cézanne's apples, it's imagetextual (*PF* 122). For Lawrence, this imagetextuality gives the "Ark cow . . . a deeper vital reality than a Cuyp cow," implying that root-vision (unlike objective curiosity) accesses this "vital reality" (*PF* 122).

Continuing to extrapolate from Lawrence's poetic "*penseés*," *Psycho-analysis* and *Fantasia* also give a privileged role to sex in their impersonal ethic. They link intercourse to the extra-individual activities that channel the circuits of the unconscious, so that sex actually transforms the blood and thereby the nature of being. They also correspondingly offer intercourse as a method for enacting the desired "fad[ing] of sight" that will produce the proper balance of vision (*PF* 194). In keeping with this focus on transformative relations that deny a Cartesian visuality, Lawrence additionally displays a decided disinterest in the gender essentialisms long mapped through the Cartesian model, just as he had in "Know Deeply." He posits that "every individual has both mother and father sparking within himself," a claim that uses reproduction to challenge autonomy and enclosed interiority. But he also posits that "biologically, . . . the rudimentary formation of both sexes is found in every individual" (*PF* 76, 126). He even goes one step further to suggest that the sexes themselves comprise an undefined complementarity rather than a set of reliable characteristics. He calls on mothers and fathers to create an emotional equilibrium for their infant and proposes that the roles productive of this balance are shifting: instead of mothers being "gentle" where fathers are "crude," parents adopt "tender[ness]" or "roughness" based on each other's inclinations and the resulting needs of the child (*PF* 90). Generalizing this principle beyond single relationships, Lawrence also explains that in the "old flow," "man ha[d] his positivity in the volitional centres [of the unconscious], and woman in the sympathetic." But "the woman is now the initiator and the man the responder" (*PF* 127). Underscoring the variability of this switch, Lawrence concludes that "[n]aturally this . . . order of things may be reversed" and that "positive and negative, passive and ac-

tive cuts both ways" in either case (127). These various statements free gender up as a set of physiologically rooted but also fungible and exchangeable
roles rather than a fixed essence or a social construction.

Lawrence's appeal to race in *Psychoanalysis* and *Fantasia* is less developed
than his consideration of gender, but it's still possible to read a similar, potentially liberating racial instability in his commitment to a balanced impersonal subjectivity. Recalling his Freudian linkage of dim eye-vision to primitive cultures in "Art and Morality," Lawrence speaks of a "negroid, sensual
will" tied to root-vision over and against any ideal, mental consciousness,
but he ultimately invests this concept with as much nuance as stereotype
(*PF* 99–100). He posits that for centuries civilized Westerners have suppressed
the negroid will, which is one part of the proper balance of the unconscious.
Moreover, because Lawrence sees the unconscious as thoroughly psychophysiological, he believes that this suppression has created physical effects,
including a thinning of the lips and a shrinking of the nose. He thus implies
that racial essences, though real, don't map cleanly onto races of people:
the "negroid" is a necessary and desirable psychophysiological component
of every human in a way that rejects discourses of racial purity; and while
negroid lips and noses exist, it's not only anthropological "Negroids" who can
have them.

It seems, then, that Lawrence's theory of impersonality explicitly invali-
dates not only the divide between mind and body and between subject and
object but also between male and female, civilized and primitive, white and
racialized Other. Yet, Lawrence's theory also manages to recuperate the
individuality traditionally secured through these divides by simply reattach-
ing it to those contours of subjectivity that he hasn't critiqued, namely, to
impersonality. *Psychoanalysis* and *Fantasia* decree, in other words, that whatever impersonality is, those very same things are by definition individual.
Thus, despite all the fluctuations and influences that attend impersonal subjectivity, and even though it's distinguished from the personality or self, individuality survives intact. Moreover, as we'll soon see, this individuality can
then give a leg up to otherwise dismissed essential identities.

Lawrence's conflation of impersonality and individuality complicates
every level of his system, beginning with the kernel of the unconscious. The
extra-individual currents of the first cell acquire new meaning through his
simultaneous claim that the "first naked unicellular organism" is not personal
but is nonetheless "an individual" (*PF* 16). Lawrence then draws this claim
into the details of his argument by remarking that "even in its profoundest,

and most elemental movements" the impersonal unconscious "is still integral and individual" (*PF* 186). As he does here, Lawrence often simply restates prior destabilizing claims in terms of individuality and coherence, relying on the multiplicity and repetitions through which he signals the flux and opacity of impersonality to excuse the discrepancies. He also works explicitly to counteract any de-individualizing implications of his own scientific systematizing. Thus, despite his detailed account of the origins of subjectivity in complex forces both within and beyond it, he insists that every organism arises in a process utterly "outside the field of mental comprehension" and manifests a "specific individual nature" that "cannot be found in any cause-and-effect process" (*PF* 17). He also complains that any "generalization" beyond the "individual" moves toward an untenable "homogenous force" (*PF* 15), and he recuperates the unconscious as the antithesis of such a force: it is "the essential unique nature of every individual creature" and "is, by its very nature, unanalyzable, undefinable, inconceivable" (*PF* 17).[20]

As Lawrence relocates individuality within the protected space of an impersonal inconceivability, he also creates a basis for resuscitating the will, and from there identity. While he asserts that "[w]e really have no will and no choice" when it comes to impersonal subjectivity, what replaces that lost will in his estimate nonetheless unfolds according to our own individual (or individualizing) design, which "acts within us, day by day unfolding us according to our nature" (*PF* 152). The virtual about-face of this intelligent design comes quickly to the rescue of traditional gender and racial identities. Though only touching briefly on race, *Psychoanalysis* and *Fantasia* turn against the instabilities of his "negroid will" by rallying his Anglo-American and seemingly imperialist readers to accept their impersonal nature, because they mustn't leave the future of the world to "China or Japan or India or Africa—any of the great swarms" (*PF* 190). Such a reassertion of white hegemony is then matched, and in much more thoroughgoing fashion, with a recovery of conventional gender and sexual binaries. Despite Lawrence's earlier contention that we all bear both male and female inside us, he now declares truculently, "A child is either male or female, in the whole of its psyche and physique. . . . Every single living cell is either male or female, and will remain either male or female as long as life lasts" (*PF* 126). He also effectively retracts his claim that sex is an undefined and variably performed complementarity by now explaining that men and women only "seem to play each other's parts": all the time, "man is purely male, playing woman's part, and woman is purely female, however manly" (*PF* 127). Even the blood, which before was impersonally transformed through intercourse, is now divided in a "dual polarity between the sexes"—and perhaps not surprisingly so, for Lawrence posits that only *hetero*sexual intercourse enacts the impersonalizing transformation and that there is no such thing as a "third sex" (*PF* 185, 126). In all of these ways, then, even a sex linked to dynamic circulations and flows manages to reassert a stolid essence. Moreover, just to make sure that this essence works only in the service of individuality, Lawrence individualizes the very category of sex. He declares that "sex [itself] is always individual. A man has his own sex: nobody else's" (*PF* 136). In other words, even the shared fact of sex among all men and all women doesn't question individuality, because every individual has a way of being either a man or a woman.

The traditional hierarchies that *Psychoanalysis* and *Fantasia* reassert at the level of gender and sexuality, and to a lesser extent race, become even steeper at the level of political systems. Here we see Lawrence's investment in individuality serve as the glue uniting impersonality to a brand of authoritarianism. Lawrence criticizes current leaders for "lov[ing] ideas" rather than individuals and suggests that a reverse economy would give rise, not to democracy, but to a much better, more impersonal "system of culminating aristocracy . . . tapering like a pyramid to the supreme leader" (*PF* 141, 191). While he democratically declares that leaders must be chosen by the people, he also posits that a proper leader, once chosen, would command the fealty of those people who would "surrender [their] individuality" to him (*PF* 137). Adding a eugenic slant to such despotism, Lawrence further contends that current cultural and political crises—which he claims result from the denial or imbalance of the impersonal unconscious—will require a massive cleansing in order to heal: "[W]e have to sink back into the darkness and the elemental consciousness of the blood. And from this rise again. But there is no rising until the bath of darkness and extinction is accomplished" (*PF* 192). Ominous as it may sound, this needed purge is, for Lawrence, not the violent genocide to come in the years following his death; it's a kind of subjective cleansing of the self, a battle like that waged in "Virgin Youth," but with a different outcome. And yet, the outward or social violence that's missing from this formulation does tellingly surface in Lawrence's final return to gender shortly thereafter, a return that also signals the patriarchy pulsing through his impersonal politics. Lawrence advises men to "make" their women "yield once more to the male leadership," for the good of the women's own impersonal unconscious and also for the manliness of the men:

"Combat her in her cocksure belief that she 'knows' . . . . Take it all out of her. . . . No man is a man unless to his woman he is a pioneer. You'll have to fight . . . to make her yield her goal to yours" (*PF* 198).

Despite Lawrence's critique of Freud, the fluctuating polarity of his slippery economy, so dominant in *Psychoanalysis* and *Fantasia* but also more subtly present in "Art and Morality" and "Introduction to These Paintings," is perhaps best summarized through Freud's theorization of *fort/da* in *Beyond the Pleasure Principle* (1920). Published by coincidence in the same year that Lawrence wrote *Psychoanalysis, Beyond the Pleasure Principle* describes a game of mastery played by Freud's grandson Ernst with his primitive yo-yo, a wooden spool with a string attached. Ernst would throw the spool over the side of his curtained crib, holding onto the string, and yell an interjection that stood roughly for *fort* (gone); then he would pull the string, bringing the spool back, and yell *da* (here). Freud argued that this distinctly visual game staged Ernst's experience of his mother's various departures. Through the game, Ernst would continually subject himself to that absence, but in a controlled environment in which he could bring about the return whenever he wanted to. Economically speaking, Ernst accepts the loss always with an eye toward a greater and more permanent gain. This structure of controlled loss for the sake of greater gain—understood in broadly social rather than simply familial Oedipal terms—captures the crux of Lawrence's theory of impersonality and its particular slippage.

In keeping with the ontological implications of his particular visuality, Lawrence renounces the various grounds for sexual and racial difference— biological, instinctual, and social. He lives, for substantial portions of his essays, with the absence of difference, but always with his hand on the string, always able to bring that spool back. And when Lawrence does bring difference back, his assertions don't act simply to reinstate those forfeited grounds for gender, sexual, and racial identity, though he does appeal to those grounds. Rather, Lawrence asserts that difference is *da*, is here, in impersonal materiality, despite its lacking any conceivable location. Without a basis for existing, but somehow existing nonetheless, gender, sexuality, and race thereby move beyond a space of reasoned demonstration; they become inevitable and unassailable, and this is the greater gain that Lawrence is after. As much as his impersonal subjectivity, and indeed the notion of modernist impersonality broadly, could offer a potential liberation from essentializing notions of embodied identities, Lawrence registers and exploits a contrary potential for instead putting these notions on a newly strong footing. It's no coincidence that his best efforts at doing so also contain some of his strongest statements in favor of authoritarian regimes, as well as his most tenuous appeals to modern science. Thus, Lawrence's initial claim to create a theory of impersonality as a "theory of human relativity" that will complement "Mr. Einstein" (*PF* 72) becomes eventually the paradoxical declaration, "I think there is no one absolute principle in the universe. I think everything is relative. But I also feel, most strongly, that in itself each individual living creature is absolute: in its own being. And that all things in the universe are just relative to the individual living creature" (*PF* 191). Where relativity had seemed at first to undo a centered subjectivity and any possibility of objective knowing, it becomes ultimately a way of reasserting an absolute and coherent individuality, as well as an abiding homocentrism.

This complex theory of impersonality and its politics inflect the fiction for which Lawrence is best known, specifically his last and most controversial novel, *Lady Chatterley's Lover*. Lawrence famously wrote to his friend Edward Garnett that his novels explore an "'intuitive physiology of matter' . . . according to whose action the individual is unrecognizable." They experiment with the "non-human in humanity" rather than the "old stable ego" and thereby "give . . . eyes" to readers so that those readers might in turn "pull the right apples," presumably Cézanne's imagetextual apples, "off the tree" (*Letters* 2:732). *Chatterley* accomplishes this impersonal work that Lawrence's letter so succinctly delineated in terms of physiology, vision, and more implicitly imagetextuality by adapting Darwinian evolutionary theory, particularly Darwin's comments on vision, into a kind of individual experiment in survival. Despite frequent claims about the sexism of *Lady Chatterley's Lover,* what's most interesting about the novel is that it posits an impersonal futurity of seeing and being and also art and identity, without reviving the *fort/da* economy of Lawrence's essays and without allowing an extreme right-wing politics to loom large. In other words, as Lawrence turns his open-endedness and multiplicity of meaning to the work of fiction, he lingers over impersonality's more destabilizing and liberatory roots.

Visual Evolution and Identitarian Futurity in
Lady Chatterley's Lover

In his 1923 essay "The Proper Study" Lawrence advocates an investigation of humanity organized not around a self or even interpersonal relations but around a "void" beyond the self that he labels "*I Don't Know.*"[21] His outline of this investigation draws multiply on scientific vocabulary. First, pointing to the need for a "proper study," he notes the limits of current scientific approaches by appealing to a notion of luminiferous ether, a theoretical medium for the propagation of radiant energies, which was at this time a recently discredited proposition. Lawrence jokes of scientific inquiry: "You start [trying] to find out the chemical composition of a drop of water, and before you know where you are, your river of knowledge is winding very unsatisfactorily into a very vague sea, called the ether" (P 720).[22] But while science can thus lead toward misdirection, Lawrence nonetheless returns to a scientific vocabulary to characterize the reconception of humanity that he values. He suggests that we might better navigate the great "ocean" of "I Don't Know" pertaining to the "unknown self" if we begin from a kind of "metamorphos[is]" (P 720, 720, 719, 720). And he explains this metamorphosis by playing on an evolutionary narrative in which land animals adapted from sea creatures, as well as on the classical four elements, which represent the phases of matter: water (liquid), earth (solid), fire (plasma), and air (gas). Lawrence declares that you must "turn into a fish, and twiddle your fins and twist your tail and grope in amazement, in a new element" (P 721). This devolutionary or re-evolutionary metaphor, in which we return along the line of descent to the earliest aquatic life, proposes that we must inhabit a different and indeed elemental material consciousness in order to study humanity and the void. In addition, it suggests that inhabiting this consciousness is in fact a biological imperative, only through which can we progress.

Lawrence elaborates on the novel's role in this transformation—and in the proper study it marks—in another essay, "Why the Novel Matters" (1925), where "matter" speaks not only to significance but also materiality. In this essay he argues that the "novel is the one bright book of life," because the novelist, unlike the highly specialized modern scientist or philosopher, traverses the whole system of "man-alive" ("WNM" 195). This broader range, Lawrence argues, does more than science or philosophy to expose the lie of any mind/body divide, the belief that we're "[m]ens sana in copore sano," a sound mind in a healthy body ("WNM" 193). Moreover, he argues that "in the novel you can see, plainly," that life is a constant flux and that one must never think of an "I"—as in "I am this, I am that"—because it halts that flux and turns one "into a stupid fixed thing" ("WNM" 197). The novel shows you "when the man goes dead" or "the woman goes inert," allowing you to "develop an instinct for life, . . . instead of a theory of right and wrong, good and bad" ("WNM" 198). This claim that the novel decenters the "I" and encourages "instincts" rather than just mental "theor[ies]" begins to suggest what will be a grounding premise for Lawrence's final novel, *Lady Chatterley's Lover:* the idea that evolutionary adaptation can occur within an individual and not simply across generations. In other words, Lawrence suggests that the novel reader can actually adapt the instincts of impersonal subjectivity and so avoid extinction in the form of "going dead."[23] Lawrence also specifically links these instincts to vision in his claim that the novel offers instruction "you can see" rather than simply cogitate: "The philosopher . . . because he can *think,* decides that nothing but *thoughts* matter," but "[t]urn truly, honorably to the novel, and *see* wherein you are *man-alive,* and wherein you are dead man in life" ("WNM" 195, 197, emphasis added). For Lawrence, the novel's mindbodily visuality means that it's more than "any Word"; it's an imagetext constituted in a negotiation of the visual and the verbal ("WNM" 196). But despite his sense that this imagetextuality offers instruction, Lawrence also emphasizes that it doesn't "stimulate [readers] into some particular direction" ("WNM" 196). This qualification aligns with his resistance to the deterministic slant of evolutionary theory and what that determinism might mean for the individual. At the same time, it also explains why Lawrence's own *fort/da* economy, with its determined trajectory, might not so clearly reign in his novels.

Perhaps more than any other novel, *Lady Chatterley's Lover* pursues the imagetextual instruction described in "Why the Novel Matters." Written as Lawrence languished with tuberculosis and indeed worried whether he could survive long enough to finish (Squires 6-7), *Chatterley* translates his anxious decline into a re-evolutionary narrative that functions as an implicit critical response to Darwin's comments on the evolution of the eye by natural selection. *On the Origin of Species* (1859) famously suggests that reason bests imagination in helping us to understand how the photosensitivity of the first elementary nerves eventually became the sophistication and sharpness of the eagle's eye. Darwin begins his chapter "Organs of Extreme Perfection and Complication" with the claim that

> To suppose that the eye, with all its inimitable contrivances for adjusting the focus to different distances, for admitting different amounts of light, and for the correction of spherical and chromatic aberration, could have been formed by natural selection, seems, I freely confess, absurd in the highest possible degree. *Yet reason tells me,* that if numerous gradations from a perfect and complex eye to one very imperfect and simple, each grade being useful to its possessor, can be shown to exist . . . then the difficulty of believing that a perfect and complex eye

could be formed by natural selection, *though insuperable by our imagination* can hardly be considered real. (186–87, emphasis added)

After tracing the evolution of the eye from simple photoreceptor cells through various invertebrate and vertebrate eyes, Darwin concludes:

> He who will go thus far, if he find on finishing this treatise that large bodies of facts, otherwise inexplicable, can be explained by the theory of descent, ought not to hesitate to go further, and to admit that a structure *even as perfect as the eye of an eagle* might be formed by natural selection. . . . *His reason ought to conquer his imagination.* (188, emphasis added)

In *Psychoanalysis* and *Fantasia* the hawk's "single point of vision" was of course a crucial illustration of the root-vision that Lawrence values. Thus, in *Chatterley* he takes on Darwin's challenge: he offers an imaginative rather than a reasoned account through which we can compare the "extreme perfection and complication" of root-vision—to use Darwin's phrase—with less adapted types of sight and so understand root-vision's relation to more and less evolved forms of impersonality. Ronald Granofsky has argued that *Chatterley*'s characters are subjects in a Darwinian experiment that tests survival skills and that Lawrence is like a gamekeeper who engages in the kind of breeding process on which Darwin famously modeled his theory of natural selection. Building on this argument, I'm proposing that Lawrence's Darwinian experiment focuses on his visual theory of impersonality and that it tests an individual's ability to adapt toward a properly impersonal mode of seeing and being.[24] *Chatterley* also exemplifies and indeed comments on how art can aid this adaptation. Its experiment and commentary together suggest both a liberatory and a conservative sociopolitical potential for impersonality but don't ultimately track in a single direction, so that the novel's formulation of gender in particular remains suggestively unstable.

Lawrence frames the broad scene of *Chatterley*'s experiment as a modern evolutionary crisis: it's post–World War I England, and the human species is in conflict with its habitat because industrial mechanization has allowed it to conceive of itself as both radically distant from and in control of that habitat. The narrower setting of the novel, the Chatterley family estate, offers a microcosm of this evolutionary crisis. Wragby encompasses an extensive ecosystem, including woods, fields, livestock, and carefully fostered game. But what funds the estate is the Chatterleys' nearby coal-mining operation, Tevershall pit, where the land is being ruthlessly pillaged: "Tevershall pit-bank was burning, had been burning for years, and it would cost thousands to put it out. So it had to burn. And when the wind was that way, which was often, the house [Wragby] was full of the stench of this sulphurous combustion of the earth's excrement" (13). In this hellish scene of waste and decay, those who work the mine or live in its midst are atavisms of a long-ago moment of evolutionary development, which Lawrence describes by slipping into a more technical language of biological taxonomy: they are each "almost . . . a creature . . . , one of the amazing crabs and lobsters of the modern industrial and financial world, invertebrates of the crustacean order, with shells of steel, like machines, and inner bodies of soft pulp" (110). Lawrence warns that in order to survive, humanity must (re)adapt to its environment, rather than trying to subdue that environment through the mechanical fruits of human reason. This adaptation means again developing a lived relation to impersonal subjectivity, which is materially united with habitat and refuses the grotesque inner/outer divide of the modern creature-machine. Lawrence's Darwinian experiment asks specifically whether two test subjects, Connie Chatterley and Oliver Mellors, can foster an impersonal connection to each other through which they might achieve the necessary adaptation. At the same time, Lawrence's write-up of this experiment persistently reflects on the role of the artistic imagination in acknowledging impersonality and thus encouraging evolutionary adaptation.

Sir Clifford Chatterley, the owner of Wragby and the Tevershall pit, personifies all of the symptoms of the modern species crisis, symptoms that unsurprisingly coincide with the habits critiqued in Lawrence's theory of impersonality. First, Clifford has returned from World War I with an injury that captures his longstanding unfitness. He has always been "apart from" or "beyond" sexual intercourse, a member of the rational "intelligentsia" who believes that civilization means "slowly eliminating the guts and alimentary system from the human being, to evolve a higher, more spiritual being" (12, 12, 10, 235). Lawrence indicates his refusal of this form of evolution—its abandonment of the body and sex—through Clifford's paraplegia, his particular visuality, and his commitment to personality. Clifford's injury means that he's cut off from those crucial lower centers of the impersonal unconscious described in *Psychoanalysis* and *Fantasia,* and he's specifically unable to engage in an impersonalizing sexual intercourse and thereby to further his family line. The motorized wheelchair he occupies as a result of his injury directly sutures his unfitness to the industrial mechanization driving the evolutionary crisis. And Lawrence draws out this crisis through Clifford's plan to produce an heir despite his injury. Clifford believes that his wife, Connie, should have a child by another man, a child that Clifford then would raise as his own, on the grounds that "connections . . . [a]nd the occasional sexual connections especially" don't really "matter" (44). Invoking the evolutionary language of "mating" and "selection" only to denigrate it, he remarks that "[i]f people don't exaggerate them [such connections] ridiculously, they pass like the mating of birds" and that he trusts Connie's "natural instinct of decency and selection" in the choice of the other man (44). Clifford's purportedly analytic approach to the question of sex suggests that the appeal to reason on which Darwin leans so heavily is actually a recipe for warping evolutionary theory.

In keeping with Clifford's dualistic belief that sex and indeed bodies don't really "matter," he also subscribes to a Cartesian visuality. In a statement that combines faith in such vision with a grandiose omniscience, Clifford presumes that "[w]hat the eye doesn't see, and the mind doesn't know, doesn't exist" (18), a belief that Lawrence mocks when he describes Clifford's "watchful look" as "a blank of insentience," a vacant stare with literally no physical sense in it (6). Lawrence also again welds Clifford's disembodiment, in this case his visual insentience, to mechanical prostheses by explaining that his "remot[e]" stare was like that of a man "looking down a microscope, or up a telescope": his "observation was extraordinary and peculiar. But there was no touch, no actual contact" (16). Unsurprisingly, given Lawrence's particular optical impersonality, Clifford's ignorance of embodied vision leads him predictably to believe that "the whole problem of life [is] the slow building up of an integral personality," that everything he owns or does is an expression of his personality, and that any resistance from Connie is an effort to "derang[e] . . . his personality" (45, 294).

Lawrence begins to frame *Chatterley* as an imaginative response against this constellation of values by linking Clifford's reasoned but distorting approach to life to inadequate forms of art. Clifford writes "very personal stories about people he had known" and approves only of those writers who "order and give shape" to "disorderly emotions" (16, 139, 139). His work reduces the embodied subject to a disembodied person and thus to a "stupid fixed thing." Clifford's counterpart in the visual arts is Connie's old friend Duncan Forbes, the abstract painter. Duncan paints the "tubes and valves and spirals" that Lawrence had rejected in "Introduction to These Paintings," and *Chatterley* correspondingly diagnoses his work as out of touch with the body and also as a "personal cult" full of "nervous self-opinion" (286). Dun-

can's forms and focus together recall the "personal conceit" of Fry's significant form and its distinct lack of imagetextuality, as detailed in "Introduction
to These Paintings."

Having diagnosed a problem that meaningfully spans both visual and
verbal representation, Lawrence answers this "personal cult" and its commitment to a purified image and opticality with *Chatterley* itself. The novel
draws the species crisis marked by Clifford's and Duncan's creativity into
a narrative, not of romance—which "Know Deeply" rejected as a mental-
personal ideal—but of new mating and correspondingly new seeing. Clifford and Connie seem at the start of the novel to be a perfect match, but
that perfection stems from their mutual and problematic abandonment of
sex. Like Clifford, Connie is uninterested in sex even before her husband's
paralysis. She believes that talking about ideas is the path to intimacy and
characterizes sex, by contrast, as "one of the curious obsolete organic processes which persisted . . . but was not really necessary" (12). Given her
similar evolutionary attitude to her husband's—one that imagines that humans are evolving beyond "organic processes"—Connie's relationship with
Clifford turns, not surprisingly, on an "intimacy which was beyond sex,"
which "was deeper, more personal" (12). Punctuating how this is in fact no
relation at all, Connie echoes Clifford's hysterical anxiety that his personality
not be deranged with her longstanding refusal to "yield her inner, free self"
(7). As Lawrence puts it in the draft of his essay "A Propos of *Lady Chatterley's Lover*" (1930), Clifford and Connie's union joins "two personalities" and
thereby removes love "from the blood into the mind," severing it from the
species' habitat, which is "the sun and the earth."[25] Such is the reason for
that union's failure.

The eventual salient difference between Clifford and Connie arises in her
recognition of this failure. Living in Clifford's enclosed, disembodied world,
Connie suffers a sharp physical decline, including a distinctly visual malady:
everything she sees is "spectral," a "simulacrum of reality" (18). These phrases
suggest the false promise of Clifford's fantasized visual immediacy and the
hollow projections of the world seen from inside a camera obscura. Connie
herself awakens to what such a Cartesian visuality denies through two experiences. First, she registers how this disembodied vision, which sharply
distinguishes interior from exterior, distances her from the material world:
"The oak-leaves to her were like oak-leaves seen ruffling in a mirror . . . [the]
primroses . . . were only shadows . . . [n]o substance . . . no touch, no contact" (18). The reference to a world "seen . . . in a mirror" evokes Clifford's

misguided commitment to an objective, mimetic image, while the closing phrase, "no touch, no contact," solidifies this connection by repeating the narrator's description of Clifford's disembodied mode of "observation," which has "no touch, no actual contact." Second, and related to the "substance" that's missing from this mode, Connie begins to intuit what Lawrence had called the "physiology of matter" in his letter to Edward Garnett. She experiences involuntary "twitche[s in] her limbs," "jerk[s of] her spine," and "violent" "beat[s]" of "her heart," as if her body were sending out signals of distinctly impersonal imperatives (20). Faced with these experiences, Connie stares at her naked body in the mirror, worries that it's "going meaningless . . . through neglect and denial," and asks herself in fundamentally Darwinian terms, "Was she fit, anyhow?" (70-71, 71). These moments reject a Cartesian visuality and tie this rejection to the origins of an adaptive relation to impersonal subjectivity. Thus, once Connie is set on this adaptive path, she correspondingly rejects Clifford's and Duncan's "ready-made" art full of "self-important mentalities" rather than "feelings" (93, 194, 194). Through this rejection, Lawrence highlights how *Chatterley* is an alternative impersonal art that can help us to escape an evolutionary dead end.

Of course, if Clifford represents all the facets of that evolutionary dead end, Lawrence must variously position Mellors, Connie's new mate, as his foil. Thus, where Clifford owns a mine and revels in the technological innovations that might encourage its greater productivity, Mellors is a former miner who has rejected such industrial exploitation of the land and its workers. While Clifford owns Wragby and treats the estate as a reflection of himself, Mellors chooses to foster Wragby's complex ecosphere as its gamekeeper. Where Clifford fashions himself as an intellectual, removed from physical labor and concerns, the no less educated Mellors doesn't allow his mental pursuits to separate him from the material world or his own instincts. Finally, and most crucially to this reading, while Clifford embraces personality and a Cartesian visuality, Mellors exudes an impersonality linked to the root-vision of *Fantasia*.

Connie senses this alternative mode of being and seeing in her earliest meetings with Mellors. He gazes at her "with a perfectly fearless, impersonal look," and she instinctively groups his "impersonal eyes" with his "swift, yet soft movements" (46, 47, 46). In other words, on some level, she understands that his vision is part of his physiology. Moreover, Connie's sudden encounter with Mellors when she comes upon him bathing creates the opportunity for her own inauguration into this embodied vision. As Lawrence puts it, Connie experiences the sight of Mellors' body as a "shock of vision in her womb," a location that roughly mirrors the very first impersonal center, the solar plexus, described in *Psychoanalysis* and *Fantasia* (66). Correspondingly, it's just after this "shock of vision" that Connie realizes that she has become unfit. And it's of course also her womb that will carry the reproductive fruits of her impersonal imperative, namely, her sexual selection of Mellors.

Impersonal adaptation is not limited to Connie, though. Like Clifford, Mellors bears the scars of a wartime illness, pneumonia contracted in the army, which has left his lungs weakened. Though Lawrence himself had this same weakness, in *Fantasia* he characterized breathing problems as the symptom of an imbalance across the impersonal centers (*PF* 98). *Chatterley* links this imbalance with the modern species crisis not only through the global decimation of the war (the context in which Mellors became ill) but also through the industrial mechanization indicated by Clifford's wheelchair. Mellors most betrays his lack of fitness when he's unable to push that chair up a steep slope, at least not without Connie's help. The sexual relationship that develops alongside this cooperative moment between Connie and Mellors enables their mutual adaptation toward a proper impersonality. The more the two are willing to efface themselves in sex, the more they experience mutual orgasms. Indeed, Connie registers these orgasms, which cleave through her consciousness and touch something unconscious in her, as a sign of the vitalistic connection and transformation between her and Mellors. These orgasms are the "extra-individual" circuit of impersonal subjectivity that Lawrence had described in *Psychoanalysis* and *Fantasia*. In addition, in keeping with "Know Deeply," Connie perceives this transformation as a kind of impersonal not-knowing. She feels that she and Mellors "knew nothing" of themselves or each other in their sexual union—that they had awakened "[a]nother self" than the personality (134, 135). Mellors seconds this feeling by contrasting his sexual union with Connie to his experience with his estranged wife, Bertha Coutts. He explains to Connie that with Bertha sex was "Self! self! self! all self!" and resulted in neither mutual orgasm nor transformation (202).

Just as importantly, both Mellors and Connie choose a visual ritual to mark the contrary success of their sexual transformation. When Connie demands, "Kiss me," Mellors "kisse[s] her . . . on the left eye," and Connie later kisses Mellors "between the eyes" (127, 127, 178). This reciprocal act of physical intimacy indicates an acknowledgment of the root-vision they now share and its importance to their impersonal connection.

In the midst of this adapted instability in both vision and subjectivity, Connie and Mellors' sexual selection repeats the sociopolitical tensions we saw in *Psychoanalysis* and *Fantasia,* particularly when it comes to gender identity. On the one hand, their postcoital conversations include a fairly radical blurring of gender roles. For instance, as the pair lie together, Connie maintains that what Mellors has "that other men don't," and what "will make the future," is the "courage of [his] own tenderness" (277). Mellors accepts this analysis, which links him to both traditionally masculine and feminine qualities—courage and tenderness—respectively. He owns his "natural physical tenderness" and suggests that this tenderness is what the men he had led in the army meant when they claimed he had "too much of the woman" in him (277). Mellors even characterizes this state of being "bodily aware" as "cunt-awareness" and suggests that having it makes him "manly" (277). Just as importantly, in the midst of this complex gender crossing, Mellors also takes up the pivotal role that Connie gives him in the species' futurity by declaring that humans, "[e]specially the English have . . . [a] crying need" for this impersonal "tenderness," and by extension the gender instability it implies (277).

On the other hand, however, Connie and Mellors' mutual submission to an impersonal imperative also includes the sense that to become no longer a person may be to occupy the more general category of one's sex. In other words, what it means to be impersonal is to be a sex rather than a self, a trajectory that recovers a stable and potentially traditional locus for gender identity in the species' futurity. When Connie claims that she's "going meaningless" in her "cold . . . and separate" relationship with Clifford, she casts that lack as her body's being "[d]isappointed of its real womanhood" (70, 72, 70). In addition, when she sees Mellors bathing, her root-vision awakens not simply in her abdomen, but rather in her "womb," a biological site of sex and reproduction. It's thus not surprising that Connie's subsequent impersonal intimacy with Mellors is predicated on her status as a woman: their union "wasn't really personal" precisely because she's "only really a female to him" (121). Likewise, Connie's praise for Mellors' "kind[ness] to the female in her"—where other men were "kind to the *person* she was but rather cruel to the female"—positions his impersonality as distinctly male and hers as once again distinctly female (121). By thoroughly suffusing the impersonal with gender in this formulation, Lawrence makes impersonal subjectivity a safe harbor for such identity. He also uses this safe harbor to shape gender in specifically conservative ways, for Mellors' masculine kindness is effectively a chivalrous magnanimity that rescues a helpless Connie from cruelty. Indeed, Lawrence later reinforces this patriarchy when Sir Malcolm Reid, Connie's father, notes that "he had always liked the female" in his daughter (274). Such a comment echoes Mellors' particular kindness and casts Connie as a passive, feminine object to be traded between the men, which is arguably the goal of Sir Malcolm's subsequent lunch with Mellors.[26]

The principal difference between *Chatterley* and Lawrence's criticism is that as the novel negotiates these dual directions for gender identity, it doesn't ultimately favor the more conservative direction, nor does it guide impersonality toward a right-wing politics. In fact, *Chatterley* uses multiple negative models of impersonality to reject *both* conservative and revolutionary political forms and to privilege the individual or the individual couple as the final site of Lawrence's own alternative. Connie and Mellors' ultimate trajectory captures what is by now an unsurprising individualism in Lawrence's impersonal aesthetic: having mated and conceived a child, they are planning a farm life together without any kind of social sanction, because Connie is unable to get a divorce and thus cannot remarry. In addition, as the two steadily move toward this choice, Connie and Mellors are confronted with alternative, more socially defined formulations of impersonality that they dismiss as inadequate to both their own and the species' survival.

Two of these alternative models, both socially conservative, are linked to Clifford, whose increasing infantilization over the course of the novel alludes to his devolution and impending extinction. The first of these models is a kind of ancestral impersonality in which the individual is swallowed up in an inherited social role. Clifford suggests this model when he proposes having a child who wouldn't be his biologically but would inherit the Chatterley name, title, estate, and social responsibilities. Such a prospect suggests an aristocracy so culturally determined and rigid as to reduce any sense of the individual to a mere "link in a chain" (43). Connie criticizes this "curious impersonality" as an "obscenely conceived . . . display" that prioritizes superficial appearance over the realities of an opaque materiality (43, 50). She imagines this brand of impersonality going extinct via a figure that suggests not only the family tree but also the tree of life and its scientific use in Darwin's branching theory of evolution: to her, the "brilliant words" of

Clifford's plan "seemed like dead leaves, crumpling up and turning to powder . . . not the leafy words of an effective life, young with energy and belonging to the tree [but] . . . the hosts of fallen leaves of a life that is ineffectual" (50). The fact that Connie's choice between Clifford and Mellors centers not only on sex but also on ways of life and their prospects for perpetuating themselves suggests the importance of evolutionary fitness in the novel. Connie decides not to raise her child within Clifford's impersonal aristocracy, though she knows that she could convince him to accept Mellors' baby as his own. By choosing Mellors for life—and by choosing a life broadly removed from inherited social structures—Connie reinforces that she and Mellors occupy an impersonal individuality apart from Clifford's systemizing ancestral impersonality.

But Clifford also offers a second conservative model of impersonality, this time in his business dealings at the Tevershall pit, where he pursues the capitalist imperative to put "industry before the individual" (180). Just as the aristocracy turns parent and child into "links in a chain," Clifford remarks that his capitalist position is "a function, a part of fate," while "the masses are a functioning of another part of fate," so that "[t]he individual hardly matters" (183). Connie condemns this capitalist impersonality for "tak[ing] away from the people their natural life and manhood, and giv[ing] them this industrial horror" in its place (182). She suggests that Clifford, and the system he represents, denies workers their materiality and individuality by commodifying them as generic units of labor. Mellors' final comments in the novel second her feelings. Casting his judgment specifically in terms of impending extinction, he declares that "the whole damned" capitalist system "is doomed" and that humans "are doomed along with it" (299). Even Lawrence's painting *Flight Back into Paradise* (1927; fig. 4.4), created as he was writing *Chatterley*, seems to chime in to reject this impersonality. The painting features a Connie-like Eve "running back into Paradise," with a "burning industrial town behind" her and a Mellors-like Adam "hold[ing] off [an] old Angel at the gate" (*Letters* 6:188n). The systemic grid of the city and its industrial works—which are burning just as the Tevershall pit is in *Chatterley*—are restraining Eve as she latches on to Adam so that he can pull her to the safety of nature. If this reimagined biblical narrative is effectively a flight toward a positive impersonality, then the painting offers Lawrence's own Cézannesque "appleyness" in place of the absolutes he associated with Satan's apple in "Art and Morality." The imagetextuality of this painting's dynamic relation with *Chatterley*, coupled with its postimpressionist commitment to

Fig. 4.4. D. H. Lawrence, *Flight Back into Paradise,* 1927. Courtesy of Robert G. Sahd, Taos, New Mexico.

a material visuality of "insignificant form," acts as a challenge not only to Clifford's capitalist impersonality but also to Duncan Forbes' "personal cult" of frozen "tubes and valves and spirals."

Connie and Mellors, and so also Lawrence, reject not only Clifford's conservative models of impersonality but a revolutionary impersonality as well. The novel proposes that although "bolshevism" is capitalism's ideological opposite, it deploys an identical and equally unacceptable logic whereby "the individual . . . must be suppressed" and "submerge[d] . . . in the greater thing, the soviet-social thing" (38). Mellors later seconds this claim by accusing a socialist impersonality of being equally entangled with the mechanized conditions of industrialism as a capitalist impersonality: "We've got these great industrial populations, and they've got to be fed, so the damn show has to be kept going. . . . Even under a Soviet you've still got to sell coal" (299).

Clarifying that the problem is one of environment and a proper relation to it, Mellors explains that what the working class really needs is to worship the god of nature and fertility: "[T]he mass of people . . . should be alive and frisky, and acknowledge the great god Pan. . . . But the colliers aren't pagan—far from it. They're a sad lot, a deadened lot of men" (300). Mellors implies that without the proper habitat, the men are in a state of decline, which is much like Sir Malcolm's earlier claim that his daughter Connie is a "bonny Scotch trout" trying to live in Wragby's choked environment for "pilchard[s]" (18). Both of these remarks suggest that if there is any system that can support the individual impersonality that Connie and Mellors, and in turn Lawrence, believe can solve the modern species crisis, it's a natural order characterized in Darwinian evolution. Thus, the life that Connie and Mellors plan for themselves, the life beyond social sanction, is an agrarian existence that promotes a material and mutually supportive relation to their habitat.

And yet, it's crucial to register that despite Connie and Mellors' clear plan, *Chatterley* doesn't offer an easy resolution. Not only that, but this uncertainty is itself part of Lawrence's impersonality, and indeed part of its modified Darwinian account as well. Though the novel launches Connie and Mellors on the path of a proper impersonality, Lawrence ends his re-evolutionary experiment before the success of his subjects' adaptation is confirmed. In other words, he sets the write-up of his imaginative experiment prior to the experiment's final results. Thus, for instance, after all of *Chatterley*'s emphasis on root-vision as a kind of seeing in touch and its comparative rejection of an intimacy in words, the novel nonetheless leaves Connie and Mellors literally out of sight and out of touch, with him writing to her from afar about their uncertain future. In addition, although Connie is pregnant, we don't see her give birth, so we have no measure of the fitness of her child compared with Mellors' shallow and materialistic daughter with Bertha, who is, significantly, also named Connie. Moreover, although Mellors is training to be a farmer, he's pursuing that training on a farm that supplies the coal industry, documenting that he hasn't yet managed to fully extricate himself or his soon-to-be family from that system. This open-endedness in *Chatterley* echoes the inevitable incompletion of Lawrence's at-hand poetry, which he suggested marks the physiology of chaos that spans the universe, including an embodied impersonal subjectivity.

But the novel's ending has an additional function as well. If Lawrence considered *Chatterley* an instrument for adapting (rather than simply representing) impersonality, and if individuals matter most in his particular brand of impersonality, then in his decision not to follow Connie and Mellors to the end of their experiment he also refuses to make them types in a larger evolutionary or fictional narrative that's neatly wrapped up for a passive reader's edification. Indeed, if individuals can themselves adapt toward impersonality, contra Darwin, then Connie and Mellors' child needn't bear so much weight in Lawrence's impersonal model or even in the species' futurity. According to Michael Squires, Lawrence worked harder in each successive version of *Lady Chatterley's Lover* to "break out of the prison of his own work" as he also broke the "old boundaries of . . . personality" (105). One might say, then, that this progressive selection for impersonality depended in part on Lawrence's granting Connie and Mellors the individuality he meant for them to model, particularly as Lawrence knew that this would be his last novel.

Lawrence's early essays put *Chatterley's* ending and its broader impersonal imperative in a particularly rich light. Juxtaposing the two gives us a final view of the flux of his impersonal aesthetic across his career and the multiple genres he worked in. In his essays on painting and psychoanalysis, Lawrence's desire to recuperate individuality was in clear tension with the destabilizing implications of the impersonality he outlined in his poetry. Those essays put the rich web of repetition and multiple meaning through which Lawrence's poetry defined impersonality in the service of consolidation. They reasserted the force not only of individuality but also of embodied identities such as gender and race through what I've termed Lawrence's *fort/da* economy. Yet in Lawrence's fiction, and specifically in *Lady Chatterley's Lover,* this economy fades without disappearing entirely. *Chatterley's* imaginative account of visual evolution promotes impersonality while also keeping embodied identities in an unresolved state of play.

This play reverberates interestingly with recent philosophical accounts of Darwinian evolution as the site of more contingency and unfixed potential than is often assumed. Elizabeth Grosz, in particular, has emphasized the fundamental indeterminacy of natural selection and the importance in sexual selection of random and individual preferences over fitness alone. In addition, while Grosz presents her reading as a way to disentangle Darwinian evolution from conservative models of biology, she doesn't allow it simply to undo gender or racial difference but instead presents it as an account of their historical production: for example, individual preferences in sexual selection (such as darker skin) can create communities that produce or sustain racial difference over time. This reverberation between Lawrence and Grosz with regard to both an open evolutionary system and embodied identities suggests that his imaginative account may well have seen in visual evolution something that Darwin's own reasoned account didn't always emphasize.

As Lawrence moved through his career-long negotiation of impersonality and its relation to a scientific vernacular of vision, he took quite a few approaches to its political implications. He fashioned impersonality at one moment as conservative and at another as the site of a more liberatory play; eventually he even attempted to move it outside an established socio-political spectrum entirely. Thus, where Loy's career negotiated an anxious ambivalence about the politics of impersonality, Lawrence tolerated multiple political possibilities in search of local, often idiosyncratic outcomes. In doing so, he offered an important microcosm of the political variability of the impersonal aesthetic as a whole.

5 Managing the "Feeling into Which We Cannot Peer"

T. S. Eliot's Impersonal Matters

[P]oetry *is* a science . . . not the mere ebullition of a personality.

Eliot, "Modern Tendencies in Poetry"

[B]eyond the nameable, classifiable emotions and motives of our conscious life . . . there is a fringe of indefinite extent, of feeling which we can only detect, so to speak, out of the corner of the eye and can never completely focus.

Eliot, "Poetry and Drama"

The writers featured in the preceding chapters are more often linked to other modernist movements than to impersonality—Pater and Field to impressionism and aestheticism, H.D. and Loy to a personalist feminism, and Lawrence to a retro-Romantic individualism. The same cannot be said for T. S. Eliot. In reserving him for this final chapter, I've worked to loosen impersonality from the critical assumptions that lie in Eliot's long shadow and to explore a new set of investments, forms, and themes for this contested aesthetic. Eliot effectively policed the perimeter of impersonality: he famously lambasted Pater as an "imperfect critic," characterized Lawrence's art as the very absence of a quintessential "moral or social sense," and posited that it was simply inappropriate to speak of Loy's *oeuvre*—to see her as a notable modernist—because her writing was too inconsistent.[1] Scholars have frequently followed Eliot's lead, even when their goal was actually to dismiss him. F. R. Leavis, for instance, championed Lawrence for answering the artistic call to express the individual will and personality, over and against any social sense, and bashed Eliot's impersonality for abandoning that call ("Lawrence After Thirty Years" 401). Even Susan Gilmore's belief

that Loy's crusade against women's relative social impersonality also rejected aesthetic impersonality seems indebted to Eliot's involvement with
the feminist literary review the *Egoist,* where he published both his marginalizing critique of Loy and his impersonal manifesto "Tradition and the Individual Talent" (1919) ("Imna, Ova, Mongrel Spy" 271). "Tradition" attacked the
ego—the pole on which the journal was flying its feminist flag—positioning
aesthetic impersonality as a potential threat to feminism.[2] Despite Eliot's
proclamations, though, he can in fact be placed within the same optical
impersonality that drives the varying aesthetic politics of Pater, Field, H.D.,
Loy, and Lawrence.

Such a rewriting challenges those critics who reduce Eliot's impersonality to a glorified balm for his various personal anxieties. According to one
reading, impersonality was a bulwark against various threats to Eliot's artistic power: a screen against prying psychological criticism (Ellmann, *Poetics
of Impersonality*); a way to sustain dominance as the unity of the authorial
self deteriorated (Buch-Jepsen); a cloak for the Romantic individualism he
claimed to shed (Langbaum); or a compensation for lacking the eccentric
personality of a successful artist (Murphy).[3] According to another reading,
impersonality was slightly more outward looking: it stemmed from Eliot's
anxious desire to hide the division between self and society (Lee) or to
reject the perceived disorder of actual life in favor of a universal ideal in
art (Ward). All of these estimates amount ultimately to the same thing: to
Steven Spender's famous polemic that Eliot's anti-expressive impersonality
was really an expression of his personality.[4] This view makes it easy to
equate modernism's impersonal aesthetic with the regressive politics that
scholars have ferreted out in Eliot's work: misogyny, racism, anti-Semitism,
and homophobia.

A few critics, however, have begun to move beyond this ample baggage
and to explore Eliot's impersonality as something more than a personal subterfuge or cryptofascism. John Paul Riquelme, Sharon Cameron, Charles Altieri, and Tim Dean have all pointed to Eliot's critique of the vanities of lyric
expressionism and his challenge to individual sovereignty. In addition, though
these scholars have tended to minimize embodiment,[5] Fabio Vericat has
recently suggested that Eliot's impersonality actually maps a radical subjectivity traceable in nervous and cognitive experience. I build on Vericat's suggestion and on this broader turn in the study of Eliot's impersonality by
tracing his participation in the modern scientific vernacular of embodied
vision.[6] Eliot himself crystallizes this participation in an iconic 1956 portrait

Fig. 5.1. Cecil Beaton, *T. S. Eliot,* 1956. Courtesy of the Cecil Beaton Studio Archive at Sotheby's, London.

by Cecil Beaton that bears out David Piper and Nuzhat Bukhari's sense that Eliot is the face of modernist impersonality (fig. 5.1).[7]

In this famed photograph, Eliot stands in professional attire before a textured glass partition in his Faber office. The light coming from a rear window falls over recesses in the glass, across Eliot's spectacles, and onto the polished cabinet on which he leans. Instead of seeing his eyes, we see the window reflected as a square of light over his glasses, even as a reflected pair of hands seems to reach for him from the cabinet top. The image is evocative of a mirror, but isn't one, just as the dim room, aperturelike window, and reflected light are together evocative of a camera obscura—the photographic camera's technological forebear—but aren't one. Indeed, this photograph works against Descartes' camera obscura model of vision by turning light into a source of opacity and multiplicity rather than of transparent enlightenment and singularity.

This effect echoes Eliot's friend J. M. Murry's description of his impersonal aesthetic as forgotten *"pièces d'identitié* [sic]," or photo ID. Murry reads Eliot's poetry not as his attempt to "cover himself with a cloud" of verse so that "he would be inviolable" but instead as a more complicated effort, by which Eliot's "substantial core" departs and "leaves in our hands" his *pièces d'identitié.*" Murry's contrasting models of impersonality (escape vs. fragmentation), coupled with his suggestive use of the French term for photo ID, sets up two notions of subjectivity: one is the willful person who can decide to leave or decide to hide (the "substantial core"); the other is a fragmented and forgotten or unknown remainder (the *"pièces d'identitié"*). Murry's verbal play casts Eliot's impersonality as the substitution of one subjectivity for another and reveals the imagetext, in the form of the photo ID, as a formal analogue for the chosen impersonal subjectivity. If we take Murry's comments as a kind of caption for Eliot's portrait, we can see that the portrait functions as a similar imagetext. Its complex depiction of visual perception, knowledge, and subjectivity is an instance of his belief that "certain images" might be able to grasp "the depths of feeling into which we cannot peer."[8] Indeed, the portrait presents Eliot's impersonal project as an effort to find those images, to make that grasp, to acknowledge those opaque and uncontrollable feelings—at least insofar as their incoherence doesn't interfere with the stolid social hierarchies that whisper from his business attire.

I locate the beginnings of Eliot's search in his early encounters with visual science and with the popular science writer J. W. N. Sullivan, who worked with Eliot at the *Athenaeum.* In his early essays on impersonality Eliot adapted Sullivan's scientific vernacular, namely, certain concepts about the nature of science, rhetoric about the relation between art and science, and even an illustrative focus on optics. But Eliot's resulting optical impersonality and its potentially liberatory social implications were a source of persistent ambivalence for him. Where Lawrence managed to exploit impersonality for conservative political ends, Eliot developed less reliable strategies for simply containing impersonality and thereby retaining traditional social hierarchies. These strategies evolve from Eliot's early poem *The Waste Land* (1922) to his verse drama *The Family Reunion* (1939), but they consistently revolve around complex bodily transformations that strive to achieve a healing rediscovery of impersonal subjectivity while still mapping it through staid gender conventions.

"New and Wonderful Visions": The Science of Eliot's Impersonality

In 1918 Eliot's wife, Viv, in addition to suffering from neuralgia and migraines, began having trouble with her vision and eventually complained of hallucinations and trance states (Trombold, "Part I" 41; "Part II" 34-35). After four years of dealing with these ailments, Eliot wrote to Pound that Viv's visual symptoms had finally been diagnosed as a cramped *sella turcica*, the saddle-shaped depression in the sphenoid bone of the skull, behind the eyes, where the pituitary gland sits (Lyndall Gordon, *T. S. Eliot* 77). A cramping of the *sella turcica* could stem from either a tumor or *hyperostosis frontalis interna*, a condition in which the bones surrounding the *sella turcica* grow beyond their normal size. In either case, this cramping can cause the pituitary to secrete an imbalance of hormones, leading to a variety of nervous disorders. It can also cause the pituitary to push against either the carotid artery or the optic chiasm, the part of the brain where the optic nerves cross. Both types of pressure can produce visual defects and delusions.

Although Viv's health problems progressively became both financially and emotionally overwhelming for Eliot, his friends nonetheless record how much he enjoyed detailing her symptoms and their causes, as he did in his letter to Pound (Trombold, "Part II" 37-38). Viv's eye troubles were likely of particular interest, because they echoed research on the psychophysiology of human vision going on at Harvard when Eliot was a student there. The philosopher Josiah Royce, from whom Eliot took a course on scientific method and who later supervised his dissertation, offered a survey of recent findings in his *Outlines of Psychology* (1903), particularly in the chapter "Mental Imagery." Royce detailed how susceptible vision and visual memory are to brain states, disturbances of the retinal field, and external stimuli. His colleague William James' *Principles of Psychology* (1890) similarly anchored its inferences regarding the human will in a survey of the recent work of optical physiologists like Hermann von Helmholtz and Ewald Hering, in addition to reporting James' own findings, for instance, on the eyes' reflex arcs and the structures of visual attention. Eliot's personal and medical encounters with such findings on embodied vision, coupled with his participation in the psychological and philosophical community that produced them, would have set the stage for his interactions with the *Athenaeum*'s science correspondent and deputy editor, J. W. N. Sullivan, as Eliot was first formulating his impersonal theory of art.

Eliot was a regular reviewer for the *Athenaeum* during his friend J. M. Murry's tenure as editor, and through Murry he became friends with Sullivan. From April 1919 to February 1921 Sullivan contributed weekly essays popularizing scientific topics, particularly in physics, and also promoting a dynamic relation between science and art.[9] Eliot gave Sullivan and Murry tickets to his lecture "Modern Tendencies in Poetry," delivered before the

Arts League of Service on 28 October 1919; in that lecture he invoked recent *Athenaeum* articles on the shared project of art and science—undoubtedly Sullivan's—as the context for his talk.[10] Written and presented between Eliot's composition of the two parts of "Tradition and the Individual Talent," "Modern Tendencies" sketches the kernel of his impersonal aesthetic and reflects on how science motivated his catalytic analogy for impersonal artistic production in that more famous essay.[11] Eliot thus effectively announces his own participation in Sullivan's scientific vernacular, suggesting that a survey of Sullivan's articles from just prior to Eliot's lecture could provide a window onto the foundational concerns of his theory of impersonality.[12]

Sullivan's articles from this period focus on the pedagogical approaches of scientific textbooks, on modern scientific method and style, and on recent research by particular scientists. At root, they all point to the intersections of science and philosophy that Eliot knew from the work of Royce and James, but they go one step further to triangulate these fields with art, the career to which Eliot had committed himself after finishing his philosophy dissertation in 1916. Sullivan posits that each of these three fields must "partake of the nature of the other two" in order to be good—that none exists in any meaningful way alone ("Place"). Perhaps not surprisingly, then, he also suggests that people learn science best through a "historic method" ("On Learning"). He calls for students to explore not only the "perfunctory 'proofs' of many modern text-books" but also the "delicate web of doubt" that is the actual lifeblood and "aesthetic value" of science ("On Learning"; "Justification" 275). According to Sullivan, modern textbooks focus exclusively on abstract formulas and thereby promote the false sense that science is (and thinks it is) an "infallib[le]" doctrine ("On Learning"). By contrast, the historic method that Sullivan advocates emphasizes an ongoing process of discovery that uncovers how science is "tentative, imaginative, courageous," rather than absolute or objective ("On Learning"). He casts this complex nature in distinctly visual terms, describing science's tentative side as "purblind . . . fumbling" and its imaginative and courageous side as the pursuit of "half-seen alternative explanations" ("Place"; "On Learning"). He also celebrates this complex nature in similarly visual terms, suggesting that even science's limits reveal to humankind "new and wonderful visions" ("Scientific Education" 885). This visual dynamic in fact becomes the bridge linking science to art, for Sullivan proposes that scientists become "poets" when their visions discern patterns among "local curiosities" of experience and construct a provisional web of relations to capture those patterns ("Place";

"Scientific Education" 885). For Sullivan, this poetic web of relations constitutes *"significant* knowledge" ("Place").

Sullivan elaborates on the role of the scientist in this process through his
remarks on style. Although he argues that science is "something in the face
of which one's individuality is lost," he also holds that the scientist's approach to knowledge isn't universal—that there's always a "personal element
in a great scientific work" ("Science and Personality" 624). Sullivan, in other
words, makes science personal-impersonal, refusing to consider personality
and impersonality as mutually exclusive forces. In addition, and crucially for
Eliot, Sullivan bears out his sense that scientists are poets by advocating the
same personal-impersonal structure for art. He argues that "the modern insistence on personalities" at the expense of the impersonal has "something
to do with the modern absence of great art" ("Science and Personality" 624).
But against this absence, and perhaps with Eliot in mind, he also reports that
the artistic "cultivation of individualities is declining" as modern art joins
with modern science to discern significant knowledge ("Science and Personality" 625).

In "A Stylist in Science," Sullivan offers the British physicist Lord Rayleigh
(John William Strutt) as a model for the modern personal-impersonal scientist. He suggests that Rayleigh belonged to a generation with "scientific imagination," in that he relied heavily on visual modeling and experimentation
rather than only abstract mathematical formula. Drawing significantly on an
account by Helmholtz, Sullivan argues that Rayleigh's style emphasizes visual schemas of scientific concepts—"some kind of imaginative picture"—
and also details the experience of constructing and conducting experiments.
Much in line with Sullivan's historic method, Rayleigh didn't seek to create
an aura of infallibility by "'command[ing]' assent"; rather, his thick description, his focus on process, and his "aesthetically as well as logically satisfy-
ing" form fostered the sense that readers themselves "could have conducted
the investigation."

Sullivan's account of Rayleigh's scientific imagination evokes his influential work on optics, which spans atmospheric physics, visual technologies,
and human vision. Rayleigh explained the light-scattering effect that causes
us to perceive the sky as blue, developed the formula for determining the
optimal diameter for a pinhole camera's aperture, and researched short-
sightedness and low-light conditions based on his own visual defects.[13]
Though Sullivan doesn't detail this work (he only briefly mentions Rayleigh's
research on pinhole cameras), he does emphasize that its "elegan[ce]" is

what makes Rayleigh a signal example of "a stylist in science," one of those scientific "poets of new and wonderful visions" ("Stylist"; "Scientific Education" 885). Cumulatively, then, Sullivan's essays manage to link the personal impersonality of the artist-scientist with an embodied vision that's not only provisional but also apt in discerning relations within experience and that promotes a stylistic ability to construct patterns that signify those relations—all concepts that Eliot adapts in his impersonal aesthetic.

Beginning with his 1919 essays "Tradition and the Individual Talent," "Humanist, Artist, and Scientist," "Modern Tendencies in Poetry," and "Hamlet," Eliot shaped this aesthetic from the premise not simply that all good poets are "interested in art, science, and philosophy" but also that "poetry is a science" ("Modern" 9, 13). These claims of course mirror Sullivan's triangulation of these same three fields and his more specific sense that scientists are poets. It's perhaps not surprising, then, that Eliot explains his reasons for this foundational equation of art and science by extending the qualities that Sullivan had laid out for modern science to modern art. Eliot posits first that poetry, as a science, requires a "historical sense," by which he means knowledge of what's come before and an effort to build upon it, as well as a feeling of provisionality created by that knowledge.[14] This complex trajectory recalls Sullivan's similarly titled "historic method." Indeed, Eliot's belief that the history of art—or "tradition," as he calls it—changes with its present study imputes to art the same dynamic nature that Sullivan had ascribed to science when he recommended the historic method to its students.[15] According to Eliot, past and present works of art are part of a continually shifting whole whose meaning changes with each new work. Tradition, in other words, doesn't simply influence new art; rather, in a more intricate relation, new art also retroactively alters the texts of tradition as the ingredients of that tradition shift. What's at stake in history, Eliot thus argues, is "a perception not only of the pastness of the past, but of its presence" (SP 38). Recalling Sullivan's focus on visual modeling, Eliot crystallizes tradition's complex provisionality in distinctly imagetextual terms: tradition is composed of "monuments" that move and "alter" in their "relations, proportions, [and] values," rather than being frozen and monolithic (SP 38).

Eliot's second of three reasons that the poet is a scientist, his famous "objective correlative," similarly echoes Sullivan's investments in perception and modeling, as well as his related notion of significant knowledge.[16] The objective correlative holds that the poet must "observ[e]," "analy[ze]," and "combin[e] . . . compounds" from "elements" of the material world, which then serve as correlatives for an embodied emotional experience, much along the lines of the patterns that constitute Sullivan's significant knowledge ("Modern" 11). While Eliot's vocabulary invokes chemistry, the more important scientific interlocutor here is contemporary physiological theories of emotion, which help him to redirect Sullivan's significant knowledge into his own concept of "*significant* emotion" (*SP* 44). Eliot casually presumes his readers' familiarity with this science when he states that he's "work[ing] out the James-Lange theory of emotion for poetry" ("Modern" 16). The James-Lange theory, developed separately by the psychologists William James and Carl Lange, proposes that emotions aren't mental-spiritual states separate from and expressed by the body; instead, they are simply the embodied experience of physiological changes. In other words, one doesn't, for instance, have a fearful inner state that's expressed by suddenly widened eyes or a quickened breath; rather, fear is no more or no less than the experience of such bodily changes—muscular tension, an elevated heart rate, perspiration. As James puts it, "[T]he feeling of the bodily changes as they occur is the emotion—the common sensational, associational, and motor elements explain all" (James and Lange 123). Eliot adopts the precise kernel of this theory when he declares that "emotion *is* the physical equivalent," that it's "the combination of what are ultimately sense-data" ("Modern" 16, 15). His objective correlative turns the mechanics of this kernel and the embodied, unwilled subjectivity that it advances into a principle of poetic composition. He proposes that poets interested in eliciting emotion must present a correlative that stimulates bodily changes. Constructing such a correlative requires poets to study not only emotion but also the autonomic systems that supply its physiological material: "the cerebral cortex, the nervous system, and the digestive tracts."[17] Only a unity of emotion with sense data can respect emotion's embodied materiality, and to fall short of it results inevitably in "buffoonery" (*SP* 49).

Eliot lays stress on the term *feeling* in explaining this process of study and representation. Not only does he begin from the premise that "all knowledge [and] all feeling is in perception"[18] but he argues that the objective correlative captures "significant emotion" only because "feelings"—which are "floating" or unstable—fuse emotion and perception (*SP* 44, 43, 43). Compounding this bonding role, the term *feeling* itself suggests both a sentiment and sense data. Eliot's use of *feeling* thus crystallizes, as it did for James and Lange before him, the inseparability of psychological and physiological systems and a consequently embodied and fluctuating subjectivity. According to Eliot, to lose track of feeling is to abstract language from perception—the source of all knowledge—and to produce what he calls mere "verbalism," a kind of literary counterpart to the sterile mathematical abstraction that Sullivan had disdained in science textbooks (*SP* 54). Eliot's objective correlative, like Sullivan's significant knowledge, instead maintains its connection to the body and offers a distinctly imagetextual amalgam of "words," "phrases," and "images" (*SP* 41). It translates Sullivan's concern with provisionality and experience into a theory of embodied, incoherent subjectivity and an aesthetic that can represent that theory.

Eliot's famous critique of Shakespeare's *Hamlet* further specifies this theory and form. He argues that Hamlet's emotions exceed the play's facts—that Shakespeare fails to produce an objective correlative—and that this renders the hero a solipsistic, inward-turning subject, cut off from even his own materiality. As an extension of this critique, Eliot declares that Hamlet's emotional excess "is doubtless a subject of study for pathologists" (*SP* 49). Given Eliot's insistence that emotion is a physiological response to stimuli, we should expect a mismatch between emotion and object to represent for him some kind of bodily disorder, and the appeal to "pathologists"—to doctors who study disease from bodily anatomy or fluids—confirms this expectation. Indeed, I want to argue that Eliot's goal in wielding this medical discourse was precisely to reconnect emotion to the body. This vernacular calls attention to the physiological systems that Eliot argues underwrite emotion, making mental imbalance a manifestation of embodiment (the implication of his James-Lange theory) that's therefore marked on or through the body (the implication of his additional pathology theory). In other words, Eliot wards off the solipsism of a dualistic, interiorized subject by reinscribing Hamlet within a contrary, embodied model of subjectivity gathered from modern science. He then clarifies the stakes of this reinscription by stretching his diagnosis to include Shakespeare as well.

According to Eliot, not only did Shakespeare suffer from the same weakness as his Hamlet but this pathology amounts to a lack of self-understanding—to an improper sense of the self. Eliot speculates that this error may have stemmed from Shakespeare's "personal experience" of reading Michel de Montaigne's "Apology of Raymond Sebond" (1576) (*SP* 49). Though Eliot doesn't elaborate on the significance of this reading, of all the works in Montaigne's *Essays* (1580) the "Apology" is the one in which he makes his boldest statements about the originality of his writing and the autonomy of his authorial identity, even though it also includes his famous skeptical motto "Que sçay-je?" (What do I know?). As Patrick Moser notes, the "Apology" "maintains that [Montaigne's] 'caprices' (i.e. the essays themselves) are 'born with him' and 'without a model' ('sans patron'). He allows for a belated correspondence between his thoughts and 'quelque humeur ancienne,' [but] seems to mock those who would automatically assume direct imitation on his part ('Voylà d'où il le print!')" (716-17). Eliot's claim that the "Apology" corrupted Shakespeare's sense of self thus seems to posit that Montaigne's literary cult of personality—over and against a model of embodied, unwilled subjectivity—blocked Shakespeare from producing an objective correlative. Such a speculation echoes Sullivan's critique of the artistic cultivation of personality.

Indeed, Eliot's third and final reason that poets are scientists is their personal impersonality. Perfectly mirroring Sullivan's description of scientists' relation to their work, Eliot declares that a poem is not a "mere ebullition of a personality"; it's simultaneously a work in which the poet "forgets himself" and which nonetheless has the "cachet of the man all over it" ("Modern" 10). Eliot argues, in other words, that unlike the "humanist," who remains centered, separate, and coherent in personality, the "artist" and the "scientist" together decenter personality with "a phase in the history of mind" that makes them "brain and intuition" rather than a singular self ("Humanist" 1015). Like Sullivan, then, Eliot regrets the concern with personality that seems to drive literature and literary criticism, the tendency to praise only "individual[ity]" and "essence" (SP 37). He argues that we gain a self only in relation to a shifting tradition. In other words, the "unique position" of the self isn't a given, and the fluctuating relations that lend it a provisional existence are an "unconscious" "inheritance" that we must work to make conscious, as far as may be.[19]

Such an argument updates basic claims in Eliot's dissertation: (1) that "[w]hen an event occurs within my world it occurs to me, but I would not be I apart from the event"; and (2) that "we have not only to interpret other souls to ourself, but to interpret ourself to ourself," because the self is "an intellectual construction" (qtd. in Freed 12, 9). Eliot turns these familiar claims into a visual-scientific vernacular that adapts Sullivan's illustrative appeal to observation and optics. He not only casts his objective correlative as a "stage of vision" but also takes a page from Sullivan's characterization of Lord Rayleigh as a personal-impersonal scientist and nominates Leonardo da Vinci, another optical scientist, as an example of the personal-impersonal artist (SP 57). Seeming to channel Pater and H.D., Eliot discusses Leonardo's visual art and science as a continual process of decentering rather than "an adventure of himself" (*Sacred Wood* 16). According to Eliot, Leonardo treated even his psychophysiological experiences as public objects rather than private events, producing from them what Eliot terms "significant emotion" and what Sullivan calls patterns among "local curiosities," or "significant knowledge."[20] Such emotion isn't devoid of personality, but neither is it simply an expression of personality: poets "escape from personality" to become a vehicle for "impressions and experiences" and thereby for "tradition," but they are also perhaps "most individual" in doing so (*SP* 43, 42, 38, 38).

Eliot's catalysis analogy is the most famous and most directly scientific formulation of this complex and unstable agency. His vernacular casts the impersonal poet alternately as the "catalyst," the shred of platinum that causes oxygen and sulfur dioxide to form sulfuric acid; as the "receptacle" in which this transformation takes place; and as the "storehouse" for elements that become part of the transformation (*SP* 41). Diversifying from this analogy, he also characterizes the artist as a "finely perfected medium" whose outputs support "material civilization," suggesting something closer to a nutrient culture for cell growth (*SP* 41; "Modern" 11). By shifting indiscriminately between these scientific roles, Eliot treats as synonymous differing agencies: "surrender" (a letting go or giving in), "sacrifice" (a kind of active giving, often to get something in return), and "extinction" (an end of self, a determinism) (*SP* 40). These isomorphs and the new "stage of vision" that they're supposed to signal build up the embodied, unwilled subjectivity that Eliot imagines, so that perception and feelings, together with the art that they enable, play simultaneously personalizing and impersonalizing roles.

To this point, Eliot's impersonal theory of art doesn't seem to move in any particular sociopolitical direction. But it does in fact open up political possibilities that would become a significant concern for Eliot's impersonal art. For example, these essays entertain the possibility that impersonality overrides cultural exclusions. Eliot ranks his personal-impersonal artist Leonardo, an illegitimate son who is "barely a citizen," far above the modern man of letters George Wyndham, whom he labels not only a member of the cult of personality but also "the aristocrat, the imperialist, the romantic, riding to hounds across his prose" (*Sacred Wood* 16). This foil distances impersonality from cultural conservatism and imperialist forms of domination.[21] Yet we can also detect in these essays an incubating anxiety about the blow that impersonality might level at social hierarchies. For example, although Eliot never identifies the pathology that he uses to wrangle Hamlet and Shakespeare back into a model of embodied subjectivity, their unmanageable emotional excess certainly looks like hysteria. This gendered illness, which takes its name from the Greek word *hystera,* for "uterus," to indicate that it resulted from an abnormal movement or disturbance of the uterus, can't help but recall Viv's host of psychophysiological health problems, which sometimes received just that diagnosis.[22] It thus seems that the embodied, impersonal observer that Eliot studied at Harvard, that he directly confronted in his care of Viv, and that formed the basis for his impersonal aesthetic was rather slippery and that he felt compelled to neutralize some of its implications with more traditional identities, particularly where questions of gender might come into play. *The Waste Land* offered Eliot an opportunity to develop strategies for pursuing his optical impersonality without giving full rein to its disorder—though with uneven success.

The Waste and Repair Land: Impersonality, but with Gender

Eliot published *The Sacred Wood,* the collection that includes "Tradition and the Individual Talent" and its "Impersonal theory of poetry," in 1920, and he began *The Waste Land* the following year (*SP* 40). Numerous threads connect *The Sacred Wood* and *The Waste Land* together: most obviously, both begin with an epigraph from Petronius' *Satyricon* (100 CE), and in Virgil's *Aeneid* (19 BCE) the Cumean Sibyl, the subject of *The Waste Land*'s epigraph, advises Aeneas to secure the Golden Bough from the Sacred Wood. Given these chronological and intertextual connections, scholars have repeatedly taken "Tradition and the Individual Talent" as an artist's statement for the ideas valued and the techniques pursued in *The Waste Land.* I follow this practice in arguing that if the Golden Bough alluded to in both *The Sacred Wood* and *The Waste Land* is part of Aeneas' epic quest, then *The Waste Land* too, even in the midst of its many opacities, features a powerful journey, and one that centers on the visual and scientific vernacular described in Eliot's essays and on the impersonal subjectivity that they chart. *The Waste Land*'s intricately woven allusions are objective correlatives meant to access and represent those impersonal systems that supply the psychophysiological material of emotion. The poem's correlatives parody a modern refusal of embodied impersonality and work to guide readers back to an impersonal mode of seeing and being. *The Waste Land* effectively suggests that we're suffering from the illness that plagued Hamlet and Shakespeare. And when the poem ends by describing its "fragments" as "shored against my [the speaker's] ruins," it's suggesting that these fragments—we might say these *pièces d'identités*—

are a way out of the sense of self that drives our illness.[23] If we can grasp these fragments, then the poem's quest is won.

Because this quest begins with an illness that Eliot had earlier coded as hysteria, its undertaking should make the implications of impersonality for gender even more pronounced as Eliot moves from poetic theory to poetic practice.[24] Indeed, *The Waste Land* reveals a delicately balanced experiment in democratizing embodiment, on the one hand, and preserving social hierarchies, particularly pertaining to gender, on the other. The poem eschews modern efforts to avoid the body by displacing materiality onto women, but it also repeatedly relies on female figures to school the reader in a proper embodiment. Eliot thus keeps a transactional structure of gender difference in play across the poem's network of speakers, subjects, and readers. The dynamics of this transaction and indeed its gender hierarchy are most striking in the relation between the poem's three dominant vehicles of impersonality: Philomel, a female guide on the path to impersonality; Tiresias, a mediating figure who has been both male and female; and Phlebas, a male traveler on Eliot's impersonal path. Eliot uses Philomel to launch the journey that Phlebas completes, so that one overshadows and ultimately replaces the other. But we'll also see that though this dynamic squeezes the universal embodiment of impersonal subjectivity into a gendered framework, Eliot finds only limited success in stabilizing that framework. This tension gives *The Waste Land* some of its complex force and offers an interesting view on Eliot's impersonal aesthetic.

The original title for *The Waste Land*, "He Do the Police in Different Voices," alludes to a minor moment in Charles Dickens' novel *Our Mutual Friend* (1864–65), one that brings together a smattering of questions about seeing and embodiment that are crucial to Eliot's poem and the quest it undertakes. In Dickens' novel, the child minder Betty Higden uses this phrase to praise her aide Sloppy for being a "beautiful reader" of the newspaper, one who can "do the Police in different voices," in other words, turn seeing into an aptly performed saying (198). Dickens reinforces this link by noting the "broad stare of [Sloppy's] mouth and eyes" (198), a description that fully unites his voice with his vision. In addition, the name Sloppy concretizes the kind of seeing at stake, for Dickens notes that Sloppy's stare "seemed to indicate . . . that in him Sloppy stood confessed"—that his vision was itself sloppy (198). This further compression roots seeing and saying alike in a disordered materiality. By turning to these odd and out-of-the-way formulations as his initial title for *The Waste Land*, Eliot suggests that we should take it too as an effort to turn embodied seeing into saying. Moreover, in Sloppy's aptitude at deciphering "writing-hand" we have a cue for the particular form of *The Waste Land*'s seeing-in-saying. While Betty can read her "Bible and most print" herself, Sloppy can also read the less standardized and more pictorial cursive script that gives Betty trouble (198). Such script, combining imagistic and textual properties, blurs one letter into another and leaves traces of the material body that produced it. If *The Waste Land* is like Sloppy—if it grasps and represents such disordered material traces—then Dickens' writing-hand points to an imagetext as a crucial form for that representation, just as it had been in Eliot's earlier essays.

Further material from *The Waste Land* manuscript points to the particular importance of the modern science and philosophy of vision in Eliot's approach to these material traces and thus again echoes those earlier essays. This context enters in particular through Tiresias, whom the manuscript casts as both a scientist deploying visual technologies and a philosopher of seeing and knowing. Such a casting reframes what might seem like a disembodied, metaphysical vision in markedly material terms and also links artistic and scientific practice in a way that both Sullivan and Eliot had endorsed. Eliot begins by likening Tiresias' visions of modern London to the observations of a microscope-wielding entomologist: the "[o]ld" and "wrinkled" Tiresias, with a mind "aberrant from the normal equipoise," turns his "observing eye" on "the manner of these crawling bugs," who lead a "swarming life" and "flit / Daily, from flat to flat," like a bee from flower to flower.[25] Though Tiresias is able to see despite being "blind" (*TWLF* 31, line 125), Eliot's description emphasizes the prophet's physical decline and "aberrant" mind, making it difficult to read his vision as disembodied.

This difficulty continues as Eliot transfigures the buggy Londoners into optical phenomena, signaling that it's a concern with scientific observation and visual technologies that animates his entomological trope. The people become a shifting "cryptogram that may be curled / Within these faint perceptions . . . / Of the movement, and the lights!" (*TWLF* 31, lines 117-19). Tiresias, in turn, becomes a codebreaker of these cryptograms, which themselves recall the imagetextual writing-hand that Sloppy so aptly deciphers. Indeed, Eliot strengthens this link by also portraying Tiresias as the turning drum of a kymograph, or wave writer, a modern visual technology whose nonmimetic images log bodily activity such as blood pressure (see fig. I.4). Tiresias' codebreaking "brain" "record[s] the jerky motions" of London's "penumbral consciousness," a penumbra being the grey shadow produced when part of a light source is obscured by an intervening body, as in a partial eclipse (*TWLF* 37, lines 8, 10, 13). Whether figured as a swarm or a penumbra, London comprises at once an extra-individual "consciousness" and autonomic bodily "motions," underscoring the opaque impersonal subjectivity under study. In addition, though in myth Tiresias has seen things that no one limited to a single body could perceive, Eliot's description of him as "throbbing between two lives"—a description that repeats in the published poem—links him to the same bodily systems and rhythms that his kymographic brain records (*TWLF* 31, line 126). Indeed, this link is further underlined by Eliot's additional use of *throbbing* to characterize what he calls "the human engine," or the inner workings of the body (*TWLF* 31, lines 123, 122). Just as importantly, the concatenation of Tiresias' roles, from scientific observer to visual decoder to optical tool, echoes the complex agency that Eliot's essays had proposed for the impersonal artist.

In addition to portraying Tiresias' scientific roles, *The Waste Land* manuscript also depicts him as a philosopher of seeing and knowing by briefly casting the reader as Plato's brother Glaucon (*TWLF* 31, line 120), whose name not only means "bright-eyed" or "owl-eyed"—suggesting a seeker of wisdom—but who's perhaps best known as Socrates' interlocutor in Plato's "Allegory of the Cave." This allegory holds that while people's perceptions are little more than shadows projected on a cave's wall, the philosopher might enable them to step out into the light, to literally enlighten them. Eliot's reference to this allegory positions the "faint" light of the "penumbral consciousness" that Tiresias records as a material counterpoint to the idealism of the Platonic Forms. While Tiresias stands apart from the buggy Londoners he observes and offers wisdom to the reader, his enlightenment is neither objective nor disembodied; it's a physiology that measures fleeting traces, and it's a philosophy born of the limitations of embodied knowledge rather than their transcendence.

Although Eliot cut some of his most explicit invocations of the science and philosophy of vision from the published *Waste Land,* the compact allusions with which he opens the poem build on the concerns about embodiment that such discourses announce. In particular, these allusions together diagnose a modern refusal of embodiment and begin to outline the poem's path back toward the body. Significantly, this diagnosis turns on the epigraph's swift conversion of visionary sight into embodied vision, much like the manuscript's portrayal of Tiresias. This epigraph from Petronius' *Satyricon* reads in translation: "For on one occasion I myself saw, with my own eyes, the Cumaean Sibyl hanging in a jar, and when some boys said to her, 'Sibyl, what do you want?' she replied, 'I want to die.'"[26] The speaker of these lines is Trimalchio, a braggart storyteller who wishes to trumpet his own education, so that the faith he declares in an objective seeing that's transparently synonymous with knowing ("I myself saw, with my own eyes") is marked from the start by misplaced confidence. The significance of the Sibyl's response to the boys becomes apparent in the context of the stories that Ovid tells of her.[27] When young, the Sibyl had petitioned Apollo for a life as long as the number of grains of sand in her hand, but she had neglected to ask also for eternal youth; her body thus grew smaller and smaller with age until she lived first in a jar—where she resides at the moment of this tale—and then ultimately consisted only of a voice. In *Satryicon* the Sibyl's response to the boys ("I want to die") suggests that in this condition she has come to prefer the one fate she had sought to avoid. In other words, she sees that the disembodiment she now faces is far worse than the embodied limit of mortality that she had once feared. The Sibyl's pronouncement, rather than delivering any of the visionary prophesies that she's capable of, attaches prophetic force to this wisdom of embodied experience. And she thus effectively endorses the disordered materiality evoked in Eliot's excised allusion to Sloppy's embodied seeing and saying, or to Tiresias' embodied scientific and philosophical observations. Just as Trimalchio seems to miss this wisdom, Eliot's epigraph implies that modernity too has disavowed its fluctuating and unwilled materiality.

The poem itself opens with an episode that holds out a solution to this problem in the form of Marie. As the world awakens from the "forgetful" "little life" that persists in winter, Marie awakens from a little life of social convention into a halting impersonal being inaugurated through the very return to the body that the Sibyl can't achieve (*TWL*, lines 6, 7). The speaker of this episode is first an "us" that refers only to an abstract community of disembodied because paradoxical perceptions: "Winter kept us warm" (*TWL*, line 5). In its next invocation, the "we" remains undefined but is located in a specific geography and in bodies: "we stopped in the colonnade,/And went on in sunlight, into the Hofgarten,/And drank coffee . . ." (*TWL*, lines 9-11). The subsequent use of the plural pronoun retroactively specifies these bodies as those of Marie (Larisch) and an unnamed interlocutor, the poetic speaker. But a new use now applies the "we" more solidly to Marie and her cousin the archduke (Rudolph of Austria):

And when we were children, staying at the archduke's,
My cousin's, he took me out on a sled,
And I was frightened. He said, Marie,
Marie, hold on tight. And down we went.
In the mountains, there you feel free. (*TWL*, lines 13-17)

This progressive embodiment of the "we" is fueled by Marie's "mixing/ Memory and desire," a phrase from Charles-Louis Philippe's novel *Bubu de Montparnasse* (1901). For Philippe, "A man who walks around carries all the things of his life and turns them in his mind. One sight arouses them, another excites them. Our flesh has kept all our memories, we mix them with our desires" (qtd. in Rabaté 213). Marie follows this prescription: her movement and observations as she tours a noble residence and its Hofgarten activate the flesh, the storehouse of our memories and the scene of our desire. By recounting a fearful but exhilarating childhood experience, she mixes memory and desire and enacts an embodied personal-impersonal subjectivity. Her palpable tension as she remembers her cousin's instructions, coupled with her exhilaration in the headlong syntax "And down we went" connects her emotion to her bodily motion. She seems to fall down into the body and into a chaotic instability that she nonetheless associates with freedom. Clarifying the implications of this "feel[ing] free," Eliot sets Marie's significant emotion against the staid conventionality of her routines, which have her departing from the mountainous space of freedom to follow the cosmopolitan trek "south for the winter" (*TWL*, line 18). More tentatively, he also contrasts this experience with Marie's initial effort to define herself firmly as a German rather than a Russian ("Bin gar keine Russin . . ." [*TWL*, line 12]), hinting that impersonal subjectivity challenges not only social habits but also a stable social identity. In all, then, this opening episode functions as Eliot's objective correlative for an authentic if momentary emotional response to corporeal fragility and its ongoing waste and repair—a fragility that the Cumaean Sibyl had sought to avoid but toward which *The Waste Land* seeks to direct the modern world.

Although Eliot offers this microcosm of his poetic project, he also makes clear that he doesn't yet consider the world ready to undertake the journey that the poem imagines. Indeed, following on the Marie episode, the speaker accuses readers of being unable to see anything of value in *The Waste Land*'s "stony rubbish" and the opaque materiality that it charts. Instead, they perceive only a "heap of broken images" and a scene "where the sun beats,/And the dead tree gives no shelter" (*TWL,* lines 20, 22, 22–23). Against this view, and repeating *The Waste Land* manuscript's remaking of Plato's "Allegory of the Cave," the speaker invites readers beneath an overhang of rock, promising as a form of enlightenment the very "shadow" that Plato sought to transcend (*TWL,* line 26). Knowledge here isn't ideal forms; it's the dregs of matter, "fear in a handful of dust" (*TWL,* line 26).[28] This crucial phrase concatenates the "ashes to ashes, dust to dust" of the burial service (invoked in the title of part 1) with both the Sibyl's wish to live as many years as the grains of sand in her hand and Marie's fearful but exhilarating fall into embodiment. Through this concatenation, Eliot promises to extend Marie's return to materiality to readers as well.

At this point *The Waste Land* begins to suggest the complex role that gender will play in fulfilling this promise. It introduces a cast of additional characters to propose a reason why readers may be unprepared for impersonality and to challenge that reason. The relations among these characters point to the common cultural and aesthetic belief that embodiment is distributed unequally across sexual difference. And the poem contests this belief in two ways: first, it parodies the idea that women's embodiment can be used to launch men into a contrary disembodiment; and second, it reverses the expectation that femininity signifies embodiment at all by instead presenting female characters who figure the modern refusal of bodies. Taken together, these parodies and reversals broach the intriguing possibility that Eliot has written gender dynamics out of his aesthetic entirely.

Eliot' parody is apparent, for instance, in the Hyacinth Girl episode, a name that situates the dialogue and events in the context of the Greek Hyacinth myth. In Ovid's account, Apollo accidentally kills his lover, Hyacinth, with a discus and in tribute transforms Hyacinth's spilt blood into a flower on which he writes a sign of his grief.[29] Eliot's speaker casts his beloved in the role of Hyacinth by overstuffing her arms with that flower, not as a sign of loving devotion but rather so that he might occupy the complementary role of Apollo. More specifically, the speaker's act pushes his beloved toward Hyacinth's untimely end, that is, toward death and the radical materiality of the corpse. The speaker's hope seems to be that if his beloved is mortal, then perhaps he can escape his mortality and make her the occasion for his self-expression, just as the immortal god Apollo recorded his grief on the hyacinth flower. This motivation, together with the speaker's related desire to vault himself into literary tradition, surface when he doesn't experience the transcendent vision and speech that he had hoped for. He uses inflated language from the *Divine Comedy* (1308-21), and particularly Dante's description when he first encounters Satan, to register that failure and to judge his beloved for it. Dante writes of the appearance of Satan: "I cannot describe it, / For all speech would fail it. / I did not die, and did not remain alive" (qtd. in *TWL* 79n). Similarly, when the Hyacinth Girl notes that her lover's floral gift had given her that name, Eliot's speaker complains:

> —Yet when we came back, late, from the Hyacinth garden,
> Your arms full, and your hair wet, I could not
> Speak, and my eyes failed, I was neither
> Living nor dead, and I knew nothing. (*TWL,* lines 37-40)

Just as Eliot condemned Hamlet for having emotion in excess of any cause, this exaggerated discourse, wherein the Hyacinth Girl becomes Satan, parodies the speaker's inability to produce an objective correlative. At the same time, it also parodies his corresponding anxiety about embodiment and understanding of poetic tradition.

The episode continues to underscore these related problems through a brief play on *The Waste Land*'s original epigraph from Joseph Conrad's *The Heart of Darkness* (1899):

> Did he live his life again in every detail of desire, temptation, and surrender during that supreme moment of complete knowledge? He cried in a whisper at some image, at some vision—he cried out twice, a cry that was no more than breath— "The horror! The horror." (*TWLF* 3)

In this epigraph the heart of darkness yields a parade of visions of "every detail of desire" and "knowledge." But in the Hyacinth Girl episode, the speaker instead "Look[s] into the heart of light"—he refuses any kind of darkness or opacity—and his looking yields not enlightenment but the single word *silence* (*TWL,* line 41). In other words, his visuality produces neither poetry nor knowledge. Eliot's layered rejection of this episode, of both its beliefs and its structures, warns the reader not to expect such a project from *The Waste Land.* Eliot's poem not only abandons artistic self-expression and a metaphysical sight but refuses efforts to escape embodiment, particularly a gendered strategy of containing the effects of materiality to women.

Eliot's second strategy for challenging traditional gender dynamics, his reversals, makes clear why those dynamics are misguided: far from occupying some disproportionate extreme of embodiment that would guarantee a contrary masculine disembodiment, women are actually equal participants in the modern refusal of materiality. The Woman in the Chair, from the opening episode of "A Game of Chess," exemplifies this reversal. The episode begins by building an expectation of this Woman's heightened embodiment by interleaving the strategic "game of chess" with the world of two historical queens: Dido, who journeys from Tyre (in Lebanon) as far as Tunisia to found Carthage, and the exotic Cleopatra, who claims to be the reincarnation of an Egyptian goddess and who wields a hypersexuality that tempts Mark Antony to neglect his duties to Rome. Surrounded by the objects of these powerful queens, the "laqueraria" of Dido and the "burnished throne" of Cleopatra, the Woman in the Chair becomes unmistakably regal, with all the mobility of the migrating Dido and the most powerful of chess pieces and with all the sensuality and indeed Oriental exoticism of Cleopatra.[30]

But if this stacking of gender, mobility, and sensuality seems to indicate embodiment, Eliot quickly buries these expectations under a thick description of the "strange synthetic perfumes" that surround the Woman and that she uses to camouflage or cancel out her bodily processes (*TWL*, line 87). These unnatural perfumes "Unguent, powered, or liquid—troubled, confused/ And drowned the sense in odours" (*TWL*, lines 88–89). The Woman thus comes to signify not simply embodiment but a modern attempt to escape embodiment. In addition, the episode ends with a reminder that this fantasized escape forecloses the dim possibility of representation and knowledge, which actually depend on materiality. The Woman's hair, a detritus formed from the body's continual waste and repair and the only actual mention of her body in the episode, first "Glowed into words, and then would be savagely still" (*TWL*, lines 110).

But even as this episode lays out and critiques the modern refusal of bodies, along with the gender dynamic that often corresponds with this refusal, it also launches the reader on a journey away from this illness by offering the poem's first real guide to an embodied impersonal subjectivity: the Athenian princess Philomel, "[s]o rudely forced" by her brother-in-law, Tereus, and later transformed into a nightingale (*TWL*, line 100). Philomel enters in the form of an artistic rendering of her transformation, hanging on the Woman's wall. She represents a material point of access for an unconscious, impersonal tradition, and Eliot casts her efforts in the same image-textual terms that repeatedly characterize his impersonal form. However, as a female guide, Philomel also hints that gender difference may not actually be absent from Eliot's impersonality. Indeed, his persistent reliance on female figures to school the reader in a proper embodiment suggests that the poem reworks rather than banishes the transactional structure of gender difference. In other words, if there's no gendered distribution of embodiment in *The Waste Land,* a gendered management of universal embodiment or of some of its social and even ontological implications nonetheless gradually emerges.

Philomel's introduction converts the commodified atmosphere of the Woman's dressing room into an imagetextual tableau. The walls of this room are decorated with art whose "staring forms" offer "withered stumps of time" that seem loyal to the traditional image/text binary and its mapping onto a supposed body/mind divide (*TWL,* lines 105, 104). The artworks' "*staring* forms" suggest that they are portraits, representational images of faces and bodies, and their "withered" temporality distances them from change and from expressive speech. But the poem immediately dispenses with the image/text binary in its claim that the forms "Were *told* upon the walls" and that they "*Leaned* out, *leaning, hushing* the room enclosed" (*TWL,* lines 105, 106, emphasis added). By associating the portraits with speech and movement, Eliot invests them with an imagetextuality, which is reinforced by the fact that they are the most living things in the room, more alive than even the Woman herself.

This reversal corresponds with Eliot's turn to Philomel, who in myth uses images woven into a tapestry to narrate her tragic tale of rape and mutilation. A picture of Philomel's transformation into a nightingale occupies the most important position over the mantle of the Woman's room. Eliot's appeal to a representation of this maker of imagetexts heightens the double coding that circulates around the other art and makes Philomel's case into an arbiter of that doubling. On the one hand, her picture seems to be the height of verisimilitude, offering an apparent "window . . . upon [a] sylvan scene" and making her into the static figure that anchors that scene (*TWL,* line 98). In addition, the violent rape that she endured suggests an apotheosis of embodiment, while her severed tongue literalizes the other artworks' "withered *stumps* of time." However, if portraits are normally supposed to freeze an identity—to secure it against aging and death—Philomel's picture is instead a record of her bodily "change" into a nightingale, and from out of that picture "still she [Philomel] cried" (*TWL,* line 102). And yet, Eliot emphasizes that "the world" doesn't register this voice of an image—the fundamental imagetextuality of all representation; instead, their "dirty ears" reduce Philomel's "inviolable voice" to the nightingale's asignifying "Jug Jug" (*TWL*, lines 103, 103, 101, 103).

Eliot continues to highlight the lesson of Philomel's song, and to help readers attend to it, through his engagement with the *Āditta Sutta,* or Fire Sermon, of the Pāli Buddhist canon, from which he takes the title of part 3 of the poem. The model of subjectivity in the *Āditta Sutta* challenges a coherent "I," much as Eliot's impersonality does. The sermon presumes a fundamental *anatman,* a non-self, and teaches disenchantment *(nibbida)* from those elements of our experience that we commonly identify as a self, namely, the conglomeration *(skandhas)* of continually forming and dissolving mindbodily phenomena.[31] But where the sermon advocates a renunciation of the senses as a way to get in touch with the non-self, Eliot emphasizes that such a plan gives rise to a cycle of repression and return that Philomel's example can instead steer us past. *The Waste Land* represents this cycle most pressingly through the legend of the Fisher King, into whom Eliot absorbs a variety of other mythical and fictional kings.

According to Jessie L. Weston and James G. Frazer, whose accounts Eliot claimed as intertexts, the legendary Fisher King is based on old vegetation rituals in which the body of a king is linked to the health of his land and his people.[32] These rituals involved a yearly practice of sacrificing a king in order to ensure the livelihood of his kingdom. In other words, in Eliot's understanding, the roots of the Fisher King legend would have represented another way of banishing embodiment, including its guarantee of death and decay, by projecting it onto a particular figure. In some versions of the vegetation ritual, moreover, the king is killed by his successor, suggesting a cycle in which materiality is rejected by one for whom it inevitably returns. In the Fisher King legend itself, the king isn't sacrificed but is instead saved by a knight who renounces the body by withstanding fleshly temptations. Eliot mixes elements of both the vegetation ritual and the subsequent Fisher King legend in "The Fire Sermon" in order to suggest that both are cyclical denials and eruptions of materiality with negative consequences.

This mixing of narratives revolves around the appearance of a king who is "fishing in the dull canal" and whose character is then developed through allusions to several additional kings (*TWL*, line 189). One of these kings is the wounded Amfortas from Richard Wagner's opera *Parsifal* (1880), suggested by an allusion to Paul Verlaine's sonnet of the same name: "Et O ces voix d'enfants, chantant dans la coupole" (*TWL*, line 202).[33] This allusion develops the milder version of bodily renunciation that Eliot reads in the Fisher King legend. In the opera, Parsifal renounces his own body by repeatedly resisting the temptations of beautiful women, which enables him to recover the sacred spear that pierced Christ's side and to use it to heal Amfortas. In *The Waste Land,* however, this renunciation of desire can't last. It's directly tied to "[t]he sound of horns and motors," an allusion to the "sound of horn and hunting" in John Day's "The Parliament of Bees" (*TWL,* line 197). In Day's poem, these sounds "bring/Actaeon" to gaze upon Diana's nakedness "in the spring" (qtd. in *TWL* 103n); and in *The Waste Land,* they "bring/Sweeney"— the frequenter of brothels in several other Eliot poems—to the brothel keeper "Mrs. Porter in the spring" (*TWL,* lines 197-98, 198). By reworking Day's lines and linking them to Parsifal's successful renunciation in Verlaine's poem, Eliot subtly suggests the cycle of bodily renunciation and return.

He alludes more fully to this cycle through the ritual origins of the Fisher King legend, which he activates in the remarks of his Fishing King:[34]

> A rat crept softly through the vegetation
> Dragging its slimy belly on the bank
> While I was fishing in the dull canal
> On a winter evening round behind the gashouse
> Musing upon the king my brother's wreck
> And on the king my father's death before him.
> White bodies naked on the low damp ground
> And bones cast in a little low dry garret,
> Rattled by the rat's foot only, year to year. (*TWL,* lines 187-95)

The opening reference to a rat crawling among "vegetation" names the sacrificial ritual that Weston identifies with the Fisher King legend. The following lines then juxtapose "the king my brother's wreck/And . . . the king my father's death" to "[w]hite bodies" and cast-off "bones," suggesting that it's precisely the repeated sacrifice of former kings that this king is "[m]using upon." The importance of repetition becomes clearer when we consider Eliot's allusion to Shakespeare's *The Tempest* (1610), and specifically to Prince (now he thinks King) Sebastian of Naples, as he mourns "the king my father's wrack" (qtd. in *TWL* 103n). Eliot's version multiplies the kings (or potential kings) by attributing the seemingly fatal wreck to the Fishing King's brother and then noting the earlier death of the Fishing King's father. In addition, Eliot again underscores the cyclicality of a banished and returning materiality in the "[r]attle" of bones that erupts perennially, from "year to year."

In all, then, the stanza emphasizes an intense cycle of bodily repression and return that Eliot takes to lie behind the milder Fisher King legend. This cycle aims for an impossible nonmaterial existence, where temporality is converted into stasis. Such an existence precludes Eliot's notion of tradition, wherein the past is perpetually transformed by the present. In addition, the illness that marks this existence—the illness that plagues the Fisher King and his lands in legend—is Hamlet's illness: an isolation from materiality. In Eliot's essays tradition and the objective correlative together sketch the contours of impersonality, both as a model of subjectivity and as an aesthetic. Their absence in the Fishing King episode suggests that the king and his people, trapped in the cycle, have no way of recognizing and representing an impersonal subjectivity.

Eliot's negative view of this cycle is borne out by the rest of "The Fire Sermon." Immediately after Verlaine's line from "Parsifal," and so Parsifal's renunciation of materiality, Eliot returns to the assault on Philomel, breaking into *The Waste Land*'s most extended version of her song:

Twit twit twit
Jug jug jug jug jug jug
So rudely forc'd.
Tereu (*TWL,* lines 203–6)

This return suggests that a repressed materiality will only result in a violent and/or unappealing sexual eruption. Correspondingly, Philomel's song becomes the entry point for a series of tales of unfortunate women who refract different aspects of her experience across a range of sociohistorical positions and against more ascetic social conventions. These women all confront a surging, distinctly illicit desire that morphs into mechanical sex, sexual violence, or both. Through an allusion to Oliver Goldsmith's *The Vicar of Wakefield* (1762), we see a rural eighteenth-century girl of meager circumstances who "stoops to folly" and is heartlessly abandoned, seemingly leading to her suicide (*TWL,* line 253).[35] In addition, we encounter a middle-class woman born in the drab Victorian suburb of Highbury, who's raped "on the floor of a narrow canoe" but who tepidly responds, "What should I resent?" (*TWL,* lines 295, 299). And most lengthily and famously, we encounter a modern urban woman working as a typist, who's so indifferent to her body that she does nothing to stop a sexual encounter in which she has no interest. Indeed, her almost mechanical embodiment is apparent in the "automatic hand" with which "[s]he smoothes her hair" and which by day maneuvers a typewriter and by night a "gramophone" (*TWL,* lines 255, 255, 256).

But even as Eliot rejects this catalog of assaults, just as he had rejected the gender dynamic that seems to underwrite them, "The Fire Sermon" also enacts an important shift in the way gender is handled in *The Waste Land.* This shift revolves around the receding role of Philomel as a recurring character along the poem's journey. Even though her song introduces these women whose experiences echo hers, and even though one of their stories includes a song that recalls hers—"Wallala leialala" (*TWL,* line 291)—Philomel doesn't actually speak of or observe these women.[36] Instead, Eliot interposes Tiresias between Philomel and the women, emphasizing in his notes that Tiresias is more than "a 'character'" and is indeed "the most important" in the poem (*TWL* 72n). Tiresias not only observes and narrates the typist in her mechanical sexual encounter with the "young man carbuncular" but declares, "I Tiresias have foresuffered all" (*TWL,* lines 231, 243). By seeing and hearing and also suffering the unfolding events, this non-character functions as an embodied impersonal subject, akin to Philomel and in keeping with his more visual-scientific iteration in *The Waste Land* manuscript.

But Tiresias and Philomel aren't simply male and female versions of the same impersonal guide. Tiresias' unique experience of having been both male and female makes him a nearly perfect prototype for preserving a transactional gender hierarchy even while insisting on universal embodiment. In Greek myth, Tiresias was temporarily transformed into a woman, gained access to an embodied knowledge through that transformation, and then returned, still enlightened, to his male state. His knowledge was linked specifically to his vision, because it ultimately led Hera to blind him and Zeus to grant him second sight.[37] However, there's a difference between Tiresias' two transformations: while he *unexpectedly* became a woman (and gained bodily knowledge) by striking apart two entwined snakes—a more than symbolic castration—he later *chose* to become a man again by repeating that action. In other words, though initially unwilled and destabilizing, Tiresias' turn as a female ultimately became an instrumental experience that continued to benefit him when he was then reinvested with the triumphant and assertive qualities of social masculinity. In Eliot's poem, this state of affairs creates a nuanced and delicate form of gender instrumentalization in which Tiresias encapsulates an embodied impersonality that crosses gender lines, while nonetheless also preserving gender difference within that impersonality.

The delicacy of this transaction is clear in Eliot's attribution of Tiresias' authority to the fact that he's an "Old man with wrinkled female breasts" (*TWL*, line 219). In one sense, this description registers that in *The Waste Land* Tiresias speaks as a man, one who retains the wisdom of his female experience but has regained the assurances of masculinity. In another sense, though, the line muddies the distinction between the male and female positions across which Tiresias' transaction takes place. Throughout the rest of the poem Eliot works to bolster the transaction rather than the indeterminacy. For just as Tiresias' experience plots this gendered transaction, his placement in the poem makes him an all-important bridge from Philomel, who now disappears, to Phlebas, the drowned Phoenician sailor, who becomes *The Waste Land*'s final impersonal guide as the poem goes on to envision an end to the cycle and a corresponding achievement of impersonal subjectivity. Tiresias thus offers a perfect condensation of Eliot's impersonal aesthetic: impersonality, but with gender.

The drowning of Phlebas inaugurates the promise of a redeemed impersonal subjectivity and even echoes Tiresias' watery death after he drinks from a tainted spring.[38] Eliot's manuscript versions of part 4, "Death by Water," introduce Phlebas as one who bore "[s]omething inhuman" and "impersonal" and suggest that his impersonality stems "[f]rom his trade with wind and sea and snow": "[A]s they/Are, he is, with 'much seen and much endured'" (*TWLF* 55, lines 4, 11, 9, 9-10). Phlebas loses this impersonality, connected as it is with embodied perception and with being coterminous with the material world, when he undertakes a journey in "Kingfisher weather" and confronts women who "charmed my senses" (*TWLF* 55, line 13; 59, line 69). Eliot's subtle references to the Fisher King legend, namely, to Percival's quest and his resistance to sexual temptation, suggest that Phlebas slips into the cycle, severing his connection with an impersonal materiality.

The published *Waste Land* doesn't record Phlebas' initial impersonality or his destructive journey; it casts his life as consumed by "the profit and loss" (*TWL*, line 314). But like the manuscript, the published poem emphasizes Phlebas' return to impersonality in death. His drowning helps him to forget the profit and loss and reunites his body with an impersonal "current under sea" (a play on *currency*) that "[p]icked his bones in whispers" (*TWL*, line 314). The speaker calls on the reader—on all "you who turn the wheel"— to "[c]onsider Phlebas, who was once as handsome and tall as you" (*TWL*, lines 320, 321). This advice to look to Phlebas confirms his status as a warning and a guide on the reader's own path toward impersonality. In addition, the reference to "the wheel" hints at the cyclical life of repression and return that's much more pronounced in the manuscript version of the episode and that blocks a relation to impersonality. Phlebas' fate documents the illusion that by "turn[ing] the wheel" one controls the cycle. He instead becomes subject to the action of a "whirlpool" whose currents return him to the bones the cycle purports to banish (*TWL,* line 318). At the same time, though, it's important to note that if Phlebas has failed to remember his own materiality, this failure nonetheless means that he, unlike the multiply assaulted Philomel, is responsible for his transformative fate. Such a fact resuscitates the gender difference of Tiresias and Philomel's relation, as Tiresias and Phlebas' shared "death by water" was already wont to do.

But it's in the final part of *The Waste Land,* "What the Thunder Said," that the exchange of Philomel for Phlebas reaches its broadest implications and that a reader suffering from a modern version of Hamlet's illness finally arrives at impersonality. While Phlebas' journey away from impersonality is cut out of "Death by Water" in the published poem, his death still guides the reader on the final leg of an explicit journey back toward impersonality through allusions to one biblical and one legendary trek: the resurrected Christ's appearance to his disciples as they travel the road to Emmaus and Percival's approach to the Chapel Perilous in the Grail legend. *The Waste Land* uses these allusions to rework the cyclical dynamic represented by the Fisher King. Eliot invokes and reconceives the idea that one figure can be sacrificed to save others (as in the founding vegetation ritual) and also reimagines the supposed threat of Percival's encounter in the Chapel (from the Fisher King legend itself).[39] In Eliot's revision, and in keeping with Phlebas' only temporarily forgotten impersonal being, Phlebas becomes the sign of an impersonal materiality that's already in those who seek it. "What the Thunder Said" casts the reader as a member of an implicitly male band of journeyers who realize in a sudden burst of insight that they already occupy the same relation to impersonality that Phebas has and therefore don't need saving. Thus, where *The Waste Land* began by warning its reader not to expect the traditional and doomed use of women's bodies to ward off materiality, its overall trajectory—from Philomel through Tiresias to Phlebas—rewards the implicitly male reader with a structurally identical use of those bodies to instead realize materiality.

"What the Thunder Said" begins by invoking the arrest and subsequent crucifixion of Christ using the same kinds of floating percepts that characterized *The Waste Land*'s opening episode about Marie:

> After the torchlight red on sweaty faces
> After the frosty silence in gardens
> After the agony in stony places
> The shouting and the crying
> Prison and palace and reverberation
> Of thunder of spring over distant mountains— (*TWL,* lines 322-27)

The floating percepts—the "torchlight red," the "sweaty faces," the "frosty silence"—are associated with the scene of Christ's betrayal and thus suggest a savior and his band of (male) disciples. These disciples, like Marie, start out as strangely disembodied. Eliot's line breaks and prepositional phrases separate or delay modifiers in relation to their subjects, heightening a feeling of disconnection, for instance, in the lines "reverberation/ Of thunder of spring." The poem installs Phlebas as the leader of this disembodied band through Eliot's reference to "He who was living [and] is now dead," a description that evokes Christ's crucifixion but more directly recalls Phlebas' own death by water (*TWL,* line 28). The band finally becomes explicit and begins to be inducted into Phlebas' transformation with the mirroring declaration that "We who were living are now dying/ With a little patience" (*TWL,* lines 329-30). As these lines' reference to death suggests, Phlebas' guidance will trigger a revelation of materiality, one strikingly similar to the Cumaean Sibyl's desire in the poem's epigraph. However, if Phlebas' guiding role motivates the poem's implicit comparison of him to Christ, he's ultimately not a figure whose actions can redeem the journeyers; instead, he marks out actions they must take on their own.

This relation is clearest in the poem's invocation of water. In *The Waste Land* manuscript, Phlebas' initial impersonality is defined by his being one with the sea to which he ultimately returns. In "What the Thunder Said," the plural speaker, who stands for the band of followers, obsessively anticipates the arrival of water, and so of impersonality, failing to recognize that it already circulates through the speaker's own articulations. More specifically, repeating Phlebas' earlier neglect of the impersonal within him, the speaker's voice as it mourns the absence of water actually reverberates with both the sound and the look of water's flows and falls:

> From doors of mudcracked houses
>   If there were water
> And no rock
> If there were rock

> And also **water**
> And **water**
> A *spring*
> A *pool* among the rock (*TWL,* lines 345-52, emphasis added)

Eliot's spacing and line breaks create the appearance of verse trickling down the page, and as *water* repeats, along with the sounds that make up that word, the trickling appears to accumulate first into a "spring" and then into a "pool." In addition, Eliot compounds the speaker's misrecognition through the band's subsequent search for even the sounds of water in the "Drip drop drip drop" of the hermit thrush's call (*TWL,* line 358).

This evocative stanza becomes a frame for a subtle rewriting of Christ's redemption of humanity. The speaker's failure to recognize the presence of water implicitly recalls the failure of Christ's disciples to recognize his presence among them on the road to Emmaus. Eliot reinforces this allusion through the speaker's questions about a mysterious presence:

> Who is the third who walks always beside you?
> When I count, there are only you and I together
> But when I look ahead up the white road
> There is always another one walking beside you
>
> . . . .
>
> —But who is that on the other side of you? (*TWL,* lines 359-65)

In this odd formulation, Phlebas' followers project their encounter with their guide always into the future—always to a place in the road where they haven't yet been—just as they search for water despite already having it. In other words, while Christ's disciples can't recognize their resurrected savior among them and thereby recognize that they have been saved, Phlebas' followers don't see that they have the impersonal materiality they seek and that there is no savior. If Christ is a version of the Fisher King, as Weston argues, then Eliot's revision questions the cycle's idea of a sacrificial proxy, particularly as it pertains to a needed impersonality.

Eliot completes this revision through his allusion to Percival's approach to the Chapel Perilous. He had many versions of the Chapel encounter to choose from, and his choice rounds out *The Waste Land*'s impersonal journey by catapulting the plural speaker past its novitiate state and into a full comprehension of impersonality. Weston's chapter on the Chapel Perilous describes versions of the Grail legend wherein Percival encounters a Black

Hand at the Chapel and must fight it for his life, as well as less common versions in which Percival does little more than wait for something to happen, to no avail. Although *The Waste Land* builds in an expectation of danger as the journeyers approach the Chapel—from encounters with "hooded hordes" to the appearance of "bats with baby faces" (*TWL,* lines 368, 379)—the arrival itself is a profoundly meaningful anticlimax. In fact, the plural speaker realizes that the Chapel is anything but Perilous and that "Dry bones," like the ones that earlier haunted the Fishing King, in fact "harm no one" (*TWL,* line 390). This realization takes the cycle of renunciation and return that Percival represents, as well as the anxiety about the body that it indicates, and empties it of all urgency and motivation. Indeed, it questions Phlebas' followers' sense that to achieve impersonal materiality is to die, as Phlebas had done. At this moment of realization regarding the presence and meaning of impersonality, water significantly comes pouring down, with "a flash of lightning. Then a damp gust/Bringing rain" (*TWL,* lines 393–94).

Given *The Waste Land*'s insistence that embodied impersonality isn't borne by one person for others but must be discovered by all, it's not surprising that the realization of Phlebas' followers doesn't guarantee that the entire world shares in their newfound sense of meaning. Indeed, as an indication of the world's continued plight, the Fishing King resurfaces in the poem's final stanzas to ask with resignation, "Shall I at least set my lands in order?" (*TWL,* line 425). More significantly, though, the poem's close suggests that even for those who have achieved impersonality, the complex role of gender within it remains an issue. This issue returns with a brief, indirect reference to Philomel through her sister, Procne, in the line "*Quando fiam ceu chelidon*" (When shall I become like the swallow) (*TWL,* line 428), from *Pervigilium Veneris* (c. 300 CE). That poem mentions "the young wife of Tereus," who was transformed into a swallow, noting that while "[s]he is singing, I am mute" and bemoaning that "being voiceless" is to "perish" (qtd. in *TWL* 122n). However, *The Waste Land* doesn't end by returning to Philomel's impersonal song. It leaves her behind again by jumping instead to Thomas Kyd's *The Spanish Tragedy,* and to Hieronymo's play within it, as a final *mise en abyme.* The allusion—"Why then Ile fit you. Hieronymo's mad againe"— announces Hieronymo's decision to create a revenge play, in which he effectively stages himself as Philomel by cutting out his tongue (*TWL,* line 431). More specifically, Hieronymo, with the help of his son's beloved, Bel Imperia, uses his play to avenge his son's murder. At the end of the play, when Hieronymo narrates the project of his art, he withholds Bel Imperia's complicity in the plot. Indeed, to finalize that silence, Hieronymo cuts out his own tongue. Eliot's allusion to Hieronymo's play bolsters gender hierarchy in the face of impersonality, both material and aesthetic. Within the network of *The Waste Land*'s allusions, Hieronymo becomes another Phlebas, another self-made and distinctly masculine version of Philomel, with no Bel Imperia in sight. And yet this allusion also duplicates the delicacy of Eliot's earlier handling of Tiresias: by becoming a self-made Philomel, by excising his tongue, Hieronymo no longer instrumentalizes the female body, but simply inhabits it, inevitably echoing Tiresias' unstable "throbbing between two lives." What this closing allusion ultimately suggests, then, is that Eliot's desire for social hierarchies will continue to vex his commitment to aesthetic impersonality. His later work must therefore continue to search for ways to perfect this negotiation.

Redeeming the Still "Unread Vision": *The Family Reunion*'s Dramatic Bodies

The copious scholarship on Eliot's early theory and practice of impersonality has often focused on two techniques by which he sought to displace the coherent and expressive lyric self: his extensive collaboration with others, most notably his work with Pound in writing *The Waste Land,* and his adoption of dramatic personae, not only in *The Waste Land* but also in earlier poems, such as "The Love Song of J. Alfred Prufrock" (1915).[40] These techniques allowed Eliot to replace his own poetic voice with that of other, often multiple speakers. Although impersonality is associated most closely with Eliot's work preceding or at least apart from his turn to verse drama, these two techniques begin to suggest how that aesthetic persisted in his work for the stage. Eliot continued to collaborate as he began writing plays: in addition to belonging to the Group Theatre, he developed most of his plays with the input of their ultimate director, Martin Browne. In addition, theater was a natural extension of Eliot's interest in dramatic personae, for he not only voiced the many characters of his plays but now added a layer of expressive instability and proliferation brought by the actors who performed the characters.

What I want to emphasize here, though, is how this continuity in Eliot's pursuit of impersonality also persists with regard to the scientific and philosophical vernacular of embodied vision that shaped his early theory, as well as his practice of it in *The Waste Land.* This vernacular informs the general understanding of verse drama that Eliot presented in his later essays, and it also surfaces strikingly in one particular play, *The Family Reunion*. To the extent that scholars have considered *The Family Reunion*, it has often been read as a record of Eliot's Anglo-Catholic conversion and thus his spiritual renunciation of the materiality that I've shown marks his impersonality.[41] But there are signs beyond *The Family Reunion* itself that Eliot's interest in vision and impersonal subjectivity continued to supply the frame for how he understood his religious as well as his dramatic turn. For instance, one of Eliot's early religious poems, "Ash Wednesday" (1930), longs to capture a still "unread vision"[42] that's strongly evocative not only of Tiresias' embodied impersonal visions in *The Waste Land* but also of Eliot's later claim that verse drama gives us a view on the "depths of feeling into which we cannot peer"—visual limits and feeling having both been key concepts for understanding impersonality in Eliot's early theory. More importantly, though, *The Family Reunion* itself revolves around a long list of allusions to Eliot's performance of impersonality in *The Waste Land:* it features a concern with visuality, embodiment, and personality; a death by water and an escape from the "human wheel"; a mother who assumes a unity between the head of her family and the health of their landed estate; and a journey that's supposed to be redemptive.[43] In keeping with the role that intertextuality plays in *The Waste Land* itself, Eliot's allusions to his earlier poem allow us to see the directions in which he took impersonality as he developed it through a new genre. In other words, these allusions suggest that *The Family Reunion* sought to "[r]edeem" the "unread vision" of impersonality through the "higher dream" of verse drama, just as "Ash Wednesday" had earlier advocated ("Ash Wednesday," lines 139, 140, 140).

One of the primary developments in Eliot's impersonality as he turned to verse drama was a more thoroughgoing social dimension. His impersonal aesthetic was always part of a social project, not least because *The Waste Land* cast impersonality as the very foundation for what Eliot hoped would be a wholesale redemption of modernity. But his mature reflections on the social function of poetry—and so of his impersonality—were further cultivated by this move to the theater. Believing that drama "cut across all the present stratifications of public taste," he came to see theater as "the ideal medium for poetry. . . , and the most direct means of [its] social 'usefulness'" (*UPUC* 146). Theater allowed him to broadcast his impersonal verse to a more popular culture. In addition, playing across the seeable and the sayable, it activated imagetextuality, a key aspect of his impersonal form, in a new and powerful way. Moreover, performance not only represented impersonal subjectivity; it directly enacted that subjectivity and showed how such an enactment was part of the social and indeed political work of literature.

Eliot points to these developments in his essays of the 1930s and 1940s on the social use of verse. In *The Use of Poetry and the Use of Criticism* (1933) he invokes Leon Trotsky to bind art to the body and to make that connection the reason for art's social function: "[A]rt is a hand-maiden. It is not a disembodied element feeding on itself, but a function of social man indissolubly tied to his life and environment" (128). Indeed, returning to the distinctly psychophysiological act of feeling that was so important to Eliot's theory of impersonality, he adds that "the material of the artist is not his beliefs as *held*, but his beliefs as *felt*" (*UPUC* 128). In "Poetry and Drama" (1951) Eliot then links feeling, and in turn the social function of art, directly to embodied vision, suggesting that "there is a fringe of indefinite extent, of feeling which we can only detect, so to speak, out of the corner of the eye and can never completely focus."[44] He argues that the "images" of verse drama, or really the imagetexts, help to develop and represent these "depths of feeling into which we cannot peer." Not only that, but in "The Social Function of Poetry" (1945) he emphasizes the broad social value of this representation, even for those who don't read poetry or go to the theater, in terms of another embodied visual analogy, seeing across distances:

> The influence of poetry, at the furthest periphery, is of course very diffused, very indirect, and very difficult to prove. It is like following the course of a bird or an aeroplane in a clear sky: if you have seen it when it was quite near, and kept your eye on it as it flew farther and farther away, you can still see it at a great distance, a distance at which the eye of another person, to whom you try to point it out, will be unable to find it. So, if you follow the influence of poetry, through those readers who are most affected by it, to those people who never read at all, you will find it present everywhere. . . for in a healthy society there is a continuous reciprocal influence and interaction of each part upon the others.[45]

Eliot goes on to associate this social work of poetry, and its persistently visual and material description, with an impersonal understanding of subjectivity in two ways. First, he makes the instability and flux of personality the very basis for poetry's urgency, saying that we "are not quite the same persons that we were a year ago" and that this perpetual change means that we "cannot afford to *stop* writing poetry," because if we do our powers of feeling "will degenerate" (*On Poetry and Poets* 10). Second, remarking specifically on his fellow modernist W. B. Yeats, Eliot commends the poetic dramatist who "out of intense and personal experience, is able to express a general truth"—an "impersonality"—indicating that poetry is socially useful precisely insofar as it's also a mode of personal impersonality.[46]

These questions of embodied visuality, impersonality, and sociality that structure Eliot's essays on verse drama also drive his own plays, and particularly *The Family Reunion*, as its plentiful allusions to *The Waste Land* cue us to realize. This early play, which subtly reworks Aeschylus' *Orestia* trilogy (458 BCE), returns specifically to the fraught gender dynamics of *The Waste Land*'s impersonality; and through the struggles of its hero, Harry, Lord Monchensey, it charts a renewed and still distinctly embodied visual attempt to advance those dynamics, even though Eliot's specifically scientific vernacular is now less pronounced. *The Family Reunion* takes the question of sameness and difference, and of social hierarchy, that plagued *The Waste Land* and diffuses it across a seeing and saying body that's simultaneously a singular and plural entity, namely, the play's chorus and the theatergoing audience itself. In addition, Eliot further refracts this diffusive strategy in the ambiguous degree to which Harry is alone or cooperating with others in his impersonal pilgrimage. These techniques together create a kind of play across unity and difference that further manages Eliot's concern with the social implications of impersonal matter.

The Family Reunion first invokes and extends the impersonal experiments of *The Waste Land* by casting Harry's mother and nemesis, Amy, Dowager Lady Monchensey, as a figure for the classical belief in the unity of seeing and knowing and for the disembodiment that accompanies that unity. This figuration begins with the play's opening, when Amy is alarmed by a maid's coming in to close the drawing-room curtains. Amy is "sit[ting] in the house" with "nothing to do but watch the days draw out," and to long for sun and light. She commands the maid, "Not yet. . . . It is still quite light/. . ./Put on the lights. But leave the curtains undrawn" (*CPP* 225). This opening characterization creates the double sense that Amy watches the world from a place of removed enclosure and that she's anxious to preserve her access from within it to light, in which she has an almost worshipful investment. This double sense begins to suggest both the camera obscura model of vision and its illusion of perfect illumination.

Amy's subsequent remarks then concretize this suggestion by associating her firmly with a desire for disembodied permanence or stasis and a corresponding transparent, objective vision. She insists that "[n]othing is changed

. . . at Wishwood," and this dictate governs everything from the grounds and the employee roster, which she won't alter, to the flowers she raises out of season, refusing the material inevitability of flux, atrophy, and death (*CPP* 228). Amy binds her efforts to control materiality to her model of vision in remarks like "I can still *see* to that," a phrase that turns vision into self-direction, and more subtly in her declaration that "I must *see* for myself. I do not *believe* you," which recalls Trimalchio's boastful seeing and knowing of the Cumaean Sibyl in *The Waste Land*'s epigraph (*CPP* 226, 265 emphasis added). Just as importantly, Amy's physician, Dr. Warburton, diagnoses a connection between her visual and her antimaterial impulses, on the one hand, and a distinctly personalist understanding of subjectivity, on the other. He tells Harry, who has recently returned to visit his family, that it's "only the force of her personality,/Her indomitable will, that keeps her alive" (*CPP* 261). Clarifying Amy's plans and the larger stakes of the play, Warburton also informs Harry, "Your mother's hopes are all centred on you" (*CPP* 262). This declaration suggests the importance of a stable center to the model of seeing and knowing that Amy stands for. But the fact that this center is specifically the Wishwood estate—and that Amy wants to secure its stability by persuading Harry, who has been away for eight years, to remain there—also alludes to the core of the Fisher King legend that *The Waste Land* modifies, a legend that presumes a connection between the king and his land.

Although Amy's plan is a very personal one, it's also crucial to the play that she's just one exponent of the modern malaise to which *The Waste Land* responded and which Harry must ultimately shake off. For instance, at the moment of Warbuton's diagnosis, a police sergeant named Winchell enters the house and not only repeatedly confuses Amy's and Harry's birthdays but remarks to Harry, "You don't look a year older/Than when I saw you last, my Lord" (*CPP* 263). Winchell's observations collapse Harry into Amy and extend her desire for a timeless, disembodied self and vision to modern society as a whole—with the police standing in for the polis. But the play's best markers of the expansiveness of this modern malaise are Amy's sisters, Ivy and Violet, and her brothers-in-law, the Honorable Gerald and the Honorable Charles Piper. If Amy tries to construct Wishwood and herself as the stable image and enlightened observer, respectively, of the camera obscura model of vision, the siblings conduct a makeshift investigation of Harry's past, particularly related to his wife's recent drowning, in which they serve as the similarly all-seeing private eye of the English detective story. Only Amy's sister Agatha, who singularly stands apart from Amy's goals, recognizes that this "is not a story of detection/Of crime and punishment, but of sin and expiation" (*CPP* 275). In other words, murder, as an individual offense, isn't the issue requiring investigation. Instead, true to the play's origins in Aeschylus' *Oresteia,* there's a broader, social ill here that needs redress.[47]

A family exchange over preparations for Harry's return to Wishwood makes clear that this ill concerns those modes of vision that refuse an opaque materiality and the impersonal lessons that it offers. Amy has demanded that the family enforce an impossible stasis by simply pretending in their interactions with Harry that time hasn't passed: "behave only/As if nothing had happened in the last eight years" (*CPP* 230). This demand leads Agatha to rebuke the family with the comment that:

> Men tighten the knot of confusion
> Into perfect misunderstanding,
> Reflecting a pocket-torch of observation
> Upon each other's opacity
> Neglecting all the admonitions
> From the world around the corner
>
> . . . .
>
> The attraction of the dark passage. (*CPP* 230-31)

Agatha's reference to "a pocket-torch of observation" links Amy's demand for a disembodied status back to her mode of vision and to its investment in a complete and perpetual light. By rejecting this investment as instead an ignorance of "opacity," Agatha associates this contrasting opacity with a disavowed materiality. Not only that, but she also emphasizes that there's an important kind of knowledge (crucial "admonitions") to be learned from this material opacity.

Harry's development across *The Family Reunion*—his move toward impersonality—is largely his increasing recognition of the knowledge that comes with Agatha's embodied point of view and of the social value it represents. From the moment he returns to Wishwood, Harry understands that his family (excepting Agatha) are "people/To whom nothing has happened," because of their distance from the body and their corresponding incapacity for experience (*CPP* 234). Harry explains that they "do not know/The noxious smell untraceable in the drains," "the slow stain [that] sinks deeper through the skin/Tainting the flesh and discolouring the bone—/This is what matters" (*CPP* 234, 235). He also understands that he's not the static "person that [his family members] have conspired to invent" and that the passage of "Time and time and time" with "no change" is not only impossible but undesirable (*CPP* 234, 233, 233). Just as importantly, Harry registers that there's something "flickering at the corner of my eye" that he can't quite grasp (*CPP* 250), an experience that not only haltingly captures Agatha's suggestions of embodied vision but also powerfully prefigures Eliot's own later contention that there's "a fringe . . . of feeling which we can only detect . . . out of the corner of the eye." The sum of these characterizations marshals the range of elements that Eliot has developed in his theory of impersonality to suggest that Harry is engaged in an ongoing struggle to approach that impersonality and that this struggle is one of the principal conflicts of the play.

The recent death of Harry's wife, which occurs prior to the opening of *The Family Reunion,* stands as the one, distinctly failed action he has taken to complete that approach. Harry initially confesses to his family that he drowned his wife, but critics have tended to presume that he mustn't have, that he only feels guilty for wanting to.[48] I'll return to the question of Harry's guilt shortly, but for now I want to focus on the reasons he offers for committing the crime, reasons that resuscitate *The Waste Land*'s complex negotiation of impersonality and gender. The fact that Lady Monchensey's drowning occurs while she and her husband are at sea points back to the death of Phlebas, raising the possibility that Harry has forced on his wife, at least in "memory and desire," the "death by water" through which the Phoenician sailor returned to impersonal subjectivity. In other words, Harry may have repeated the program of gender instrumentalizing that occurs in *The Waste Land* in his effort to achieve impersonality. This suggestion is indeed borne out by his specific remarks about his wife's death. Speaking of his desire for something more than the life his family lives, Harry notes, "One thinks to escape / By violence," and then quickly adds that it was "[f]or a momentary rest from the burning wheel / That cloudless night in the mid-Atlantic / When I pushed her over" (*CPP* 235). These remarks evoke the warning in "Death by Water" to "all those who turn the wheel," that is, all those who are trapped in the cycle that Eliot's impersonality seeks to transcend. However, as Harry's anxious state at the outset of the play makes clear, his attempt to use the sacrifice of his wife to secure impersonality for himself comes to nothing, just as Phlebas' death doesn't grant impersonality to his followers. The specifically gendered nature of Harry's instrumentalization nonetheless betrays an ambivalence that Eliot will continue to negotiate in the play: an interest in accessing impersonality, which precludes an instrumentalizing dynamic, on the one hand, and an interest in preserving gender, which depends on that kind of dynamic, on the other. Harry's effort to access but also contain impersonality fails in this case, leaving the question of what Harry, and in turn Eliot, can do to overcome this failure.

The answer lies partly in Harry's differently instrumentalizing relation to Agatha. By the end of *The Family Reunion* he has explicitly echoed her dismissal of the family's supposedly all-seeing investigation, discerning that their "inquest" merely "predict[s] the minor event" rather than what's beyond the individual (*CPP* 268). He has also distinguished himself from this tendency by adding:

> I was like that in a way, so long as I could think
> Even of my own life as an isolated ruin
>
> . . . .
>
> But it begins to seem just part of some huge disaster,
> Some monstrous mistake and aberration
> Of all men, of the world . . . (*CPP* 268)

Just as importantly, Harry casts his shift away from the world's "monstrous" individualism in the same embodied visual terms as Agatha. He explains to his family that the answer to the "ruin" of modern life lies not "in getting rid of what can't be got rid of," namely, the material flux and opacity that Agatha had pointed to, "But in a different vision" (*CPP* 275). Like Agatha, he describes this different vision as a break from Amy's camera obscura model of seeing and being. He suggests that this vision has relocated him from an "awful privacy" to a life "in public," effectively from an enclosed individuality to a shared impersonality (*CPP* 267). He also suggests that this relocation saved him from the "circular desert" and the "burning wheel" from which his wife's death had failed to release him; with this new vision, "the chain broke" and the "wheel stop[ped]" (*CPP* 277). In all of these ways, Harry makes Agatha's embodied point of view into a template for his own impersonal transformation. Yet if his relation to his wife was inadequate to achieve and manage impersonality, his admittedly less assertive instrumentalizing of another female figure is unlikely to be a sufficient substitute. Thus, Eliot needs to find impersonal strategies that exceed Harry and Agatha entirely. He finds these strategies first in his particular deployment of those aunts and uncles against whom Harry defines himself.

These relatives—Ivy, Violet, Charles, and Gerald—have a curious double role in the play. Most of the time, they are distinct characters, clearly marked according to hierarchical social positions. Ivy, for instance, has little more to do than arrange Amy's hothouse flowers and grasp spastically at the privileges of class status, while Gerald enjoys a bumbling prestige as a former colonel in the British colonial service. Both lead the conventional kind of "little life" that typifies Marie's separation from impersonal embodiment at the opening of *The Waste Land*. And to the extent that their lives differ, it's according to rigid patriarchal norms. Indeed, these norms are reinforced by the fact that Amy and her siblings are all women, while her deceased husband and his siblings are all men. Periodically, though, these siblings and siblings-in-law also come together to form *The Family Reunion*'s chorus. Still wearing the visage of their individual selves, and in some cases having just delivered lines as those selves, the siblings nonetheless express in this communal form an unconscious knowledge about their lives that they don't exhibit as individuals. This knowledge in fact leads them to challenge some of their own individual positions in ways that echo Agatha and Harry. For instance, recalling Harry's condemnation of the wheel on which modern humanity lives, the chorus describes its members as existing inside the "very restricted area" of their narrow "circle of . . . understanding" (*CPP* 291). In addition, echoing Harry's sense that his family knows nothing of what has "happened," the chorus asks: "What is happening outside of the circle? / And what is the meaning of happening?" (*CPP* 291). Indeed, the chorus even gestures toward the impersonality that lies beyond its members' restrictive individual existence, conceding finally that all "have suffered far more than a personal loss" (*CPP* 291). In these ways the chorus functions, on the one hand, as a group of clearly marked individuals who perform and sustain social hierarchies of gender, class, and more implicitly race (given Gerald's colonial service). On the other hand, though, this group is also an embodiment of impersonal subjectivity, a sensing being that understands things that individuals as such can't grasp. The chorus' formal construction, its simultaneous singularity and plurality, thus struggles for an impossible-to-resolve balance between impersonality and the social hierarchies against which impersonality seems to work, hierarchies that Eliot still very much values. This balance forms specifically in the eyes of the audience, who observe the characters' shift from individuals to chorus and back again.

But the audience isn't simply observing *The Family Reunion*'s balancing act; it's also ultimately a part of that balancing act. The audience's incorporation begins with an early comment by the chorus that its members are "actors" who "play an unread part" in Amy's "pantomime" (*CPP* 231). This vague sense of a play within a play, a kind of *mise en abyme,* displays the chorus' impersonal awareness of the "monstrous farce" that is Amy's effort at stasis but also extends to an awareness of the siblings' role in *The Family Reunion* itself (*CPP* 231). The chorus shares this meta-awareness with the audience, puncturing the latter's passive observation of the play's events and thereby folding its members into the play as well. In other words, the audience members aren't able to inhabit the kind of enclosed space of disembodied observation that Amy cherishes; instead, they are nudged closer to the knowledge of opacity offered by Agatha and Harry. If this positioning creates an experience of what is for Eliot embodied impersonality, it also sets the stage for the audience to play a role much like that of the chorus in *The Family Reunion*'s impersonal transitions. The audience is similarly both a unified body and a set of individual and socially mapped bodies—a multiplicity that once again allows social hierarchies to persist alongside impersonality.

Eliot builds the audience's active impersonal awareness through the aunts and uncles' investigation of Harry's wife's drowning. When they ask Harry's valet, Downing, to provide evidence about his employer's movements on the night of Lady Monchensey's death, Downing reports that Harry's calm presence on the ship deck exonerates him of any crime: "While I took my turn about, for near half an hour / He stayed there alone, looking over the rail. / Her Ladyship must have been all right then, / Mustn't she, Sir? or else he'd have known it" (*CPP* 241). Although the family doesn't recognize that Downing's conclusion doesn't follow from his evidence, the audience (who have also become de facto investigators) can't help but realize that he only begs the question rather than resolving it. In other words, Downing's report proves that Harry stood where his wife went overboard and thus that he could have pushed her, or at the very least not tried to save her. By realizing this uncertainty, audience members confront for themselves the strange commitment to a plainly false transparency that's presumed in the investigation on stage. Moreover, via this confrontation, audience members are aligned with Agatha's indictment of that transparency and with Harry's eventual agreement with her as well. In other words, the opacity that the audience registers in the investigation becomes a kind of objective correlative for the opacity of impersonal subjectivity that both Agatha and Harry gesture toward. This experience provides the audience with a basis for reading Harry's ultimate decision to leave Wishwood on an unspecified journey very differently from the way his family read it. In keeping with their belief in a disembodied subject and a transparent, objective vision, the family see that journey, very conventionally, as a Christian mission. Not only does Harry reject this transcendent reading but he refuses to replace it with his own account of what his next steps entail. Audience members, having earlier departed from the family's view, are poised to recognize this incompleteness as itself part of the flux and opacity of the impersonal subjectivity that Harry seeks. In other words, the audience can see Harry's journey as an impersonal one.

As *The Family Reunion* nears its conclusion, Eliot seems to bank on the audience's induction into the incoherent nature of impersonality as an aid to one more effort to double-code his characters as simultaneously both impersonal and socially marked. This last effort revolves around Harry's relation to Agatha regarding the question of his journey. Over the course of the play, Agatha's impersonal instruction has stemmed from the premise that "[w]e must try to penetrate the other private worlds," that to "rest in our own suffering/Is evasion of suffering" (*CPP* 268). Harry performs this refusal of solipsism—alongside a powerful refusal of the gendered instrumentalizing apparent in his wife's murder—in his eventual belief that he and Agatha are in a "common pursuit of liberation" from the "human wheel" (*CPP* 273). Agatha, however, quickly recasts this joint impersonal pursuit as Harry's singular project, claiming that he has already "crossed the frontier," while she "wander[s] in the neutral territory/Between two worlds" (*CPP* 284, 285). The catch here is, of course, that Agatha herself labels these positions (even for Harry), so she's somehow both the ultimate impersonal perceiver and a distinctly limited perceiver of impersonality. Through this paradoxical simultaneity, Eliot condenses his elaboration of impersonality and his management of its implications into a single character: Agatha is at once a privileged embodiment of impersonal subjectivity and also a woman who defers that privilege to her male nephew. This condensation creates a kind of confused authority that's at once patriarchal and not, impersonal and not. Although this condensation appears to advertise an impossible incoherence that surfaces when impersonality meets social hierarchies like gender, audience members have been taught to read incoherence as impersonal, which acts to justify this odd moment.

The end of the play—the immediate aftermath of Harry's departure on his journey—echoes this strategy one last time. On the one hand, Harry has gone off to experience impersonality, while Agatha and her younger counterpart, Harry's cousin Mary, are left to a distinctly gendered life at a women's college. On the other hand, Agatha closes by recasting this rather patriarchal trajectory in terms of the "common pursuit of liberation" that Harry had earlier imagined. She explains to Mary that the modern illness marked by Amy's plans will be ended

> By intercession
> By pilgrimage
> By those who depart
> In several directions
> For their own redemption
> And that of the departed— (*CPP* 293)

The implication of Agatha's final words—and she does, significantly, have the final words in *The Family Reunion*—is that multiple negotiations and directions rather than any one savior are needed for a modern recovery of impersonality. According to this reading, Agatha and Mary do have a part to play, but it's left open-ended whether the various parts (for example, "intercession" versus "pilgrimage") are equal, or equally available to all. This final uncertainty in the play again points to the opaque nature of impersonal subjectivity, even as that nature again allows Eliot to reach for impersonality, but with gender. While some of the possibilities of *The Family Reunion*'s "common . . . liberation" don't quite stabilize social hierarchies, as Eliot might like, the play does represent a significant development on his earlier efforts in *The Waste Land*.

Ultimately, Eliot's late analogy of the social influence of poetry to seeing across distances is also useful for appreciating the reach of impersonality across the full arc of his career. It's not hard to grasp the visual-scientific vernacular at work in Eliot's first theorizations of impersonal art, or in his imagetextual investigations of impersonality in *The Waste Land,* especially its manuscript. But with that recognition in place, it becomes possible to track this vernacular as it moves to a distance at which it isn't instantly recognizable. We can see, for instance, that Eliot's early discussion of monuments that move lingers not only in his broad turn to drama but specifically in *The Family Reunion*'s critique of visual transparency and stasis; and we can recognize Eliot's objective correlative as a way to understand how *The Waste Land*'s impersonal instruction persists in *The Family Reunion*'s attempts to orchestrate the audience's experience. These developments point to the importance of vision, materiality, and science throughout Eliot's career. Rather than reading impersonality simply as a screen for Eliot's personality, we can thus see that the rich set of visual languages traced throughout this book

were part of his vocabulary, that they motivated his uneven politics of impersonality, and that they even explain his strong investment in verse drama,
though it wasn't his most successful medium.

Placed alongside one another, Walter Pater, Michael Field, H.D., Mina
Loy, D. H. Lawrence, and T. S. Eliot together show the broad reach and significance of modernist impersonality. First, they provide a context for thinking differently about literary modernism in relation to modern science—once
again taking on the bogeyman of C. P. Snow's "two cultures" divide. Their
scientific vernacular of vision elaborates and adapts optics, visual culture,
and image-text relations to ask important questions about what it means to
be, to see, and to know and also about how the answers might change the
way we live and relate to one another. Second, this group of writers, together with the context they lay bare, brings to the surface the complicated
politics of impersonality, which have generally gone unrecognized. Impersonality bolstered a range of liberatory and conservative social goals, from
challenging racial and gender essentialisms, to defending individuality, to
reinvigorating claims to universality. Regardless of their particular political
aims, though, all of the writers considered here confronted an inability to
fully control their impersonal aesthetics. Some struggled against certain
implications of an impersonal subjectivity that they didn't wish to acknowledge, while others, however much they wanted to follow those implications
out, struggled with the fact that the complexity of such a subjectivity made
it impossible to fully understand and represent it. In other words, modernist
impersonality's particular object of study meant that the aesthetic would inevitably be a rocky encounter rather than a completely malleable discourse.

Of course the scientific vernacular of vision—and indeed the way that
aesthetic impersonality marshals it to consider ontology—didn't simply dis-
appear with the end of literary modernism. Indeed, we can see its legacy in
continued efforts to rethink materiality in the present. The concepts toward
which impersonality gravitated in reconceiving personhood echo strikingly
in current new materialisms, particularly affect theory. Modernist impersonality and affect theory both attend to the nature of being by asking a set
of visually inflected questions about the interdependence of bodily fluctuations, sensations, feelings, mental states, and objects of the mind; moreover,
both show that personality is the shifting product of these phenomena, not
the site of autonomy or even a coherent interiority. The following afterword
explores these continuities in order to crystallize the stakes of both projects
and to suggest future directions for affect theory as well.

Afterword: Modernist Futurity
The "Creative Contagion"
of Impersonality and Affect

> The notion of a visual or tactile beauty that might be
> impersonal, dislinked from the need to present a first-
> person self to the world, came as news to me—late, late
> news. But exciting! My fingers were very hungry to be
> handling a reality, a beauty, that wasn't myself, wasn't
> any self, and didn't want to be.
>
> Eve Kosofsky Sedgwick, *The Weather in Proust*

This book has intentionally not offered an affect theory of modernist impersonality. The terms and structures I've attributed to impersonality instead arise strictly from modernism and its scientific vernacular. But optical
impersonality does constitute a sort of prehistory for current affect theory. And to turn to this connection now is to make what Brian Massumi has
called a "trans-situational linkage" (239). Such a linkage involves a "reconstellation of concepts," a process of extracting ideas from their usual relations in their home system and bringing them together instead with ideas
from another system (17). Some of the most important ideas about affect
come from Massumi himself, who is strongly influenced by Gilles Deleuze,
and from Eve Kosofsky Sedgwick, who is more loosely influenced by the
psychologist Silvan Tomkins' Basic Emotions paradigm. Attending to the
trans-situational linkage between impersonality and these particular thinkers reveals what happens to impersonality—its beliefs, concerns, and forms—
after modernism. Without suggesting that impersonality and affect theory
are synonymous, or even entirely isomorphic, this reconstellation points to
avenues of new and future growth that may arise from their joint consideration.

A Shared Visual Vernacular: Affect Theory's Impersonality

The "affect" of affect theory is perhaps best grasped by analogy to the difference between energy and matter. Affect, like energy, is a capacity that hasn't yet been channeled to any particular purpose. As Eric Shouse puts it, affect is a "non-conscious experience of intensity," a moment of "unformed and unstructured potential" (¶5). This "intensity" or "potential" is just as embodied as physical energy: it consists in correlated sets of responses involving facial muscles, the viscera, the skeleton, the respiratory system, vocalizations, and changes in blood flow that together register "the particular gradient . . . of stimulation impinging on the organism" and correspondingly augment or diminish the body's capacity to act (¶6). In other words, affect includes both one's degree of sensitivity to the world—that is, one's capacity to *be affected*—and the degree of one's ability to act in the world—that is, one's ability to *affect*. With this meaning in mind, most of the characteristics that affect theorists assign to affect fall into place. As an intensity or potential, affect is about variability, movement, and futurity rather than a positioned body or psychological state. It's unlike any particular action, arrival, or emotion because it exists before will and consciousness. In Massumi's terms, affect is an excess that's not accounted for by the "'discursive' body" and "its signifying gestures" (2).

As Massumi's claim suggests, affect theory is typically taken as a riposte to poststructuralist theory. Teresa Brennan, however, has usefully situated it within a much longer intellectual history whose terms overlap with the history of impersonality. Brennan's basic premise is that affect both undermines the supposed binary between self and world and suggests that subjects can be motivated by intentions that aren't entirely their own but that are frequently owned after the fact. She argues that the idea of affect faded from scientific and philosophical discussion when "the individual, especially the biologically determined individual, came to the fore" in the eighteenth century, alongside the rise of "objectivity" (2). Affect wasn't conducive to the establishment of this individual, who was formulated around the subject/object divide. And this ill fit thus required a purging of affect: the objective subject was supposed to calculate more and feel, and even sense, less. Brennan maintains, moreover, that the heightened preoccupation with vision beginning in the eighteenth century—the *siècle des lumières,* or century of light—precipitated the declining interest in affect. True to that preoccupation, vision became the only sense to attain some sort of objective status, as its function at a distance seemed capable of keeping subject and object separate. The recent return to affect, Brennan thus concludes, requires and indeed facilitates a demotion of the individual as a visual construction.

This set of claims is closely akin to Walter Pater's argument in *The Renaissance,* where he called for readers to recognize the failings of the longstanding and distinctly cloistered camera obscura model of the subject-observer. But if Brennan and Pater are both critical of how vision and the individual were historically intertwined, they differ on how long that history lasted. For Brennan, modern vision and visual science continued to perpetuate the problem of the individual; their subject/object binary determined what bodily processes could be admitted to consciousness and continually filtered out affect as inconsistent with that binary. Pater, on the other hand, believed that only a mistaken, disembodied understanding of vision produced the problem of the sequestered individual—and indeed that this problem was already being solved by the new physiology of vision in the later nineteenth century. Perhaps it seems surprising, then, to connect affect theory to modernism's optical impersonality. Even if both are interested in the same kind of human subject, and specifically in what's left out of that subject, in one case vision and science are the problem and in the other they are (also) the solution. But we've already seen, through the case of D. H. Lawrence and his critique of a modern "kodak-vision," that a fraught or even critical relation to modern visuality was no obstacle to developing an optical impersonality. And with affect theory too—setting aside what I think are the flaws of Brennan's history of vision—optics and even a corresponding discourse of imagetextuality have played a meaningful role, particularly in those threads elaborated by Massumi and Sedgwick.

Massumi's approach to optics is part of a broader engagement with the sciences, one that takes them not as a source of factual constraint but as a philosophical provocation. This approach shares a good deal with modernist impersonality's scientific vernacular of vision. Stylists of impersonality adapted propositions and experiments from the science and philosophy of embodied vision and from a related modern visual culture in order to elaborate their own formal and thematic theorizations of subjectivity. This adaptation led to a scientific engagement that didn't always depend on technical accuracy. We might recall, for instance, the moment in *Parade's End* when Ford Madox Ford makes an error in his representation of color-opposite (or negative) afterimages, or Ezra Pound's vortex-driven descriptions of imag-

ism, which characterize the vibrations and intensities of impersonal subjectivity in terms of a then recently obsolete notion of the ether. Neither Ford's
error nor Pound's datedness ultimately compromises their resulting imagetexts of impersonal subjectivity; Ford still memorably maps Tietjens' impersonal being onto his embodied seeing, and Pound still usefully captures an
unseen material chaos within and beyond the subject. Massumi's *Parables
for the Virtual* (2002) makes an explicit virtue of this vernacular style of engagement. He declares at the outset that he's not concerned about getting
everything right about the science he discusses, because he doesn't want
simply to annex the study of affect to the sciences. Rather, he argues that a
repurposed scientific concept carries a residue of activity from its former
role, so that it has a kind of readiness to arrive and relay in certain ways. He
describes this residue as a "scientific affect," and he's more interested in
exploring and exploiting such affects than in technical accuracy (20). Such a
focus is evocative, for instance, of T. S. Eliot's selective appeal to the popular
science writer J. W. N. Sullivan's ideas about the nature of science, rhetoric
about the relation between art and science, and illustrative focus on optics
as Eliot first began to develop his impersonal aesthetic.

Indeed, this illustrative focus is equally crucial to Massumi's scientific re-
purposing. Although he considers findings from a variety of scientific fields,
he returns to optics, and specifically modern optics, across the full arc of
Parables for the Virtual, perhaps echoing back through its Deleuzian framework to Lawrence, the modern impersonalist to whom Deleuze frequently
signaled his indebtedness.[1] Massumi focuses most extensively on two areas
of modern optical study: the *Ganzfeld,* or total field, of vision experiments,
pursued mainly from the late 1920s to the mid-1960s; and David Katz's experiments with color memory in the first decade of the twentieth century.
Both experiments are quite representative of modern optics in the way that
they explore vision as physiological and decidedly not objective. In other
words, this isn't the optics, or more broadly the visuality, that Brennan has
in mind in her history of affect, but it's very much the science that crucially
informed modernism's impersonal aesthetic.

Massumi turns first to the *Ganzfeld* experiments, which sought to isolate
the elemental physical and physiological conditions of vision. These experiments assumed that the most elemental aspect of vision is the act of light
striking the retinas and inferred that white light, which contains the full
spectrum of color, would therefore be the most complete version of this act.
Experimenters thus arranged for white light to strike their subjects' entire

retinas uniformly and thereby to capture the full spectrum of light across the entire visual field. This "pure" visual experience, however, resulted in three unpredicted and startling results: (1) temporary blindness; (2) subjects' sense that they were floating out of their bodies, "literally los[ing] their selves" in what Massumi records as an act of "depersonalization"; and (3) the inability to construe things as objects, so that "the objective conditions of vision exclude object vision" (145, 145, 146). Riffing on the experiments' results, Massumi hypothesizes that the subjects were arrested at an experience of visual intensity and were unable to convert that intensity into the objects of everyday visual sensation. He locates this intensity in degrees of depth, brightness, and saturation, as well as in levels of endogenous retinal firings and eye jitter. And he argues that by forcing subjects to perceive these intensities, or affects, themselves, the *Ganzfeld* experiments exposed the "conditions of [the] emergence of vision" (152). Massumi contrasts these conditions of emergence to the "empirical conditions of vision" that the experimenters were interested in, and he thus argues that the experiments inadvertently exposed the doubling of vision. They showed that what the subject consciously perceived was a belated addition to an unconscious affect, a "visually unperceived from which vision emerges" (155). Moreover, playing on the idea of addition, Massumi contends that our conscious percepts are actually "excess seeings" or "oversights" (155). In other words, the clean forms that our percepts offer are "hallucinations" overlaid on a much more chaotic visual field, so that what remains "unperceived"—the experience rather than the product of vision—is ironically the only element of seeing that we can treat as a "given" (155).

Returning more directly to questions of subject and object, Massumi also explains that what generates these "oversights" is the difference between the chaotic speed of affect and the "sluggishness of the body's reactions" (149). Much as the eyes and brain fuse the quick series of stills presented in film into the fluid motion of one figure, the persistence of vision and other lagging mindbodily reactions generate the consolidated objects or products of vision that we recognize. Moreover, he argues that our sense of these objects allows us to create a retroactive confidence in the similar coherence of our own bodies. In Massumi's hands, then, the psychophysiology of vision works much as it did for the modernists: it lays bare a set of autonomic operations that compose what he calls a "depersonalize[ed]" subjectivity (145). Indeed, Massumi's philosophy of visual misfires is strikingly similar to Mina Loy's poem "The Ceiling," in which optical floaters and afterimages become a springboard for thinking about being and knowing beyond the confines of the personality and beyond the guarantees of perceptual objectivity. Similarly, Massumi's idea that the body itself is formed retroactively— that it isn't the preexisting context or location for an event but is instead posited in the unfolding of an event—recalls Pater's claim that the body is "but an image of ours" (*R* 186-87); it also recalls Lawrence's distinction between the chaotic "physiology of matter" and the coherence presumed in everyday "kodak-vision," in which one "makes himself in his own image" (*Letters* 2:732; "AM" 165, 165).

Massumi expands upon these philosophical questions in discussing his second modern optical experiment, Katz's work on visual memory. Katz's experiment asked subjects to match the color of various familiar objects from memory. (Significantly, the object that most interests Massumi is the color of a friend's eyes.) Not only did subjects fail to achieve matches but their memories consistently exaggerated the color of the objects in question. For Katz, this exaggeration amounted to simple empirical error. Moreover, when he revealed those errors to his experimental subjects, both he and they treated the errors as personal, a memorial excess that the subjects added to perception because of their emotional investment. According to Massumi, though, this experiment and its conclusions point to how our standard sense of subjectivity and objectivity keeps us from recognizing the workings of affect and leads us to transform it too quickly into the personal. He argues that vision's imperceptible affects, its open "potential," enable emotional influences in the first place (232). In other words, the workings of vision are irreducible to objectively measurable elements, such as the difference between the actual blue of a friend's eyes and the "too blue" recollection of them (210). Massumi elaborates on this open potential in two key ways. First, he argues that any experience of the world is "logically and ontologically prior to its participants"; that is, experience puts things into relation, and that relation allows the "objects and subjects involved in the unfolding event [to] come into definition only retrospectively" (232, 231). Second, Massumi also argues that there's a "fringe of active indetermination" regarding the particular relation that the various elements of an experience will leap into. For both reasons, the outcome of any experience has a "constitutive . . . vagueness" built into it (231). Thus, Massumi argues that for Katz to describe the "vagueness" of vision as individual error is for him to misrecognize affect as personal and also to reduce the territory that being and perception actually encompass. "[D]on't take it personally," Massumi quips (221).

Massumi's effort to draw out the unrecognized implications of a modern physiological optics, coupled with his specific insistence on vagueness as a lodestar for modeling seeing and being beyond the personal, recalls the indeterminacy of many of modernism's impersonal imagetexts. H.D.'s *Borderline* pamphlet is but one example. It describes *Borderline,* including its actors and the process of making the film, in terms of an indeterminate middle space, one where the actors are neither professionals nor amateurs, where the director is neither American nor European, where the style is neither ultra-abstract nor realistic, and where even the setting is just some border town or other. In H.D.'s estimate, these indeterminate aspects of the film's form and production visualize the vagueness of impersonal being by both performing and enabling what her director Kenneth Macpherson calls a "special nervous reflexive response" that's distinct from all "individual attractions" ("Introduction to 'The Fourth Dimension in the Kino,'" 182). Such appeals to indeterminacy in modernism's optical impersonality reverberate in Massumi's passing description of vision's vagueness as an "impersonality of experience" that characterizes an "impersonal subjectivity" (211, 212). Moreover, H.D.'s specific location of indeterminacy in an in-between space echoes even more strongly in Massumi's call for scientists to attend to the "impersonal" "middle" that's typically excluded from experimental results (220). Thus, while Massumi doesn't appear to recognize the historical significance of the term *impersonal,* his use gestures at a linkage, if not an actual lineage, between modernist impersonality and current affect theory.

Indeed, as a kind of glue for this linkage, Massumi later remarks that art, not unlike his theory, is concerned with "the qualitative expression of self-transforming life activity," that is, with the vague vivacity of affect (248). In addition, he defines avant-garde art in particular through its refusal to present that "qualitative expression as personal" and also its "disjunctive" rather than artificially "smooth" conjoining of the various moments and levels of the artwork (251). Any of the impersonal stylists examined in the previous chapters might be understood in these terms: their scientific vernacular of vision qualitatively expresses impersonal affects, and their imagetextuality is a formal program for enacting the disjunction that Massumi notes. Imagetextuality, and more broadly the relation between images and texts, is in fact the one aspect of modernist impersonality that doesn't directly concern

Massumi. Instead, it's Eve Sedgwick's affect theory, or more specifically her own late artistic practice of that theory, that resuscitates this formal component of impersonality.

In its early days, Sedgwick's theory actually followed Teresa Brennan's line by distancing affect from the visual. Probably the best example is her discussion of the artist Judith Scott's wrapped sculptures, one of which appears, embraced by Scott herself, on the cover of Sedgwick's *Touching Feeling* (2003). Sedgwick celebrates Scott's work as the product of a "creative idiom" that lies beyond both personhood and ordered rationality, or in Sedgwick's words, beyond an "obscuring puppy fat of personableness" and even "coherent sense."[2] Sedgwick explicitly detaches this idiom from vision, arguing that in Scott's relation to her sculptures the "sense of sight is seen to dissolve in favor of that of touch" (*TF* 22). This affective turn to touch, Sedgwick argues, "makes nonsense out of any dualistic understanding of agency and passivity" (*TF* 14). Aside from her skepticism of vision, many of Sedgwick's remarks, from her valorization of a move beyond the person to her confident antidualism, sound like crucial elements of modernist impersonality. Indeed, years later, Sedgwick's reflections on her own late effort to turn her affect theory into an aesthetic practice elaborate on the cues she associates with Scott's work by linking them more explicitly to a discourse of impersonality. Just as importantly, though, Sedgwick's own late art practice isn't at all antivisual. Rather, it focuses on what I call *imagetextiles*, objects that function complexly as text, image, and tactile object, so that touch has become a part of what I've discussed as imagetextuality rather than an alternative to it.

In her posthumous volume *The Weather in Proust* (2011) Sedgwick insists that unlike her work as a literary critic, her artistic practice didn't involve the construction of an identity—or even the deconstruction of one. She describes her art as a "meditative practice" on the "possibilities of emptiness," and she explains this emptiness by contrasting her public profile as a queer theorist to her more anonymous work in textile art, noting sardonically that she's not "overendowed with either natural facility or acquired skills" as an artist.[3] Sedgwick's supposed lack of personal skill becomes a metonym for the depersonalization signaled in her art. Indeed, she ultimately attaches the term *impersonality* to this art: emptiness is a "spacious framework of impermanence in which ideas, selves, and other phenomena can arise in new relations," and these new relations include "a visual or tactile beauty that might be impersonal, dislinked from the need to present a first-

person self to the world" (*WP* 70-71, 71). Sedgwick's association of emptiness and its new relations with the potential of touch suggests that it refuses
the "dualistic understanding of activity and passivity" that she had already
attributed to that modality. But Sedgwick's art also adopts a formal program, the imagetextile that accompanies emptiness to challenge dualism
further. She draws attention to this aspect of her work when she argues that
though the grammatical properties of language, such as active and passive
voice, insist on dualism no matter what her words say, she can't simply exclude language from her art, because that would only "consolidate the dualism between language and 'real' materiality" (106). Refusing this image/text
binary and the dualism of body and mind that it maps, Sedgwick's imagetextiles instead make the seeable and the sayable part of those relations among
"ideas, selves, and other phenomena" that are shifting in her art, and it's
through this antidualism that visuality becomes part of the potential she
sees in touch rather than being opposed to it.

Sedgwick's affective art richly recalls elements of multiple modern stylists of impersonality. For instance, in valuing emptiness as a remove from "a
first-person self," she echoes Loy's definition of impersonality as an "anti-
thesis of self-expression." And her practice of pitting her artistic weaknesses
against a consolidation of her personhood recalls the impersonality that
Katharine Bradley and Edith Cooper pursued in their stringent collaboration as Michael Field. Even her gradual assimilation of vision to the antidualism of touch suggests the way that Lawrence's "root-vision" not only rejects
Cartesian dualism but exemplifies that rejection through the idea of a vision
that's in touch.

In keeping with these connections to modernist impersonality, Sedgwick's antidualism is consistently shaped by a scientific interest in human
psychophysiology, and as she moves toward an imagetextile practice and an
increased visuality, this interest moves more specifically toward optics. In
Touching Feeling her primary scientific touchstone is Silvan Tomkins' Basic
Emotions paradigm, which she suggests "underpin[s] most of the approaches"
in that volume (*TF* 18). She argues that to engage Tomkins' theory of "psychology and materiality at the level of affect is also to enter a conceptual
realm that is not shaped by lack nor by commonsensical dualities of subject
versus object or of means versus ends" (*TF* 18, 21). But as Sedgwick develops
her own affective art practice, she looks beyond psychology also to physics
and visual technologies to shape her sense of being and knowing. One piece

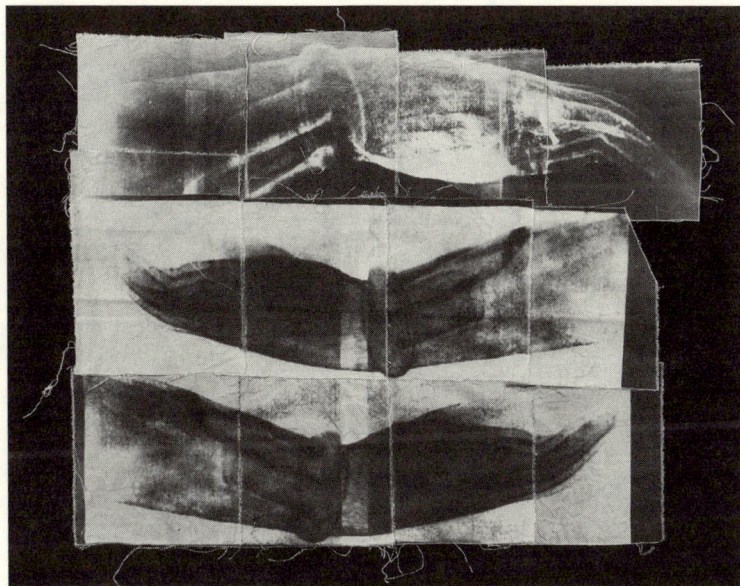

Fig. A.1. Eve Kosofsky Sedgwick, *Fractured Bodhisattva,* c. 2002. Photograph by Kevin Ryan. Courtesy of H. A. Sedgwick.

that registers this expansion is *Fractured Bodhisattva* (fig. A.1), from Sedgwick's 2002-3 *Bodhisattva Fractal World* exhibition.

Fractured Bodhisattva depicts the extended hand of a wooden Guanyin statue in a cascading series of vertical and horizontal inversions. Guanyin is an East Asian Bodhisattva, a figure who "registers a singular aspect or ema-nation of the Buddha," in this case compassion, as well as a broader "aiming toward enlightenment" (*WP* 102). Echoing T. S. Eliot's appeal to the non-dualism of the Buddhist *Āditta Sutta,* or Fire Sermon, in *The Waste Land,* Sedgwick explains in her artist statement about the exhibition that Guanyin both exists in and indicates a nondualistic dimension of being that's "not self, not other, not both self and other, and not neither self nor other" (*WP* 104). She goes on to describe her attraction to this figure, and the being and knowing it represents, in terms of two scientific discourses meaningful to modernist impersonality. The first, fractal mathematics, is already announced in her exhibition title. Fractals are recursive shapes, like a snowflake: they comprise parts that reproduce the shape of the whole, and although they are continuous, their sharp and complex cusps aren't understandable using classical tools of mathematical analysis such as differential equations. These characteristics, as Sedgwick explains, mean that fractals "refuse the classical geometrical definitions" and certainties of knowing that were long the basis for privileging the "illusion" of "perspectival realism" (90)—and, I would add, a corresponding camera obscura model of vision as well. Thus, just as Loy found in non-Euclidean geometry an invigorating imaginative space in which to reconceive the seeing subject as fundamentally impersonal, Sedgwick takes fractals as a useful framework for understanding impersonal affect. She argues that Guanyin exists dynamically "along the defile of fractal dimension," an affective expanse beyond any kind of self, let alone self-other relation (93).

The second, not unconnected scientific discourse that Sedgwick links to Guanyin is the work of the modern quantum physicist David Bohm, who eventually became interested in the affinity of physics and Buddhism. Akin to my earlier distinction between energy and matter as a model for affect, Bohm's later philosophy discusses a "holomovement" of energy in the universe as the physical underpinning of the Buddhist notion of emptiness and imagines this energy as an "implicate order" (qtd. in *WP* 101). Sedgwick suggests not only that Guanyin's being is in this holomovement but also that Bohm's physics is a universal formulation of impersonal affect. Bohm thus functions for Sedgwick much as Einstein functioned in the "alert science" of Lawrence's impersonality. Both Lawrence and Sedgwick sought in their scientifically inflected art to show that "we move and move for ever, in no discernible direction, [so] there is no center to the movement, to us" ("AM" 167).

Beyond the thematics of Guanyin, though, Sedgwick's *Fractured Bodhisattva* also shares affinities with modernism's optical impersonality in its use of distinctly modern visual technologies. The piece comprises numerous uneven squares of fabric, each bearing one portion of a cyanotype of an x-ray of Guanyin's hand, which is then twice inverted and repeated. Cyanotype, or blueprinting, is a primitive photo-printing technique invented in 1842 and popular well into the twentieth century; the generally more familiar x-ray, or solid-penetrating electromagnetic radiation, was discovered in 1895, developed for medicine around 1908, and first used artistically and art historically in the late 1920s. Sedgwick's piece highlights the messiness of both of these modern technologies' replications: she compounds the smears of over- and underexposure in the cyanotype and the shadows of the tape used to secure the x-ray by also retaining creases in her fabric, unevenly over-

lapping her squares, neglecting to cut loose or dangling threads, and refrain-
ing from making an overall hem. These elements together create a sense of
mediation, incompletion, materiality, and opacity that resists the "illusion-
ary three-dimensional space of the sculptur[e]" itself (*WP* 93). Indeed, Sedgwick's redundant repetition of the x-ray seems to underscore the irony of
trying to see into a statue, which necessarily has no interiority and which in
this case, portrays a non-individualizing, nondualistic symbol. The cumula-
tive result of these techniques closely recalls Loy's description of *Die Irma,*
or rather Richard Oelze's drawing *Frieda* (fig. 3.9), in her novel *Insel.* It also
thereby echoes Loy's alter-ego Mrs. Jones' description of Insel's detritus rays
(fig. 3.8), which seemed to surround Irma, as well as Jones' sense that his
impersonal being was a kind of photographic *Entwicklung,* or development.

But though we see in *Fractured Bodhisattva* the imagetextual images that
grew out of the new physiology of vision in the later nineteenth century,
what we don't see there is Sedgwick's specific tendency to combine images,
textiles, *and* text. *I Have Always Known,* a second work from Sedgwick's *Bodhisattva Fractal World* exhibition, is more representative in that respect (fig.
A.2). This imagetextile is her version of a Buddhist prayer flag. *I Have Always
Known* offers an English translation of a haiku written by the seventh-century
Japanese poet and Zen practitioner Ariwara no Narihira about death. Sedgwick's artist statement links this poem to her impersonal sense of affect by
noting that she chose it because its "first person" exists at the tenuous "edge
of decomposition" (*WP* 111). She also suggests that her particular form in *I
Have Always Known* works to draw out this affective state. By putting the
haiku on a prayer flag, Sedgwick has converted it into a mantra, which is
"performative" rather than "express[ive]" or "propositional"; it doesn't consolidate a speaker in its saying (*WP* 105). Indeed, a prayer flag is supposed to
imprint its message on the air as it blows in the wind, acting as an imagetextual "promulgation of . . . something that simply exists . . . by no one, to no
one, in a kind of unanswerable impersonality" (*WP* 106). *I Have Always
Known* thus displaces the grammatical structures of agency and passivity, of
expression and receipt, that Sedgwick finds so difficult to avoid in language
alone.

The piece further elaborates its imagetextuality in its textiled mixing of
the temporal and spatial qualities traditionally assigned to image and text.
The cloth of the flag, and so the field for its mantra, features *shibori,* a Japanese tie-dying technique in which cloth is bound into a three-dimensional
shape and then dyed. Though the cloth is ultimately returned to its two-

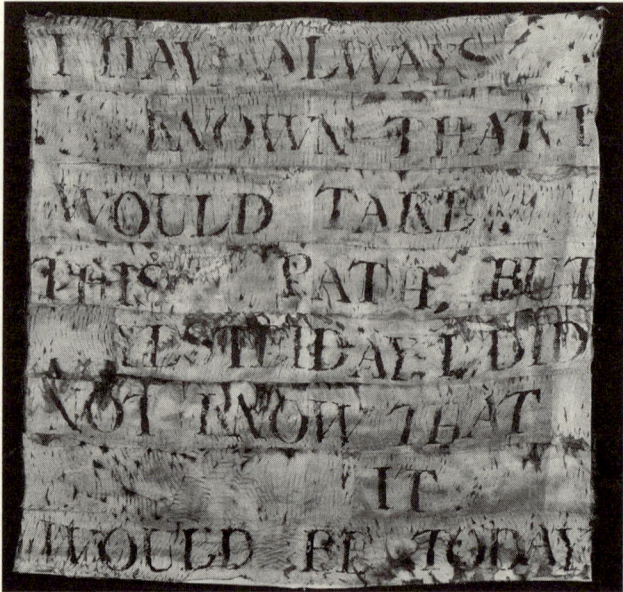

Fig. A.2. Eve Kosofsky Sedgwick, *I Have Always Known,* c. 2002. Photograph by Kevin Ryan. Courtesy of H. A. Sedgwick.

dimensional form, its creases and color patterns bear the memory of that higher-dimensional shape, existing effectively as a "between-dimension[al]" trace of "time" and "space" (*WP* 90). Ariwara's poem-turned-mantra is sten-ciled over the top of the dyed fabric as individual letters. Words accrue, often a bit crooked or only hazily outlined, and it's not always possible to detect where the text begins and ends in relation to the *shibori* pattern. This lack of differentiation creates a sense of spatialization and opacity, which is redoubled in the text's compression owing to the flag's limited width. The heavy enjambment, uneven spacing, and unexpected indentation of the lines break up the linearity of the text into looser forms, or images. Sedgwick emphasizes that these processes of construction that generate the flag's appearance mean that the artist's will is no longer controlling the artwork. Instead, as the difference between image and text becomes hard to sustain, and as material opacities become part of the creative process, art decenters will for both artist and audience alike. "The will . . . is only one determinant of the art that emerges—and often not the most important determinant,"

Sedgwick explains (*WP* 83). Such an explanation recalls H.D.'s desire for an art, "not of persons," but of the subjective recesses beyond the "frail, too-high, too inaccessible brink" of the "*will*" (*Wing Beat* announcement). Correspondingly, Sedgwick argues that as the will's powers are deflated, its territory is given over to affect's "reservoir of potential" (101)—or in the language of modernist impersonality, to H.D.'s "over-mind," Lawrence's "chaos alive," or Eliot's "fringe of indefinite extent."

Even this cursory review of Massumi's and Sedgwick's work thus shows that the terms of modernist impersonality form a ready constellation with recent affect theory. The payoff of this constellation is great: it makes clear that impersonality—its scientific roots, theoretical commitments, and image-textual form—wasn't a peripheral movement that can easily be written out of histories of modernism, whether literary or otherwise. Instead, impersonality is a persistent way of thinking about science, art, being, perceiving, and knowing. Massumi and Sedgwick together make this persistence clear in their effort to describe a new materialist ontology and epistemology by turning to modern optics and physics and to modern visual culture and its technologies and by producing a scientific vernacular of vision and an image-textual art. This historical payoff alone makes the linkage of impersonality and affect theory of interest. But it also raises the question of what theoretical implications this linkage may have for both impersonality and affect.

Open Ended: Affecting Impersonality, Impersonalizing Affect

By uprooting examples of modernist impersonality's theory and practice and reconstellating them with strikingly similar examples of affect theory and practice, we get more than simply a view on impersonality's potentially formative role in postmodern ontology and epistemology. We also gain a two-way transmission in which the particular rhythms of impersonality and affect—removed from the full regularity of either system—begin to make new conceptual connections. Massumi has argued that such connections can serve as "creative contagions," opening and sustaining new areas of intellectual growth and eventually producing a new "incipient system" (19). He advocates leaving such systems open and incomplete in order for that growth to happen. While I haven't actually arranged impersonality and affect into even an incipient system, I want to close by identifying two areas of growth that such an open system might enable.

The first area involves the way affect theory understands politics, or rather how that understanding may help to explain both the political nature of impersonality and why this nature has been overlooked. First, Massumi suggests that the qualities of affect create a variety of politics that's not reducible to ideology but that can certainly impinge on ideology. More specifically, he argues that politicians can communicate with people directly at the level of affect: they can eschew ideological argument, and make no particular effort to activate emotion or identification, but still achieve a kind of "abstractive" and "asignifying intensity" that's received by constituents and actualized along whatever sets of meaning are desirable to them (41). This actualization is the moment at which a politician can achieve ideological effects through "non-ideological," affective means (40). Such a relation between the ideological and the non-ideological is useful for challenging at least one of the existing critical readings of modernist impersonality: the sense that it's an aesthetic escape route not only from the self but from the entire sociopolitical scene in which the self is constructed. If we understand modernist impersonality at its most basic level as tapping into and representing something like affect, or what Massumi himself has called an "impersonal subjectivity," then we can understand how it could be political in *all* of its formulations without being reducible to the political direction of any *one* formulation, let alone any one text. Indeed, impersonality may be political most precisely and most radically because of that irreducibility. Moreover, such an irreducibility might account for the ways in which individual stylists of impersonality must circle back to acknowledge the revolutionary limits of their aesthetic (H.D.), or express ambivalence about whether impersonality can be closed off from conservative directions (Loy), or repeatedly scramble to contain its more liberatory instabilities (Eliot).

We can develop this argument a bit further by turning to another of Massumi's claims, namely, his sense that understanding affect's intensity as political but not ideological can actually alter the way politics works and that the academic field of cultural studies is suited to enabling this alteration. Massumi suggests that affect directs us to see politics as an "ecological undertaking," one that continually gives rise to unique yet symbiotic "forms of life" that accrue around but exceed fluctuating self-interests (255). In addition, he proposes that cultural-studies scholars could facilitate this symbiotic process, because they aren't "a determinable constituency," nor do they represent one (254). More specifically, Massumi believes that the sheer "anomaly of [such] an affectively engaged yet largely disinterested" participant in the political ecology would allow cultural studies to be an "intercessor" in the different directions of unfolding experience—what Massumi calls political "process lines," meaning particular political issues and events (255). In other words, cultural studies would promote the sense that politics is more than an aggregate of self-interests: it's also an "overpersonal excess of ongoing transformation" (253). The field would "side with" and thus serve as a space for that complex "symbiosis," rather than promoting any political position (255). Though Massumi's sketch remains quite general, I want to suggest that the kernel of modernist impersonality—the one that reverberates across different political positions—may amount to another such space. By rigorously undoing so many forms of identity, difference, and enclosure, impersonality may offer a political ecology, in the sense of a space that brings together "processually unique and divergent forms of life" rather than just a community of identical or even similar interests (255). What various individual modernists may add to that space and its visual cultural studies is the modulating transformations, the different "process lines," that attempt to address particular (self-)interests but are themselves also put into "ongoing transformation" (256, 253). Indeed, this symbiotic relation may actually be what modernist impersonality most rightly is. Such an account challenges not only those who see impersonality as forsaking politics but also those who instead pigeonhole it as a conservative or even cryptofascist aesthetic because of its connections to Pound and Eliot.

If affect theory helps to explain the politics of modernist impersonality, then impersonality may also be in a position to reciprocate. More specifically, as a second area of "creative contagion," impersonality may offer affect theory a way out of the vexed temporal issue of the prepersonal. Affect theory's broader temporal language has recently spurred attacks, most notably by Ruth Leys, who has complained that when affect theorists champion a non-ideological politics, they imply that reason, beliefs, and intentions must always be belated and thus not entirely effectual arrivals to political action. The notion of the prepersonal lies at the root of this belatedness. Following Gilbert Simondon's theory of individuation, Massumi suggests that the "dimension of the emergent," where affect is believed to reside, is fundamentally "prepersonal" (34).[4] He bases this conclusion on the idea that affect is by definition prior to form and that the individual or person is such a form. He explains that affect exists in a "different topology and causal order" from "formed entities" like the person, whose topology includes conventionalized circuits of action and reaction, linear time, and a variety of higher cognitive functions. Massumi exemplifies these ideas using the so-called "missing half second" of Benjamin Libet's neuroscientific research on intention (28). Libet asked his experimental subjects to move one of their fingers at a time of their own selection and to note the time on a clock when they made the decision to engage in that movement. The results identified an apparent lag between the time when an intentional decision was registered in neural activity and the time when the subjects indicated consciousness of that decision. Because this half-second appeared in the context of decision making, Massumi uses it to imply that voluntary action precedes the sphere of conscious thought and so the topology of the person. The missing half-second, in other words, records an "overfull" space of the prepersonal, an emergent causal order, from which the will or consciousness subtracts (29). Leys' critique of affect theory zeroes in on this interpretation of Libet's research, rightly noting that it makes no sense. Libet's subjects consciously intended to move their finger from the moment he asked them to do so, and it's therefore very difficult to single out some moment without intention that clearly precedes their decision regarding when to perform that movement. There's thus a more complex relation between intensity and intention than the "prepersonal" leaves room for.

However, if there's no missing half-second, there is in fact an unrecognized gap between Massumi's own argument about affect and the prepersonal temporality that he uses to describe that argument. I suggest that the complexity of Massumi's theory is better served by the concept of the impersonal—a term much less used and less theorized by Massumi, but one that dissolves this gap and thus at least a portion of Leys' critique. In its most rigorous form, Massumi's theory posits that intensity isn't "presocial," because the body "infolds *contexts*," including "volitions and cognitions" that are situated in the world (30). More specifically, he maintains that intensity incorporates "social elements, but mixes them with elements belonging to other levels of functioning and combines them according to a different logic" (30). Massumi's insistent rejection of the hard temporality of the *pre-* is convincing here and so should preclude his resuscitation of that *pre-* later. In other words, if intensity itself isn't presocial, then it's hard to understand why affect is prepersonal. By slipping back into the problematic language of the prepersonal, Massumi slips in his reasoning too. Noting that the brain's participation in an event "precedes recognition," he concludes that it also then "precedes cognition," as if *recognition* and cognition were the same thing and, ironically, as if there were no temporal gap between them (231).

Modernist impersonality offers a different formulation that might resolve this problem. If the *pre*personal frames affect simply as what's "before" or "in advance" of the personal, the impersonal speaks less linearly of what conditions the personal and what the personal tries to condition.[5] Moreover, impersonality includes the complex incoherence of the social, which is itself a site of intensity rather than just the routing of intensity along a particular path. H.D., for example, describes a social and biological matrix within which personality shifts and accrues, and she emphasizes how the social experience of watching a film offers a space of intensity that can reshape its viewers. Impersonality is thus not strictly before or without intention, even as it speaks to qualifications and meanings that aren't fully controlled, either socially or personally. In addition, impersonality doesn't understand intention only as a higher-order cognitive phenomenon, like recognition. Lawrence's impersonal imperatives, for instance, are most basically a set of psychophysiological and relational intentions that permeate every person, whether they are acknowledged and owned or not. Indeed, modernism's sense of impersonality is much in line with the expanded definition of intention offered by another affect theorist, William Connolly, in response to Ruth Leys' critique: "intentional tendencies emerge through a history of exchanges between an open, layered body/brain network and the wider culture," and a "specific intention on the way is often replete with pluripotentiality"; not only that, but "our consciousness plays a less consummate role" in consolidating intention than it "typically credits itself for doing" (793–94, 794, 794). The fact that the impersonal can capture Massumi's refusal of the presocial as well as Connolly's expanded sense of intention suggests that the aesthetic history of impersonality could play a useful role in affect theorists' continued explorations.

This lesson applies just as well to scholars of modernism and of modern science and technology studies. An important premise for Massumi is that current empirical frameworks are impoverished and therefore reduce our understanding of being as often as they advance it. These frameworks privilege "entropy, closure, and [the] stability of formed perceptions" without recognizing that they are "provisional, but a beat in a rhythm" (160). Scientists, in other words, set out in search of particular findings—with particular notions of subjectivity and objectivity and particular forms of measurement in mind. Because they are unprepared to recognize intensities that don't fit their expectations, they either don't see affect at all or else render it a meaningless anomaly; in both cases, they winnow being down to the personal. As Massumi puts it, they fail to see that "the truth of the experience isn't reducible to its objectification (and personification)" (221).

My premise in this book has been that scholars of modernism and of modern science and technology studies have participated in a similar winnowing down: they have reduced modernist impersonality and what it stands for and have limited the forms that the modern popularization of science must take. I have sought to expand the canon of writers who pursued modernist impersonality; to recognize its engagement with pressing social, scientific, and philosophical issues; and to appreciate its adaptation to many political positions. At the same time, this new account of impersonality pushes for an enlarged study of aesthetic engagements of science. I've argued that modernist impersonality is an optical impersonality not only because some of its stylists dealt directly with an important shift in the science of vision but because all of its stylists participated in a much more pervasive visual-scientific vernacular, one that allows for indirect and subtle engagements with the premises and implications of a physiological optics, even at the level of literary form. By becoming attuned to this broader range of participation—and indeed the way that it should make us think differently about twentieth-century image-text relations—we gain an expanded history of modernism as well as expanded models of how science and aesthetic culture continue to interact.

Notes

Introduction. Eye Don't See

1. I take the term *imagetext* from W. J. T. Mitchell, esp. *Picture Theory*.

2. See, for example, Attridge. In his commentary on impressionism Ford repeatedly discusses, at times contradictorily, the effort to represent and also move beyond personality. In "On Impressionism" (1913), for instance, he writes both that his method is a "frank expression of personality" and that he sedulously "avoid[s] letting his personality appear in the course of his work" (262, 269). Thus, it is an oversimplification to link literary impressionism exclusively with personality.

3. Lukács of course broadly rejected what he saw as modernism's refusal to confront an objective reality (namely, a social and political reality), beginning with impressionism and culminating in surrealism. Fredric Jameson offers an influential formulation of this same argument as early as *Fables of Aggression* (1979), as does Erich Kahler, who coined the influential phrase *inward turn* to refer to modernism.

4. See Daston and Galison on philosophical discussions of the subjectivity of color (273–83).

5. The physiologist Ewald Hering developed the basic theory of color opponency in 1892, and the ophthalmologist Émile Javal theorized saccadic motion in 1878. For a brief introduction to the human visual system, see David M. Miller; and Richard L. Gregory.

6. Two key terms here and throughout this book are *visuality* and *vernacular*. As Hal Foster aptly explains, if vision is the "mechanism" and "datum" of sight, then visuality is vision's "historical techniques" and "discursive determinations." The histories of vision and visuality together suggest the many differences between "how we are able, allowed, or made to see, and how we see this seeing or the unseen therein" (ix). As Katherine Pandora has argued, the phrase *scientific vernacular* signals "a broader sense of the history of 'everyday scientific knowledge,'" beyond simply the direct narratives of scientists themselves. It is "a kind of 'intellectual common' where social and theoretical comment can circulate without regard for scientific propriety" (491, 492).

7. Hereafter, emphasis is original unless otherwise noted.

8. The "two cultures" narrative derives from the physicist and novelist C. P. Snow's 1959 Rede lecture of that title, a lecture that bemoans a contemporary split between the sciences and the humanities. As their titles suggest, Isobel Armstrong's *Victorian Glassworlds* and Flint's *Victorians and the Visual Imagination* focus on the nineteenth century. Willis extends into the Edwardian period but focuses only on the genre fiction of Sir Arthur Conan Doyle and H. G. Wells. Firmly modernist studies like Craig Gordon's or those by Bruce Clarke don't consider ocular science. An important exception to this trend is James Krasner's *Entangled Eye,* though it concentrates more on evolutionary narrative.

9. See Crary's *Techniques of the Observer,* in which he points to the first decades of the nineteenth century as a moment when the truth of vision became grounded in the density and materiality of the body, thereby marking the birth of modern visuality. Also see Foucault's *The Order of Things,* in which he describes the nineteenth century as the moment when the system of thought no longer existed outside and beyond humanity but instead had physiological conditions.

10. On Kepler's theory and influence, see Lindberg; and Wade and Finger.

11. Martin Jay writes of the ocularcentrism of Western philosophy: "The development of Western philosophy cannot be understood . . . without attending to its habitual dependence on visual metaphors of one sort or another. From the shadows playing on the walls of Plato's cave and Augustine's praise of the divine light to Descartes's ideas available to a 'steadfast mental gaze' and the Enlightenment's faith in the data of our senses, the ocularcentric underpinnings of our philosophical tradition have been undeniably pervasive" (186).

12. Even though Descartes' description rejects visual semblance (because he locates the eye as a site of error), his sense of the corrective force of intuition is based largely on visual metaphors. In other words, he effectively transfers the properties of the visible to a kind of mental schematism, resulting in an objective mental vision.

13. See Wade and Finger and, more extensively, Atherton on Descartes' physiological experiments and speculation, as well as Lokhorst on the pineal gland.

14. On this shift, see Langer; and Wettlaufer.

15. On this representational history, see Hagstrum; Ray Frazer; Park; and Mitchell, *Iconology.*

16. See Daston and Galison's chapters "Mechanical Objectivity" and "Structural Objectivity" for more on these two scientific approaches to objectivity.

17. On this cultural mapping of the representational "selves" attributed to image and text, see esp. Mitchell, *Iconology.*

18. On Helmholtz and related optical physiologists' scientific influence and popularization, see Bowler and Morus; Schiemann; Dember; Beer; and Pastore, "Helmholtz on the Projection or Transfer of Sensation." Though Helmholtz's *Physiological*

Optics wasn't translated into English until 1924, its arguments appeared in popular science journals like *Nature* and *Mind*, as well as more generalist magazines like the *Fortnightly Review*, following its original German publication. Helmholtz himself paved the way for such popularizing through his Popular Lectures of 1868, which were translated into English in 1873.

19. On the influence of these gadgets, see esp. Horton; Isobel Armstrong; and Lightman, "Visual Theology."

20. On the broad popular interest in recording technologies, see Gitelman. On "x-ray mania" in particular, see Natale; and Cartwright. As a marker of that mania, I would note that obtaining an x-ray of one's hand was a popular fad in the early twentieth century, and such images could be purchased at fun fairs and amusement parks.

21. On the graphic recording image in scientific modernism, see Brain.

22. For more on Pepper and popular science, see Lightman, *Victorian Popularizers*.

23. For the former approach, see Crary, *Suspensions of Perception* and *Techniques of the Observer;* and Cartwright. For the latter, see Otter. Otter's recent study offers a more nuanced history of the new physiology of vision than do Crary's works. It's much in line with that offered here, though this book moves in different political directions.

24. See esp. Jacobs, which argues that literary modernism worked to recover a transparent observer by creating an interior gaze through which an expert viewer could access concealed truths in others.

25. See Nancy Armstrong; Steiner; and Mitchell, *Iconology*.

26. Benjamin, "Little History of Photography" 512. See also Benjamin, "Work of Art in the Age of Mechanical Reproduction," for more on the optical unconscious. Interestingly, the latter essay implicitly connects a modern imagetextuality with the optical unconscious. Its epigraph announces that "our fine arts were developed, their types and uses were established, in times very different from the present," and the "physical component" in them "can no longer be . . . treated as it used to be," having been affected by "modern knowledge and power" (Valéry, qtd. on 217). Benjamin specifies this new understanding as art's fundamental imagetextuality, beginning with the later nineteenth-century rise of illustrated magazines and a new importance given to the titles of paintings and moving through to modern film, "where the meaning of each single picture appears to be prescribed by the sequence of all preceding ones" (226). Just as this book does, Benjamin ties this imagetextuality to a "hidden political significance" and also to a decentering of humanity in the move away from portraits and also from allowing a detached, autonomous contemplation on the part of the viewer (226).

27. "Personality, n. and adj.," def. 1a, *OED Online*. Further references to this entry mention only this definition. See also Williams 194-97.

28. The quoted terms are part of Susman's catalog of the most popular adjectives

to describe personality, as they appear in self-help manuals in the first decades of the twentieth century (217). On Hollywood's "picture personality," a concept I'll return to in chapters 2 and 3, see deCordova.

29. In Victorian political thought, *character* referred to a mental or moral constitution and reputation linked particularly to masculinity (Collini). On the modern shift from character, see Susman; and Nicholson. I'll return to this shift in chapters 1 and 3.

30. Crary, *Suspensions of Perception* 65–70.

31. "Im-²" and "in-, *prefix*³," *OED Online.*

32. In addition to the critics I discuss below, see Allan; and Gilmore.

33. In addition to the critics I discuss below, see Coste; and Bort.

34. As a point of clarification, Dean's reading (in "The Other's Voice"; "Paring His Fingernails"; and "T.S. Eliot") does posit a role for the body in the *process* of achieving impersonality but nonetheless imagines that impersonality itself is disembodied.

35. In *A Singular Modernity* Fredric Jameson discusses this loss of faith as a "taboo" on "older forms of the self" and a "programmatic movement away . . . from personal identity" (135). He links this loss to a modernist tendency toward "depersonalization," and he refuses any reading of that tendency as "some resignation to an impossibly 'alienating condition'" (132, 133). Instead, he argues that it is an "original and productive response to it" (133). This book positions modernism's aesthetic impersonality as one formulation of this invigorating modernist depersonalization.

36. See "im-¹" and "in-, *prefix*²," *OED Online.*

Chapter 1. A Protomodern Picture Impersonality

1. Pater, "Prosper Mérimée" 15, 31. Pater published his lecture in the *Fortnightly Review* in December 1890, and his friend Charles Lancelot Shadwell reprinted it, with only a few variants, in *Miscellaneous Studies* (1895) after Pater's death.

2. On Pater as a kind of personalist protomodernist, see Eribon; Dowling, "Walter Pater"; Dellamora, "Critical Impressionism"; Davis; and Love (who all variously focus on a modern homoerotic aesthetic), as well as Matz; and Katz (who both describe modernist impressionism).

3. H.D. had a volume of Field's poetry and a biography of Field in her library at her death ("H.D.'s Library Index"). W. B. Yeats not only knew Bradley and Cooper personally from 1902 but wrote a review of *Sight and Song* for *The Bookman* and invited the women to submit their play *Deirdre* (1918) for production at the Abbey Theatre (Emma Donoghue 112). Yeats' papers also include an unpublished review of Field's *The Father's Tragedy; William Rufus; Loyalty or Love?* (1885) (*Uncollected Prose of W. B. Yeats* 1:225). The art critic Roger Fry had tea with Bradley and Cooper at least once (Field, *Works and Days* 267; hereafter cited as *W&D*, referring to the 1933 collection of excerpts from Bradley and Cooper's twenty-eight-volume journal. For

portions of the journal not in that collection, I cite the manuscript in the British Library).

4. I use a plural pronoun, in this case *their,* to refer to Field, as I find the use of *he* misleading, not only because Bradley and Cooper were two women rather than one man but also because *Michael Field* was more than just a pseudonym for the pair: Field also was part of a complex public performance.

5. In "Walter Pater and the Matter of the Self" Dowling similarly discerns Pater's effort to register that the human subject is material and that the self is an artifact of culture and materiality. However, she sees this effort as at odds with contemporary science and philosophy.

6. "Leonardo da Vinci" was originally published in the *Fortnightly Review* in November 1869 and appeared in the first edition of *The Renaissance* (hereafter cited as *R*).

7. Pater may have read Michelet's book as early as 1864 (Inman, *Walter Pater's Reading* 75), but he had certainly read it by 1869, because he quotes from it in his Leonardo essay. He read Quinet in early 1865 (77). Other texts that contribute to Leonardo's nineteenth-century reputation and that Pater read include Charles Clément's *Michelangelo, Leonardo da Vinci, and Raphael* (1861) and Arsène Houssaye's *History of Leonardo da Vinci* (1869) (197–212).

8. The phrase "chief organ" is Leonardo's; it appears in his "Treatise on Painting," from the Codex Urbinas manuscript (8a–9a), and is reprinted in *The Literary Works of Leonardo da Vinci* (1:56).

9. In his discussion of perspective, Leonardo writes that "when the images of illuminated objects penetrate into a very dark chamber by some small round hole," "you will receive these images on a white paper placed within this dark room and rather near to the hole, and you will see all the objects on the paper in their proper forms and colours. . . . [O]bjects transmit their images or pictures, intersecting within the eye" in the same way (D Manuscript, 8a, reprinted in *The Literary Works of Leonardo da Vinci* 1:142). See Pedretti 133–37 for additional instances of this analogy in Leonardo's notebooks. On Leonardo's optics, see Pastore, *Selective History;* and Wade and Finger.

10. The final quotation is Bacon's definition of *subtilitas naturae* in *Novum Organum,* aphorism 10. It doesn't appear in *The Renaissance,* but it is the definition Pater invokes when he uses Bacon's phrase.

11. The conclusion derives from the last six paragraphs of Pater's "Poems by William Morris" (hereafter cited as "PWM").

12. On Goethe's color theory, see Crary, *Techniques of the Observer* 67–74. When multiple lights, each of a different color, shine on the same spot on a white surface, the light reflecting from that spot is an additive mixture because it contains multiple colors. Different additive mixtures work with the color receptors in the eye to produce colored shadows when a solid object intervenes between the light and the surface. Chromatic aberration is a failure to focus all colors on the same convergence

point. It appears as little streaks of color at the boundaries between the light and dark parts of an image.

13. Pater read *The Vocation of Man* in 1860 (Inman, *Walter Pater's Reading* 14), and he discusses Fichte as one of the seminal figures of modern skepticism in his unpublished essay "The History of Philosophy" 5, 10.

14. These phrases appear in "PWM" 311, 311, 301 but not in Pater's conclusion. The argument that these phrases capture is, however, consistent with the conclusion.

15. Early critiques of *The Renaissance* on hedonistic grounds include Colvin's review in the *Pall Mall Gazette,* Oliphant's review in *Blackwood's Magazine,* and Courthope's review in the *Quarterly Review.* Critics even as late as Meisel fell in with this reading, but it has more recently been challenged.

16. "The School of Giorgione" was first published in the *Fortnightly Review* in 1877 and added to the 1888 edition of *The Renaissance.* Though Evans speculates in the *Letters of Walter Pater* (8n1) that a draft of this chapter was the essay Pater canceled from the first edition, that canceled essay is not extant. Regardless, we can assume that this last-added chapter reflects any evolution in Pater's aesthetic between 1869, when he wrote "Leonardo," and 1877, when he published "Giorgione."

17. Matthew Arnold, "On Translating Homer" (1862), 1:140.

18. This statement appears in the *Fortnightly Review* version of "The School of Giorgione" but not in the version published in *The Renaissance* (R 241).

19. Again, this elaboration appears only in the *Fortnightly Review* version (R 242).

20. Henry James wrote of Pater in a letter to Edmund Gosse of 13 December 1894, shortly after Pater's death, that he had been "the mask without the face" and so left everyone wanting "more of an inside view" of his "personal history" (3:492). More recently, Denis Donoghue has similarly characterized a quest to discover Pater over and against his "rare visib[ility]" and his seeming "to have taken literally his favorite motif of evanescence" (23). See also Shuter; and Love.

21. Wallen makes the former argument, Adams the latter.

22. When Pater uses the word *unconscious,* he likely has in mind Karl Robert Eduard von Hartmann's *Philosophy of the Unconscious* (1869), which he read in 1877 (Inman, *Walter Pater and His Reading* 230). Hartmann claimed that the universe was ruled by the unconscious in absolute, physiological, and relative forms. The first accounts for the mechanics of the physical universe; the second, for the underlying origin, evolution, development, and mechanisms of material life; and the last, for the origin of conscious mental life.

23. Cooper quotes Spencer to Bradley as early as 1880, and the women met him in 1890 (*W&D* 131–33). On Bradley's involvement with the antivivisection movement, see Sturgeon 21.

24. Bradley and Cooper's correspondence mentions Winckelmann, Lessing, and Ruskin (*Fowl and the Pussycat* 9, 96, 56–58, 172; hereafter cited as *F&P*). Prior to their research for *Sight and Song,* their correspondence also records multiple trips to the

British Museum (10-11, 130) and the Grosvenor (3). Bradley journeyed to the Uffizi and the Louvre in 1880 (15, 21-23), and both women went again (and to other museums on the Continent) during their research.

25. Cooper uses the same language when she talks about the collaboration. After receiving Bradley's revisions of her work, she writes in their joint journal: "Gradually my tremendous sorrow expresses itself through a hollow in the rocky mass of unloosened sobs. The beautiful architecture of [our verse play] *The World at Auction* . . . has been violated. . . . I would rather have lost an ear or had a nostril split. . . . I am silence. I am a despair" (qtd. in Locard 7). In addition to this lament's violence, Cooper's last phrase reduces her "I" to an affect ("despair"), one made generic and free floating by her use of an indefinite article ("a despair").

26. Cooper uses this same mosaic figure in an 1884 letter to Robert Browning, where she writes that "the scenes of our play are like mosaic-work—the mingled, various product of our two brains" (*W&D* 3).

27. For examples of the former school, see Laird; and Thain, *Michael Field and Poetic Identity*. For examples of the latter, see Chris White; and Vanita.

28. Michael Field published more than thirty verse dramas, and their journal features references to twenty-six more (per Treby's list in the *Michael Field Catalogue*). As far as we know, only one play was performed, and with Bradley and Cooper's involvement: *A Question of Memory*, on 27 October 1893 at Jack Grein's Independent Theatre in London. However, we also know that Bradley and Cooper worked to get *Deidre* produced in 1903 and sent *Equal Love* (1894) to the actress Ellen Terry, hoping that she would star in it (Emma Donoghue 85). These efforts were likely part of a broader pattern.

29. Critics have tended to link the name Michael exclusively to Bradley, so that Michael Field announces the union of Bradley (Michael) and Cooper (Field). However, as Bickle points out (*F&P* xxix), the women applied the name to each other, suggesting a greater instability in the signature.

30. For the former school, see Fraser; and Lysack. For the latter, see Vadillo; and Ehnenn. Vadillo posits that Field seeks a transparent, objective vision and therefore argues that Field's project opposes Pater's. Ehnenn instead insists that Field rejected objectivity, but she also sees that rejection as antiscience.

31. My thanks to Debra Hawhee for this translation.

32. Field records the line from Flaubert in French; the translation is mine. Interestingly, the French word for "characters"—*personnages*—more directly announces Flaubert's (and in turn Field's) concern with personality and impersonality in writing. Indeed, it's also significant that this dialectic that Field points to in Flaubert is the same one that Pater notes in "Prosper Mérimée": " 'It has always been my rule to put nothing of myself into my works,' says another great master of French prose, Gustave Flaubert; but luckily as we may think, he often failed in thus effacing himself, as he was too aware. 'It has always been my rule to put nothing of myself into my works

. . . yet I have put much of myself into them': and where he failed Mérimée succeeded" (36).

33. On the industrialization and mechanization of visual images, both in a museum context and elsewhere, see Beegan.

34. On Morelli's method and its influence, see Wollheim.

35. On Correggio's appeal to the then newly unearthed *Laocoön,* see Campbell.

36. According to Postle, the term *fancies* was first used in 1737 to describe Philip Mercier's paintings, which combined portraits of everyday people with elements of storytelling. In the nineteenth century, Sir Joshua Reynolds used the phrase *fancy pictures* to describe Thomas Gainsborough's similar work.

37. Cooper drafted a plan for a second volume of *Sight and Song,* and the pair wrote at least a few ekphrases for that volume (Vicinus 336).

Chapter 2. Images of Incoherence

1. The only other completed work in the "Borderline cycle" is the novella *Kora and Ka,* which was published alongside *The Usual Star.* Both novellas contain autobiographical elements of H.D.'s relationship with the film director Kenneth Macpherson, which I discuss in more detail below.

2. An important exception to the critical neglect of H.D.'s affiliation with science is her lengthy engagement of Freudian psychoanalysis. Numerous studies explore this engagement, including Hirsh; Buck; Chisholm; and Edmunds. Beyond psychoanalysis, Vetter's recent book *Modernist Writings and Religio-Scientific Discourse* is part of a new effort to trace H.D.'s dialogue with contemporary sciences of the body, primarily sexology and eugenics.

3. H.D.'s maternal grandfather, the Reverend Francis Wolle, was a pioneer in microbotany, and her father, Charles Doolittle, was a professor of astronomy and mathematics and the director of Flower Observatory at the University of Pennsylvania.

4. The first descriptor is Buck's (1), the latter two Laity's (*H.D.* 21, 4). Laity's argument is perhaps more important here because she characterizes H.D. as an antimodernist owing to her embrace of Pater's "cult of personality" over and against the "normative male masks, purgative conceptions of the female image, . . . and closed self-referential linguistic theories" of modernism (ix, xii). In this book I challenge the sense that Pater and H.D. were alike invested in personality in any simple way, that H.D. was antimodernist, and that impersonality was somehow singularly masculinist or opposed to subjectivity.

5. Rives has recently proposed a more complex dialectic for H.D.'s impersonal aesthetic, arguing that it moves between impersonality, as a bid for an objective poetic authority, and an "intense engagement with others that presupposes a personality in the first place" (47–48). This move is distinctly recursive and corrective, as an ethical process of surrendering personality becomes the basis for impersonal author-

ity, but that authority is also tempered by considering others. Even there, though, we see an underwriting binary between personality and impersonality and a sense that the latter takes objectivity as its possible goal.

6. H.D. had a volume of Field's poetry and their biography in her library at her death ("H.D.'s Library Index"). Her library also included a number of Pater's source texts for *The Renaissance,* such as Giorgio Vasari's *Lives of the Artists,* as well as a number of subsequently published but related books, such as Leonardo da Vinci's *Note-Books,* which includes his anatomical studies of the human eye. See Laity, *H.D.,* on H.D.'s extensive intertextual references to Pater.

7. H.D. uses the phrase *personal-impersonal* in an unpublished essay about the 1927 short film *Wing Beat* ("Wing Beat" 1), but it also comports closely with her laudatory remarks about Sappho's personal-impersonal poetry, cited in the epigraph to this chapter.

8. Pound cites Pater's famous claim in "The School of Giorgione" that "all arts approach the conditions of music," the slight miswording being Pound's (153).

9. This account of imagism, which I subsequently connect to Tiffany's, differs sharply from those of Ross and Gage, wherein imagism is obsessed with the purity and accuracy of vision and tries to lend those traits to the modern poet.

10. The physicist Peter Guthrie Tait translated Helmholtz's 1858 essay on vortex-motion into English in 1867 and also popularized Helmholtz's broader work in *The Unseen Universe* (1875). In the *OED,* the compound entries for *vortex*—including "vortex-motion," "vortex-matter," "vortex-filament," "vortex-line," and "vortex-ring"—all list Helmholtz as the originator, firmly linking him with the term. For more on potential links between Pound's vorticism and Helmholtz's vortex, see Pfannkuchen; and Ian F. A. Bell.

11. Pound wrote under both pseudonyms for the *Egoist* in 1914.

12. See Pfannkuchen for a quick summary of physicists' use of Helmholtz's ideas to theorize both the nature of ether as an ideal fluid and also the construction of atoms, then believed to be matter's most basic constituent. Such theorizations were eventually debunked by Einstein's theory of special relativity, which was proposed in 1905 but took time to become established in physics.

13. Eileen Gregory usefully traces H.D.'s appeal to classical statuary and connects it to Pater's earlier aesthetic. However, while her larger thesis is that H.D. seeks spiritual integrity and an authentic and autonomous poetic expression as a woman, I argue that H.D.'s concern with visual art (like Pater's before her) focuses on the visual body as a model of impersonal subjectivity. Such a focus works against the notions of autonomy, authenticity, and integrity that Gregory's reading emphasizes and is more in line with Comentale's analysis of modernist classicism.

14. *Collected Poems* 12–14, lines 1–2, 3, 5, 7 (hereafter cited as *CP*).

15. The neurophysiologist Sir Charles Scott Sherrington coined the term *proprioception* in 1906.

16. For a thorough discussion of H.D.'s challenge to Ellis and to sexology more broadly, see Pappas.

17. As already noted, H.D. had a copy of Edward McCurdy's *Leonardo da Vinci's Note-Books* (1908) in her library at her death. The volume is inscribed "Hilda Aldington, 1918," so she owned it when she wrote *Notes*. The Beinecke catalog of her library states that the book was much read.

18. Codex Atlanticus 138a, reprinted in *The Literary Works of Leonardo da Vinci* 1:138.

19. Perhaps most famously, Freud, who would later become H.D.'s friend and analyst, compared adult female sexuality to a "dark continent" in *The Question of Lay-Analysis* (1926).

20. See Pound's poem "The Ballad of Mulberry Road" and the accompanying note in Weinberger.

21. It's perhaps useful to note Pound's poem "The Tree" (1908), in which the speaker, like Daphne, Baucis, Philemon, and others in classical mythology, is metamorphosed into a tree. For Pound, this unwilled metamorphosis marks embodiment and opacity over and against the possibility of a pure, transparent image, whether perceptual or artistic.

22. See Mackail's introduction to *Select Epigrams*.

23. Though the published edition of *Notes* reads "script of the golden Plate," the second and fourth drafts read "golden Plato," which makes more sense in context.

24. The Eleusinian mystics were an ancient Greek cult of Demeter, whose yearly rites were kept secret but involved visions and a conjuring of the afterlife. Plato discusses their rites in the *Meno,* and H.D. refers to them at multiple moments in *Notes.*

25. As examples of Sachs' work in *Close Up* see "Film Psychology" and "Kitsch."

26. For further details, see Guest; Friedberg, "Approaching *Borderline*"; and Marcus, introductions.

27. Cartwright, for example, broadly aligns early film motion studies with modern cubism, but she also points specifically to the fact that a number of these motion studies were exhibited in 1924 at the Vieux-Colombier theater in Paris, where they captivated avant-garde filmmakers like Germaine Dulac, Luis Buñuel, and Jean Painlevé.

28. As examples of the way *Close Up* attends to scientific films and the scientific origins of film see Bryher's "Mechanics of the Brain," a review of V. I. Pudovkin's film on Pavlov's conditioned reflex research; Hellmund-Waldow's "Educational School Films," which bemoans a decline in the support for scientific films; Herring's "Tachyscope, Daedalum, and Fantoscope," which discusses early film technologies; and Blakeston's "Medical Films," a write-up on Kodak's scientific film catalog.

29. "Graphic method" is the name given to Étienne-Jules Marey's chronophotography. See Cartwright 12–13, as well as Frank, for further discussion. Frank is particu-

larly interesting in this context because he discusses Marey's graphic method of film as a "new language" (11), underscoring a sense of imagetextuality.

30. See Rose as an influential example of this scholarly trend.

31. H.D., "Cinema and the Classics" 108, 108, 105 (hereafter cited as "CC"). This essay appeared serially in July, August, and November 1927.

32. In 1907 Ries made one of the first time-lapse films of the sea urchin's fertilization and development. Another example would be the French medical researcher Jean Comandon's early films of syphilis spirochete. A slightly later and more popular example from science would be Percy Smith's "Secrets of Nature" series, produced by British Instructional from 1922 to 1933. For more on these and other films, see Landecker; and Gaycken.

33. See Cartwright 33 on the careful construction of blank backgrounds in motion studies.

34. See Cartwright, chap. 4, on this point.

35. Critics who read H.D. as actively, if unconsciously, racist include Walton, Lawson, and Nies. Those who read her as explicitly antiracist include Friedman ("Modernism") and Debo.

36. See Ida B. Wells' famous diagnosis of the American South's use of this myth to justify lynching.

37. I take the phrase "atavistic image" from Eng, who similarly uses it to characterize Freud's association of the racialized savage with a frozen, transparent image. The other quotations are from *Totem and Taboo* 3.

38. The published essay reads "duped," but the manuscript and proof read "doped."

39. H.D.'s involvement with *Borderline*'s playlist and publicity is recorded in her letters to Paul and Eslanda Robeson, who appear in the film (Debo 378).

40. "Confessions—Questionnaire" 364-66. H.D. writes, "I should like to work the Debrie camera which I can't. I can do a little work on the small cameras and some of it will be incorporated in the big film that we are busy on" (364).

41. Despite Macpherson's compromise, U.S. Customs confiscated the *Borderline* reels when he sent them for scheduled screenings in October 1931 (Friedberg, introduction 220).

42. It's likely that H.D. also wrote *The Story,* because she definitely wrote the longer exegetical pamphlet available for purchase by those who rented *Borderline* or attended a screening.

43. For a sampling of these two scholarly readings, see, in addition to Debo, Walton; Friedman, "Modernism"; Carby; and McCabe.

44. "Introduction to 'The Fourth Dimension in the Kino,'" 182. Macpherson makes this remark about montage in general rather than about *Borderline*'s montages specifically.

45. On the collaborative nature of H.D.'s scrapbook, see Vetter, "Representing 'A Sort of Composite Person.'"

46. H.D., *Borderline: A POOL Film with Paul Robeson* 221 (hereafter cited as *BP*).

47. In H.D.'s "Writing on the Wall" notebook, which precedes the first typescript of this section of *Tribute to Freud,* she recounts how Freud inscribed a copy of his Leonardo essay to H.D. and wonders, "Was it 'by chance or intention' that he linked me in his creative, vivid discrimination" with the "greatest of living renaissance innovators, thinkers and artists?" This remark appears at the end of section 8 in the notebook, added onto the published end of that section in *Tribute.*

48. Freud, "Leonardo da Vinci" 122, 132, 75, 122 (hereafter cited as "LM").

49. I should point out that Freud's chain of associations begins from a translation error that substitutes "vulture" for "kite." In other words, Freud believed that Leonardo's memory was about a vulture hitting him with its tail, and "in the hieroglyphics of the ancient Egyptians the mother is represented by a picture of a vulture" ("LM" 88). On this translation error, see the editor's note preceding the essay ("LM" 61).

Chapter 3. Getting Impersonal

1. In addition to Gilmore, see Stauder; Kouidis; Conover; and Elizabeth Arnold. Such criticism ignores Loy biographer Carolyn Burke's warning that scholarly "expectations about what constitutes a 'woman's voice' may . . . put earmuffs on our capacity to hear more impersonal or non-personal voices" ("Supposed Persons" 132).

2. Burstein argues that what she calls "cold modernism" is a "world without selves" in which the mind is only "physical" (2). The result is a "surface" reality wherein "the mind has no secrets, and the world beyond presents itself as wholly knowable, and already known" (1).

3. On the popularization of relativity, see Bowler. On the intersections of modern physics and literary and artistic modernism, see Mook and Vargish; Henderson, *Duchamp in Context* and *Fourth Dimension;* Parkinson; and Clarke, *Energy Forms.* I return to the specific arguments of Henderson and Parkinson below.

4. Nicholls; Stauder; Kouidis; and Zelazo, among others, have detailed Loy's interest in the contingent nature of perceptual images. But none have aligned this interest with an investment in modernist impersonality; indeed, Stauder has argued that Loy's image-driven aesthetic is distinctly not impersonal (208).

5. Here I'm invoking Burke's biography *Becoming Modern* (hereafter cited as *BM*). For a concrete example of the threat that Loy registers, see below, chap. 5, n. 2, which discusses Eliot's editorial policies at the *Egoist.*

6. Lyon has valuably traced Loy's appeal to the contrary (but sometimes intersecting) rhetorics of futurism and feminism. She concludes that Loy "fashioned a lexicon and a style that was avant-garde *by virtue of* its amalgamation" of these two rhetorics and that this amalgamation "collaps[ed] the cultural dichotomies of art and morality, production and reproduction, revolution and reform, performance and biology" ("Mina Loy's Pregnant Pauses" 382).

7. Weininger claims that woman has no ego and that the artistic genius is he who has the most conscious, most continuous, most individual ego. Simmel likewise portrays the alienated nature of cultural institutions as inimical to an unmediated feminine identity.

8. Luhan sent "Aphorisms on Futurism" to Stieglitz in April 1914, and it was published in June. She sent Loy the Myers volumes sometime before 1919, but likely in 1914, not long after she left Florence, where she had met Loy. Loy only read the Myers in late 1919, but the title itself bespeaks Luhan's interest in personality (see Loy, letter to Luhan, February 1920).

9. For details on Luhan's salon, see her memoir *Movers and Shakers,* chaps. 1 and 2.

10. We might extend this affiliation back to Michael Field as well, because Bradley and Cooper were both friends with Ellis.

11. For a broader discussion of Loy's inventions and fashions in the context of a modern effort to rethink personality, see Burstein.

12. See *BM* 118n. Burke reports that Loy's "carriage improved so noticeably that she came to resemble the straight-backed Edwardian ladies with whom she socialized" (ibid.).

13. These and other facts about Mensendieck and her system derive from Veder, in this case "Expressive Efficiencies" 829–30.

14. By 1922 there were 142 documented Mensendieck teachers in Europe. It's unclear whether Loy attended classes or simply read one of Mensendieck's early books, either *Body Culture of Women* (1906) or the revised *Body Culture of Woman* (1912).

15. Loy, *Auto-Facial-Construction* 165 (hereafter cited as *AFC*).

16. On liberalism's presumption of a disembodied, autonomous (male) subject, particularly in the context of a rights discourse, see Wendy Brown; and Kittay.

17. This history of the "picture personality" in film derives from deCordova, though he doesn't focus specifically on the face.

18. Tim Armstrong has similarly pointed to *Auto-Facial-Construction*'s simultaneous investment in self-presentation, which presumes a stable self that exists to be expressed, and self-construction, which presumes a fluctuating self continually in the process of being made (120–23).

19. For more on Myers' parapsychology, see Alvarado; and Owen.

20. I date "The Child and the Parent" to the later 1920s for two reasons. First, the narrative mentions Kotex, created by Kimberly-Clark in 1921 and only popularized in the mid-twenties. Second, in a note on the back of a draft page Loy records that this was her "first try at writing of childhood," meaning that it precedes another such narrative, "Goy Israels," drafted in the 1930s.

21. All references to "The Child and the Parent" cite chapter rather than page numbers because the manuscript's pagination is inconsistent and the ordering of sections within chapters is at times unclear. The memoir has two parts, "The Child"

and "The Parent," the second beginning with chapter 7. According to Loy's outline—which is cut off due to the page's having been torn—there were (or were to have been) at least sixteen chapters. The extant draft begins with chapter 3 and runs through chapter 12 but is often fragmented.

22. On these scientific debates and the proliferation of non-Euclidean models in modern art, see Parkinson, chap. 2; and Henderson, *Fourth Dimension*. The phrase "idea-image" is Parkinson's. Henderson points, significantly, to Hermann von Helmholtz's foundational role in popularizing the curvature of space in his *Popular Lectures on Scientific Subjects* (1873), in which he also discusses a physiological optics (10–15).

23. The phrase "in his entirety" is not part of this sentence in the typescript draft. It is included, however, in a variant of this passage seemingly misplaced in a folder titled "Static" in the Mina Loy Papers. I incorporate the phrase here because it clarifies the distinction Loy is making between the person and the subject.

24. Vetter's reading departs from mine insofar as she sees Loy's career-long aesthetic (including her appeal to the "Cosmopolitan Jew") as dedicated to a spiritual monism that has overcome the body.

25. It's worth noting that Loy's comparison of Stein to Curie may have been suggested by Stein's own studies: she worked with the philosopher William James and the psychologist Hugo Münsterberg at the Harvard Psychological Laboratory and with the neuroanatomist and embryologist Franklin Mall at the Johns Hopkins Medical School. Indeed, Loy may have been drawn to Stein's poetics exactly for this background, namely, for her investigations at Harvard into secondary personalities and automatic writing.

26. On Curie's life and in particular the false portrayal of her as a Jew, see Quinn.

27. A number of scholars have pointed out that Stein's Jewishness is complicated, not least by her friendship with the Vichy official Bernard Faÿ (years after Loy's essay). But Maria Damon has proposed that Stein's Jewishness nonetheless manifests itself in her "language practice"—that her repetition, circularity, and unconventional syntactic and semantic constructions are part of a "Jewish intellectual tradition" that considered it a "religious obligation" to "push language" (492, 499). As we'll see, Loy's analysis strikingly prefigures this reading.

28. Loy prefigures Stein's own similar connection in "Lecture II: Narration" (1935), 106.

29. On Oelze's life and art, see Jaguer.

30. These comments are part of Lo's opening statement in part 4 of "Mi and Lo."

31. Jones declares to Insel: "I give you the key [to my apartment]—dinner—My man Godfrey—the loan on your picture . . . you are the living confirmation of my favorite theories" (159). At the beginning of the following chapter, the two go to a bar "after the Powell film" (160), clarifying that Jones did indeed have in mind Gregory La Cava's *My Man Godfrey,* with William Powell in the title role.

32. The first phrase, "one point of contact," is from the published novel (65), but

"eye-caves" and "boney structure around the eye" are from drafts 1 and 2. The published novel (from the draft 3 typescript) uses the less specific word *temple* in place of both phrases (65). Later in the published novel, Loy returns to this idea of impersonality being behind the eyes and of Insel's desire to access and express it when she describes Insel as "leaking out of himself . . . that ominous honey he stored behind his eyes" and "into which it was his constant, his distraught concern to withdraw" (102).

33. This speculation appears in "Insel," drafts 1 and 2: "the coincidence of our both having evoked this in our work may be the explanation for the telepathic pictures he conveyed to me."

34. A butterfly's appositional eyes actually send incomplete (and inverted) images from each of its many lenses—images that are then unified in the brain—rather than offering numerous replications of the full visual field, as in Loy's painting. The semi-accurate nature of Loy's scientific vernacular of vision here recalls Ford's semiaccuracy in depicting Tietjens' visual experience in *Parade's End*.

35. Loy actually uses the word *spectator* in draft 2 but not in the published novel. That said, the published version repeatedly emphasizes Jones' status as a passive audience for Insel's lived and creative surrealism.

36. Loy was the Paris agent for her son-in-law Julien Levy's New York gallery and in that capacity acquired or shipped works for multiple United States–based interests, including the Museum of Modern Art in New York. As I note below, she shipped Oelze's painting *Expectation* to MoMA, and *Frieda* is contemporary with it.

37. For more on this cover and the Atget photograph featured in it, see Hopkins 48.

38. On Loy's dealings with *Expectation* and her related letter to Fabienne, see *BM* 385.

39. Gaedtke's sense that *Insel* dramatizes a Freudian analytic scene through Jones and Insel's relationship and that this scene ultimately involves shared burdens and risks, rather than the asymmetrical power dynamic of doctor and patient, maps well onto my evaluation, though I don't take psychoanalysis to be as crucial a visual discourse for Loy as Gaedtke does.

40. Loy in fact directed her anxieties specifically against Lawrence's *Women in Love* (1920), along with T. S. Eliot's *The Waste Land,* in an unpublished and undated essay on unsatisfied women in literature that is part of her "Notes on Literature."

Chapter 4. D. H. Lawrence's Impersonal Imperative

1. The first quotation is from *"Psychoanalysis and the Unconscious" and "Fantasia of the Unconscious"* 95 (hereafter cited as *PF*). The second is reported in Lawrence's friend Aldous Huxley's introduction to the 1932 edition of Lawrence's letters (xv).

2. Lawrence took science courses at Nottingham University College and taught science during his years at Davidson Road School (1908–11). In addition, as Rose Marie

Burwell catalogs, he read widely among scientific texts, including Darwin's *Origin of Species* (1859), T. H. Huxley's *Man's Place in Nature* (1863), Ernst Haeckel's *Riddle of the Universe* (1901), William James' *Pragmatism* (1907), and Albert Einstein's *Relativity: The Special and General Theory* (1920), as well as books on psychoanalysis by Freud, Jung, Trigant Burrow, Rudolf Steiner, and A. A. Brill.

3. See Clarke "Different Sun" and *Energy Forms;* Granofsky; Craig Gordon; Hoshi; Seelow; Wallace; and Wutz.

4. On Lawrence's shaping focus on vision and visual culture, see Stewart; Alldritt; Kushigian; and Taylor. Against this trend, see Seelow (80-82) and Burack ("Mortifying the Reader"), who read him as hostile to the dominating influence of vision in modern culture.

5. "Chaos in Poetry," *Phoenix* 255-62 at 261; *PF* 65. *Phoenix* is hereafter cited as *P*.

6. Lawrence, "Why the Novel Matters," *Study of Thomas Hardy* 193-98 at 197 (hereafter cited as "WNM").

7. *Complete Poems* 615-19 at 617, 615 (hereafter cited as *CP*).

8. Lawrence wrote the preface around August 1919, and the precise degree of his knowledge of relativity at this time is unclear. However, he expressed familiarity with the theory less than two years later, in an April 1921 letter, and actively sought to deepen that familiarity (Burwell 258). He asked his friend S. S. Koteliansky to send him a book of Einstein's, which Koteliansky did and which he duly read (*Letters* 4:2249, 2257). On Lawrence's repeated but varying appeals to relativity, see Clarke, *Energy Forms* 208-21.

9. For Helmholtz's optical experiments using the anorthoscope, see *Physiological Optics* 2:187-89, 221-24. Plateau developed the anorthoscope from his own research into the effect of colors on the retina and the observational distortion of moving images (see Verriest). For a brief discussion of modernist form and the particular visuality of an anorthoscope, see Ellmann, *Nets of Modernism* 105-6.

10. See Krasner for a discussion of Lawrence's visuality in relation to early twentieth-century gestalt psychology, namely, their shared understanding of figure and ground in form perception. Though Krasner doesn't draw out the connection, modern gestalt psychologists, like Kurt Koffka and Wolfgang Köhler, actually returned to Helmholtz's earlier anorthoscopic experiments.

11. Lawrence, "Introduction to These Paintings" 198 (hereafter cited as "ITP").

12. See, for instance, Crary, *Suspensions of Perception* 6-7, on the link between the new physiology of vision in the nineteenth century and the rise of painterly impressionism and postimpressionism.

13. Lawrence, "Art and Morality," *Study of Thomas Hardy* 163-68 at 167 (hereafter cited as "AM").

14. *P* 699-718 at 704, 714, 710, 714.

15. Fry actually appropriated the phrase *significant form* from Clive Bell, who de-

scribed it first in his introduction to the English section of the second postimpressionist exhibition (1912), but Lawrence seems to know of the concept only from Fry.

16. I've already noted that Lawrence read Einstein as he was writing *Psychoanalysis and the Unconscious*. He also brushed up on his knowledge of physiology at this time. In a May 1918 letter, he asked his friend Edith Eder for "a book which describes the human nervous system, and gives a sort of map of the nerves of the human body" (*Letters* 3:1570). Such reading indicates the importance of both scientific fields, physics and physiology, to his understanding of impersonal subjectivity.

17. In addition to Freud, Lawrence read the American Jungian analyst Trigant Burrow, who sent copies of his papers to Lawrence following their first contact in 1919. The two men corresponded numerous times. Lawrence's familiarity with psychoanalysis also came from several more mediated fronts. He was close friends with the English analysts Barbara Low and David Eder, and his wife, Frieda, had had an affair with the German analyst Otto Gross in 1907-8 and was quite familiar with Gross' work. On these various points, see Steele's introduction to *PF*, as well as Craig Gordon.

18. Burrow, "Psychoanalysis in Theory and Life" (qtd. in *PF* xxxiii). Lawrence knew this essay by January 1920.

19. From 1909, Lawrence and H.D. were both part of Ford's circle of "les jeunes" and contributors to his *English Review*, but they don't seem to have met until a 1914 dinner hosted by the imagist Amy Lowell. The two had become friends by 1915. Indeed, in 1917 H.D. hosted the Lawrences in her London flat after wartime officials forced the couple from their coastal cottage in Cornwall owing to Frieda's German birth. By mid-1918, however, the friendship had largely ceased, in part because of H.D.'s complex feelings for Lawrence. Still, as an indication of a lasting and mutual influence, H.D.'s novel *Bid Me to Live* (1933-50) features a character named Rico who's modeled on Lawrence, and Lawrence's novel *Aaron's Rod* (1922) features a character named Julia Cunningham who's modeled on H.D. On Lawrence and H.D.'s friendship, see Guest; and Worthen. Guest briefly and with some alarm registers the similarities between H.D.'s *Notes* and Lawrence's philosophy (120).

20. Perhaps the best crystallization of how Lawrence's impersonality works both for and against individuality—and also of how it shores up this contradiction—is a moment in his early draft of "John Galsworthy" (1928), in which he declares: "Paradoxical as it may sound, the individual is only truly himself when he is unconscious of his own individuality, when he is unaware of his own isolation, when he is not split into subjective and objective, when there is no *me or you*, no *me or it* in his consciousness, but the *me and you*, the *me and it* is a living *continuum*, as if all were connected by a living membrane" (*Study of Thomas Hardy* 249-52 at 249). Here to be "individual" is to be "unaware" of "individuality," indeed to have no "you" or "me" and to be part of a "continuum" of "living membrane."

21. *P* 719-23 at 722, 721.

22. By suggesting that Lawrence is playing on an increasing disbelief in a lumi-niferous ether (a disbelief fueled by the theory of relativity), I'm not suggesting that he doesn't elsewhere still rely on the ether as a generative concept, whether gathered from the esoteric philosopher P. D. Ouspensky's *Tertium Organum* (1924) or Einstein's continued (though different) use of the term in papers like "Concerning the Aether" (1924). On Lawrence's uses, see Clarke, *Energy Forms* 186-92.

23. For more on Lawrence's tendency to extend adaptation from the species to the individual, see Granofsky.

24. My argument has a complement in Krasner's earlier analysis of Darwin's nar-rative eye—the way that Darwin uses the evolution of the eye as a figure for the dynamism and multiplicity of evolution, on one the hand, and the nonetheless lim-ited human vision that it produced, on the other. For Krasner, modernist writers like Lawrence followed Darwin in filtering their considerations of nature through an em-bodied visual perception rather than an omniscient point of view. Krasner briefly discusses *Lady Chatterley's Lover*, but his focus is on how the novel's portrayal of na-ture parallels a field theory of energy and perception espoused in modern gestalt psychology. The connection to Darwin is thus less direct than in my account of *Chat-terley* as an evolutionary narrative that adapts a Darwinian visuality to advocate for an optical impersonality.

25. These phrases are from MSII, held at the Harry Ransom Humanities Research Center, University of Texas, Austin. They appear in Squires' explanatory notes to "A Propos" in *Chatterley* (370).

26. I've focused on gender here because that's the identity most pressing in the novel. But we might register a similar tension in *Chatterley*'s few references to race. On the one hand, a newly adapted Connie wonders in response to Clifford's invest-ment in "an English spring": "Why not an Irish one, or Jewish?" (184). In other words, Connie's shift toward an embodied impersonality corresponds with her move away from racial essentialism via her belief that England's spring needn't be distinctly Anglo. Indeed, we might even go one step further and surmise that if Connie's im-personal adaptation marks a path for the species' futurity, then her thought suggests that racial hybridity is actually desirable for the species' fitness. When Connie first ponders the idea of having a child at Clifford's instigation, she does in fact think that if she is to find someone who is not a "male huma[n] . . . But *a man*," "he would have to be a foreigner: not an Englishman, still less an Irishman. A real foreigner" (64).

On the other hand, Mellors in one of his postcoital conversations with Connie, uses sex as a site for promoting a racial essence and purity. He valorizes "black women" for being the only females who are sexually in touch (204). But he also ex-plains that this bodily awareness is of no benefit to his own impersonal subjectivity, because "we're white men: and they're a bit like mud" (204). Though an association with earth is elsewhere positively impersonal in the novel, here it's a negative marker of race and a way of distinguishing one race from another. Thus, the dual directions that the novel proposes for racial identity within its model of impersonality remain unresolved.

Chapter 5. Managing the "Feeling into Which We Cannot Peer"

1. The first phrase is from "Imperfect Critics" (*Sacred Wood, and Major Early Essays* 10–26 at 14). The second phrase is from *After Strange Gods* 13. Eliot minimizes the value of Loy's poetry in "Observations."

2. In questioning a simple opposition of Eliot and Loy, I don't mean to elide the former's chauvinism. Eliot did in fact write to his father of his editorship at the *Egoist:* "I struggle to keep the writing as much as possible in Male hands, as I distrust the Feminine in literature" (*Letters* 1:203–5 at 204). Such an attitude gives credence to Loy's early anxiety that if an impersonal art emphasized the instability of the human subject (rather than a stable individuality), then it could run counter to women's efforts to refuse the passivity often ascribed to them.

3. If Eliot's critique of Pater, Lawrence, and Loy has helped to obscure their shared practice of an optical impersonality, his actions have likewise fueled readings of his impersonality as subterfuge. His will forbade any official sanction of the publication of his letters or a biography, and earlier, when he discovered that his friend Emily Hale had given her letters from him to Princeton University, he burnt her letters to him, deleting the other side of the exchange (see Murphy).

4. Spender writes: "But an escape from personality, which is an escape from emotion, *is* an expression of personality" (159). In addition, contrary to a notion of aesthetic impersonality, the chapter in which Spender offers this reading of Eliot is called "Three Individualists," of which Eliot is one.

5. In "T. S. Eliot, Famous Clairvoyant," Dean argues that Eliot challenges individual sovereignty through a process of bodily alienation, and Cameron posits that Eliot offers a web of fleeting but recurring percepts unattributable to any subjectivity. The other cited scholars tend to focus on linguistic strategies or performances rather than materiality. Even Altieri, who suggests that Eliot's speaker is always under observation and so denied the eloquence of invisibility, is only metaphorically concerned with vision and embodiment.

6. In his unpublished dissertation, Warren Reed likewise posits a connection between Eliot's early aesthetic and modern scientific notions of visual embodiment, but he argues that this connection was quickly severed with Eliot's Anglo-Catholic conversion in 1927.

7. Piper argues that Eliot's portraits are visual signs of a "sober-suited extinction of personality" (191), while Bukhari posits that like Eliot's art, they announce the lack of any coherent self.

8. Eliot, *Use of Poetry and the Use of Criticism* 141 (hereafter cited as *UPUC*).

9. On Sullivan's role in popularizing modern science in Britain, see Bowler.

10. See Whitworth 153 on the first point. Whitworth also traces how Eliot adapts Sullivan's *Athenaeum* articles.

11. See Peter White for a timetable of the composition of "Tradition" and "Modern Tendencies," the latter of which was published in an Indian journal called *Shama'a* and has never been reprinted.

12. My survey focuses on six of Sullivan's essays published in 1919: "The Place of Science" (11 April), "The Justification of the Scientific Method" (2 May), "On Learning Science" (4 July), "A Stylist in Science" (11 July), "Science and Personality" (18 July), and "Scientific Education" (12 September).

13. For more on Rayleigh's optics, see Lindsay.

14. "Tradition," in Eliot, *Selected Prose* 37–44 at 38 (collection hereafter cited as *SP*).

15. Reinforcing that Sullivan's historic method was a likely source for Eliot's historical sense, Eliot first began to formulate his concept in a letter of 11 July 1919 to his friend Mary Hutchinson (*Letters* 1:316–18). Sullivan's essay "On Learning Science," in which he first uses the phrase "historic method," had appeared the previous week, on 4 July, suggesting that it was fresh in Eliot's mind.

16. "*Hamlet,*" in Eliot, *SP* 45–49 at 48.

17. This explanation is part of Eliot's continued elaboration of his impersonal aesthetic after 1919, here in "The Metaphysical Poets" (1921) (*SP* 59–67 at 66).

18. This premise appears in "The Perfect Critic" (1920) (*SP* 50–58 at 55).

19. These ideas are from Eliot's later elaboration of tradition in "The Function of Criticism" (1923) (*SP* 68–76 at 68).

20. Another claim from Eliot's dissertation is meaningful here, not least for its appeal to both optics and feelings. Eliot argues that "so far as feelings are objects . . . they exist on the same footing as other objects: they are equally public, they are equally independent of consciousness. . . . [M]y experience is in principle essentially public. My emotions may be better understood by others than by myself; as my oculist knows my eyes" (qtd. in Freed 2).

21. Eliot saw himself in much the same terms as he saw Leonardo, namely, as a "metic," a stranger "admitted to the city (originally of Athens) because of his utility" and "granted rights and franchises although rarely admitted fully into the communal mysteries" (Rabaté 212). Early on, this description might stem simply from Eliot's recent relocation to Britain. But he continued to draw on it much later. For instance, in a February 1938 letter to the theater director Martin Browne, Eliot writes, "[Y]ou are much more at home, naturally, in foxhunting society than I am" (qtd. in Browne 102). Given that Browne wasn't of the gentry, Eliot's foil seems more about an ongoing desire to lay claim to the metic's decentered view, a desire that parallels Loy's valorization of the exile impersonalist.

22. On the gendering of hysteria, see Maines. On Viv's diagnoses, see Seymour-Jones.

23. *The Waste Land,* line 430. This and subsequent quotations from the published poem are from *The Annotated Waste Land* (hereafter cited as *TWL*).

24. For a recent summary of scholarly readings of Eliot's approaches to gender and also a summary of some of those approaches, see Pondrom.

25. From the facsimile edition of *The Waste Land* 31, lines 126, 126, 114, 111; 33, line 143; 31, line 106; 33, lines 157-58 (hereafter cited as *TWLF*).

26. This translation is Rainey's (*TWL* 75n), with the exception of "jar" for *ampulla,* which he translates as "cage."

27. See *Metamorphoses* 14.101-53.

28. The speaker's promise to ". . . show you something different from either / Your shadow at morning striding behind you / Or your shadow at evening rising to meet you" (*TWL,* lines 27-29) invokes and counters Job 8:9, which posits that our life is a mere shadow compared with the transcendence of death in heaven. The speaker offers a "handful of dust" rather than a heavenly afterlife.

29. *Metamorphoses* 10.163-220.

30. The episode begins, "The Chair she sat in, like a burnished throne" (*TWL,* line 77), alluding to Shakespeare's *Antony and Cleopatra* (1603-7): "The barge she [Cleopatra] sat in, like a burnished throne" (qtd. in *TWL* 88n). Eliot subsequently describes the "laquearia" (*TWL,* line 92) of the Woman's room, and his note refers readers to Virgil's *Aeneid* 1.726-27,which describes Dido's banquet hall: "Blazing torches hang down from the gilded ceiling, / And vanquish the night with their flames" (qtd. in *TWL* 89n). On the Orientalism of Eliot's many references to Cleopatra during his career, see McCombe.

31. On the *Āditta Sutta*'s model of being and Eliot's appeal to it, see Kearns; and Hauck.

32. For Eliot's comments on Jessie Weston and James Frazer, see his introduction to the notes to *The Waste Land* (*TWL* 71).

33. This allusion exactly repeats the closing line of Verlaine's poem.

34. I use the name Fishing King here and throughout to refer to the character that Eliot creates, as opposed to the Fisher King legend, which Eliot draws on to construct his king.

35. Much like Philomel, Olivia Primrose, the seduced girl of Goldsmith's novel, retells her tale in a song. The line that Eliot cites ("When lovely woman stoops to folly") is from that song, which ends with a call to suicide. Olivia is soon reported dead, though that report is false.

36. Eliot's note suggests that the song of the three Thames daughters, modeled on the three Rhine daughters in Wagner's *Ring of the Nibelung* (1853), begins with line 266 and that each daughter speaks in turn (*TWL* 73n). The implication, then, is that

the woman who's raped in a canoe on the Thames is one of these daughters and that the "Wallala leialala" song is part of her story.

37. In Ovid, Hera and Zeus ask Tiresias to settle their argument regarding who enjoys sex more, men or women, with Tiresias' authority stemming from the fact that he has been both. Tiresias sides with Zeus, stating that women enjoy sex more, and Hera angrily strikes him blind. Zeus lightens the burden of blindness by granting Tiresias second sight (*Metamorphoses* 3.316–38).

38. See Pausanias 11.33.1.

39. Eliot points to these structuring allusions in his notes (*TWL* 73n).

40. On these two trends, see, for instance, Badenhausen; and Reed. Badenhausen also discusses Eliot's theatrical collaborations.

41. Various elements of the play have fed this reading. For example, Wishwood, the family estate depicted in the play, echoes the name Wychwood, the "ancient haunted forest" that Eliot walked through on the evening before his religious confirmation; and this forest in turn recalls the pagan sacred wood that provided the name of Eliot's first essay collection, featuring "Tradition and the Individual Talent" (William Force Stead, qtd. in Lowe 79). It can thus be tempting to conclude that the rejection of Wishwood by the play's hero, Harry, Lord Monchensey, announces Eliot's own rejection of his *Sacred Wood* and its impersonal theory of art in favor of a metaphysical spiritual redemption.

42. *Complete Poems and Plays* 60–67, line 140 (hereafter cited as *CPP*).

43. *The Family Reunion*, in *CPP* 224–93 at 273.

44. *SP* 132–47 at 145.

45. *On Poetry and Poets* 3–16 at 12.

46. "Yeats" (1940), *On Poetry and Poets* 295–308 at 299.

47. The *Oresteia* tells of Orestes' murder of his mother, Clytemnestra, as revenge for her murder of her husband, Agamemnon, in part because of Agamemnon's sacrifice of their daughter Iphigenia. The principal theme is the cultural shift from personal vendetta to a social system of litigation.

48. The scholarly presumption that Harry didn't murder his wife begins with the early readings of Grover Smith (200–202) and Martin Browne (108, 128). And these readings are in turn informed by Eliot's own description of Lady Monchensey's death scene in a March 1938 letter to Browne. Eliot suggests that as Harry's wife stands on the ship deck, "trying to play one of her comedies with him," she "overdoes it, and just at that moment, plump, in she goes. Harry thinks he has pushed her; and certainly, he has not called for help, or behaved in any normal way" (qtd. in Browne 108). Even if Eliot's clarification, which of course doesn't appear in the play, suggests that Harry didn't push his wife, it still gives him a share of responsibility in her drowning, because he didn't try to help her.

Afterword. Modernist Futurity

1. On Deleuze's various appeals to Lawrence, see Masschelein.

2. Sedgwick, *Touching Feeling* 24 (hereafter cited as *TF*).

3. Sedgwick, *Weather in Proust* 69, 69, 83 (hereafter cited as *WP*).

4. Massumi first links affect with the prepersonal in his translator's note to Deleuze and Guattari's *Thousand Plateaus,* where he defines affect as a "prepersonal intensity corresponding to the passage from one experiential state of the body to another and implying an augmentation or diminution in that body's capacity to act" (xvi). The prepersonal parallels Simondon's "preindividual."

5. See "pre-, *prefix,*" *OED Online.*

Bibliography

Ackroyd, Peter. *T. S. Eliot: A Life*. New York: Simon & Schuster, 1985.

Adams, James Eli. *Dandies and Desert Saints: Styles of Victorian Masculinity*. Ithaca, NY: Cornell University Press, 1995.

Albright, Daniel. *Personality and Impersonality: Lawrence, Woolf, and Mann*. Chicago: University of Chicago Press, 1978.

Allan, Tuzyline Jita. "A Voice of One's Own: Implications of Impersonality in the Essays of Virginia Woolf and Alice Walker." In *The Politics of the Essay: Feminist Perspectives*, edited by Ruth-Ellen Boetcher Joeres and Elizabeth Mittman, 131-47. Bloomington: Indiana University Press, 1993.

Alldritt, Keith. *The Visual Imagination of D. H. Lawrence*. London: Arnold, 1971.

Altieri, Charles. *The Art of Twentieth-Century American Poetry: Modernism and After*. Oxford: Blackwell, 2007.

Alvarado, Carlos S. "On the Centenary of Frederic W. H. Myers' *Human Personality and Its Survival of Bodily Death*." *Journal of Parapsychology* 68 (2004): 3-43.

Anderson, Amanda. *The Powers of Distance: Cosmopolitanism and the Cultivation of Detachment*. Princeton, NJ: Princeton University Press, 2001.

Angell, Henry C. *How to Take Care of Our Eyes*. Boston: Roberts Brothers; New York: Boericke & Tafel, 1878.

Armstrong, Isobel. *Victorian Glassworlds: Glass Culture and the Imagination, 1830-1880*. Oxford: Oxford University Press, 2008.

Armstrong, Nancy. "Modernism's Iconophobia and What it Did to Gender." *Modernism/modernity* 5, no. 2 (1998): 47-75.

Armstrong, Tim. *Modernism, Technology and the Body: A Cultural Study*. Cambridge: Cambridge University Press, 1998.

Arnold, Elizabeth. Afterword to Loy, *Insel*, 179-81.

Arnold, Matthew. "On Translating Homer." In vol. 1 of *The Complete Prose Works of Matthew Arnold*, edited by Robert H. Super, 97-216. Ann Arbor: University of Michigan Press, 1960.

Atherton, Margaret. "How to Write the History of Vision: Understanding the Relationship between Berkeley and Descartes." In *Sites of Vision: The Discursive Construction of Sight in the History of Philosophy,* edited by David Michael Levin, 139-66. Cambridge, MA: MIT Press, 1999.

Attridge, John. "'I Don't Read Novels . . . I Know What's in 'em': Impersonality, Impressionism, and Responsibility in *Parade's End.*" In Reynier and Ganteau, *Impersonality and Emotion,* 97-107.

Auerbach, Jonathan. *Body Shots: Early Cinema's Incarnations.* Berkeley: University of California Press, 2007.

Babbitt, Irving. *The New Laokoön: An Essay on the Confusion of the Arts.* Boston: Houghton Mifflin, 1910.

Bacon, Francis. *Novum Organum.* In vol. 1 of *The Works of Francis Bacon,* edited by James Spedding, Robert Leslie Ellis, and Douglas Denton Heath. London: Longman, 1861.

Badenhausen, Richard. *T. S. Eliot and the Art of Collaboration.* Cambridge: Cambridge University Press, 2005.

Barney, Natalie Clifford. *Adventures of the Mind.* Translated by John Spalding Gatton. New York: NYU Press, 1992.

Barthes, Roland. "The Death of the Author." In *Image—Music—Text,* translated by Stephen Heath, 142-48. New York: Hill & Wang, 1977.

Bederman, Gail. *Manliness & Civilization: A Cultural History of Gender and Race in the United States, 1880-1917.* Chicago: University of Chicago Press, 1995.

Beegan, Gerry. *The Mass Image: A Social History of Photomechanical Reproduction in Victorian London.* New York: Palgrave Macmillan, 2008.

Beer, Gillian. "Helmholtz, Tyndall, Gerard Manley Hopkins: Leaps of the Prepared Imagination." In *Open Fields: Science in Cultural Encounter,* 242-72. Oxford: Oxford University Press, 1996.

Bell, Clive. *Art.* New York: Capricorn, 1958. First published 1914.

Bell, Ian F. A. *Critic as Scientist: The Modernist Poetics of Ezra Pound.* London: Methuen, 1981.

Bell, Michael. "D. H. Lawrence and the Meaning of Modernism." In *Rethinking Modernism,* edited by Marianne Thormälen, 132-48. New York: Palgrave Macmillan, 2003.

Benjamin, Walter. "Little History of Photography." In *Walter Benjamin: Selected Writings,* vol. 2, *1927-1934,* edited by Michael W. Jennings, Howard Eiland, and Gary Smith, translated by Rodney Livingston et al., 507-30. Cambridge, MA: Belknap Press of Harvard University Press, 1999.

———. "The Work of Art in the Age of Mechanical Reproduction." In *Illuminations: Essays and Reflections,* edited by Hannah Arendt, translated by Harry Zohn, 217-51. New York: Schocken Books, 2007.

Berman, Louis. *The Glands Regulating Personality: A Study of the Glands of Internal Secretion in Relation to the Types of Human Nature.* Rev. ed. New York: Macmillan, 1928.

Black, Michael. *D. H. Lawrence: The Early Fiction*. Basingstoke, UK: Macmillan, 1986.

Blackwood's Magazine. Unsigned review of *Studies in the History of the Renaissance*, by Walter Pater. November 1873, 30:604-9.

Blakeston, Oswell. "Medical Films." *Close Up* 10, no. 2 (June 1933): 198-99.

Borderline. Directed by Kenneth Macpherson. Performed by Paul Robeson, Adah Robeson, Robert Herring, Bryher, and Helga Dorne (H.D.). POOL, 1930.

Bort, Françoise. "Emotion and the Immemorial." In Reynier and Ganteau, 63-74.

Bowler, Peter J. *Science for All: The Popularization of Science in Early Twentieth-Century Britain*. Chicago: University of Chicago Press, 2009.

Bowler, Peter J., and Iwan Rhys Morus. *Making Modern Science: A Historical Survey*. Chicago: University of Chicago Press, 2005.

Brain, Robert M. "Representation on the Line: Graphic Recording Instruments and Scientific Modernism." In *From Energy to Information: Representation in Science and Technology, Art, and Literature*, edited by Bruce Clarke and Linda Dalrymple Henderson, 155-77. Stanford, CA: Stanford University Press, 2002.

Brake, Laurel, Lesley Higgins, and Carolyn Williams, eds. *Walter Pater: Transparencies of Desire*. Greensboro, NC: ELT, 2002.

Brennan, Teresa. *The Transmission of Affect*. Ithaca, NY: Cornell University Press, 2004.

Brooker, Jewel Spears. "Writing the Self: Dialectic and Impersonality in T. S. Eliot." In Cianci and Harding, *T. S. Eliot and the Idea of Tradition*, 41-57.

Brown, Judith. "*Borderline*, Sensation, and the Machinery of Expression." *Modernism/modernity* 14, no. 4 (2007): 687-705.

Brown, Wendy. *States of Injury: Power and Freedom in Late Modernity*. Princeton, NJ: Princeton University Press, 1995.

Browne, Martin. *The Making of T. S. Eliot's Plays*. Cambridge: Cambridge University Press, 1969.

Browning, John. *How to Use Our Eyes; and How to Preserve Them By the Aid of Spectacles*. London: Chatto & Windus, 1883.

Bryher [Annie Winifred Ellerman]. "Mechanics of the Brain." *Close Up* 3, no. 4 (October 1928): 27-30.

Buch-Jepsen, Niels. "What Happened to the Author? Modernist Impersonality and Authorial Selfhood." In *From Homer to Hypertext: Studies in Narrative, Literature, and Media*, edited by Hans Balling and Anders Klinkby Madsen, 77-94. Odense: University of Southern Denmark, 2002.

Buck, Claire. *H.D. & Freud: Bisexuality and a Feminine Discourse*. New York: St. Martin's, 1991.

Bukhari, Nuzhat. "The Distinguished Shaman: T. S. Eliot's Portraits in Modern Art." *Modernism/modernity* 11, no. 3 (2004): 373-424.

Bullen, Barrie. "Walter Pater's *Renaissance* and Leonardo da Vinci's Reputation in the Nineteenth Century." *Modern Language Review* 74, no. 2 (April 1979): 268-80.

Burack, Charles M. "Mortifying the Reader: The Assault on Verbal and Visual Consciousness in D. H. Lawrence's *Lady Chatterley's Lover.*" *Studies in the Novel* 29, no. 4 (1997): 491–511.

———. "Revitalizing the Reader: Literary Technique and the Language of Sacred Experience in D. H. Lawrence's *Lady Chatterley's Lover.*" *Style* 32, no. 1 (1998): 102–26.

Burke, Carolyn. *Becoming Modern: The Life of Mina Loy.* New York: Farrar, Straus & Giroux, 1996.

———. "Mina Loy's 'Love Songs' and the Limits of Imagism." *San Jose Studies* 13, no. 3 (Fall 1987): 37–46.

———. "Supposed Persons: Modernist Poetry and the Female Subject." *Feminist Studies* 11, no. 1 (Spring 1985): 131–48.

Burrow, Trigant. *The Social Basis of Consciousness: A Study in Organic Psychology Based Upon a Synthetic and Societal Concept of the Neuroses.* London: K. Paul, Trench, Trubner, 1927.

Burstein, Jessica. *Cold Modernism: Literature, Fashion, Art.* University Park: Pennsylvania State University Press, 2012.

Burwell, Rose Marie. "A Catalogue of D. H. Lawrence's Reading from Early Childhood." *D. H. Lawrence Review* 3, no. 3 (1970): 193–299.

Cahan, David, ed. *Hermann von Helmholtz and the Foundations of Nineteenth-Century Science.* Berkeley: University of California Press, 1994.

Camboni, Maria. "Between Painting and Writing: Figures of Identity in H.D.'s Early Poetry." In *H.D.'s Poetry: "The Meanings That Words Hide,"* edited by Maria Camboni, 35–62. New York: AMS, 2003.

Cameron, Sharon. *Impersonality: Seven Essays.* Chicago: University of Chicago Press, 2006.

Campbell, Stephen J. *The Cabinet of Eros: Renaissance Mythological Painting and the Studiolo of Isabella D'Este.* New Haven, CT: Yale University Press, 2004.

Carby, Hazel. *Race Men.* Cambridge, MA: Harvard University Press, 1998.

Cartwright, Lisa. *Screening the Body: Tracing Medicine's Visual Culture.* Minneapolis: University of Minnesota Press, 1995.

Chadwick, Whitney. *Women Artists and the Surrealist Movement.* New York: Thames & Hudson, 1995.

Chinitz, David E., ed. *A Companion to T. S. Eliot.* West Sussex, UK: Wiley-Blackwell, 2009.

———. *T. S. Eliot and the Cultural Divide.* Chicago: University of Chicago Press, 2003.

Chisholm, Dianne. *H.D.'s Freudian Poetics: Psychoanalysis in Translation.* Ithaca, NY: Cornell University Press, 1992.

Cianci, Giovanni, and Jason Harding, eds. *T. S. Eliot and the Concept of Tradition.* Cambridge: Cambridge University Press, 2007.

Clarke, Bruce. "A Different Sun: The Allegory of Thermodynamics in D. H. Lawrence."

In *Myth and the Making of Modernity*, edited by Michael Bell and Peter Poellner, 81–98. Amsterdam: Rodopi, 1998.

———. *Energy Forms: Allegory and Science in the Era of Classical Thermodynamics.* Ann Arbor: University of Michigan Press, 2001.

———. "Mabel Dodge Luhan and the Lawrencean Aether." *Paunch* 69–70 (1999): 123–35.

Coates, John. "Pater as Polemicist in 'Prosper Mérimée.'" *Modern Language Review* 99, no. 1 (January 2004): 1–16.

Collini, Stefan. "The Idea of 'Character' in Victorian Political Thought." *Transactions of the Royal Historical Society* 35 (1985): 29–50.

Colvin, Sidney. Review of *Studies in the History of the Renaissance*, by Walter Pater. *Pall Mall Gazette*, 1 March 1873, 11–12.

Comentale, Edward P. "Thesmophoria: Suffragettes, Sympathetic Magic, and H.D.'s Ritual Poetics." *Modernism/modernity* 8, no. 3 (2001): 471–92.

"Confessions—Questionnaire." In *The Little Review Anthology*, edited by Margaret Anderson, 349–83. New York: Hermitage, 1953.

Conley, Katharine. *Automatic Woman: The Representation of Woman in Surrealism.* Lincoln: University of Nebraska Press, 1996.

Conlon, John J. *Walter Pater and the French Tradition.* Lewisburg, PA: Bucknell University Press, 1982.

Connolly, William E. "The Complexity of Intention." *Critical Inquiry* 37, no. 4 (Summer 2011): 791–98.

Connor, Rachel. "Textu(r)al Braille: Visionary (Re)Readings of H.D." In *Body Matters: Feminism, Textuality, Corporeality*, edited by Avril Horner and Angela Keane, 199–208. Manchester, UK: Manchester University Press, 2000.

Conover, Roger. Foreword to Loy, *Insel*, 9–15.

Coste, Bénédicte. "'The Perfection of Nobody's Style': Impersonality and Emotion in Pater's 'Prosper Mérimée.'" In Reynier and Ganteau, *Impersonality and Emotion*, 29–42.

Courthope, W. J. Review of *Studies in the History of the Renaissance*, by Walter Pater. *Quarterly Review* 141 (January 1876): 69.

Crary, Jonathan. *Suspensions of Perception: Attention, Spectacle, and Modern Culture.* Cambridge, MA: MIT Press, 1999.

———. *Techniques of the Observer: On Vision and Modernity in the Nineteenth Century.* Cambridge, MA: MIT Press, 1990.

Crowe, J. A., and G. B. Cavalcaselle. *History of Painting in North Italy.* 2 vols. London: J. Murray, 1871.

Cunningham, Bonnie Wilde. "Bearing the Pain: Anaesthetics of Impersonality in Modernist Fiction." PhD diss., Brandeis University, 1994.

Daniel, Samuel. *The Complete Works in Verse and Prose of Samuel Daniel.* Edited by

Alexander B. Grosart. Vol. 3, *The Dramatic Works*. New York: Russell & Russell, 1963.

Davis, Michael F. "Walter Pater's 'Latent Intelligence' and the Conception of Queer 'Theory.'" In Brake, Higgins, and Williams, *Walter Pater*, 61-85.

Damon, Maria. "Gertrude Stein's Jewishness, Jewish Social Scientists, and the 'Jewish Question.'" *Modern Fiction Studies* 42, no. 3 (1996): 489-506.

Darwin, Charles. *The Origin of Species: A Facsimile of the First Edition*. Annotated by James T. Costa. Cambridge, MA: Belknap Press of Harvard University Press, 2009.

Daston, Lorraine, and Peter Galison. *Objectivity*. New York: Zone Books, 2007.

Dean, Tim. "The Other's Voice: Cultural Imperialism and the Poetic Impersonality in Gary Snyder's *Mountains and Rivers without End*." *Contemporary Literature* 41, no. 3 (Spring 2000): 462-94.

———. "Paring His Fingernails: Homosexuality and Joyce's Impersonalist Aesthetic." In *Quare Joyce,* edited by Joseph Valente, 241-72. Ann Arbor: University of Michigan Press, 1998.

———. "T. S. Eliot, Famous Clairvoyante." In Laity and Gish, *Gender, Sexuality, and Desire in T. S. Eliot,* 43-65.

Debo, Annette. "Interracial Modernism in Avant-Garde Film: Paul Robeson and H.D. in the 1930 *Borderline*." *Quarterly Review of Film and Video* 18, no. 4 (2001): 371-83.

deCordova, Richard. *Picture Personalities: The Emergence of the Star System in America*. Urbana: University of Illinois Press, 2001.

Deleuze, Gilles, and Félix Guattari. *Anti-Oedipus: Capitalism and Schizophrenia*. Translated by Robert Hurley, Mark Seem, and Helen R. Lane. London: Continuum, 2004.

———. *A Thousand Plateaus: Capitalism and Schizophrenia*. Translated by Brian Massumi. Minneapolis: University of Minnesota Press, 1987.

Dellamora, Richard. "Critical Impressionism as Anti-Phallogocentric Strategy." In *Pater in the 1990s,* edited by Laurel Brake and Ian Small, 127-42. Greensboro, NC: ELT, 1990.

———. *Masculine Desire: The Sexual Politics of Victorian Aestheticism*. Chapel Hill: University of North Carolina Press, 1990.

Dember, William N. *Visual Perception: The Nineteenth Century*. New York: John Wiley & Sons, 1964.

Dickens, Charles. *Our Mutual Friend*. London: Penguin Classics, 1997.

Dollimore, Jonathan. *Sexual Dissidence: Augustine to Wilde, Freud to Foucault*. Oxford: Oxford University Press, 1991.

Donald, James, Anne Friedberg, and Laura Marcus, eds. *Close Up, 1927-1933: Cinema and Modernism*. Princeton, NJ: Princeton University Press, 1998.

Donoghue, Denis. *Walter Pater: Lover of Strange Souls*. New York: Knopf, 1995.

Donoghue, Emma. *We Are Michael Field*. Bath: Absolute, 1998.

Dowling, Linda. *Hellenism and Homosexuality in Victorian Oxford.* Ithaca, NY: Cornell University Press, 1994.

——. "Walter Pater and the Matter of the Self." In *Die Modernisierung des Ich,* edited by Manfred Pfister, 64-73. Passau, Germany: Wissenschaftsverlag Rothe, 1989.

"Do You Strive to Capture the Symbols of Your Reactions?" *New York Evening Sun,* 13 February 1917.

Edmunds, Susan. *Out of Line: History, Psychoanalysis, & Montage in H.D.'s Long Poems.* Palo Alto, CA: Stanford University Press, 1994.

Ehnenn, Jill. "Looking Strategically: Feminist and Queer Aesthetics in Michael Field's *Sight and Song.*" *Victorian Poetry* 43, no. 1 (Spring 2005): 109-54.

Ehrenfels, Christian von. "On *Gestalt*-Qualities." Translated by Mildred Focht. *Psychological Review* 44, no. 6 (November 1937): 521-24.

Eliot, T. S. *After Strange Gods: A Primer in Modern Heresy.* New York: Harcourt, Brace, 1934.

——. *The Annotated Waste Land with Eliot's Contemporary Prose.* Edited by Lawrence Rainey. 2nd ed. New Haven, CT: Yale University Press, 2005.

——. *The Complete Poems and Plays, 1909-1950.* London: Harcourt, Brace, 1967.

——. "Humanist, Artist, and Scientist." *Athenaeum,* 10 October 1919, 1014-15.

——. *The Letters of T. S. Eliot.* Edited by Valerie Eliot. Vol. 1. New York: Harcourt, Brace Jovanovich, 1988.

——. "Modern Tendencies in Poetry." *Shama'a* 1, no. 1 (April 1920): 9-18.

——. "Observations." *Egoist* 5, no. 5 (May 1918): 69-70.

——. *On Poetry and Poets.* New York: Farrar, Straus & Giroux, 1957.

——. *The Sacred Wood, and Major Early Essays.* Mineola, NY: Dover, 1998.

——. *Selected Prose of T. S. Eliot.* Edited by Frank Kermode. San Diego: Harcourt, 1975.

——. *The Use of Poetry and the Use of Criticism.* 1961. Reprint, Cambridge, MA: Harvard University Press, 1961.

——. *The Waste Land: A Facsimile and Transcript of the Original Drafts Including the Annotations of Ezra Pound.* Edited by Valerie Eliot. San Diego: Harcourt, 1971.

Ellmann, Maud. *The Nets of Modernism: Henry James, Virginia Woolf, James Joyce, and Sigmund Freud.* Cambridge: Cambridge University Press, 2010.

——. *The Poetics of Impersonality: T. S. Eliot and Ezra Pound.* Cambridge, MA: Harvard University Press, 1987.

Eng, David. *Racial Castration: Managing Masculinity in Asian America.* Durham, NC: Duke University Press, 2001.

Eribon, Didier. *Insult and the Making of the Gay Self.* Translated by Michael Lucey. Durham, NC: Duke University Press, 2004.

Feldman, Jessica R. *Gender on the Divide: The Dandy in Modernist Literature.* Ithaca, NY: Cornell University Press, 1993.

Fernihough, Anne. *D. H. Lawrence: Aesthetics and Ideology.* Cambridge: Cambridge University Press, 1993.

Fichte, Johann Gottlied. *The Vocation of Man* (1800). In *Popular Works of Johann Gottlieb Fichte,* translated by William Smith, vol. 1. London: Trübner, 1899.

Field, Michael [Katherine Bradley and Edith Cooper]. *The Fowl and the Pussycat: Love Letters of Michael Field, 1876-1909.* Edited by Sharon Bickle. Charlottesville: University of Virginia Press, 2008.

———. *Sight and Song.* London: Elkin Mathews & John Lane, 1892.

———. "Walter Pater (July 30, 1894)." *Academy* 46 (11 August 1894): 102. Reprinted in *Walter Pater: The Critical Heritage,* edited by R. M. Seiler, 280. London: Routledge & Kegan Paul, 1980.

———. "Works and Days." 30 vols. British Library, London. Add. MSS 46776-46804B.

———. *Works and Days: From the Journal of Michael Field.* Edited by T. Sturge Moore and D. C. Sturge Moore. London: John Murray, 1933.

Fletcher, Robert P. "Reframing an 'unmitigated guide-book': Yeats, Berenson, and the Sexual Politics of the Picture-Poem in Michael Field's *Sight and Song.*" Unpublished manuscript, 2003.

Flint, Kate. *Victorians and the Visual Imagination.* Cambridge: Cambridge University Press, 2000.

Ford, Ford Madox. *Parade's End.* London: Penguin Classics, 1982.

———. "On Impressionism." In *The Good Soldier: A Tale of Passion,* edited by Kenneth Womack and William Baker, 260-80. Toronto: Broadview, 2003.

Foster, Hal. Preface to *Vision and Visuality,* edited by Hal Foster, ix-xiv. New York: Dia Art Foundation, 1988.

Foucault, Michel. *The Order of Things: An Archaeology of the Human Sciences.* New York: Vintage, 1994.

Frank, Robert G. "American Physiologists in German Laboratories, 1865-1914." In *Physiology in the American Context,* edited by Gerald L. Geison, 11-46. Bethesda, MD: American Physiological Society, 1987.

Fraser, Hilary. "A Visual Field: Michael Field and the Gaze." *Victorian Literature and Culture* 34 (2006): 552-71.

Frazer, James G. *The Golden Bough: A Study in Magic and Religion.* Abr. ed. New York: Macmillan, 1950.

Frazer, Ray. "The Origin of the Term 'Image.'" *ELH* 27, no. 2 (June 1960): 149-61.

Freed, Lewis. "T. S. Eliot's Impersonal Theory of Poetry and the Doctrine of Feeling and Emotion as Objects." *Yeats Eliot Review* 17, no. 1 (Winter 2001): 2-18.

Freud, Sigmund. *Beyond the Pleasure Principle.* Translated by C. J. M. Hubback. 1922. Reprint, Eastford, CT: Martino Fine Books, 2010.

———. *The Interpretation of Dreams.* Translated and edited by James Strachey. 1953. Reprint, New York: Avon, 1965.

———. "Leonardo da Vinci and a Memory of His Childhood." In Freud, *Standard Edition,* 11:59-137.

———. "A Note on the Unconscious." In Freud, *Standard Edition,* 12:255-66.

———. *The Question of Lay-Analysis.* In Freud, *Standard Edition,* 20:183-250.

———. *The Standard Edition of the Complete Psychological Works of Sigmund Freud.* Translated and edited by James Strachey. 24 vols. London: Hogarth, 1956-74.

———. *Totem and Taboo: Some Points of Agreement Between the Mental Lives of Savages and Neurotics.* Translated and edited by James Strachey. New York: Norton, 1950.

Friedberg, Anne. "Approaching *Borderline.*" In King, *H.D.,* 369-90.

———. Introduction to pt. 5. In Donald, Friedberg, and Marcus, *Close Up, 1927-1933,* 212-20.

Friedman, Susan Stanford. "Modernism of the 'Scattered Remnant': Race and Politics in the Development of H.D.'s Modernist Vision." In King, *H.D.,* 91-116.

———. *Penelope's Web: Gender, Modernity, H.D.'s Fiction.* Cambridge: Cambridge University Press, 1990.

———. *Psyche Reborn: The Emergence of H.D.* Bloomington: Indiana University Press, 1981.

Gaedtke, Andrew. "From Transmissions of Madness to Machines of Writing: Mina Loy's *Insel* as Clinical Fantasy." *Journal of Modern Literature* 32, no. 1 (2008): 143-62.

Gage, John T. *The Arresting Eye: The Rhetoric of Imagism.* Baton Rouge: Louisiana State University Press, 1981.

Gaycken, Oliver. *Devices of Curiosity: Early Cinema and Popular Science.* Oxford: Oxford University Press, forthcoming.

Gilmore, Susan. "Imna, Ova, Mongrel, Spy: Anagram and Imposture in the Work of Mina Loy." In Shreiber and Tuma, *Mina Loy,* 271-317.

———. "Not Quite a Lady: Mina Loy, Edna St. Vincent Millay, H.D., Gwendolyn Brooks and the Poetics of Impersonation." PhD diss., Cornell University, 1995.

Gish, Nancy K. "Discarnate Desire: T. S. Eliot and the Poetics of Dissociation." In Laity and Gish, *Gender, Desire, and Sexuality in T. S. Eliot,* 107-29.

Gitelman, Lisa. *Scripts, Grooves, and Writing Machines: Representing Technology in the Edison Era.* Stanford, CA: Stanford University Press, 1999.

Goethe, Johann Wolfgang von. *Theory of Colours.* Translated by Charles Lock Eastlake. Cambridge, MA: MIT Press, 1970.

Gordon, Craig. *Literary Modernism, Bioscience, and Community in Early Twentieth Century Britain.* New York: Palgrave, 2007.

Gordon, Lyndall. *Eliot's Early Years.* New York: Farrar, 1977.

———. *T. S. Eliot: An Imperfect Life.* London: Vintage, 1998.

Goulet, Andrea. *Optiques: The Science of the Eye and the Birth of Modern French Fiction.* Philadelphia: University of Pennsylvania Press, 2006.

Granofsky, Ronald. *D. H. Lawrence and Survival: Darwinism in the Fiction of the Transitional Period.* Montreal: McGill-Queen's University Press, 2003.

Grant, Madison. *The Passing of the Great Race, or, The Racial Basis of European History.* New York: Charles Scribner's Sons, 1918.

Greenberg, Clement. "Towards a Newer Laocoön." *Partisan Review* 7, no. 4 (July–August 1940): 296–310.

Gregory, Eileen. *H.D. and Hellenism: Classic Lines.* Cambridge: Cambridge University Press, 1997.

Gregory, Richard L. *Eye and Brain: The Psychology of Seeing.* 4th ed. Princeton, NJ: Princeton University Press, 1990.

Grosz, Elizabeth. *The Nick of Time: Politics, Evolution, and the Untimely.* Durham, NC: Duke University Press, 2004.

Guest, Barbara. *Herself Defined: The Poet H.D. and Her World.* New York: Doubleday, 1984.

Hacking, Ian. *Mad Travellers: Reflections on the Reality of Transient Mental Illness.* Charlottesville: University of Virginia Press, 1998.

———. *Rewriting the Soul: Multiple Personality and the Sciences of Memory.* Princeton, NJ: Princeton University Press, 1995.

Hagstrum, Jean H. *The Sister Arts: The Tradition of Literary Pictorialism and English Poetry from Dryden to Gray.* Chicago: University of Chicago Press, 1958.

Haraway, Donna. "Situated Knowledges: The Science Question in Feminism and the Privilege of Partial Perspective." *Feminist Studies* 14, no. 3 (Autumn 1988): 575–99.

Harlan, George C. *Eyesight, and How to Care for It.* Philadelphia: Lindsay & Blakiston, 1879.

Harries, Karsten. "Descartes, Perspective, and the Angelic Eye." *Yale French Studies* 49 (1973): 28–42.

Hartmann, Karl Robert Eduard von. *The Philosophy of the Unconscious; Speculative Results According to the Inductive Method of Physical Science.* Translated by William Chatterton Coupland. 1884. Reprint, Westport, CT: Greenwood, 1972.

Hauck, Christina. "Not One, Not Two: Eliot and Buddhism." In Chinitz, *Companion to T. S. Eliot,* 40–52.

H.D. [Hilda Doolittle]. "Autobiographical Notes." H.D. Papers.

———. *Borderline: A POOL Film with Paul Robeson.* In Donald, Friedberg, and Marcus, *Close Up, 1927–1933,* 221–36.

———. "Cinema and the Classics." In Donald, Friedberg, and Marcus, *Close Up, 1927–1933,* 105–20.

———. *Collected Poems, 1912–1944.* Edited by Louis L. Martz. New York: New Directions, 1983.

———. *HERmione.* New York: New Directions, 1981.

———. *Notes on Thought and Vision.* New York: City Lights Books, 1982.

———. "Notes on Thought and Vision." Draft 2. H.D. Papers.

———. "Notes on Thought and Vision." Draft 4. H.D. Papers.

———. "Notes on Thought and Vision." Page proofs. H.D. Papers.

———. *Paint It Today.* Edited by Cassandra Laity. New York: NYU Press, 1992.

———. *Tribute to Freud.* New York: New Directions, 1974.

———. *The Usual Star.* Dijon, France: Imprimerie Darantiere, 1934.

———. "*Wing Beat.*" H.D. Papers.

———. "Writing on the Wall" notebook. H.D. Papers.

———. "The Wise Sappho." In H.D., *Notes on Thought and Vision.*

[H.D.?]. *The Story.* H.D. Papers.

———. *Wing Beat* announcement. *Close Up* 1, no. 1 (July 1927): 15.

H.D. Papers. Yale Collection of American Literature, Beinecke Rare Book and Manuscript Library, Yale University.

"H.D.'s Library Index." H.D. Papers.

Heidegger, Martin. "The Age of the World Picture." In *The Question Concerning Technology and Other Essays,* translated by William Lovitt, 115-54. New York: Harper Perennial, 1982.

Hellmund-Waldow, E. "Educational School Films." *Close Up* 2, no. 3 (March 1928): 60-69.

Helmholtz, Hermann von. *Helmholtz's Treatise on Physiological Optics.* 3rd ed. Edited and translated by James P. C. Southall. 2 vols. New York: Dover, 1962.

———. "On the Integrals of the Hydrodynamical Equations Which Express Vortex-Motion." Translated by Peter Guthrie Tait. *Philosophical Magazine* 33 (1867): 485-512.

———. *Popular Lectures on Scientific Subjects.* Translated by E. Atkinson. London: Longmans, Green, 1873.

Henderson, Linda Dalrymple. *Duchamp in Context: Science and Technology in the Large Glass and Related Works.* Princeton, NJ: Princeton University Press, 1998.

———. *The Fourth Dimension and Non-Euclidean Geometry in Modern Art.* Princeton, NJ: Princeton University Press, 1983.

———. "Modernism and Science." In vol. 1 of *Modernism,* edited by Astradur Eysteinsson and Vivian Liska, 383-403. Amsterdam: John Benjamins, 2007.

Herman, David. "1880-1945: Re-minding Modernism." In *The Emergence of Mind: Representations of Consciousness in Narrative,* edited by David Herman, 243-70. Lincoln: University of Nebraska Press, 2011.

Herring, Robert. "Tachyscope, Daedalum, and Fantoscope." *Close Up* 10, no. 1 (March 1933): 79-80.

Hirsh, Elizabeth A. "Imaginary Images: 'H.D.,' Modernism, and the Psychoanalysis of Seeing." In *Signets: Reading H.D.,* edited by Susan Stanford Friedman and Rachel Blau DuPlessis, 430-51. Madison: University of Wisconsin Press, 1990.

Hita, Michèle. "Emotion vs. Impersonality: Action/Reaction in D. H. Lawrence's *Women in Love.*" In Reynier and Ganteau, *Impersonality and Emotion,* 53-62.

Hopkins, David. *Dada and Surrealism: A Very Short Introduction.* Oxford: Oxford University Press, 2004.

Horton, Susan R. "Were They Having Fun Yet? Victorian Optical Gadgetry, Modernist Selves." In *Victorian Literature and the Victorian Visual Imagination,* edited by

Carol T. Christ and John O. Jordan, 1-26. Los Angeles: University of California Press, 1995.

Hoshi, Kumiko. "Modernism's Fourth Dimension in *Aaron's Rod:* Einstein, Picasso, and Lawrence." In *Windows to the Sun: D. H. Lawrence's "Thought-Adventures,"* edited by Earl Ingersoll and Virginia Hyde, 99-117. Cranbury, NJ: Rosemont, 2009.

Hulme, T. E. *Selected Writings.* Edited by Patrick McGuinness. New York: Routledge, 2003.

Hume, David. *A Treatise of Human Nature.* 2nd ed. Edited by L. A. Selby-Bigge, revised and edited by P. H. Nidditch. Oxford: Oxford University Press, 1978.

Humm, Maggie. *Modernist Women and Visual Cultures: Virginia Woolf, Vanessa Bell, Photography and Cinema.* New Brunswick, NJ: Rutgers University Press, 2003.

Huxley, Aldous. Introduction to *The Collected Letters of D. H. Lawrence.* New York: Viking, 1932.

Huxley, Thomas Henry. *Lessons in Elementary Physiology.* 1866. New ed. London: Macmillan, 1881.

Huyssen, Andreas. "The Disturbance of Vision in Vienna Modernism." *Modernism/modernity* 5, no. 3 (1998): 33-47.

Inman, Billie Andrew. "The Intellectual Context of Walter Pater's 'Conclusion.'" *Prose Studies* 4, no. 1 (1981): 12-30.

———. *Walter Pater and His Reading, 1874-1877; with a Bibliography of His Library Borrowings, 1878-1894.* New York: Garland, 1990.

———. *Walter Pater's Reading: A Bibliography of His Library Borrowings and Literary References, 1858-1873.* New York: Garland, 1981.

Jacobs, Karen. *The Eye's Mind: Literary Modernism and Visual Culture.* Ithaca, NY: Cornell University Press, 2001.

Jaguer, Edouard. *Richard Oelze.* New York: Lafayette Parke Gallery, 1991.

James, Henry. Letter to Edmund Gosse. 13 December 1894. *Letters of Henry James.* Edited by Leon Edel. 4 vols. Cambridge, MA: Harvard University Press, 1974-82.

James, William. *The Principles of Psychology.* Edited by Frederick H. Burkhardt, Fredson Bowers, and Ignas K. Skrupskelis. 3 vols. Cambridge, MA: Harvard University Press, 1981.

James, William, and Carl Lange. *The Emotions.* Edited by Knight Dunlap. Baltimore: Williams & Wilkins, 1922.

Jameson, Fredric. *Fables of Aggression: Wyndham Lewis, the Modernist as Fascist.* Berkeley: University of California Press, 1979.

———. *The Political Unconscious: Narrative as a Socially Symbolic Act.* Ithaca, NY: Cornell University Press, 1982.

———. *A Singular Modernity: Essay on the Ontology of the Present.* New York: Verso, 2002.

Jay, Martin. *Downcast Eyes: On the Denigration of Vision in Twentieth-Century French Thought.* Berkeley: University of California Press, 1993.

J.S. "*Borderline:* An Experiment in Silent Films." *Manchester Guardian,* 14 October 1930, 8.

Judovitz, Dalia. "Vision, Representation, and Technology in Descartes." In *Modernity and the Hegemony of Vision,* edited by David Michael Levin, 63–86. Berkeley: University of California Press, 1993.

Kafka, Franz. *The Trial.* Translated by Willa Muir and Edwin Muir. New York: Knopf, 1950.

Kahler, Erich. *The Inward Turn of Narrative.* Princeton, NJ: Princeton University Press, 1973.

Katz, Tamar. *Impressionist Subjects: Gender, Interiority, and Modernist Fiction in England.* Urbana: University of Illinois Press, 2002.

Kearns, Cleo McNelly. *T. S. Eliot and the Indic Traditions: A Study in Poetry and Belief.* Cambridge: Cambridge University Press, 1987.

Keats, John. "Ode on a Grecian Urn." In *John Keats: Complete Poems,* edited by Jack Stillinger, 282–83. Cambridge, MA: Harvard University Press, 1991.

———. "Ode to Psyche." In *John Keats: Complete Poems,* edited by Jack Stillinger, 275–76. Cambridge, MA: Harvard University Press, 1991.

Khalip, Jacques. "Pater's Sadness." *Raritan* 20, no. 2 (Fall 2002): 136–58.

King, Michael, ed. *H.D.: Woman and Poet.* Orono, ME: National Poetry Foundation, 1986.

Kittay, Eva Feder. *Love's Labor: Essays on Women, Equality, and Dependency.* New York: Routledge, 1999.

Koffka, Kurt. *Principles of Gestalt Psychology.* London: Kegan Paul, 1935.

Kofman, Sarah. *Camera Obscura: Of Ideology.* Translated by Will Straw. Ithaca, NY: Cornell University Press, 1999.

Köhler, Wolfgang. *Gestalt Psychology.* New York: Liveright, 1947.

Kouidis, Virginia M. *Mina Loy: American Modernist Poet.* Baton Rouge: Louisiana State University Press, 1980.

———. "Prison into Prism: Emerson's 'Many-Colored Lenses' and the Woman Writer of Early Modernism." In *The Green American Tradition: Essays and Poems for Sherman Paul,* edited by H. Daniel Peck, 115–34. Baton Rouge: Louisiana State University Press, 1990.

Krasner, James. *The Entangled Eye: Visual Perception and the Representation of Nature in Post-Darwinian Narrative.* Oxford: Oxford University Press, 1992.

Krauss, Rosalind E. *The Optical Unconscious.* Cambridge, MA: MIT Press, 1993.

Kushigian, Nancy. *Pictures and Fictions: Visual Modernism and the Pre-War Novels of D. H. Lawrence.* New York: Lang, 1990.

Laird, Holly. *Women Coauthors.* Urbana: University of Illinois Press, 2000.

Laity, Cassandra. *H.D. and the Victorian Fin-De-Siècle.* Cambridge: Cambridge University Press, 1996.

——. "T. S. Eliot and A. C. Swinburne: Decadent Bodies, Modern Visualities, and Changing Modes of Perception." *Modernism/modernity* 11, no. 3 (2004): 425-48.

Laity, Cassandra, and Nancy Gish, eds. *Gender, Sexuality, and Desire in T. S. Eliot.* Cambridge: Cambridge University Press, 2004.

Landecker, Hannah. "Microcinematography and the History of Science and Film." *Isis* 97, no. 1 (2006): 121-32.

Langbaum, Robert. *The Poetry of Experience: The Dramatic Monologue in Modern Literary Tradition.* New York: Random House, 1957.

Langer, Susanne. *Philosophy in a New Key.* Cambridge, MA: Harvard University Press, 1957.

Larmore, Charles. "Descartes' Empirical Epistemology." In *Descartes: Philosophy, Mathematics, and Physics,* edited by Stephen Gaukrager. Sussex, UK: Harvester, 1980.

Laurent, Henri. *Personality: How to Build It.* Translated by Richard Duffy. New York and London: Funk & Wagnalls, 1916.

Lawrence, D. H. *The Complete Poems of D. H. Lawrence.* Herefordshire, UK: Wordsworth Editions, 1994.

——. "Introduction to These Paintings." In *D. H. Lawrence: Late Essays and Articles,* edited by James T. Boulton, 182-217. Cambridge: Cambridge University Press, 2004.

——. *Lady Chatterley's Lover.* Edited by Michael Squires. Cambridge: Cambridge University Press, 1993.

——. *The Letters of D. H. Lawrence.* Vol. 2. Edited by George J. Zytaruk. Cambridge: Cambridge University Press, 1981.

——. *The Letters of D. H. Lawrence.* Vol. 3. Edited by James T. Boulton and Andrew Robertson. Cambridge: Cambridge University Press, 1979.

——. *The Letters of D. H. Lawrence.* Vol. 4. Edited by Warren Roberts, James T. Boulton, and Elizabeth Mansfield. Cambridge: Cambridge University Press, 1987.

——. *The Letters of D. H. Lawrence.* Vol. 6. Edited by James T. Boulton, Margaret H. Boulton, and Gerald M. Lacy. Cambridge: Cambridge University Press, 1991.

——. *Phoenix: The Posthumous Papers of D. H. Lawrence.* Edited by Edward D. McDonald. New York: Penguin, 1978.

——. *"Psychoanalysis and the Unconscious" and "Fantasia of the Unconscious."* Edited by Bruce Steele. Cambridge: Cambridge University Press, 2004.

——. *Study of Thomas Hardy, and Other Essays.* Edited by Bruce Steele. Cambridge: Cambridge University Press, 1985.

——. "Virgin Youth" (1916). In *The Complete Poems of D. H. Lawrence,* edited by Vivian de Sola Pinto and Warren Roberts, 2:909. London: Heinemann, 1972.

Lawson, Andrew. "Helen in Philadelphia: H.D.'s Eugenic Paganism." In *Evolution and Eugenics in American Literature and Culture, 1880-1940,* edited by Lois A. Cuddy and Claire M. Roche, 220-39. Lewisburg, PA: Bucknell University Press, 2003.

Leavell, Linda. "Nietzsche's Theory of Tragedy in the Plays of T. S. Eliot." *Twentieth-Century Literature* 31, no. 1 (Spring 1985): 111-26.

Leavis, F. R. *Anna Karenina, and Other Essays*. New York: Pantheon Books, 1968.

———. "Lawrence after Thirty Years." In *D. H. Lawrence,* edited by H. Coombes, 398–407. London: Penguin, 1973.

———. "Lawrence Scholarship and Lawrence." In Leavis, *Anna Karenina, and Other Essays*.

Lee, Brian. *Theory and Impersonality: The Significance of T. S. Eliot's Criticism*. London: Athlone, 1972.

Leighton, Angela. *Victorian Women Poets: Writing Against the Heart*. Charlottesville: University of Virginia Press, 1992.

Leonardo da Vinci. *The Literary Works of Leonardo da Vinci*. Edited by Jean Paul Richter. 2nd ed. 2 vols. London: Oxford University Press, 1939.

Lessing, Gotthold Ephraim. *Laokoön: An Essay on the Limits of Poetry and Painting*. Translated by Edward Allan McCormick. Baltimore: Johns Hopkins University Press, 1984.

Levenson, Michael. *A Genealogy of Modernism: A Study of English Literary Doctrine, 1908-1922*. Cambridge: Cambridge University Press, 1984.

Leys, Ruth. "Affect and Intention: A Reply to William E. Connolly." *Critical Inquiry* 37, no. 4 (Summer 2011): 799–805.

———. "The Turn to Affect: A Critique." *Critical Inquiry* 37, no. 3 (Spring 2011): 434–72.

Lightman, Bernard. *Victorian Popularizers of Science: Designing Nature for New Audiences*. Chicago: University of Chicago Press, 2007.

———. "The Visual Theology of Victorian Popularizers of Science: From Reverent Eye to Chemical Retina." *Isis* 91, no. 4 (2000): 651–80.

Lindberg, David C. *Theories of Vision from al-Kindi to Kepler*. Chicago: University of Chicago Press, 1976.

Lindsay, Robert Bruce. *Lord Rayleigh: The Man and His Work*. New York: Pergamon, 1970.

Locard, Henri. "Works and Days: The Journals of 'Michael Field.'" *Journal of the Eighteen Nineties Society* 10 (1979): 1–9.

Locke, John. *An Essay concerning Human Understanding*. Edited by Peter H. Nidditch. Oxford: Clarendon, 1975.

Loizeaux, Elizabeth Bergmann. *Twentieth-Century Poetry and the Visual Arts*. Cambridge: Cambridge University Press, 2008.

Lokhorst, Gert-Jan. "Descartes and the Pineal Gland." In *The Stanford Encyclopedia of Philosophy,* edited by Edward N. Zalta. Accessed 10 January 2013. http://plato.stanford.edu/archives/sum2011/entries/pineal-gland/.

London, Bette. *Writing Double: Women's Literary Partnerships*. Ithaca, NY: Cornell University Press, 1999.

London Quarterly Review. Unsigned review of *Studies in the History of the Renaissance,* by Walter Pater. July 1873, 28:505–7.

Love, Heather K. *Feeling Backward: Loss and the Politics of Queer History.* Cambridge, MA: Harvard University Press, 2007.

Low, Lisa. "Refusing to Hit Back: Virginia Woolf and the Impersonality Question." In *Virginia Woolf and the Essay,* edited by Beth Carole Rosenberg and Jeanne Dubino, 257–73. New York: St. Martin's, 1997.

Lowe, Peter. " 'Doing a Girl In': Re-Reading the Asceticism of T. S. Eliot's *The Family Reunion." Religion and Literature* 38, no. 4 (Winter 2006): 63–85.

Loy, Mina. "Aphorisms on Futurism." *Camera Work* 45 (January [June] 1914): 13–15.

———. "Aphorisms on Futurism." Printed leaf from *Camera Work,* with pencil emendations by Loy. Mina Loy Papers.

———. "Arthur Cravan is Alive!" In Loy, *Last Lunar Baedeker,* 317–22.

———. *Auto-Facial-Construction.* In Loy, *Lost Lunar Baedeker,* 165–66.

———. "The Ceiling." Mina Loy Papers.

———. "The Child and the Parent." Mina Loy Papers.

———. "The Child and the Parent." Outline. Mina Loy Papers.

———. "Feminist Manifesto." In Loy, *Lost Lunar Baedeker,* 153–56.

———. "Film-Face." In Loy, *Lost Lunar Baedeker,* 125.

———. "Gertrude Stein." *Transatlantic Review* 2, no. 3 (1924): 305–9 and no. 4 (1924): 427–30.

———. "A Hard Luck Story." Mina Loy Papers.

———. *Insel.* Edited by Elizabeth Arnold. Santa Rosa, CA: Black Sparrow, 1991.

———. "Insel." Draft 1. Mina Loy Papers.

———. "Insel." Draft 2. Mina Loy Papers.

———. Letter to Mabel Dodge Luhan. N.d. [1914]. Mabel Dodge Luhan Papers.

———. Letter to Mabel Dodge Luhan. N.d. [1915]. Mabel Dodge Luhan Papers.

———. Letter to Mabel Dodge Luhan. February 1920. Mabel Dodge Luhan Papers.

———. Letter to Mabel Dodge Luhan. 3 July [1920]. Mabel Dodge Luhan Papers.

———. Letter to Carl Van Vechten. N.d. [1915]. Carl Van Vechten Papers, Yale Collection of American Literature, Beinecke Rare Book and Manuscript Library, Yale University.

———. *The Last Lunar Baedeker.* Edited by Roger L. Conover. Highlands, NC: Jargon Society, 1982.

———. *The Lost Lunar Baedeker.* Edited by Roger L. Conover. New York: Farrar, Straus & Giroux, 1996.

———. *Lunar Baedeker & Time-Tables.* Edited by Jonathan Williams. Highlands, NC: Jargon Society, 1958.

———. "Mi and Lo." Mina Loy Papers.

———. "Notes on Literature." Mina Loy Papers.

Loy, Mina, Papers. Yale Collection of American Literature. Beinecke Rare Book and Manuscript Library, Yale University.

Luhan, Mabel Dodge. *Movers and Shakers*. Albuquerque: University of New Mexico Press, 1985.

Luhan, Mabel Dodge, Papers. Yale Collection of American Literature, Beinecke Rare Book and Manuscript Library, Yale University.

Lukács, György. "The Ideology of Modernism." In *The Meaning of Contemporary Realism*, translated by John Mander and Necke Mander, 17-46. London: Merlin, 1963.

Lyon, Janet. *Manifestos: Provocations of the Modern*. Ithaca, NY: Cornell University Press, 1999.

———. "Mina Loy's Pregnant Pauses: The Space of Possibility in the Florence Writings." In Shreiber and Tuma, *Mina Loy*, 379-401.

Lysack, Krista. "Aesthetic Consumption and the Cultural Production of Michael Field's *Sight and Song*." *Studies in English Literature* 45, no. 4 (Autumn 2005): 935-60.

Mackail, J. W., ed. and trans. *Select Epigrams from the Greek Anthology*. London: Longmans, Green, and Co., 1890.

Macpherson, Kenneth. "As Is (Nov. 1930)." In Donald, Friedberg, and Marcus, *Close Up, 1927-1933*, 236-38.

———. "An Introduction to 'The Fourth Dimension in the Kino.'" *Close Up* 6, no. 3 (March 1930): 175-84.

———. "A Negro Film Union—Why Not?" In *Negro: An Anthology*, edited and abridged with an introduction by Hugh Ford, 205-7. New York: Ungar, 1970. First collected and edited by Nancy Cunard in 1934.

Maines, Rachel. *The Technology of Orgasm: "Hysteria," the Vibrator, and Women's Sexual Satisfaction*. Baltimore: Johns Hopkins University Press, 1999.

Mandel, Charlotte. "Magical Lenses: Poet's Vision Beyond the Naked Eye." In King, *H.D.*, 301-17.

Marcus, Laura. Introductions to pts. 3 and 6. In Donald, Friedberg, and Marcus, *Close Up, 1927-1933*, 96-104 and 240-46.

Marey, Étienne-Jules. *Le mouvement*. Paris: Masson, 1894.

Masschelein, Anneleen. "Rip the Veil of the Old Vision Across, and Walk Through the Rent: Reading D. H. Lawrence with Deleuze and Guattari." In *Modernism and Theory: A Critical Debate*, edited by Stephen Ross, 23-39. New York: Routledge, 2009.

Massumi, Brian. *Parables for the Virtual: Movement, Affect, Sensation*. Durham, NC: Duke University Press, 2002.

Matz, Jesse. *Literary Impressionism and Modernist Aesthetics*. Cambridge: Cambridge University Press, 2001.

Mauss, Marcel. "A Category of the Human Mind: The Notion of Person; the Notion of Self." Translated by W. D. Halls. In *The Category of the Person: Anthropology, Philosophy, History*, edited by Michael Carrithers, Steven Collins, and Steven Lukes, 1-25. Cambridge: Cambridge University Press, 1985.

McCabe, Susan. *Cinematic Modernism: Modernist Poetry and Film.* Cambridge: Cambridge University Press, 2005.

McCombe, John. "Cleopatra and Her Problems: T. S. Eliot and the Fetishization of Shakespeare's Queen of the Nile." *Journal of Modern Literature* 31, no. 2 (2008): 23–38.

Meisel, Perry. *The Absent Father: Virginia Woolf and Walter Pater.* New Haven, CT: Yale University Press, 1980.

Mensendieck, Bess M. *"It's Up to You."* New York: Mensendieck System Main School, 1931.

———. *Körperkultur der Frau: Praktisch Hygienische und Praktisch Asthetische Winke.* Munich: F. Bruckmann, 1906.

———. *Look Better, Feel Better.* New York: Harper, 1954.

———. *The Mensendieck System of Functional Exercises.* Portland, ME: Southworth-Anthoensen, 1937.

Merleau-Ponty, Maurice. "Eye and Mind." Translated by Caleton Dallery. In *The Primacy of Perception: And Other Essays on Phenomenological Psychology, the Philosophy of Art, History, and Politics,* edited by James M. Edie, 159–90. Evanston, IL: Northwestern University Press, 1964.

———. *The Visible and the Invisible.* Edited by Claude Lefort. Translated by Alphonso Lingis. Evanston, IL: Northwestern University Press, 1968.

Mikics, David. *A New Handbook of Literary Terms.* New Haven, CT: Yale University Press, 2007.

Miller, Cristanne. *Cultures of Modernism: Gender and Literary Community in New York and Berlin.* Ann Arbor: University of Michigan Press, 2005.

Miller, David M. *The Wisdom of the Eye.* San Diego: Academic, 2000.

Miller, Tyrus. *Late Modernism: Politics, Fiction, and the Arts Between the World Wars.* Berkeley: University of California Press, 1999.

Millett, Kate. *Sexual Politics.* London: Sphere Books, 1971.

Mitchell, W. J. T. *Iconology: Image, Text, Ideology.* Chicago: University of Chicago Press, 1986.

———. *Picture Theory: Essays on Verbal and Visual Representation.* Chicago: University of Chicago Press, 1994.

Monroe, Harriet. "The Editor in France." *Poetry* 23 (1923): 95–96.

Mook, Delo E., and Thomas Vargish. *Inside Modernism: Relativity Theory, Cubism, Narrative.* New Haven, CT: Yale University Press, 1999.

Morelli, Giovanni. *Italian Painters: Critical Studies of Their Works.* Translated by Constance Jocelyn Foulkes. 2 vols. London: John Murray, 1892–93.

Morris, Adalaide. *How to Live / What to Do: H.D.'s Cultural Poetics.* Urbana: University of Illinois Press, 2003.

Moser, Patrick. "Literary Identity in Montaigne's 'Apologie de Raimond Sebond.'" *French Review* 77, no. 4 (March 2004): 716–27.

Mottram, V. H. *The Physical Basis of Personality*. Harmondsworth, UK: Penguin, 1944.

Murphy, Russell Elliott. "T. S. Eliot and Impersonality: The Evidence in the Letters." *CIEFL Bulletin* 3, nos. 1-2 (July-December 1991): 1-13.

Murry, J. M. Review of *Arts and Letters: An Illustrated Quarterly*, edited by Frank Rutter and Osbert Sitwell. *Athenaeum*, 11 July 1919, 605.

Mutz, Diana C. *Impersonal Influence: How Perceptions of Mass Collectives Affect Political Attitudes*. Cambridge: Cambridge University Press, 1998.

Myers, Frederic W. H. *Human Personality and its Survival of Bodily Death*. 2 vols. London: Longmans, Green, 1903.

My Man Godfrey. Directed by Gregory La Cava. Performed by William Powell, Carole Lombard, Alice Brady, Gail Patrick, Eugene Pallette, Jean Dixon, Alan Mowbray, Pat Flaherty, Robert Light, Mischa Auer, and Grady Sutton. Universal Pictures, 1936.

Natale, Simone. "The Invisible Made Visible: X-rays as Attraction and Visual Medium at the End of the Nineteenth Century." *Media History* 17, no. 4 (2011): 345-58.

Nead, Lynda. *The Haunted Gallery: Painting, Photography, Film c. 1900*. New Haven, CT: Yale University Press, 2007.

News and Gossip. *Creative Art*, 2 February 1933, 87.

Nicholls, Peter. "'Arid Clarity': Ezra Pound, Mina Loy, and Jules Laforgue." *Yearbook of English Studies* 32 (2002): 52-64.

Nicholson, Ian A. M. "Gordon Allport, Character, and the 'Culture of Personality,' 1897-1937." *History of Psychology* 1, no. 1 (1998): 52-68.

Nies, Betsy L. *Eugenic Fantasies: Racial Ideology in the Literature and Popular Culture of the 1920s*. New York: Routledge, 2002.

Nietzsche, Friedrich. *Human, All Too Human*. Translated by R. J. Hollingdale. Cambridge: Cambridge University Press, 1986.

North, Michael. *Camera Works: Photography and the Twentieth-Century Word*. Oxford: Oxford University Press, 2005.

Oliphant, Margaret Wilson. Review of *Studies in the History of the Renaissance*, by Walter Pater. *Blackwood's Magazine* 30 (November 1873): 604-9.

Otter, Chris. *The Victorian Eye: A Political History of Light and Vision in Britain, 1800-1910*. Chicago: University of Chicago Press, 2008.

Ouspensky, P. D. *Tertium Organum: A Key to the Enigmas of the World*. Translated by Nicholas Bessaraboff and Claude Bragdon. New York: Knopf, 1945.

Ovid. *Metamorphoses*. Translated by Rolfe Humphries. 1955. Reprint, Bloomington: Indiana University Press, 1983.

Owen, Alex. *The Place of Enchantment: British Occultism and the Culture of the Modern*. Chicago: University of Chicago Press, 2004.

Oxford Book of Modern Verse, 1892-1935. Edited by W. B. Yeats. Oxford: Oxford University Press, 1936.

Pandora, Katherine. "Knowledge Held in Common: Tales of Luther Burbank and Science in the American Vernacular." *Isis* 92, no. 3 (2001): 484-516.

Pappas, Robin. "H.D. and Havelock Ellis: Popular Science and the Gendering of Thought and Vision." *Women's Studies: An Interdisciplinary Journal* 38, no. 2 (2009): 151-82.

Park, Roy. "'Ut Pictura Poesis': The Nineteenth-Century Aftermath." *Journal of Aesthetics and Art Criticism* 28, no. 2 (Winter 1969): 155-64.

Parkinson, Gavin. *Surrealism, Art, and Modern Science: Relativity, Quantum Mechanics, Epistemology.* New Haven, CT: Yale University Press, 2008.

Pastore, Nicholas. "Helmholtz on the Projection or Transfer of Sensation." In *Studies in Perception: Interrelations in the History of Philosophy and Science,* edited by Peter K. Machamer and Robert G. Turnbull, 355-76. Columbus: Ohio State University Press, 1978.

———. *A Selective History of Theories of Visual Perception, 1650-1950.* Oxford: Oxford University Press, 1971.

Pater, Walter. "Dante Gabriel Rossetti." In *Appreciations, with an Essay on Style,* 228-42. London: Macmillan, 1889.

———. "The History of Philosophy." Houghton Library, Harvard University. bMS Eng 1150.

———. *Letters of Walter Pater.* Edited by Lawrence Evans. Oxford: Oxford University Press, 1970.

———. "Poems by William Morris." *Westminster Review* 90 (October 1868): 300-312.

———. "Prosper Mérimée." In *Miscellaneous Studies: A Series of Essays,* 11-37. 1895. Reprint, London: Macmillan, 1924.

———. *The Renaissance: Studies in Art and Poetry, the 1893 Text.* Edited by Donald L. Hill. Berkeley: University of California Press, 1980.

———. "Style." In *Walter Pater, Three Major Texts,* edited by William E. Buckler, 393-413. New York: NYU Press, 1986.

Pausanias. *Description of Greece.* Translated and edited by James G. Frazer. 1897. Reprint, New York: Biblio & Tannen, 1965.

Pearson, Norman Holmes. "The American Poet in Relation to Science." H.D. Papers.

Pedretti, Carlo. *Commentary on "The Literary Works of Leonardo da Vinci."* Berkeley: University of California Press, 1977.

Pfannkuchen, Antje. "From Vortex to Vorticism: Ezra Pound's Art and Science." *Intertexts* 9, no. 1 (Spring 2005): 61-77.

Piper, David. *The Image of the Poet: British Poets and their Portraits.* Oxford: Clarendon, 1982.

Pondrom, Cyrena. "Conflict and Concealment: Eliot's Approach to Women and Gender." In Chinitz, *Companion to T. S. Eliot,* 323-34.

Postle, Martin. *Angels and Urchins: The Fancy Picture in Eighteenth-Century British Art.* Nottingham, UK: Djanogly Art Gallery and Lund Humphries, 1998.

Potamkin, H. A. "Personality of the Player: A Phase of Unity." *Close Up 6*, no. 4 (April 1930): 290–97.

Potter, Rachel. "T. S. Eliot, Women, and Democracy." In Laity and Gish, *Gender, Desire, and Sexuality in T. S. Eliot*, 215–33.

Pound, Ezra. *The Spirit of Romance*. London: Owen, 1960. First published in 1910.

———. "The Tree." In *Personae: The Shorter Poems of Ezra Pound*. Rev. ed. Prepared by Lea Baechler and A. Walton Litz. New York: New Directions, 1990.

———. "VORTEX." *Blast* 1 (20 June 1914): 153–54.

———. "The Wisdom of Poetry." *Forum* 47 (April 1912): 497–501.

Prins, Yopie. *Victorian Sappho*. Princeton, NJ: Princeton University Press, 1999.

Quema, Anne. "A Genealogy of Impersonality." *Philosophy and Literature* 18 (1994): 109–17.

Quinn, Susan. *Marie Curie: A Life*. New York: Simon & Schuster, 1995.

Rabaté, Jean-Michel. "Tradition and T. S. Eliot." In *The Cambridge Companion to T. S. Eliot*, edited by David Moody, 210–22. Cambridge: Cambridge University Press, 1994.

Rancière, Jacques. *The Future of the Image*. Translated by Gregory Elliott. New York: Verso, 2007.

Reed, Warren A. "The Eye and the Tongue: T. S. Eliot, Modernism, and the Rhetoric of Vision." PhD diss., Rutgers University, 1995.

Reid, Thomas. *An Inquiry into the Human Mind*. Edited by Timothy Duggan. Chicago: University of Chicago Press, 1970.

Reynier, Christine, and Jean-Michael Ganteau, eds. *Impersonality and Emotion in Twentieth-Century British Literature*. Montpellier, France: Université Montpellier III, 2005.

Riley, Denise. *Impersonal Passion: Language as Affect*. Durham, NC: Duke University Press, 2005.

Ripley, William Z. *The Races of Europe: A Sociological Study*. New York: D. Appleton, 1937.

Riquelme, John Paul. *Harmony of Dissonances: T. S. Eliot, Romanticism, and Imagination*. Baltimore: Johns Hopkins University Press, 1991.

Rives, Rochelle. *Modernist Impersonalities: Affect, Authority, and the Subject*. New York: Palgrave Macmillan, 2012.

Rorty, Richard. *Philosophy and the Mirror of Nature*. Princeton, NJ: Princeton University Press, 1979.

Rose, Jacqueline. *Sexuality in the Field of Vision*. New York: Verso, 1986.

Ross, Andrew. *The Failure of Modernism: Symptoms of American Poetry*. New York: Columbia University Press, 1986.

Royce, Josiah. *Outlines of Psychology*. 1903. Reprint, London: Macmillan, 1906.

Sachs, Hanns. "Film Psychology." In Donald, Friedberg, and Marcus, *Close Up, 1927–1933*, 250–54.

——. "Kitsch." *Close Up* 9, no. 3 (September 1932): 200–205.

Saville, Julia F. "The Poetic Imaging of Michael Field." In *The Fin-de-Siècle Poem,* edited by Joseph Bristow, 178–206. Athens, OH: Ohio University Press, 2005.

Schiemann, Gregor. *Hermann von Helmholtz's Mechanism: The Loss of Certainty.* Translated by Cynthia Klohr. New York: Springer-Verlag, 2008.

Schuchard, Ronald. *Eliot's Dark Angel: Intersections of Life and Art.* New York: Oxford University Press, 1999.

Sedgwick, Eve Kosofsky. *Touching Feeling: Affect, Pedagogy, Performativity.* Durham, NC: Duke University Press, 2003.

——. *The Weather in Proust.* Edited by Jonathan Goldberg. Durham, NC: Duke University Press, 2011.

Seelow, David. *Radical Modernism and Sexuality: Freud/Reich/D. H. Lawrence and Beyond.* New York: Palgrave Macmillan, 2005.

Seymour-Jones, Carole. *Painted Shadow: The Life of Vivienne Eliot, First Wife of T. S. Eliot.* New York: Knopf, 2001.

Shakespeare, William. *The Complete Works of William Shakespeare.* Herefordshire, UK: Wordsworth Editions, 1996.

Shouse, Eric. "Feeling, Emotion, Affect." *M/C Journal* 8, no. 6 (Dec. 2005). http://journal.media-culture.org.au/0512/03-shouse.php.

Shreiber, Maeera, and Keith Tuma, eds. *Mina Loy: Woman and Poet.* Orono, ME: National Poetry Foundation, 1998.

Shuter, W. F. "The 'Outing' of Walter Pater." *Nineteenth-Century Literature* 48, no. 4 (March 1994): 1–30.

Siegel, Jonah. "'Schooling Leonardo': Collaboration, Desire, and the Challenge of Attribution in Pater." In Brake, Higgins, and Williams, *Walter Pater,* 133–50.

Simmel, Georg. "The Metropolis and Mental Life." In *Georg Simmel: On Individuality and Social Forms,* edited by Donald N. Levine, 324–39. Chicago: University of Chicago Press, 1971.

Simondon, Gilbert. "The Genesis of the Individual." In *Incorporations,* edited by Jonathan Crary and Sanford Kwinter, 297–319. New York: Zone Books, 1992.

Smith, Carol H. *T. S. Eliot's Dramatic Theory and Practice.* Princeton, NJ: Princeton University Press, 1963.

Smith, Grover. *T. S. Eliot's Poetry and Plays: A Study in Sources and Meaning.* 2nd ed. Chicago: University of Chicago Press, 1974.

Snow, C. P. *The Two Cultures.* Cambridge: Cambridge University Press, 1993.

Snyder, Joel. "Visualization and Visibility." In *Picturing Science, Producing Art,* edited by Caroline A. Jones and Peter Galison, 379–97. New York: Routledge, 1998.

Sophocles. *Sophocles I: Three Tragedies (Oedipus the King, Oedipus at Colonus, Antigone).* Edited by David Grene and Richard Lattimore. 2nd ed. Chicago: University of Chicago Press, 1991.

Spencer, Herbert. *The Principles of Biology.* 2 vols. 1864–67. Reprint, New York: D. Appleton, 1897.

Spender, Stephen. *The Destructive Element.* London: Jonathan Cape, 1935.

Squires, Michael. *The Creation of "Lady Chatterley's Lover."* Baltimore: Johns Hopkins University Press, 1983.

Stauder, Ellen Keck. "Beyond the Synopsis of Vision: The Conception of Art in Ezra Pound and Mina Loy." *Paideuma* 24, nos. 2–3 (Fall–Winter 1995): 195–227.

Steele, Bruce. Introduction to Lawrence, *"Psychoanalysis and the Unconscious" and "Fantasia of the Unconscious."*

Stein, Gertrude. "Aux Galeries Layfayette." *Rogue* 1 (March 1915): 13.

———. *Geography and Plays.* Madison: University of Wisconsin Press, 1993. First published in 1922.

———. "Lecture II: Narration." In *The Poetics of the New American Poetry,* edited by Donald Allan, 104–14. New York: Grove, 1973.

Steiner, Wendy. *The Colors of Rhetoric: Problems in the Relation of Modern Literature and Painting.* Chicago: University of Chicago Press, 1982.

Stewart, Jack. *The Vital Art of D. H. Lawrence: Vision and Expression.* Carbondale: Southern Illinois University Press, 1999.

Stockard, Charles R. *The Physical Basis of Personality.* New York: Norton, 1931.

Sturgeon, Mary C. *Michael Field.* New York: Arno, 1976.

Suleiman, Susan Rubin. *Subversive Intent: Gender, Politics, and the Avant Garde.* Cambridge, MA: Harvard University Press, 1991.

Sullivan, J. W. N. "The Justification of the Scientific Method." *Athenaeum,* 2 May 1919, 274–75.

———. "On Learning Science." *Athenaeum,* 4 July 1919, 559.

———. "The Place of Science." *Athenaeum,* 11 April 1919, 176.

———. "Science and Personality." *Athenaeum,* 18 July 1919, 624–25.

———. "Scientific Education." *Athenaeum,* 12 September 1919, 885–86.

———. "A Stylist in Science." *Athenaeum,* 11 July 1919, 593.

Susman, Warren I. "'Personality' and the Making of Twentieth-Century Culture." In *New Directions in American Intellectual History,* edited by John Higham and Paul K. Conkin, 212–26. Baltimore: Johns Hopkins University Press, 1979.

Sword, Helen. *Engendering Inspiration: Visionary Strategies in Rilke, Lawrence, and H.D.* Ann Arbor: University of Michigan Press, 1995.

Tait, Peter Guthrie, and Balfour Stewart. *The Unseen Universe.* London: Macmillan, 1875.

Taylor, Oliver. "Lawrence and Merleau-Ponty: Movement, Perception, and *Rapport.*" *Etudes Lawrenciennes* 37 (2007): 167–99.

Terada, Rei. *Feeling in Theory: Emotion after the "Death of the Subject."* Cambridge, MA: Harvard University Press, 2003.

Teukolsky, Rachel. "The Politics of Formalist Art Criticism: Pater's 'School of Gior-gione.'" In Brake, Higgins, and Williams, *Walter Pater*, 151-69.

Thain, Marion. *"Michael Field": Poetry, Aestheticism, and the Fin de Siècle.* Cambridge: Cambridge University Press, 2007.

——. *Michael Field and Poetic Identity.* London: Eighteen-Nineties Society, 2000.

Thormählen, Marianne. "'My Life for This Life': T. S. Eliot and the Extinction of the Individual Personality." In *T. S. Eliot at the Turn of the Century*, 120-32. Lund, Swe-den: Lund University Press, 1994.

Tiffany, Daniel. *Radio Corpse: Imagism and the Cryptaesthetic of Ezra Pound.* Cam-bridge, MA: Harvard University Press, 1995.

"Towards the Unknown: Six Points of View." Interview with William Carlos Williams, Mina Loy, Marianne Moore, Archibald MacLeish, Harold Rosenberg, and Lee Ver-Duft. *View* 1, nos. 11-12 (February/March 1942): 10-11.

Treby, Ivor C. *The Michael Field Catalogue.* Bury St. Edwards, Suffolk, UK: De Black-land, 2000.

Trombold, Chris Buttram. "The Bodily Biography of T. S. Eliot, Part I." *Yeats Eliot Review* 15, no. 1 (Fall 1997): 2-9, 36-44.

——. "The Bodily Biography of T. S. Eliot, Part II." *Yeats Eliot Review* 15, no. 2 (Spring 1998): 27-44.

Tyndall, John. *Six Lectures on Light.* London: Longmans, Green, 1873.

Vadillo, Ana Parejo. *Women Poets and Urban Aestheticism.* New York: Palgrave Mac-millan, 2005.

Vanita, Ruth. *Sappho and the Virgin Mary: Same-Sex Love and the English Literary Imagi-nation.* New York: Columbia University Press, 1996.

Veder, Robin. "The Expressive Efficiencies of American Delsarte and Mensendieck Body Culture." *Modernism/modernity* 17, no. 4 (2011): 819-38.

——. "Seeing Your Way to Health: The Visual Pedagogy of Bess Mensendieck's Physical Culture System." *International Journal of the History of Sport* 28, nos. 8-9 (2011): 1336-52.

Vericat, Fabio. "Less Love and More Feeling: Radical Personality in T. S. Eliot's 'Im-personal Theory of Art.'" In Reynier and Ganteau, *Impersonality and Emotion*, 109-17.

Verriest, Guy. "The Life, Eye Disease, and Work of Joseph Plateau." *Documenta Oph-thalmologica* 74, nos. 1-2 (1990): 9-20.

Vetter, Lara. *Modernist Writings and Religio-Scientific Discourse: H.D., Loy, and Toomer.* New York: Palgrave Macmillan, 2010.

——. "Representing 'A Sort of Composite Person': Autobiography, Sexuality, and Collaborative Authorship in H.D.'s Prose and Scrapbook." *Genre* 36, nos. 1-2 (Spring/Summer 2003): 107-30.

——. "Theories of Spiritual Evolution, Christian Science, and the 'Cosmopolitan Jew': Mina Loy and American Identity." *Journal of Modern Literature* 31, no. 1 (2007): 47-63.

Vicinus, Martha. "'Sister Souls': Bernard Berenson and Michael Field (Katherine Bradley and Edith Cooper)." *Nineteenth-Century Literature* 60, no. 3 (2005): 326-54.

Virgil. *The Aeneid.* Translated by Robert Fitzgerald. New York: Vintage Classic, 1990.

Vivas, Eliseo. *D. H. Lawrence: The Failure and Triumph of Art.* London: Allen & Unwin, 1961.

Wade, Nicholas J., and Stanley Finger. "The Eye as an Optical Instrument: From *Camera Obscura* to Helmholtz's Perspective." *Perception* 30 (2001): 1157-77.

Wagner, David, ed. *Icons, Texts, Iconotexts: Essays on Ekphrasis and Intermediality.* Berlin: W. de Gruyter, 1996.

Wallace, Jeff. *D. H. Lawrence, Science, and the Posthuman.* Basingstoke, UK: Palgrave Macmillan, 2005.

Wallen, Jeffrey. "Physiology, Mesmerism, and Walter Pater's 'Susceptibilities of Influence.'" In Brake, Higgins, and Williams, *Transparencies of Desire,* 72-93.

Walton, Jean. *Fair Sex, Savage Dreams: Race, Psychoanalysis, Sexual Difference.* Durham, NC: Duke University Press, 2001.

Ward, David E. "The Cult of Impersonality: Eliot, St. Augustine, and Flaubert." *Essays in Criticism* 17 (1967): 169-82.

Weil, Simone. "Human Personality." In *The Simone Weil Reader,* edited by George A. Panichas, 313-39. New York: David McKay, 1977.

Weinberger, Eliot, ed. *The New Directions Anthology of Classical Chinese Poetry.* New York: New Directions, 2003.

Weininger, Otto. *Sex and Character: An Investigation of Fundamental Principles.* Translated by Ladislaus Löb. Edited by Daniel Steuer and Laura Marcus. Bloomington: Indiana University Press, 2005.

Wells, Ida B. *Southern Horrors and Other Writings: The Anti-Lynching Campaign of Ida B. Wells, 1892 -1900.* Edited by Jacqueline Jones Royster. New York: Bedford/ St. Martin's, 1997.

Weston, Jessie L. *From Ritual to Romance.* Garden City, NY: Doubleday, 1957.

Wettlaufer, Alexandra. *In the Mind's Eye: The Visual Impulse in Baudelaire, Diderot, and Ruskin.* Amsterdam: Rodopi, 2003.

Wexler, Joyce. "The Uncommon Language of Modernist Women Writers." *Women's Studies* 25, no. 6 (1996): 571-84.

White, Chris. "'Poets and Lovers Evermore': Interpreting Female Love in the Poetry and Journals of Michael Field." In *Sexual Sameness: Textual Differences in Lesbian and Gay Writing,* edited by Joseph Bristowe, 26-43. New York: Routledge, 1992.

White, Peter. "'Tradition and the Individual Talent' Revisited." *Review of English Studies* 58, no. 235 (2007): 364-92.

Whitworth, Michael. "*Pièces d'identité:* T. S. Eliot, J. W. N. Sullivan and Poetic Impersonality." *English Literature in Transition* 39, no. 2 (1996): 149-70.

Wiegman, Robyn. *American Anatomies: Theorizing Race and Gender.* Durham, NC: Duke University Press, 1995.

Williams, Raymond. *Keywords: A Vocabulary of Culture and Society.* Oxford: Oxford University Press, 1976.

Willis, Martin. *Vision, Science, and Literature, 1870-1920: Ocular Horizons.* London: Pickering & Chatto, 2011.

Wilmer, Clive. "The Later Fortunes of Impersonality: 'Tradition and the Individual Talent' and Postwar Poetry." In Cianci and Harding, *T. S. Eliot and the Concept of Tradition,* 58-71.

Wollheim, Richard. "Giovanni Morelli and the Origin of Scientific Connoisseurship." In *On Art and the Mind,* 177-201. Cambridge, MA: Harvard University Press, 1974.

Woolf, Virginia. *Between the Acts.* Edited by Melba Cuddy-Keane. New York: Harcourt, 2008.

Worthen, John. *D. H. Lawrence: The Life of an Outsider.* Cambridge: Cambridge University Press, 2005.

Wutz, Michael. "The Thermodynamics of Gender: Lawrence, Science, and Sexism." *Mosaic: Journal for the Interdisciplinary Study of Literature* 28, no. 2 (June 1995): 83-108.

Yeats, William Butler. *Per Amica Silentia Lunae.* In *Mythologies,* 317-69. New York: Touchstone, 1998.

———. Review of *The Father's Tragedy; William Rufus; Loyalty or Love?,* by Michael Field. In Yeats, *Uncollected Prose,* 1:225.

———. Review of *Sight and Song,* by Michael Field. In Yeats, *Uncollected Prose,* 1:225-27.

———. *The Uncollected Prose of W. B. Yeats.* Edited by John P. Frayne and Colton Johnson. 2 vols. New York: Columbia University Press, 1970-76.

Zelazo, Suzanne. "'Altered Observation of Modern Eyes': Mina Loy's Collages and Multisensual Aesthetics." *Senses and Society* 4, no. 1 (2009): 47-74.

Index

Isn't it sort b old hat to return to mod'st impersonality as
evacue'n d r self? ok to see linke w/ neo

2-3: mod'sts blend subject, percept, object d rough stats d at
combine seen d sayable

— (H.D)

83 — argues d at HD does ≠ reject imp'y for subj'y but posits a
nexus d social d organic imperatives c/in wh identities take
shape d fluctuate // unbounded seeing subject (in later wr'g)

86 — HD apparently life long reader d science

Loy;